Consciousness and the Computational Mind

Explorations in Cognitive Science
Margaret A. Boden, editor

1. *Mental Processes: Studies in Cognitive Science*
   H. Christopher Longuet-Higgins

2. *Psychosemantics: The Problem of Meaning in the Philosophy of Mind*
   Jerry Fodor

3. *Consciousness and the Computational Mind*
   Ray Jackendoff

Consciousness and the Computational Mind

Ray Jackendoff

Published in cooperation with
The British Psychological Society

A Bradford Book
The MIT Press
Cambridge, Massachusetts
London, England

Second printing, 1989

© 1987 Massachusetts Institute of Technology

This book was set in Palatino by Asco Trade Typesetting Ltd., Hong Kong, and printed and bound by The Halliday Lithograph in the United States of America.

Library of Congress Cataloging-in-Publication Data

Jackendoff, Ray S.
  Consciousness and the computational mind.

  (Explorations in cognitive science; 3)
  "A Bradford book."
  Bibliography: p.
  Includes index.
  1. Human information processing.   2. Cognition.   3. Consciousness.   I. Title.
II. Series.
BF444.J33   1987   153   87-2661
ISBN 0-262-10037-1

to my parents

Contents

Introduction   xi
Acknowledgments   xv

PART I
The Phenomenological Mind and the Computational Mind   1

Chapter 1
The Phenomenological Mind   3
1.1 Varieties of Experience   3
1.2 Positions on the Mind-Body Problem   7
1.3 Externalization, Form, Qualia, and the Unconscious   12

Chapter 2
The Computational Mind   15
2.1 The Computer Analogy   15
2.2 Attractions of the Computational Mind; *Theory I*   16
2.3 The Mind-Mind Problem   18
2.4 Positions on the Mind-Mind Problem; *Theory II*   21
2.5 Corollaries of Theory II   24

Chapter 3
Preliminaries to Description of the Computational Mind   29
3.1 Justification of the Computational Mind   29
3.2 Computational Theories and Computer Theories   33

Chapter 4
Forms of Information   37
4.1 Structure and Process   37
4.2 The Importance of Structure to Learning and Memory   39
4.3 A Constraint on Syntactic Structure   42
4.4 Lashley's Observation; *Theory III*   45
4.5 Levels of Structure   47
4.6 The Disunity of Awareness; *Theory IV*   51

PART II
The Language Faculty and What It Expresses   55

Chapter 5
Levels of Linguistic Structure   57
5.1 Phonological Structure   57
5.2 The Psychological Reality of Formalism   64
5.3 The Relation of Phonological Structure to Lower Levels   66
5.4 Syntactic Structure   68
5.5 Transformations and Processing   72
5.6 Phonological Segmentation: Intonation and Stress   74
5.7 Correspondence Rules and the Lexicon   81
5.8 Summary   85
5.9 Language Acquisition and Innateness   86

Chapter 6
Language Processing   91
6.1 The Logical Structure of Language Perception and Production   91
6.2 Holistic and Top-Down Influences in Language Understanding   96
6.3 Lexical Access during Speech Perception   103
6.4 The Time Course of Language Production   104
6.5 Bidirectionality in the Language Processor   108
6.6 Levels of Representation in Short-Term Linguistic Memory   110
6.7 The Function of Short-Term Linguistic Memory   113
6.8 The Selection Function of Short-Term Linguistic Memory   115
6.9 Summary; *Theory V-A*   119

Chapter 7
Boundary Conditions on Conceptual Structure   121
7.1 Meaning as a Component of the Computational Mind   121
7.2 Connections to Other Faculties   124
7.3 Approaches Ruled Out by the Mentalist Postulate   126
7.4 Reference and Intentionality   127
7.5 Truth   128

Chapter 8
Some Elements of Conceptual Structure   135
8.1 Categorization   135
8.2 The Noncategorical Nature of Categorization   139
8.3 Preference Rule Systems   143
8.4 Ontological Claims: Some Major Categories of Concepts   148
8.5 Generalization of Spatial Concepts to Abstract Domains   152
8.6 Final Remarks   158

PART III
Nonlinguistic Faculties   161

Chapter 9
Levels of Visual Structure   163
9.1 The Problem of Vision   163
9.2 The Form of Marr's Inquiry into Vision   168
9.3 The Primal Sketch and 2½D Sketch   170
9.4 The 3D Model   174
9.5 Visual Imagery and the Imagery Debate   179
9.6 Remarks on Visual Processing   185

Chapter 10
The Connection between Language and Vision   193
10.1 Preliminary Correspondences   193
10.2 The 3D Model as a Central Representation   194
10.3 Visual Identification and Categorization   198
10.4 The use of 3D Models in Word Meanings   200
10.5 Enriching the Conceptual-3D Connection   202
10.6 Summary   207
10.7 Special-Purpose Capacities That Draw on Vision   208

Chapter 11
Levels of Musical Structure   213
11.1 What Is Musical Cognition?   213
11.2 Tonal Systems   216
11.3 The Musical Surface   217
11.4 Grouping and Metrical Structure   219
11.5 Time-Span and Prolongational Reductions   224
11.6 Musical Understanding versus Linguistic and Visual
      Understanding   232
11.7 Musical Understanding and Musical Performance   234
11.8 Musical Affect; Toward a Level of Body Representation   236
11.9 Remarks on Musical Processing   239

Chapter 12
The Modularity of the Computational Mind   247
12.1 Summary of the Levels   247
12.2 Hierarchies and Headed Hierarchies   249
12.3 Fundamental Computational Principles   251
12.4 Larger-Scale Commonalities across Language and Music   253
12.5 What Part of Music Is Specifically Musical?   256
12.6 General Characteristics of the Processors   258
12.7 Fodor's Modularity Thesis   260
12.8 A Finer-Grained View of Modularity   262

12.9   Central Processes   265
12.10   Acquisition of Modules: Innateness versus Learning   268
12.11   Summary   270
12.12   Perception and Cognition   271

PART IV
The Phenomenological Mind and the Computational Mind,
continued   273

Chapter 13
Processing Precursors to Consciousness   275
13.1 Review of *Theories I–III*   275
13.2 The Role of Modality-Specific Levels: Review of *Theory IV*   277
13.3 Short-Term Memory and the Selection Function; *Theory V*   278
13.4 The Role of Attention in Awareness; *Theory VI*   280

Chapter 14
The Intermediate-Level Theory of Consciousness   285
14.1 Some Theories of the Form of Awareness   285
14.2 The Form of Linguistic Awareness; *Theory VII*   287
14.3 The Form of Musical Awareness   292
14.4 The Form of Awareness in Visual Perception   293
14.5 The Form of Awareness in Visual Imagery; *Theory VII*
        Generalized   296
14.6 Remarks on "Sensation," Touch, Pain, Hunger, and the Self   298
14.7 The Unity of Entities in Awareness   300

Chapter 15
Amplifications of the Intermediate-Level Theory   303
15.1 The Affects; *Theory VIII*   303
15.2 How Is Introspection Possible?   311

Chapter 16
Closing Thoughts   319
16.1 Inexpressible Thoughts and Knowledge   319
16.2 How Does Language Aid Thought?   322
16.3 Last Overview   325

Appendix A
A Second Correspondence Rule between Intonation and Syntax   329

Appendix B
Possible Enrichment of the $2\frac{1}{2}$D Sketch   331

References   339

Index   351

Introduction

The central question of this book is, it seems to me, one of the most fundamental issues of psychology: What makes our conscious experience the way it is? To approach this question, I take very seriously the motivating premise of contemporary cognitive science—that the mind can be thought of as a biological information-processing device—and I explore the degree to which the character of experience can be explained in terms of the forms of information in the mind and the processes this information undergoes.

In order to develop this approach, I first have to say what I believe mental information is, such that it can have a form, and how its form could matter to experience or to anything else. This is the burden of part I of the book, which scouts the foundations of cognitive science and makes some preliminary hypotheses about the relation of mental computation to consciousness.

At the level of generality of part I, though, one can see only the overall form of a solution. To achieve more precise results, it is necessary to do a great deal of homework on detailed properties of mental information structures and their interactions. The middle two parts of the book are devoted to this task.

Part II deals with language. Beginning with the well-studied areas of phonology and syntax, I discuss why generative linguists in the tradition of Chomsky find it rewarding to study the pure form of mental representations, and why linguistic theories are theories of psychology. I have found that many psychologists, philosophers, and computer scientists labor under views of linguistic theory originating in the late 1960s, views that call for reconsideration in light of more recent research. In particular, phonological theory has undergone a major revolution in the past ten years; I consider it now to surpass syntax in its sophistication in dealing with issues of representation. My discussion of linguistic theory is meant to convey the flavor of this research and to show how it substantially revises our notions of the relationships among levels of representation.

I then demonstrate the consequences of a hard-line view of linguistic form for language processing. Again there are prejudices from other fields to be overcome. I show that these are unfounded, in that they presume the wrong sorts of dependencies between linguistic form and the processes that derive it. I then develop an approach to processing that is consonant both with linguistic theory and with everyday and experimental evidence about speech perception and speech production.

Part II then turns to what language expresses: meaning, or conceptual structure. Here I advocate a view, developed more fully in my *Semantics and Cognition*, that the structure of meaning ought to be pursued on the same first principles as phonology and syntax. This leads to a decisive break with most of the philosophical tradition on meaning; but in compensation it yields several basic results about the organization of thought and its relation to language.

Part III extends the framework developed for language to two other faculties, vision and music. In the chapters on vision I draw heavily on the work of the Marr school and also on work on visual imagery by Shepard, Kosslyn, Cooper, and others. My reading of Marr's approach is, I find, not altogether like everyone else's; I am more heavily influenced by the parallels with linguistic theory and have taken care to bring them out. The major new contribution of these chapters is the beginning of a connection between Marr's theory of visual representation and my own theory of linguistic meaning. This connection not only solves important problems for both theories: it also makes possible for the first time a serious answer to the fundamental question of how we manage to talk about what we see.

The inclusion of music in this volume is a by-product of my ongoing research in collaboration with the composer and music theorist Fred Lerdahl, reported in detail in our *Generative Theory of Tonal Music*. Although there is a tradition of research on the psychology of music stretching back to Helmholtz, and although psychology of music is now beginning to come into its own, such research seems often to be treated as somehow less serious than research on language, reasoning, or vision—as a kind of "dessert" to more central inquiry. I think the reasons for such treatment are more sociological than scientific. Carrying out and understanding research on music requires a certain degree of musical literacy, more than individuals generally expect of themselves in a culture where music is regarded basically as a source of casual amusement. In addition, there is a strong bias against even mentioning the "emotional" overtones of music in the context of "hard science." Nevertheless, I have become convinced that musical cognition is as much a part of psychology as are language and vision and that an exploration of the musical faculty presents crucial points of comparison and contrast with these other two.

Part III concludes with an examination of Fodor's hypotheses concerning the modularity of mind. With the more detailed and comprehensive treatment of mental representations worked out in previous chapters, it proves possible to revise and refine Fodor's conception in several important respects. If anything, the mind proves to be considerably more modular than Fodor has envisioned.

Having arrived at some understanding of the computational mind, we can then go back more insightfully to issues of phenomenology in part IV. The central hypothesis I arrive at is called the *Intermediate-Level Theory of Consciousness*: the form of awareness is derived neither from "sense-data" in the traditional sense nor from the form of thought, as many have guessed, but rather—in each separate faculty of the mind—from a level of representation intermediate between the most peripheral (sensation-like) and the most central (thought-like). Put so baldly, this may not seem an exceptional conclusion. However, it is at odds with every statement I have encountered on the nature of consciousness; it is shown superior to them all in accounting for many simple facts of experience that other investigators either have failed to observe or could not make any sense of. On the other hand, the Intermediate-Level Theory cannot be properly formulated, much less understood, without an overview of the computational mind as a whole, derived from the empirical study and comparison of the representations in a number of faculties—an overview that is created for the first time in parts II and III. I therefore hope that this book can serve to deepen significantly the foundations of psychology, while putting a number of venerable philosophical problems on a more empirical basis.

Because this book involves so many interwoven threads from what are usually considered separate disciplines, it has posed intimidating problems of exposition. On the one hand, it is necessary to speak to practitioners of each of the constituent disciplines, trying to persuade them that the pieces they are working on belong in my jigsaw puzzle and that certain modifications to standard views are justified for the sake of coherence in the larger scheme of things. On the other hand, the very same material must be presented in a form that is both highly condensed, for reasons of space, and also accessible to specialists in all the other disciplines. In addition, fitting everything together sometimes requires certain pieces about which we know very little, so I am on occasion reduced to conjecture based only on the structure of the theory. Finally, there are many relevant topics that have been heavily studied—attention, multiple personalities, split-brain patients, and the whole tradition of phenomenology, to mention only four—whose neglect I can defend only by pleading limitations of time and will.

I have tried to cope with these expository difficulties by keeping the major issues as clear and prominent as possible, by assuming little previous knowledge on the part of the reader, and by being frank when ignorance has forced me to speculation. Still, the result is inevitably demanding. I can only trust that readers will join me sympathetically in the effort of putting the puzzle together, and that those who feel their own interests unduly slighted will be understanding in light of the magnitude of the task I have set myself. Much of the manuscript has been read (with some enjoyment, I gather) by Brandeis University undergraduates in my courses on Consciousness and Introduction to Cognitive Science, so I hold some hope that the work will be accessible and interesting to a broad audience.

Some friends who have read this manuscript have felt its portrayal of the mind excessively mechanical for their taste, in particular giving rather short shrift to the sense of free will. I could just reply that I have gone in the directions that scientific inquiry has led me, and leave it at that. Such a reply would be evasive, however; I am perfectly aware that no science, whatever its protestations of objectivity, is ideology-free. I should address what is really at stake.

The ideology behind this work, as far as I can verbalize it, is far from mechanical. It is deeply opposed to the narrow associationist view of human nature that pervades much of contemporary cognitive psychology, most artificial intelligence research, and indeed the lore of our culture at large, which tends to acknowledge value only insofar as it can be externalized. This work proceeds from and substantiates the assumption that our internal contribution to the world we know is as rich, complex, and vital as the contribution of "external reality" and that human knowledge and values are rooted in our biological heritage. It follows that research in the social and "behavioral" sciences must be sensitive to the dictates of human nature: there can be no science of behavior without a rigorous, sophisticated science of mind.

It is moreover important to recognize that, even if a theory such as the one developed here may start to explain the nature of our experience, it cannot explain it *away*. We are still human beings, fated—or privileged—to live our lives through the perspective provided by *these* minds and *these* bodies. Our sense of personal autonomy and our deep pleasure in doing a good piece of work are as real for us, and as full of value, as the sky and the sunrise. We do well to cherish them, and to strive to assure everyone the opportunity to do so.

Acknowledgments

Pride of first acknowledgment must go to the Center for Advanced Study in the Behavioral Sciences, where I had the privilege of spending the year 1983–84 as a Fellow. In this beautiful and pampering environment, with its pride in encouraging intellectual exploration and growth, I was given the leisure to learn what I needed to learn in the course of formulating and drafting this work. I am deeply grateful to the administration and staff of the Center for nurturing not only the Fellows but also the atmosphere and traditions of the institution.

I am especially indebted to my colleagues at the Center for making the year intellectually and personally so enriching. In particular, David Olson organized an ad hoc workshop on language and cognition that continued throughout the year and kept strangely evolving into a workshop on consciousness. Though we continued throughout the year to disagree violently—and some of the arguments got pretty heated—I think we all came to understand and respect the others' point of view a great deal more than when we started. Indeed, toward the end of the year, when some visitors came to give talks, we found to our surprise that we all had the same objections: evidently we had, without noticing it, developed a common framework. In addition to David, I must especially thank Lynn Cooper, Carol Krumhansl, James Cutting, Mardi Horowitz, Christopher Peacocke, Stephen Stich, Robert Seyfarth, Barbara Smuts, Hersch Leibowitz, and Elizabeth Traugott for being invaluable sources of information and insight, for being willing to have my half-baked ideas bounced off them, even when they were not sure they wanted to listen, for letting me listen to their own ideas, half-baked or not, and for innumerable shared cups of coffee and walks in the cow-pasture.

Plenty of other people have contributed ideas, advice, and encouragement to this project. Those who stand out in my mind are John Macnamara, Lila Gleitman, Morris Halle, David Swinney, Leonard Talmy, Dan Dennett, Roger Shepard, Steve Pinker, Lucia Vaina, Steve Kosslyn, Merrill Garrett, Barbara Landau, and my colleagues at Brandeis University Jim Lackner, Ricardo Morant, Edgar Zurif, and Moira Yip. Fred Lerdahl, Jerry Feldman, Edgar Zurif, Sparky Jackendoff, and John Macnamara offered

extensive comments on portions of the manuscript, which I hope I have put
to good use. As will be seen, the framework I have developed here owes a
great deal to Dan Dennett's *Brainstorms*, to Jerry Fodor's *Language of
Thought* and *Modularity of Mind*, to David Marr's *Vision*, and particularly to
my teacher Noam Chomsky's *Aspects of the Theory of Syntax* and *Reflections
on Language*.

I owe thanks also to Judy Woodman, who deciphered my chaotic drafts
into legible form, to Armand Qualliotine, who wrote out the musical
examples, and to Amy Jackendoff, who helped with the bibliography.
Harry and Betty Stanton of Bradford Books have been a continuing source
of encouragement and good will. And, although it will probably embarrass
her, I must express my gratitude to Anne Mark, who, as my copy editor in
this and many previous works, has made the process of production almost
a pleasure.

A few passages in the book have been borrowed from *Semantics and
Cognition, A Generative Theory of Tonal Music*, and my paper "Grammar as
Evidence for Conceptual Structure." A version of parts of chapters 7 and 8
is to appear in *Versus*; parts of chapters 9 and 10 are to appear in *Cognition*.
I have stolen one irresistibly apt figure of speech in chapter 2 from Richard
Brautigan.

Financial support for this work came in part from National Science
Foundation Grants BNS 76–22943 to the Center for Advanced Study in
the Behavioral Sciences and IST 81–20403 and IST 84–20073 to Brandeis
University.

Elise has said that she doesn't deserve my thanks this time. Nothing
could be further from the truth. Even if one's reality comes ultimately from
within, there is still a need to have it validated from without, especially
when traveling in disputed or uncharted territories. Elise has been my
Reality Check, a continuing source of comfort and strength. My thanks
to her go beyond words, though, as she always says, words do help
sometimes.

PART I

The Phenomenological Mind and the
Computational Mind

Chapter 1
The Phenomenological Mind

Two senses of the words "mind" and "mental" are in use today. One, which might be called the *phenomenological* notion of mind, pertains to the mind as the seat of conscious awareness, the experiencing of the world and of our own inner lives that each of us carries on, inaccessible to others. The other, which I will call the *computational* notion of mind, treats the mind as an information-bearing and information-processing system. The mind in this sense acts as the locus of understanding, knowledge, reasoning, and intelligence.

In ordinary common sense these two notions of mind seem inseparably yoked together: intuitively, my conscious mind is where my perception and my thinking take place. How could someone *know* something without being *aware* of it? And how could someone be aware of something without knowing it? However, it has become increasingly clear over the last thirty years or so that these questions are far from rhetorical. The problem of consciousness has proved to be quite distinct from that of how we understand and reason. In this chapter and the next we will see why a single notion of mind is incapable of encompassing both.

1.1 Varieties of Experience

To give an idea of what is encompassed by the phenomenological mind, I would like to cast my net fairly widely in considering the domain of entities of which we can be aware. It is worth trying to conjure up the full space of possibilities in order to see how rich a world is within our awareness.

To start, of course, there are all the perceivable objects in the world— not physical objects *per se*, but objects *as we experience them*. This qualification is crucial: we would experience the world very differently if our eyes were sensitive to different wavelengths of electromagnetic radiation, if we were three millimeters tall, or if we had sonar like a bat or a bloodhound's sense of smell.

Then there are the experiences of our own bodies: the pain in your toe, the hunger in your gut, the itch behind your ear, the tension in your arm.

Like the objects of the world, these experiences come with a sense of "reality." But there are also lots of experiences that come with different kinds and degrees of "unreality."

Consider acts of imagination, for example. Try to imagine two little green Martians materializing through the wall of the room you're now sitting in, muttering "Yup, yup, yup, uh-huh, uh-huh..." Or imagine your mother yelling at you to clean up your room. These imagined entities and their actions form as much a part of your experience of the moment as do the "real" objects of perception, but they are experienced as "unreal." Between these two extremes are a number of experiences somewhat harder to classify. I'll try to distinguish some of them very roughly.

The events of *dreams* are usually experienced as real though possibly incongruous, but they are remembered as unreal. By contrast, *illusions* are experienced as real but incongruous, and memory or subsequent experience does not change that impression. In addition to the standard visual illusions, it is worth noting the body illusion of the "phantom limb," where an amputee experiences convincing but incongruous sensations in the limb that is not there. *Hallucinations* are, I suppose, experienced in varying degrees of "reality" and "congruity"; the more one tends to experience and/or remember them as real and congruous, the more one tends to be classified by society as psychotic (or magical, depending on the society).

All these objects of awareness appear in what might be called *primary* awareness. A second layer of experience involves awareness of oneself and of one's interaction with the objects of primary awareness; I will call this *reflective* awareness. Contrast the examples in (1.1), reports of primary awareness, with those in (1.2), reports of reflective awareness.

(1.1)   a. Hey, there's a dog!
        b. Train's coming!
        c. That smells terrible!
        d. You're awful!
        e. Ouch! My toe hurts!

(1.2)   a. I see a dog!
        b. I hear/see a train coming!
        c. That smells terrible to me!
        d. I hate you!
        e. I have/feel a pain in my toe!

These may not seem so different, and in many cases they are interchangeable in use. But notice how the sentences in (1.2) inject the experiencer into the picture and are thereby in some way slightly less direct and emphatic.

This distance between primary and reflective awareness varies in immediacy. In the case of visual or auditory awareness of external objects, we tend to utilize expressions of reflective awareness when there is some possibility of doubt: "I *see* a dog, but is there really one there?" That is, reflective awareness permits the qualification "but I could be wrong."

In cases (c) and (d) the gap seems narrower. Still, the reports of reflective awareness in (1.2), by bringing in the observer, acknowledge the possibility of someone else arriving at a different evaluation: "This is *my* reality," not "This is reality, take it or leave it." In the case (e) of body sensations there is still less of a gap, if any. Contrast, for instance, "It doesn't hurt anymore" with "I don't feel the pain anymore." If these differ at all, it is because the latter suggests the odd possibility that the pain is still there but I just don't feel it. (See Dennett 1978c for discussion.)

There are further varieties of reflective experience that seem to have no counterpart in primary experience. I am thinking for instance of the experience of *emotions*. Compare feeling happiness to feeling pain. A possible parallel for happiness to (1.1e) might be "Yay! There's (that) happiness again!" This is strange indeed. If the happiness has any location, it's in my *self* and therefore by definition an object of reflective awareness.

The sense of *will* would also seem to belong to reflective experience. For example, "I raised my arm" involves the essential *me* and is therefore reflective. A corresponding primary experience might be "My arm is going up" or, perhaps more believably, "My knee jerked when the doctor knocked it with the hammer." But such expressions, especially the former, tend to have an undercurrent of "even though I'm not making it move" where the *disclaimer* of will expresses reflective awareness too.

It would be nice to go on to ask, What varieties of experience are ideas, thoughts, beliefs, desires, and the like? But these cases are too complicated and encrusted with dogma to permit the sort of brief discussion I have maintained so far, so I will beg off for now; part IV will offer some suggestions.

This bestiary should give an idea of the denizens of the phenomenological mind. I am not for the moment concerned with questions of whether people *really* have such experiences (see Dennett 1976); let us assume that they do. Nor am I insisting on my way of breaking them up, such as my particular way of dividing them between primary and reflective experience. The point is only to see how many different phenomena are to be encompassed. If some of them go, there will no doubt be others to take their places.

I do wish, though, to hew closely to the notion of consciousness as *experience* and to distinguish sharply between "conscious awareness" and "intelligent sensitivity." For instance, from observing the flexible and innovative reactions of animals to various situations, we may well conclude, with Köhler (1927), Griffin (1981), and many others, that animals in many respects display considerable intelligence and cannot be driven by bundles of simple reflexes. But this is quite different from saying that they have conscious experiences, as Griffin goes on to claim. I can be conscious of a tree branch outside my window without having any appreciable intelligent reaction to it; contrariwise, I can react intelligently and flexibly to, say, a social situation of which I become aware only in retrospect—I "did something smart without realizing it." In short, intelligent behavior, whether in animals, people, or computers, need neither imply nor be implied by the presence of awareness.

On the other hand, the line can be drawn too finely. Some writers on consciousness appear to use the term to encompass only reflective awareness. Jaynes (1976, chapter 2), for instance, speaks of consciousness as a "metaphor" for the structure of the world, including the self as actor and deliberator. Among the characteristics of consciousness in his sense are the detection of one's own emotions and the ability to discriminate between reality and hallucination—functions that have been localized here in reflective awareness. Similarly, Dawkins (1981) writes, "Perhaps consciousness arises when the brain's simulation of the world becomes so complete that it has to include a model of itself." And Hofstadter (in Hofstadter and Dennett 1981, 281–282) asks, "Could it be valid to suppose that the magic of human consciousness somehow arises from the closing of a loop whereby...a true representational system perceives its own state in terms of its repertoire of concepts[?]" These both suggest only reflective or self-awareness, not the primary consciousness of the external world. By contrast, I wish to include both varieties of consciousness here.

Various other criteria for awareness seem to me also off the mark. For example, it would be inaccurate to identify the contents of consciousness with the contents of attention. Paying attention to something may result in focusing or heightening one's awareness of it, but, as Dennett (1978a) and Crook (1980) point out, one can also be *vaguely* aware of something, that is, aware of it without attending to it. In fact, the converse of this criterion is more likely the case: it is hard to imagine paying attention to something without first being aware of it.

Other authors, such as Jerison (1973), stress the importance of the projection of future events, or imagining—the necessity of being able to conjure up an internal representation of reality. Similarly, Griffin (1981, 144) speaks of "awareness as the possession of mental images" for flexible pattern-matching; Bruner (1983, 215) calls consciousness "a vehicle for making present the absent." But such emphasis on imagery is too narrow: primary awareness of the physical world might as well be called "a vehicle for making present the *present*." Again, the conditions have been reversed: being able to have images is sufficient, not necessary, for being conscious.

Still another common criterion for awareness is the notion that someone is only aware of something if he can tell us about it. For example, Dennett

(1969) advocates systematically recasting the locution "aware of an X" as "aware that there is an X"—that is, treating awareness as an attitude toward a proposition. As a result, when he grapples with the issue of visual imagery (1978b), the best he can come up with is an account of *beliefs that one has experienced a visual image*, a propositional attitude that is some steps removed from actually experiencing a visual image. Having the propositional attitude may depend on or be a sign of having had the experience, but it is not the experience itself.

More generally, there are many genuine aspects of experience that simply cannot be reported in any detail. Consider: "These two wines taste different." "But *how* do they taste different?" "It's hard to say: try them yourself." Is the speaker *unaware* of the difference because all he can say is that they're different? Or: "What does it feel like when you do a double back flip on the trampoline?" "It's hard to say, but when you can do one you'll know when it feels right and when it doesn't." Is the instructor talking nonsense? Have generations of gymnastics and dancing and tennis and violin teachers who have used such language been talking nonsense? I would like to think they have not—on the contrary, such teaching appeals to the student's own developing awareness, even if the language is too impoverished to express the experience. (If this sounds like remarks of Wittgenstein (1953) and Polanyi (1958), the resemblance is partly premeditated.)

There is of course a drawback in admitting the possibility of such experiences: they severely threaten the coherence of phenomenological discourse. It is perhaps less dangerous to rule them out of existence, or at least out of bounds. But they are part of what a theory of experience must encompass. For those who don't like to live dangerously, there are plenty of other things to study. If we want to study experience, though, we will have to find ways around this fundamental difficulty.

I have no prescriptions to offer. What seems to be called for is a developing sensitivity to the phenomena. We must find an acceptable descriptive balance between the rigidity of operationalism, which forces us to throw out too much of value, and the various self-indulgences of mysticism, turn-of-the-century introspectionism, and psychiatric free association. In order to raise the level of discourse, it is necessary to be sufficiently rigorous both about the rest of one's psychology and about its connection to phenomenological issues. That is what I will attempt to achieve here.

1.2 Positions on the Mind-Body Problem

Let us begin with traditional approaches to the description of the phenomenological mind. The classical way of stating the puzzle is as the *mind-body problem*: there seem to be these two domains, the physical world and the mental world of experience, but how do they interact with one another?

Descartes, to whom the modern formulation of the problem is due, thought not only that the physical world could causally affect the mental world but also that the mental domain, which included for him the will, could affect the physical domain. It was through the possession of a mentality that humans were to be separated from the beasts, who functioned only as mechanical devices of the physical world. Moreover, since the mental domain need not in principle be linked to the physical, one could imagine the mind as surviving the death of the body, in convenient consonance with religious tradition.

Descartes's *interactionist* theory is in many respects closer to common-sense intuition than other solutions to the mind-body problem (I find it is the one my undergraduate students *want* to believe), and in recent times it has been advocated by such prominent figures as Popper and Eccles (1977) and Sperry (1976). But it is not the position of choice for most psychologists and philosophers today. One major objection to it is its invocation of nonphysical causes within the physical world, in violation of the physical laws of conservation of energy. A second difficulty, which overlaps and includes the first, is its appeal to a nonphysical domain per se, which because of its private, personal nature cannot be investigated by natural science. It inevitably smells mystical or at least antiscientific. Depending how far one is willing to grant these objections, one arrives at one of four other major positions on the mind-body problem.

The least reductive of these is the *epiphenomenalist* thesis, which grants the first objection but denies the second. It claims that the mental domain retains its existence independent of the physical world, but that causal relations go only from physical to mental and not the other way round. In this view, then, the elements of our conscious awareness are causally determined by what goes on in our brains but cannot themselves have any effect on behavior. The mental world is, as it were, a puppet manipulated by the physical brain backstage; our consciousness is an epiphenomenon.

The difference between the interactionist and the epiphenomenalist views of the mind-body interaction is crudely diagrammed in figures 1.1 and 1.2. Time moves from left to right; arrows indicate causation. The difference lies in the connections from brain-state$_1$ in S to brain-state$_2$ in S and from S's experience of O to S's decision to kick O. In the interactionist theory the mental domain alone provides the connection; in the epiphenomenalist theory the physical domain alone provides the connection.

Notice how epiphenomenalism already severely undermines our common sense about the nature of mind, for it claims that the connections among our conscious thoughts are only apparent. They are not made in the mental domain: they must rather be made by the physical connections

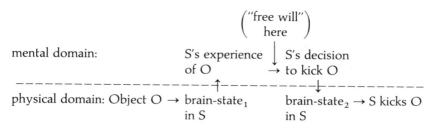

Figure 1.1
Interactionism

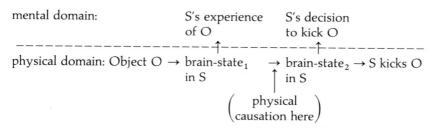

Figure 1.2
Epiphenomenalism

among brain events, which "throw off" apparently related elements into consciousness. Moreover, since the brain is governed by physical laws, that which appears to us as "free will" must in fact be determined by physical causation, which seems more deterministic than we would like to believe ourselves to be.

This apparent loss of free will, with its attendant reduction in one's sense of human dignity, seems a high price to pay to maintain the integrity of physical causation. This is a major reason for the intuitive attraction of interactionism. Nevertheless, most philosophers of mind have been willing to pay the price. (Hence a source of intellectual splintering: out of the apparent incompatibility of free will and noninteractionist doctrines of mind, moral philosophy gets divorced from philosophy of mind. Dennett (1984) explores this dilemma, proposing a solution that I find both congenial to the view of mind being developed here and also humane.)

Another alternative to epiphenomenalism is *parallelism*, in which the mental and physical domains proceed side by side in a relation of correspondence, as in figure 1.3 (double-headed arrows signify correspondence). Though parallelism seems to admit mental connections between mental

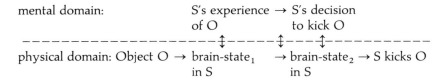

Figure 1.3
Parallelism

states, reflection suggests that this is only by virtue of sleight-of-hand. For this theory only makes more pointed the objections against positing distinct mental and physical domains. By what natural laws could a nonphysical domain be related to the physical world; in particular, how does the mental domain come to be connected specifically to *brains*? (Without invoking the special powers of a deity, of course.)

The notion of parallel causation in the two domains is especially suspicious: why should physical causation in the brain happen to have a counterpart in an entirely separate metaphysical domain? Furthermore, if mental causation parallels physical (that is, deterministic) causation, can "free will" actually be so free after all? So parallelism does not really provide a way out of the objections to epiphenomenalism.

In pursuit of further alternatives, we leave these *dualist* theories and look at *materialist* theories, which reject the notion of a separate mental domain. Such theories immediately defuse the question of how there can be a nonphysical domain and how it comes to be connected with brains, but they create their own problems.

The most extreme materialist theories are the varieties of *behaviorism*, which in less radical versions deny the utility to science of studying experience ("methodological behaviorism") and in more radical versions deny the very existence of conscious experience ("radical behaviorism"). All there is to study is the bodily states and behavior of organisms— including the verbal reports organisms give us about experiences, mythical though these might be. The obvious problem with such theories for me is that they deny *my* experience, which I feel certain I have and which I would like to understand. I imagine you feel the same way.

Somewhere between behaviorism and the dualist theories lies the *identity theory*, which admits the existence of conscious experience but holds that the distinction between mental and physical events is purely one of mode of description. Just as the terms "heat" and "molecular kinetic energy," for instance, turn out to be only different ways of talking about the same phenomenon, the identity theory predicts that "S's experience of O" and

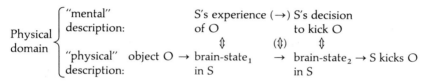

Figure 1.4
Identity theory

"brain-state$_1$ in S" will turn out to be just different descriptions of the same phenomenon; the latter will be a *reduction* of the former to physical terms. What we call "mental states" or "experiences" are how brain states feel from the inside of the organism that is in those states; experiencing O is "what it is like" (in the sense of Nagel 1974) to be an S in brain-state$_1$. Figure 1.4 diagrams this theory (double arrows here denote equivalence); it is very similar to the way Searle (1983, 270) diagrams his view.

Note how similar this diagram is to that of parallelism. The only difference is that this theory treats the two domains not as two *actual* domains but rather as two ways of describing the *same* domain. It leaves open the possibility (enclosed in parentheses in figure 1.4) of talking about mental connections between mental events but (unlike parallelism) provides a principled account of them: "mental connections" are the "mentalistic" way of describing causal connections among brain states.

In short, like the dualist theories and unlike behaviorism, a complete identity theory will offer an account of mental states. But unlike all the other theories, it offers the hope of reducing the mental descriptions to physical ones. For this reason it is probably the most highly favored today.

Yet doubts remain. As a counterpart of the dualist's problem with the connection of mental to physical events, the identity theorist has the problem of explaining how physical events can "feel like" anything— without reinvoking a mysterious "experiencer" over and above the brain. And of course, since experience is physically determined, we apparently lose free will again.

As we will see, many other questions about the phenomenological mind are intertranslatable between dualist and identity-theory positions. Thus, one begins to get the sense that not much has been gained by the identity theory beyond metaphysical comfort: there is not so much *empirical* difference.

I have glossed over many subtle variants of each of these positions and ignored other positions of less direct interest to us here. (Churchland (1984) provides an admirable and much more extensive survey; I am also indebted to Rorty (1979) for clarification of many points in this section and the next.) What is important in the present context is to understand the flavor of the problem and to see how it arises in response to the distinction between the physical world and the phenomenological mind.

1.3 Externalization, Form, Qualia, and the Unconscious

Whichever view one takes of the mind-body problem—other than radical behaviorism, which simply denies the phenomena—a number of important problems must be dealt with. The first I will call the *externalization* of experience—the fact that my experiences may be *of* things external to me. This fact may seem so obvious as to be almost beneath notice. But I believe it is fundamental.

For the moment consider just perception. The blueness of the sky is *out there in the sky*; the pain is *in my toe*. In a dualist theory the problem is to say how the mind, linked to the brain, comes in contact with—grasps—external reality. (Descartes and especially Berkeley worried about this a great deal.) In an interactionist theory, where the mind has some powers of its own, one can imagine it reaching out to the world and grasping its character. A parallelist mind and especially an epiphenomenalist mind seem more constrained, stuck to what is going on in the brain; for them, externalization seems a tougher nut. In the identity theory it is downright paradoxical (as pointed out rather mildly in Brandt 1960): the identity theory claims that the experienced blueness *in the sky* is identical with a state of neurons *in my brain* and that the experienced pain *in my toe* is identical with another state of neurons *in my brain*. How can the same thing be in two different places?

The problem comes more into focus if we consider mental phenomena other than veridical perception. Consider hallucinations, or our imagined Martians coming through the wall. In both cases things are experienced "out there" that have no physical basis. Also, consider the experience of a tune running through your head or of "holding a picture before your mind's eye": whatever is going on in the brain, there surely is no room in it for loudspeakers or projection screens, much less for a little person in there to listen or watch. In dualist terms cases like these must consist of mysteriously "grasping" something that isn't there. In the identity theory the location of all these experienced entities is different from the location of the brain states to which they are supposed to be identical. (Note that this applies even to the tunes and pictures in the head, barring the unlikely eventuality that the neurons responsible for the images take up exactly the same space in the skull as do the phenomenal images themselves.) Thus, none of the positions on the mind-body problem is particularly attractive here.

A case that mixes the previous two arises when we imbue an external object with illusory properties. One such example is seeing a picture as three-dimensional; another is perceiving a talking parrot (or computer) as intelligent by virtue of the noises it emits. I have come across no discussion of such cases in the context of the mind-body problem, and I find it difficult to drum up a plausible story within any of the theories. The moment the going gets rough, it seems as if the substance of these theories begins to wear thin pretty quickly.

In short, the problem of externalization, when extended across the varieties of experience, turns into the general question, How do things and their properties, real or not, come to be experienced where they are? The interactionist theory may look a little more promising in the case of perception and the identity theory a little better in the case of illusion; but none of the theories looks very good overall. For the moment let's not push any harder.

A related and more widely appreciated problem concerns how experienced entities come to have the *form* they do. What makes the square look square and the triangle triangular? Again, an interactionist theory can appeal to the mind "reaching out and grasping reality," but misperception, illusion, and imagery reveal the emptiness of such a solution. Folk wisdom (perpetuated, I suspect, by elementary science education) suggests that we experience the square by virtue of the brain viewing the square image on the retina. But, as realized as early as Hume and emphasized in our time by Gibson, nothing is *viewing* the retina: there's no further optical equipment back there and no further apparatus to do the viewing. Rather, the retina just sends some millions of nerve impulses to the brain, and somehow the unitary experience of the square must be caused by, or parallel to, or identical with these impulses.

The Gestalt psychologists, particularly Köhler (1940, 1960) tried to get around this problem by claiming that the unity of form in experience was due not to the actions of individual neurons but rather to the holistic effects of electrical fields in the brain. Although this approach appeared to answer certain problems about illusory perception, it clearly did not have enough structure to account for the richness of experience: how could electrical fields have that much complexity? Clearly we are getting nowhere with this problem either.

A third problem concerns the *qualia* in awareness: the blueness of blue, the saltiness of salt, the painfulness of pain, and so forth. In any of the dualist theories these can be ascribed, I suppose, to the mental domain, though this is essentially license to let them remain mysterious. In the identity theory the mystery is again more explicit: how does neural activity come to "feel like" blueness or saltiness or painfulness? It is one thing to provide neurological *distinctions* among qualia—to say that one bunch of neurons is activated for blue, another for red, another for saltiness—but quite another to explain how blueness *as you or I experience it* arises from what our brains are doing. This problem is often regarded as the real nut to crack in understanding consciousness, but I find it on a par with the problems of externalization and form.

The last problem I will bring up for now concerns the notion of *unconscious* mental states. At the outset we took the phenomenological mind to be the seat of *conscious awareness*. (I follow for instance Brandt (1960), whose opening definition seems altogether standard: "It is useful to stipulate ... 'F is a particular mental fact' ... to mean the same as 'F is temporal, and something is directly aware of F.'") If this is the sense in which "mental" is understood, it is easy to see how Freud, for example, could be seen as incoherent in speaking of an unconscious mind—mental states of which one is by definition unaware. (Of course, there were certainly other reasons to resist his position as well: many people seem to feel threatened by the notion of unconscious thought, out of sight and hence apparently out of one's control. To the extent that inaccessible thoughts and knowledge are felt as a threat to one's rationality and personal integrity, one will have a stake in rejecting the possibility of unconscious mental states.) I see little point in elaborating possible moves within the framework laid out so far. The next chapter will suggest the beginnings of a more principled approach, and profuse detail will develop as we go along.

Contemporary American psychology makes little reference to the phenomenological mind. It is perhaps symptomatic of this gap that, to choose a random example, Gleitman's prestigious introductory text (1981) contains no discussion at all of awareness or consciousness, despite the great intrinsic interest it would presumably have for beginning undergraduates. Yet William James (1890) devotes several chapters to the topic. What happened in the interim, I think, is that the field was overwhelmed by the radical behaviorist reaction to the phenomenological excesses of Wundt and his followers, and talk of mind largely disappeared for some forty or fifty years. When the recovery from behaviorism came, though, the traditional notion of mind was still left pretty much to the philosophers, and an entirely different notion surfaced, to which we now turn.

Chapter 2
The Computational Mind

2.1 The Computer Analogy

The computational theory of mind grows out of the conception of the brain as an information-processing device, analogous to a computer. In comparison with earlier analogies—brain as hydraulic mechanism, as steam engine, as telephone switchboard—the computer analogy has been remarkably successful in capturing the general public's imagination (see Turkle 1984) as well as in generating fruitful programs of research.

Two properties of computers recommend the analogy. First, the information content of data and programs (especially those written in high-level languages) can be stated independently of physical instantiation in any particular computer. For example, a FORTRAN program will run on more or less any machine, whether built out of vacuum tubes, transistors, or chips. Thus there is a sense in which, like the mind, the information in the computer is autonomous—inhabits a separate domain—from the (mere) hardware that supports computation. Second, the ways in which programs are organized—in terms of goals and subgoals, self-monitoring and self-modification—resonate with commonsense intuitions about the organization of problem solving, learning, and other cognitive tasks. (In addition, the speed and accuracy of computers at tasks like calculation and graphics generation cannot be followed in real time by humans and hence can lead to an impression of intelligence.)

Very crudely, then, the computer analogy suggests the following hypothesis: just as we need not deal with the actual wiring of the computer when writing our programs, so we can investigate the information processed by the brain and the computational processes the brain performs on this information, independent of questions of neurological implementation. This approach is often called *functionalism*; the idea behind this term is that the function rather than the physical substance of the brain is significant in studying the mind.

Such inquiry has occupied much of cognitive psychology and linguistics since the early 1950s. And although it was common even earlier to speak of computers as "electronic brains," the earliest reference I have come across that makes explicit the analogy to *minds* is Putnam's "Mind and Machines" (1960). It is now routine to speak of the information in the brain as *mental representations* and of the processes operating on such representations as *mental processes*. In short, the mind is taken to stand to the brain as the software and data of the computer stand to the hardware.

2.2 Attractions of the Computational Mind; *Theory I*

Let us see how well this computational notion of the mind corresponds to the traditional phenomenological notion. To begin with, both kinds of mind seem to inhabit a domain of description separate from that of the physical device, though both are causally dependent on the characteristics and states of the physical device. Moreover, thinking in computational terms is a fruitful way to achieve the sort of abstractness and generality that seems necessary to describe not only our conscious life but also the behavior of animals of any substantial degree of complexity (see section 3.1). In particular, the units of a high-level computational account, such as objects, organized actions, and goals, correspond much more closely to the intuitive units of consciousness than do any presently known descriptions of neural activity.

The computer analogy also offers an attractive way to treat the notion of the unconscious mind. In chapter 1 we saw that the unconscious offers a paradox to the definition of the mental as that which is experienced: how can something be an experience and yet *un*experienced? However, if "mental" is defined in terms of information processing instead, a rather satisfying result emerges. Consider memory, for example. A computer stores a great deal of information, only some small part of which is being actively used at a given time. Similarly, the moment-by-moment kaleidoscopic shifts in information being actively processed in the brain correspond intuitively to the ever-changing stream of consciousness, whereas inactive stored information can be regarded as unconscious—but still mental.

As Putnam (1960) points out, the computer analogy also helps explain how one can know something without being aware that one knows it. Suppose that in order to know some fact F, a machine must contain some configuration of computational states C. Then, for the machine to be *aware* of knowing F, it must be *aware of being in configuration C*. But that requires the realization of some further computational state C' that checks whether C is present. If C is present without C', the machine knows F but is not aware of knowing F. That is, the computational device's self-monitoring is a set of processes beyond those responsible for ordinary interaction with the world. We thus see the emergence of a distinction like that between primary and reflective awareness.

A computer may carry on several tasks at once, some of which involve higher-level goals or forms of organization and some of which are more subsidiary. Since the same is true of the brain (in fact, much more so—see section 3.2), it is tempting to divide the computational mind up into black boxes and identify some especially important one as the locus of consciousness. Then one's hypothesis, roughly, is that information and/or processing that is active within this particular black box is conscious and the rest is unconscious. Thus, the conscious and the unconscious parts of the mind are of the same essential character, built out of information and the processes that operate on it.

Let us codify this approach as Theory I, the first of a series of theories we will develop in an attempt to gradually refine the problem of consciousness.

Theory I
The elements of conscious awareness consist of information and processes of the computational mind that (1) are active and (2) have other (as yet unspecified) privileged properties.

Something like Theory I is common in the literature, in many disparate guises. Minsky (1968) sees consciousness as the "supreme organizer" that can access and debug other faculties; Dennett (1969) identifies the elements of consciousness as the contents of the speech center; Johnson-Laird (1983, 465) says, "The contents of consciousness are the current values of parameters governing the high-level computations of the operating system"; Frith (1981) speaks of consciousness as a monitor system, a higher-level system that directs subroutines, controlling and selecting; Mandler (1984, 89) wants to think of the contents of consciousness as mental products that are undergoing a particular mode of processing. All of these are in a sense anticipated by William James (1890, 288):

Consciousness consists in the comparison of [simultaneous possibilities] with each other, the selection of some, and the suppression of the rest by the reinforcing and inhibiting agency of attention. The highest and most elaborated mental products are filtered from the data chosen by the faculty next beneath, out of the mass offered by the faculty below that, which mass in turn was sifted from a still larger amount of simpler material, and so on.

The disagreements among these views lie largely in how to spell out proviso (2) in Theory I—what part of the active mind is privileged. One thing they have in common, though, is their unquestioned identification of consciousness with an especially high-level representation or process. This choice corresponds to the traditional intuition that the conscious mind is connected with the will, with the initiation and coordination of action, with the ability to make rational choices, and ultimately with one's sense of personhood. It is difficult to see this as at all controversial. But since Part IV will eventually come to question it, we had better observe right away that it is no more than an assumption, subject in principle to empirical examination.

However, that is not the issue I want to take up at the moment. At stake is a much more basic clarification of the relation of the phenomenological mind to the computational mind.

2.3 The Mind-Mind Problem

The problem is this: just because the computational mind and the phenomenological mind are both different domains of description from the physical body, this does not mean they are the *same* domain.

Optimists on this issue (such as Hofstadter (1979), if I read him properly) say that if a nervous system (or a computer) can just achieve some sufficient degree of complexity, consciousness will somehow miraculously emerge. In fact, though, I find it every bit as incoherent to speak of conscious experience as a flow of information as to speak of it as a collection of neural firings. It is completely unclear to me how computations, no matter how complex or abstract, can add up to an experience.

Hofstadter's position, like some others, arises in part from confusing consciousness with self-consciousness (that is, reflective awareness). The latter involves (at least) the combination of ordinary consciousness with self-reference. Self-reference, of course, is a capacity common to people, certain kinds of computer languages, and ordinary sentences such as "The sentence I am now uttering is ten words long"; it has nothing to do with consciousness per se. Hofstadter, preoccupied with self-reference, neglects the other essential components of self-awareness. Then, finding both recursive self-reference and consciousness mind-boggling (and even inspiring of religious awe!), he uncritically identifies the former as the source of the latter.

More sober consideration suggests that the leap from self-reference to self-consciousness to consciousness is unwarranted. Consider the problem of qualia. As Block (1978) points out, no computational theory gives the slightest idea of how to get blueness or saltiness or painfulness out of computations. Like neurological accounts, computational accounts may provide the right *distinctions*—they may, as it were, give the phenomenological mind the cue to produce experiences of blue at the right times and experiences of red at the right times. But that is not the same as producing the experiences themselves.

With the problem of form there is little more hope. Certainly, "propositional" representations of the general form "X is square" (including semantic networks as well as language-like representations—see section

8.1) provide no basis for the *experience* of squareness, whatever their virtues in other respects. Representations more geometric in character have been proposed to account for visual imagery (Shepard and Cooper 1982; Kosslyn 1980; see section 9.5), and these seem at first blush more satisfactory. But, as we will see, the force behind these proposals is only that such representations can encode the proper distinctions among geometric forms, not that they can account for the experience of forms per se. It is only by slipping into thinking of them as "pictures in the head," viewed by the "mind's eye," that we trick ourselves into believing otherwise.

Finally, the externalization of experience creates the same problems for the computational mind as it does for the neurological brain. I experience objects out there *in the world*, and pain *in my toe*, not computational states in my brain. The computational mind may well express the distinctions among the locations of experienced objects, but it is hard to see how it can literally put them there.

A curiously distorted version of these points appears in Searle's (1980) widely cited attempt to refute the computational theory of mind. The argument centers on *intentionality*, which Searle defines as "that feature of certain mental states by which they are directed at or about objects and states of affairs in the world" (p. 424). He argues correctly that all a computer can do is manipulate its own internal symbols; it cannot understand those symbols as connected to an external reality. From the point of view of the machine the symbols are not symbols *for anything*—they are just meaningless marks. Thus, the computer's states are not intentional in Searle's sense. He concludes that "the brain's causal capacity to produce intentionality cannot consist in its instantiating a computer program, since for any program you like it is possible for something to instantiate that program and still not have any [intentional] mental states. Whatever it is that the brain does to produce intentionality, it cannot consist in instantiating a program since no program, by itself, is sufficient for intentionality" (p. 424).

If we strip away the jargon, I think Searle's argument can be seen as a displacement of a more fundamental and gut-level claim: that running a computer program does not produce consciousness. What makes us believe that our mental states are intentional in Searle's sense is that we experience the things in the world that our thoughts are about. What makes us believe that a computer's states are not intentional is that we can't imagine how the computer could experience the world. In short, Searle's peculiar "causal capacity of the brain to produce intentionality," which is lacking in computers and in computational theories, seems to be a euphemism for conscious awareness.

A survey of the varieties of experience suggests in fact that intentionality in Searle's sense is the wrong place to locate the problem. If intention-

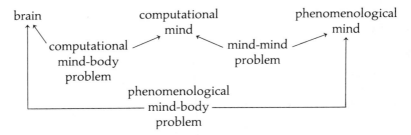

Figure 2.1
Domains of psychology and their relations

ality concerns the relation between mental states and the (real) world, it leaves no room for the "aboutness" of mental states that produce images or hallucinations. That is, a theory that focuses on the intentionality of mental states suffers from the same difficulty as the theories of mind that involve "grasping" external reality, as discussed in section 1.3. A more inclusive formulation might take intentionality to be the property of (computational) mental states whereby they are related to the world as experienced, whether real or not. But then it boils down again to the issue of consciousness. (I return to this and intimately related issues in sections 7.4. and 7.5.)

In this reading of Searle, then, I take him to be making (albeit indirectly) the same point I have been pressing here: the computational mind offers no explication of what a conscious experience is. This is not necessarily reason to reject the computational mind, as Searle does. But it is reason to limit the claims one makes about the power of the computer analogy.

The upshot is that psychology now has not two domains to worry about, brain and mind, but three: the brain, the computational mind, and the phenomenological mind. Consequently, Descartes's formulation of the mind-body problem is split into two separate issues. The "phenomenological mind-body problem" (our concern in chapter 1) is, How can a brain have experiences? The "computational mind-body problem" is, How can a brain accomplish reasoning? In addition, we have the mind-*mind* problem, namely, What is the relationship between computational states and experience? Figure 2.1 sketches these relationships.

From this vantage let us return to Putnam's (1960) claim that seeing the brain as an information processor solves the mind-body problem. What Putnam has actually done is to discover that functionalism provides an *approach* to the computational mind-body problem; he neglects the phenomenological mind-body problem altogether. A *solution* to the computational mind-body problem would tell us how the information structures and processes of the computational mind are neurally instantiated, that is, how the software runs on the hardware. Since at the moment we know relatively little about either the software or the hardware in the requisite fine detail (for example, how the neurons accomplish visual identification or sentence comprehension), Putnam's claim of a solution would seem somewhat premature.

However, we do understand the problem fairly well in principle. We can hope for at least what Fodor (1975) has called *token reductionism*. A description of this sort would be able to say that such-and-such a computational structure or process taking place in such-and-such an individual on such-and-such an occasion is instantiated by such-and-such neural structures or processes in that individual's nervous system. On the other hand, it does not seem reasonable to hope for what Fodor calls *type reductionism*, in which one could say, for instance, that the concept *grandmother* is instantiated in everyone in exactly the same way. A position somewhere between these two is probably the best we can expect: token reduction for many kinds of structures and processes, type reduction for others (for instance, the low-level visual system), and beyond this some taxonomy of types (for instance, that such-and-such types of information and processes are localized in such-and-such an area of the brain and performed by such-and-such arrangements of neural architecture).

Whatever the ultimate outcome on these issues, the overall form of the solution to the computational mind-body problem is clear. Just as we say that a computer program is a way of specifying the operation of the machine in terms of its functional organization, so we can regard the computational mind as an abstract specification of functional organization in the nervous system—even if, at the moment, we cannot translate from this description into hardware terms. Hence, if one were to choose which theory of the mind-body relationship applies to this case, the appropriate answer would clearly be an identity theory: the computational mind is another way of describing the brain. It would make little sense to adopt a "behaviorist" position prohibiting discourse about information structure; it would make even less sense to adopt an "epiphenomenalist" position in which somehow the information processing went on in a metaphysically distinct domain.

2.4 Positions on the Mind-Mind Problem; *Theory II*

Such clarity as there is in this relationship vanishes, it seems to me, when we turn to the relation of the computational mind to the phenomenological mind. Rather, we are in the same situation as we were with the phenomenological mind-body problem. Although the computational theory of mind may be of help in elucidating the units and distinctions that are present to experience, and although the organization of the phenomenological mind may be more closely paralleled by the computational mind than by raw

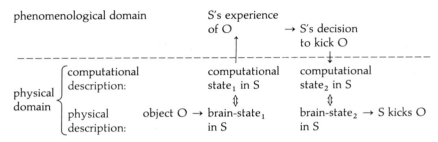

Figure 2.2
Computational interactionism

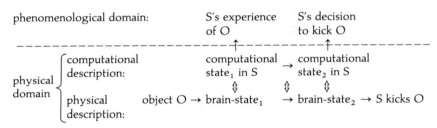

Figure 2.3
Computational epiphenomenalism

neurophysiology, we still have gotten nowhere with the essential nature of consciousness itself.

One can still, for instance, conceive of an interactionist theory of the phenomenological mind, in which it is a separate metaphysical domain with its own causal powers, acting on and being acted on by the computational mind/brain, as in figure 2.2. Such a theory, though formulable, rather mocks the spirit of the computational theory of mind. The whole point of speaking in terms of computational states is to explicate the logical connections among states of mind, and an interactionist theory denies that such logical connections need exist.

More congenial to a computational approach, but still within a dualist framework, would be an epiphenomenal theory, in which computational states cause conscious states but not the other way round, as in figure 2.3. (The form of a parallelist variant of this should be obvious.)

Alternatively, one can formulate a materialist, or identity, theory (as in figure 2.4) in which the phenomenological mind is just a third way of

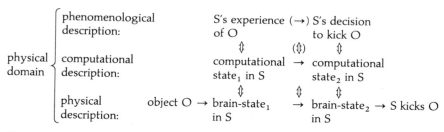

Figure 2.4
Computational identity theory

describing the physical domain: conscious experience is what it "feels like" to be the device in the relevant computational states.

As in the traditional mind-body problem, there is not much basis for choosing between these alternatives. The identity theory might be more acceptable to the modern scientific mind—though, as observed in chapter 1, the explication of "feels like" still is utterly mysterious. Again, the identity theory might more readily imply that a computer would be conscious if it duplicated the computational states of the human brain. But as this is more a matter of ideology—and people come down in different ways on the possibility of computer consciousness—we can hardly consider this a telling point.

For the present, then, I find it methodologically prudent not to choose between the views illustrated in figures 2.3 and 2.4. Accordingly, Theory I must be modified to allow for the distinction between the computational mind and consciousness. Theory II is a preliminary formulation.

Theory II
The elements of conscious awareness are caused by/supported by/ projected from information and processes of the computational mind that (1) are active and (2) have other (as yet unspecified) privileged properties.

The difference between this and Theory I is the substitution of *are caused by/supported by/projected from* for *consist of*. It is in this purposely vague predicate that the mysterious part of the mind-mind problem is localized, and I wish not to be held responsible for defining it. As we will see, the rest of Theory II is open to empirical investigation, and our theories from here on out will be refinements of it.

We will envision awareness, then, as an *externalization* or *projection* of some subset of elements of the computational mind. Insofar as diagrams of this situation make any sense, the form of the theory we are seeking can be

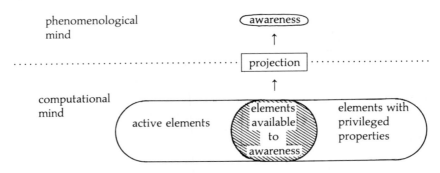

Figure 2.5
Schematization of Theory II

schematized as shown in figure 2.5. The horizontal dotted line in the figure represents the metaphysical divide between the two minds. This diagram leaves open the character of projection, the mapping from computational mind to phenomenological mind—in particular, whether it "causes" awareness, as in the epiphenomenal theory (figure 2.3), or whether it is merely a change of point of view, as in the identity theory (figure 2.4).

The issue that can be addressed, however, is the selection of privileged representations. In refining Theory II, then, we will try to constrain the set of elements available to awareness, so as to find just that set that can account for the character of experience.

2.5 Corollaries of Theory II

Two corollaries of Theory II should be made explicit, in order to set ground rules and make clear the range of possibilities I wish to consider.

Hypothesis of Computational Sufficiency
Every phenomenological distinction is caused by/supported by/projected from a corresponding computational distinction.

This means that the organization of awareness is determined by the supporting computational mind. The hypothesis is stated in terms of *distinctions* rather than *elements* because, as seen in section 2.3, we do not know how to derive the elements of awareness per se from computations. Rather, the best we can expect is that where a difference appears in awareness, it corresponds to a difference in computational state: for instance, seeing red comes from a different computational state than seeing blue or tasting saltiness.

Viewing this hypothesis from a different angle, it says that the world we are aware of is just that which the brain/computational mind is capable of representing. Insofar as this world is veridical, we will claim that it is because evolution has provided the right distinctions in the computational mind. George Miller has put this beautifully: "The crowning intellectual accomplishment of the brain is the real world.... all [the] fundamental aspects of the real world of our experience are adaptive interpretations of the really real world of physics" (Miller 1980, 222).

The empirical force of this hypothesis is to bring phenomenological evidence to bear on the computational theory. The computational theory must be sufficiently expressive (must contain sufficient distinctions of the proper sorts) to make the world of awareness possible. Thus, if there is a phenomenological distinction that is not yet expressed by our current computational theory, the theory must be enriched or revised.

Notice, however, that the conditionality of the hypothesis goes only in one direction: not every computational distinction causes/supports/projects a phenomenological distinction. This one-way conditionality is what makes possible unconscious computation. The hope is that in the course of refining Theory II we can determine exactly *which* computational distinctions emerge into awareness. The second corollary of Theory II makes the point even more strongly.

Hypothesis of the Nonefficacy of Consciousness
The awareness of an entity E cannot *in itself* have any effect on the computational mind. Only the computational states that cause/support/project E can have any such effect.

This hypothesis is in effect an explicit rejection of the interactionist position. It says that all explanation of computational effects must take place in computational terms: there are no causal connections from the phenomenological mind to the computational. Thus, it is impossible to mount explanations of the form "Because X is present in consciousness, computation Y takes place." Rather, the only possible construal of such an explanation is in terms of the computational states responsible for X's being present to consciousness: "Because information Z and processes W are active and of the privileged sort (and hence, by the way, cause/support/project X in awareness), Y takes place." That is, the explanation must fall back on properties of the computational states themselves, independent of whether they produce awareness.

There are two ways to view these consequences of Theory II. The stronger is as an empirical claim about causality.

Empirical Noninteractionism
The elements of the computational mind and their causal interactions will turn out to be sufficient to explain the character of experience.

The weaker is as a stricture on scientific methodology.

Methodological Noninteractionism
The only kind of causal relations we know how to investigate empirically are physical and computational, so in the interests of scientific
coherence we will seek to explain the elements of the computational
mind and their causal interactions in those terms, disallowing explanations in terms of phenomenological causation.

In terms of how we actually do our research, the two interpretations of
Theory II and its corollaries are equivalent. In particular, they both prevent
us from accepting arguments to the effect that, because one cannot imagine
how phenomenon X could be caused by neural or computational devices, phenomenological causation must be at work. (Such arguments are
mounted by Eccles in Popper and Eccles 1977.) Without a coherent notion
of what could possibly be meant by "phenomenological causation," this
kind of argument amounts essentially to an appeal to magic.

Adopting either interpretation of Theory II, by contrast, we are led to
seek a computational distinction responsible for phenomenon X. We attribute lack of success to our lack of imagination, not to the magic workings
of the phenomenological mind. The only place where Theory II admits the
possible insufficiency of computational explanation is in the causation/sup-
port/projection of experience by computational distinctions—the fundamental mystery of the mind-mind problem.

Within the scheme of Theory II, then, it is a category error to speak of
"conscious representations" and "conscious processes" versus "unconscious
representations and processes," as is common in the literature. *No* representations and processes are conscious—they are in the computational mind,
not the phenomenological mind. The only sense that can be made of this
locution is as shorthand for "representations and processes *projected into*
consciousness" versus "representations and processes not projected into
consciousness." In order to keep matters as clear as possible, I will avoid
this shorthand.

Yet another way of looking at Theory II and its corollaries is as a claim
that consciousness is *causally inert*. This may seem harmless enough until
we realize its ugly consequence: *Consciousness is not good for anything.* The
only way it can be good for anything is for it to have effects, and such
possibility has just been denied. Again, the only construal of "Consciousness is good for purpose X" within Theory II is as "The computational
states that cause/support/project consciousness are good for purpose X,"
which does not exactly have the same ring of victory to it.

Thus, we must for example reject speculation like Griffin's (1981, 144):
"Awareness [is] the existence of internal images available for comparison
with current sensory input." Mental images are phenomenological and
cannot be compared with anything, without invoking the objectionable

"mind's eye" or "little man" in the phenomenological mind. The only comparison possible is between the computational representations resulting from current sensory input and the computational representations that cause/support/project mental images. In other words, it is not the mental images that are efficacious but rather the representations that give rise to them. Similar objections obtain to the quotation from William James in section 2.2, "Consciousness consists in the comparison of [simultaneous possibilities] with each other, . . ." and to the view of Bruner (1983, 215): "[Consciousness is] an instrument for the analysis of necessity and trouble." Consciousness cannot compare or analyze; only the computational mind can.

I myself am not too happy about this consequence. Consciousness seems too important to one's life—too much fun—to conceive of it as useless: imagine how miserable it would be to sleepwalk through life as an unconscious zombie! (Nagel (1974) would reply: "It wouldn't be like anything!" That's even more disturbing; one might as well be a brick or a package of frozen peas or a bus transfer.) Nevertheless, to grant consciousness purpose requires it to have causal efficacy, which in turn forces one to embrace interactionism, a move I find myself constitutionally incapable of.

The reader is therefore enjoined to suspend any preconceptions about the purpose of consciousness. They will only serve as distraction from the empirical evidence to follow. In any event, part IV will show that standard speculations about the purpose of consciousness along the lines pursued by Griffin, James, and Bruner are seriously off the mark, so the issue is not merely methodological.

Chapter 3

Preliminaries to Description of the Computational Mind

Aside from drawing analogies to computers as information processors, chapter 2 was rather vague about the nature of the computational mind. Before embarking on a detailed description of the parts of it germane to the problem of consciousness, the subject of parts II and III, we need a clearer picture of what there is to describe.

3.1 Justification of the Computational Mind

What licenses us to consider the brain a device that *contains mental representations*?[1] When we construct formal theories of other devices such as planetary systems, weather patterns, or digestion, our theories are taken only as mathematical reconstructions or simulations of how the devices behave. We do not claim that the planets, for instance, are solving differential equations whose solutions tell them where to move next. We do not attribute to the stomach "digestive representations" by which it calculates how to deal with the latest input from the esophagus. Why then can we feel justified in claiming that the brain is different, that it actually *is* doing computations? Isn't a formal theory of mind better thought of as just another complex calculating device to predict how the brain will behave?

A possible answer grows out of further exploration of the computer analogy. Compare a formal description of a computer's behavior with that of, say, an electric motor. The motor's description will not claim that the motor is doing calculations, but the computer's description may well mention a putative program the computer is running and explicit calculations the computer carries out. The computer is said to have internal representations, the motor is not. What makes the difference?

Here we are on clearer ground than in the contrast between brains and stomachs. Both motors and computers contain lots of identical components arranged into larger functional units. In a motor the individual windings in each coil function in mass action; for purposes of description their actions

---

1. This section owes a great deal to a couple of violent arguments I had with John Searle in winter 1984 and also to a frustrating experience reading Fodor 1984.

can just be summed to derive the action of the coil. Moreover, the switching of the current among the coils is a function not of their electrical states but of the physical position of the commutator.

In a computer, though, things are quite different. The power of the computer lies in the fact that the state of each binary switch (or "flip-flop") is independent of the states of the others. Thus, the action of larger components is not a sum or average of the actions of the parts; rather, it depends on the precise combinatorial properties of the parts. Furthermore, each part's changes of state depend on combinatorial properties of the other parts.

This difference in function dictates a radical difference in the appropriate form of description for the two devices. Whereas the description of a motor can idealize away from single windings, speaking of the mass action of its components, that of a computer must explicitly mention the state of each component and their combinatorial interactions. Moreover, the complexity of the combinatorial properties overwhelms that of individual parts in contributing to the overall description of the device's behavior. This leads to the independence of much of the description from the physical instantiation: any device with the same combinatorial properties will have the same set of possible states and will go through the same sequence of states. Since the combinatorial properties are formal rather than physical, we will have arrived at a computational description.

Just such a difference obtains between the stomach and the brain. Whereas the cells of the stomach group into larger components that can be regarded as functioning en masse, the cells of the brain function much more independently, and the function of each is determined by combinatorial properties of all the many other cells with which it interacts. Thus, a description of brain function, unlike a description of stomach function, must encode the combinatorial behavior of its small-scale components. Again, the complexity due to the formal combinatorial properties is much more significant in the overall description than the complexity of individual components, leading us to say that by virtue of its organization, the brain instantiates a set of formal properties—again a computational description.

A common objection to computational approaches to the brain involves evolutionary continuity. If humans have computational minds, then what about monkeys? dogs? turtles? fish? ants? flatworms? hydra? Or even, following Fodor (1984), what about paramecia, for goodness sake? Where can we draw a principled line? And if we can't, then how can we coherently claim that humans have minds and paramecia don't?

The account just given for why the brain has a computational mind provides (what I find) a reasonable reply to this line of attack. Look again at machines. There are evidently some people who are willing to consider something as simple as a thermostat to be a computing device; but surely its computational description is not very revealing of its behavior—we want to know by what *physical* means it switches the furnace on and off. At the other extreme of complexity is the computer, whose behavior involves the combinatorial properties of millions of switching devices of a relatively small number of different types. Here the description of the individual components takes a back seat to the description of their interactions, and so the computational description is dominant. (Still, of course, the physical components must be described in the end.)

Between these two extremes lie many kinds of machines of many degrees of complexity. If complexity grows by increasing the connections among elementary units in regimented ways (that is, if one doesn't just add wires and components in big tangles), there comes a point where physical descriptions are less revealing than formal combinatorial descriptions. This is actually not a discrete point in the scale of complexity but more a pragmatic range. My old textbook on sequential machines (Moore 1964) is poised right in this transition range, on the boundary of sequential switching circuits and finite automata, and here (physical) circuit diagrams can be found rubbing shoulders unashamedly with (computational) state transition diagrams.

It seems reasonable to suppose that a similar transition occurs in description of animal behavior as one moves up the phylogenetic scale. With the simplest organisms the major task of description is biological and chemical in nature; a computational description is not very revealing. It is only as animals come to develop nervous systems whose combinatorial properties are significant—where response is not of a massed character—that it becomes interesting to treat the combinatorial properties as a formal system instantiated by the organism. I do not know enough about the nervous systems of lower animals to conjecture intelligently about the transition area, but given the things insects and spiders and squids do, I would imagine it is below them and perhaps above earthworms and conches. In this transition area one would expect simple but nontrivial computational descriptions in alternation with complete but fairly formidable neurophysiological descriptions.

The same is to be expected in the description of small isolable components in the nervous systems of more complex creatures. No one could get very excited about a computational description of a reflex arc, for example: there aren't any combinatorial properties of interest. However, the transition area emerges in a work like Gallistel's (1980) *The Organization of Action*, where simpler (though still surprisingly sophisticated) behaviors such as insect walking are described in neurophysiological terms, but where it is argued that more complex behaviors such as the homing ability of the digger wasp must be described in terms of computational representations. Similarly, the more peripheral parts of the visual system have proven amenable to neurophysiological description. But as one moves in toward the brain, where massive interconnection is the rule, description in terms of functional organization becomes increasingly necessary, in part because the relevant neuroanatomy has not been discovered, but also because neural structure per se becomes less dominant within the complexity of the system.

We see therefore that a computational theory of the brain is a different sort of theory than the formal description of planets, hurricanes, thermostats, or stomachs, and that the need for such a theory arises from the combinatorial characteristics of the device. Moreover, the computational mind can be seen as an emergent characteristic in the course of evolution, as nervous systems grow in size and connectivity.

It almost goes without saying that there are consequences for the theory of consciousness. If Theory II is correct and the computational mind is responsible for the distinctions present to consciousness, then where there is no computational mind of interest, there is no consciousness of interest. Thus, we can agree with Globus (1976, 290) that "there is no place to unarbitrarily draw a line ... in a hierarchy of systems increasing in complexity, above which we can say that mind [that is, consciousness] occurs and below which it does not. The notion that awareness somehow emerges at only the highest orders of complexity is human chauvinism at its worst." Yet we can find reason to reject his assertion (p. 290) that "The difference between the minds intrinsic to rock and [human] brain is such that the mind intrinsic to brain is myriad billions of times more aware than that of rock, but still, the difference is *only quantitative* [his italics]." According to Theory II, the relevant transition is not from inanimate to animate but within the animal kingdom, following the emergence of a computational mind; a rock does not encode distinctions. However, change "rock" to "flatworm" in Globus's passage and it takes on some plausibility.

There is another consequence, of greater methodological importance. If the brain is a combinatorial rather than a mass-action device, it follows that no research technique that depends primarily on measuring mass action in the brain can yield detailed understanding of brain function. I have in mind techniques such as EEGs and CAT scans, which can detect localized activity in various parts of the brain; such measures, though useful, can give only a generalized idea of what is going on. The detailed combinatorial properties of the areas in question must be investigated in order to understand how they function. It also follows that measuring the activity of individual neurons does not in itself reveal much, for it is the interaction of each neuron with the others that is responsible for the behavior of the device.

That is not to say that such research is uninteresting. But given the nature of the device, these techniques alone, no matter how refined, are not going to lead to an account of the contents of thought and of conscious experience. Thus I see work in contemporary neuroscience as a complement to, not a potential replacement for, research on the computational mind.

3.2 Computational Theories and Computer Theories

The previous section made clearer what I mean by a computational theory of a device: a theory of the formal combinatorial interactions of the device's functional components. I wish now to distinguish the class of such theories from a narrower class of *computer* theories, theories that encompass all contemporary general-purpose computers. One of the important contributions of neuroscience is that it enables us to place the mind outside the domain of devices covered by computer theories. At the same time it sets quite different boundary conditions on an adequate theory of mind.

Here are four well-known differences between brains and computers whose roots lie in rather elementary facts of neuroscience.

1. *Digital versus quasi-digital functional units.* The basic functional unit of a computer is a binary switch with two states, on and off. The basic functional unit of a brain is a neuron. It was argued by McCulloch and Pitts (1943) that "the activity of the neuron is an all-or-none process"—that is, binary and digital also. Under this idealization they were able to prove mathematically that the computational power of a brain is comparable to that of a computer. McCulloch and Pitts's idealization is based on the fact that when a neuron fires, it always fires in the same way; and for a period after it fires, it is in a "refractory period" during which it cannot fire again. On the other hand, it now appears that rate and pattern of firing, which are continuously variable, also can play a role in neural interactions (Kandel and Schwarz 1981, 23, 162; Anderson 1984, 362, 366). Thus, the action of neurons is only "quasi-digital": there are discrete threshold effects but also ranges of continuous analog behavior. As far as I know, there is no mathematics for large-scale computational devices built out of such units, comparable to the theory of computability for finite-state automata. (Minsky and Papert 1969 might be along the right lines.) Such devices might well have characteristics quite unexpected from the point of view of standard finite-state machines, including computers. (This difference is noted as early as Von Neumann 1958.)

It might be objected that a computer could be programmed to behave in quasi-digital fashion. True enough; but in order to behave functionally like the brain, the neurons would have to be so simulated one by one, a forbidding amount of digital computation. Anything less would be just a description of brain behavior on the order of hurricane or stomach descriptions—nontrivial of course, but nevertheless not an instantiation of the computational mind.

2. *Serial versus massively parallel computation.* The standard architecture for digital computers has always included a central processor that retrieves information from a passive memory, operates in it, and replaces it in memory. The central processor is itself capable of carrying out only one operation at a time; multiple tasks can be carried out simultaneously only by interleaving their sequences of operations. The speed of the machine is increased by increasing the number of sequential operations it can perform per second.

By contrast, no anatomical basis has been found in the brain for a distinction between central processor and memory. Rather, every neuron seems to act like a little independent processor. Consequently, computation in the brain can be carried out in massively parallel fashion, with many processes going on at once and mutually affecting each other. Since the response time of neurons (in particular, the transmission time across synapses) is relatively slow compared to the cycle time of a modern computer, speed of computation must be achieved by means other than brute speed of the component devices. This is particularly critical in tasks involving sensorimotor coordination like hitting a 90 mph baseball and in rapid motor tasks like playing the Rachmaninoff Third Piano Concerto or, for that matter, speaking. In such tasks motor coordination must be achieved within tolerances of 20 milliseconds or less.

Such parallel behavior can to a certain extent be simulated on a serial computer, at great computational expense. But again the result is a description and not an instantiation of the computational mind.

Recent work in computer science has led to the development of "connectionist" machines, computers with a large number of independent but interacting processors (Feldman and Ballard 1982; Rumelhart and Zipser 1985; Ackley, Hinton, and Sejnowski 1985). Such machines do not fall within what I have called "computer theories" and are in some respects more like the brain. Although these machines are of great intrinsic interest, in my opinion they have not yet been applied to enough hard problems of psychology to be able to tell whether they will yield significantly new theories of natural (as opposed to artificial) intelligence.

3. *General-purpose versus specialized hardware.* The standard computer memory is equipotential; that is, the same information can be encoded at any location in it. On the other hand, brain functions are heavily localized, suggesting that there is a great deal of "hardware" differentiation. These localizations seem to be biologically determined, since they are by and large the same across individuals. The major known exception is hemispheric dominance, which is reversed in some left-handers but which is still determined at least partly by heredity (and certainly not by chance or learning!). It is true that, in case of brain damage, brain functions can be shifted around somewhat, especially in the very young. But the baseline

fact, from which these are deviations, is that the brain does not display the equipotentiality of the general-purpose computer memory.

This raises the possibility that the brain has corresponding "software" specializations as well—that is, that the computational mind contains many components, each of which has its own "language" devoted to a special purpose. Since parts II and III will be devoted to developing such a position, I will say nothing further here beyond bringing it up as a premonition of things to come.

4. *Immutability versus change in hardware.* If a computer undergoes a change in behavioral patterns, we can be certain that the change is in the program, not in the physical structure of the computer (barring equipment failure or outside intervention by a repairman). In particular, internally induced behavioral changes ("learning") are caused by one part of the program changing another part.

In the brain, by contrast, there is far less clear-cut division between "software" and "hardware" change. If the reactivity of a synapse changes, is this a change in "program" or "wiring"? If a neuron grows new connections, as happens at least during growth, is this a change in "program" as well as in "wiring"? And so forth. In addition, computational functions in the brain are affected by blood flow, hormonal action, and the like, which have no counterpart in computer function. Thus the brain undergoes a great deal of "hardware" change with corresponding effects on the mind.

This means that ultimately it is less feasible to separate computational considerations entirely from their physical instantiation in the brain than might be expected from the computer analogy. In particular, one should be suspicious of claims like Minsky's (quoted in Huyghe 1983, 34) to the effect that we could build emotions into computers if we cared to. One might build superficial simulations (hurricane-like descriptions) without too much difficulty, but actually instantiating the mechanisms of emotion would, I suspect, require a radical change in the entire conception of the physical device.

In addition to these differences between brain and computer mechanisms, differences in task-specific behavior should give us pause. The sort of thing I have in mind concerns not large-scale cognitive tasks ("A computer could never write Shakespeare!") but ordinary, everyday ones like remembering things. Some memory tasks are trivial for people but so far have eluded programming technology—for instance, quickly recovering the context-appropriate sense of an English word from a vocabulary of tens of thousands, many of which have several senses. Other memory tasks are trivial to program but strenuous for a human unaided by pencil and paper. One example is the game of "Concentration," which begins with a matrix of 50 or so face-down cards. Players take turns turning over two cards. If they match, the player who turned them over gets to keep them; otherwise, they are turned face-down again. The player with the most cards at the end wins. Obviously, if the players can write down the values and locations of cards as they are uncovered, the game is simple, and a computer program on such principles would be child's play. But without external aids the game requires tremendous self-discipline and attention—more than I can usually muster for my daughter's pre-bedtime recreation!

Why should some things that are so easy for people be so hard for computers, and vice versa? One is led to speculate whether there might not be some fundamental differences in computational organization from which the behavioral differences follow as natural consequences.

None of the differences cited in this section leads immediately to a theory of the computational mind, of course. I mention them here as a caution against too literal interpretation of the computer metaphor and as reasons to remain open to computational theories different in character from what we know how to program. At the same time these sorts of facts serve as important boundary conditions on the study of the computational mind: we would like neuroscience to explain certain fundamental aspects of computational organization, and we would like computational organization to explain the character of people's behavior in everyday tasks.

Chapter 4
Forms of Information

We are gradually getting ready for the description of the computational mind. Chapter 3 differentiated this task from neuroscience and from artificial intelligence. In this chapter we must unfortunately differentiate it from much of cognitive psychology. On the other hand, we will become a bit clearer about how the computational mind is related to consciousness.

4.1 Structure and Process

In approaching the computational mind, one may begin with either of two complementary strategies. Both are in the end essential to a complete theory, but it is important to appreciate their distinctness.

The strategy that follows more immediately from the computational analogy is to seek a theory of *processing*. This strategy is predominant in contemporary cognitive psychology, as well as in research on computer simulation of human capacities. In this mode of description, one asks, What is the computational mind doing, and with what internal resources? A processing theory will include a set of procedures or algorithms (analogous to a computer program) that process, store, and retrieve information and can send information on to other procedures. The theory will claim that these are the procedures carried out by the computational mind.

Typically, processing theories have addressed questions such as these: What possible procedure for retrieving words from memory accords with the speed at which humans do it? To what extent does the syntactic analysis of a sentence—or the analysis of a visual scene—proceed without drawing on one's general knowledge of the world? What procedure could restrict the number of strategies one has to try in proving a mathematical theorem or in making a move in chess? What sorts of shared processing facilities are implied by the fact that such-and-such a task interferes with speed or accuracy on *this* task but not *that* one? That is, the focus is primarily on the machinery deployed in ongoing, dynamic mental processes. Not surprisingly, this paradigm of research has been called by its practitioners the *information-processing* approach.

There is, however, a tendency within this approach to neglect the *content* of the information being processed. Although nobody explicitly recommends the analogy, sometimes one gets the impression that information is to be thought of as a sort of abstract liquid that is poured from one memory receptacle into another, that is filtered free of unwanted detail, and that overflows into forgetfulness if the receptacle into which it is being poured is already full. This approach is certainly encouraged by formal information theory (Shannon and Weaver 1949), which is concerned primarily with the *quantity* of information that can be transmitted by different sorts of devices.

However, such an approach cannot tell us how different kinds of information (visual versus auditory, episodic versus semantic, and so on) differ from each other. They might just as well be different-colored liquids. Even more important, it cannot tell us how information of the *same* sort is differentiated—for instance, how the visual appearance of a guitar is differentiated from that of a banana. (Recall that this cannot be accomplished by any direct kind of link to the real world out there; rather, the world as we perceive it is the product, not the source, of such differentiation.)

The point of this caricature of information-processing theories is that a theory of processing, when it gets into any detail at all, must come to grips with the question, What is the *form* of the information that is being processed, stored, or retrieved? This question is at the heart of the second approach to the computational mind—what I will call the *structural* approach. Here the basic issue is to determine what categories, distinctions, and relations must be represented in mental information structures in order to account for human behavior and experience. This approach thus abstracts away from processing and concentrates on what there is to be processed. (To return to the computer analogy, if a processing theory is about programs, a structural theory is about the nature of the internalized data structures on which the programs operate.)

A structural theory in the sense intended here is what Chomsky (1965) calls a "theory of competence" and Marr (1982) calls a "computational theory." The reader should be cautioned, however, that Chomsky's opposition of competence to "performance" is not the same as my opposition of structural to processing theories: Chomsky has used "performance" in a wider sense, to include not only processing but also effects of world knowledge, low-level slips of the tongue, and even biological constraints such as the finiteness of the human life span (which stands in the way of producing sentences over a trillion words long). The fact that "performance" has been used more or less as a theoretical garbage can has, I believe, stood in the way of the understanding of Chomsky's notion of competence. Once the lines are drawn more narrowly—a competence or structural theory as a description of the form of the information being processed, and a processing theory as a description of how the information is processed—the role of the competence theory in an overall theory of the computational mind becomes clearer.

The only branch of psychology where tradition sanctions the distinction between structural and processing theories is the study of language, where *linguistics* is the study of the structure of language and *psycholinguistics* is the study of language processing. In other areas of psychology such as attention, memory, and visual perception one typically finds rather perfunctory discussion of information structure only as a prelude or postlude to extensive treatment of processing.

In fact, psychologists and computer scientists studying language have often expressed indifference or even hostility to the idea of studying linguistic competence per se (for recent examples, see Kintsch 1984 and Schank and Birnbaum 1984). I think the experience of the last thirty years has shown this attitude to be a methodological mistake, for the nature of the structure to be derived can constrain the choice of process, decisively eliminating otherwise attractive choices. In one well-known case, Chomsky's (1957) discussion of the *structure* of language showed that a *processing* theory could not be formulated in terms of the then-popular Markov devices. Marr (1982) makes a similarly forceful point within the theory of vision, showing that theories of visual processing have repeatedly failed because there was no theory of the form of the information the visual system must compute in order to carry out the tasks it does.

To be sure, processing theories can affect structural theories as well—for instance, in Bresnan and Kaplan's (1982) arguments for a nontransformational generative grammar, the better to conform to the needs of current parsers (but see also Berwick and Weinberg's (1984) reply). However, my focus here will be on theories of structure, and I therefore want to show that it is worth thinking hard about the structure of information used in various tasks before attempting to develop theories of processing. To that end, the next two sections will be devoted to rather simple illustrations of the importance of linguistic structure.

4.2 The Importance of Structure to Learning and Memory

Consider the well-worn experimental paradigm espoused by learning theorists of a generation and more ago: the perception and memory of lists of nonsense syllables such as (4.1).

(4.1)   taf tib ine eth yob zup sif

The reason such sequences were of interest, I gather, is that they were supposedly stimuli for which subjects had no previous association and therefore could serve well for studying learning under "purest" conditions. The existence of previous associations, such as experience with the English language, is evidently what makes (4.2a) and (4.2b) easier to perceive and remember. Such associations were taken to contaminate the learning process.

(4.2)   a. dog fat bit boy one sly the
         b. one sly boy bit the fat dog

Now notice that there is a qualitative difference between (4.2a) and (4.2b) as well. (4.2b) will be far easier to memorize and recall, since it forms a sentence of English and (4.2a) does not. Yet (4.2b) is not a sentence that a subject is likely to have heard and memorized before, so what might the "associations" be that so radically facilitate its perception and recognition?

Another way to improve performance on (4.1), as noted by Epstein (1961, 1962), is to impose grammatical structure on its nonsense words, as in (4.3).

(4.3)   a taf tib is inely ething the yob zups and sifs

(Such structure is familiar from Lewis Carroll's "Jabberwocky": "'Twas brillig, and the slithy toves/Did gyre and gimble in the wabe....") Though (4.3) contains all the nonsense syllables of (4.1) plus more, Epstein shows that it is easier to learn and remember sequences like (4.3) than sequences like (4.1). Thus, grammatical structure, independent of meaning, can also facilitate processing.

To twist the problem a little further, observe that (4.1) itself is not as devoid of structure as one might at first imagine. The syllables in (4.1) are possible syllables of English: one can imagine them being unusual words one has never heard of. Contrast (4.1) with (4.4a), which contains pronounceable but non-English syllables, and with (4.4b), which contains (relatively) unpronounceable combinations of three letters.

(4.4)   a. tfa bze ngo pzu ebm kvi egl
         b. tfx lsf cmr sbg qpt wvl nmh

I don't have to do the experiment in order to be fairly certain that subjects will find (4.4a) more difficult in all ways than (4.1), and (4.4b) more difficult still. Finally, we can dissolve the "associations" due to English orthography by presenting sequences like (4.5), which are radically more difficult than (4.1)–(4.4).

(4.5)   **ԷՍՐ ՍՐՆ ՈհՑ ԱԴՐ ԿԵՑ ՍՐՆ ՈհՍ**

Now let us ask, Which of these sequences, if any, involves "pure" learning?

The point of this group of examples is that it is impossible to study processes of perception and memory without asking what structures the subjects impose on the material being perceived and remembered. Some kinds of structure, such as words and letters of the alphabet, can be viewed for a first approximation as memorized items stored whole. But other kinds of structure cannot be so viewed, since they can be imposed on stimuli one has never encountered before. Such is the case with the notion "possible sentence of English," which differentiates (4.2b) from (4.2a), and with the notion "possible word of English," which differentiates (4.1) from (4.4a). For cases like these we need a more substantial approach to structure to account for the way it facilitates processing.

These remarks clearly echo Chomsky's (1957) well-known observation that the *creative* use of language—the ability to understand and produce sentences one has never heard before—is the most basic issue that must be faced in thinking about the psychological implementation of linguistic structure. Chomsky notes that mastery of English cannot require one to have memorized the set of possible English sentences, because that would require both an infinite memory capacity and an infinite time for exposure to the set. Therefore, one's ability to identify and produce novel sentences of English must be attributed to the internalization of a set of principles, or *rules*, that collectively characterize what is involved in sentencehood.

The analogous point about possible *words* of English, on which I have drawn in the contrast between (4.1) and (4.4), is due to Halle (1978). Here the argument is more subtle and in some ways more striking. Evidently, even in a case that apparently involves no more than memorization—the learning of the vocabulary of English—speakers have extracted generalizations about the sound structure of English words. They are typically unable to state these generalizations explicitly and in fact are typically unaware of having extracted them. Nevertheless, by observing the difference between (4.1) and (4.4a), we can infer that English speakers have internalized and can make use of general principles of word structure.

Another piece of evidence for the same point comes from the spontaneous speech errors known as *spoonerisms*, in which sounds are erroneously exchanged among words. One of the most robust findings in the study of speech errors (see, for example, Fromkin 1971 and Garrett 1975) is that spoonerisms observe the principles of word structure, even when they produce nonsense words. For example, one frequently finds errors like the change from (4.6a) to (4.6b), in which the underlined sounds are exchanged. But one never finds something like the change from (4.6c) to (4.6d), which contains the cluster *vl*, impossible in English though pronounceable. Rather, the *v* is automatically and unconsciously changed to *f* as in (4.6e) to produce an allowable configuration. (This example is from Fromkin 1971.)

(4.6)   a. st̲r̲ictly sp̲eaking
         b. spictly st̲reaking
         c. p̲lay the v̲ictor
         d. v̲lay the pictor
         e. flay the pictor

In other words, even when errors take place, the principles of English word structure are adhered to no matter what. Thus these principles must be playing some active role in speech production.

I am stressing word structure rather than sentence structure here in order to help defuse an argument often raised against Chomsky's notion of a competence theory: How can one possibly make a claim about the internalization of principles of English sentence structure, their "psychological reality," without describing their realization in actual processing? Shouldn't the proper theory just describe what one does when one speaks and perceives sentences, bypassing all the superfluous machinery of an internalized task-independent grammar?

This argument has a certain appeal in the case of sentence structure, where we know that active rule-governed processing must take place. But consider the principles of word structure. What seems curious, at least superficially, is that there is no apparent need for such principles in the active use of language (as there is for principles of sentence formation), since they pertain only to items that are individually memorized. We have no immediate insight into their role in ordinary speech; they surface overtly only in ecologically useless tasks like learning nonsense syllables or producing spoonerisms. Nevertheless, performance on such tasks shows that the rules are indeed internalized. Moreover, the fact that they are invoked in tasks that speakers do not normally perform suggests that they cannot be so closely task-bound as to be unstatable outside of their role in processing ordinary speech.

In short, we have good reason to believe in the psychological reality of the rules of English word structure, whatever their particular use in English word processing.

4.3 A Constraint on Syntactic Structure

Let me present a slightly more extended example that brings·out the importance of a theory of structure that is independent of processing considerations.

In a common interrogative construction of English, a *wh*-word such as *who, what,* or *when* appears at the beginning of the sentence; its functional role in the sentence is indicated by a "gap" where a normal declarative sentence would have lexical material. For instance, in *Who did you see?* the verb *see* normally occurs with a following direct object; the gap in this position indicates that *who* functions as direct object. In *Who did you talk about Bill to?* the gap is the object of *to*, whereas in *Who did you talk about to Bill?* the gap is the object of *about*.

This configuration for *wh*-questions is quite general, but there turn out to be a number of cases in which it breaks down. One of the most blatant was first explored in detail by Ross (1967). Contrast (4.7a) with (4.7b) and (4.8a) with (4.8b).

(4.7) a. What do you like to eat peanut butter and?
            (Answer: I like to eat peanut butter and *mustard*.)
       b. What do you like to eat peanut butter with?

(4.8) a. What will Harry spread on the hot dogs and serve the drinks?
            (Answer: Harry will spread *ketchup* on the hot dogs and serve the drinks.)
       b. What will Harry spread on the hot dogs before serving the drinks?

Speakers of English will intuitively recognize that the (a) sentences are deviant. Yet they are, at least superficially, no more complex than the (b) sentences, and they are constructed on the basis of the same general strategy as any other *wh*-question. Thus, there is an apparent loss of generality here that cries out for explanation.

Ross isolates the structural condition under which this sort of deviance occurs: it occurs when a gap inside a coordinate construction indicates the function of an element (in this case *what*) outside the coordinate construction. The gap in (4.7a) is within the coordinate construction *peanut butter and x*; by contrast, there is no coordination in (4.7b), and the gap is the object of the preposition *with*. Hence (4.7a) violates Ross's constraint and (4.7b) does not. Similarly, the gap in (4.8a) is within the coordinate construction *spread x on the hot dogs and serve the drinks*, whereas (4.8b) contains no coordination, since *before serving the drinks* is a subordinate clause. Ross calls this condition the *Coordinate Structure Constraint*.

Two putative explanations of these facts suggest themselves immediately. The first is that (4.7) and (4.8) "make no sense"; that is, they are semantically deviant in some way. But in fact we know precisely what these sentences *should* mean, as indicated by the possible answers given with the examples and by the close paraphrases in the (b) sentences. So this attempted line of explanation will not wash. A second possibility is to say that one has never heard sentences like these before, so one is not equipped to process them. But this line fails also when we realize that most sentences we hear in our life have never been uttered before. What should single these sentences out for special treatment, such that lack of exposure is criterial? (Moreover, as a practicing linguist, I have been dealing with sentences like these for over twenty years and they never get to sounding better!)

The importance of this deviance is intensified by two additional facts. First, given all the kinds of mistakes children make in learning English, they never seem to come up with sentences like (4.7a) and (4.8a). Second, all languages of the world that have the same sort of question construction as English obey the very same constraint. These observations suggest that the Coordinate Structure Constraint has nothing to do with how language is learned but rather that it is an automatic consequence of human cognitive capacity in general or of human linguistic capacity in particular. What is curious about the constraint is that it serves no (as yet discovered) function. It appears to be just an arbitrary kink in the system that prevents us from being able to express certain things in certain ways.

The Coordinate Structure Constraint is one of the simpler of a wide range of limitations that restrict the generality of principles of sentence structure. Such constraints have become a major preoccupation of syntactic theorists (see, for example, Chomsky 1972, chapter 2; 1975, chapter 3; 1981), and it is not hard to see why: they are phenomena that most clearly reflect the organization of language, independent of questions of communicative function, utility, social interaction, and learning. Moreover, it is doubtful that they could have been discovered—and certain that they could not be fruitfully explored—in a mode of theoretical description that stressed processing considerations at the expense of the study of structure per se. (The argument is sometimes advanced that the study of such constraints is of no interest in designing computer implementations of natural languages. This may be true, but if so, it only shows the magnitude of the difference in goals between the study of artificial intelligence and the study of natural intelligence.)

To return to my main theme: I have tried to show the virtues of separating the theory of the computational mind into two modes of description. The processing mode needs no recommendation, since obviously a computational theory calls for a description of process. On the other hand, despite the fact that Chomsky has been arguing the point for nearly three decades, more recently joined by Marr, the importance of theories in the structural mode is still widely disputed. I have argued here (1) that the availability of structure has a facilitating effect on processing; (2) that particular structures must be available for a number of tasks; (3) that we can find evidence for structure even when we are not sure what processing purpose it serves; and (4) that the study of structure per se reveals organization that could not be envisioned within the framework of a process description.

All of this, of course, only serves as methodological justification for undertaking a description in the structural mode. I in no way intend to suggest that processing is to be ignored. However, there is a further reason to concentrate on structure rather than process, to which we now turn.

4.4 Lashley's Observation; *Theory III*

In his provocative "Cerebral Organization and Behavior" (1956) Karl Lashley discusses the relationship of consciousness to neurophysiology. Although his paradigm does not include a computational mind mediating between neural and phenomenological description, the following passage nonetheless speaks eloquently to the problems we face here.

> *No activity of mind is ever conscious.* [Lashley's italics] This sounds like a paradox, but it is nonetheless true. There are order and arrangement, but there is no experience of the creation of that order. I could give numberless examples, for there is no exception to the rule. A couple of illustrations should suffice. Look at a complicated scene. It consists of a number of objects standing out against an indistinct background: desk, chairs, faces. Each consists of a number of lesser sensations combined in the object, but there is no experience of putting them together. The objects are immediately present. When we think in words, the thoughts come in grammatical form with subject, verb, object, and modifying clauses falling into place without our having the slightest perception of how the sentence structure is produced.... Experience clearly gives no clue as to the means by which it is organized. (Lashley 1956, 4)

Let us see what this passage says in our terms. Theory II in section 2.4 proposed that the character of the phenomenological mind is to be explicated by virtue of active, privileged elements of the computational mind being made available to consciousness, while other elements remain unconscious. Lashley is pointing out that computational activity—processing—is *always* unconscious: what is revealed to consciousness is the *consequence* of processing, namely an information structure. This means that if there is to be a relation between computation and awareness, it will be most directly revealed by a theory of structure rather than by a theory of processing. Thus, for our purposes there is still another vital reason to pursue a theory in a structural mode of description.

A quick caution: There is no question that we are aware of ongoing processes in the world and within ourselves, and this might be hastily taken to refute Lashley's point. However, more careful consideration is necessary. When we are aware of an object in motion, for instance, we are still not aware of the processes within us that give rise to this perception. That is, such awareness is based on a dynamic information structure, not on a mental process per se. Similarly, in awareness of one's own thought one experiences a succession of information structures, plus perhaps a sense of effort, but not the computational processes that give rise to the succession. Hence, this objection shows only that a theory of consciousness must include an account of the computational structures involved in process perception and process conceptualization; it does not show that we are aware of computational activity itself. Thus Lashley's point stands.

We therefore can refine Theory II to incorporate Lashley's Observation, by claiming that only structures, not processes, support distinctions in awareness.

Theory III
The distinctions present in conscious awareness are caused by/ supported by/projected from information structures in the computational mind that (1) are active and (2) have other (as yet unspecified) privileged properties.

In light of Lashley's Observation, consider a widely held view of consciousness as a sort of "executive function" in the mind. I have already mentioned some exponents of this view: Minsky's (1968) notion of a "supreme organizer," Frith's (1981) treatment of consciousness as a high-level monitor system, Bruner's (1983) idea of "an instrument for the analysis of necessity and trouble." There are various ways to read this position. In the worst case it seems to fall back on a Cartesian interactionism, claiming that the phenomenological domain itself has the function of directing processing in the computational domain. (Most of the authors quoted would probably deny this reading, though it is likely the reading most appealing to common sense and is explicitly adopted by Popper and Eccles (1977).) However, we ruled out such an interactionist account in chapter 2, with the Hypothesis of the Nonefficacy of Consciousness. Suppose, then, that we read this position in a less objectionable fashion—say, that the processes of the central executive support the form of consciousness. In this case it still violates Lashley's Observation that processes are never available to consciousness. And surely this is intuitively correct: we generally have no awareness at all of the processing that lies behind a judgment—only of the emergence of the result and perhaps of some intermediate results along the way. So this reading of the position is untenable as well.

Finally, one can read it along the lines suggested by the quotation from Johnson-Laird given earlier (1983, 465): "The contents of consciousness are the current values of parameters governing the high-level computations of the operating system." Here Johnson-Laird ascribes consciousness to information structures, not to processes, so his proposal, unlike the others, does conform to Lashley's Observation. Thus, this reading of the "executive" theory is still within the class of theories we will consider. We will take it up again in chapter 14, when we have a better understanding of the forms of information in the computational mind.

4.5 Levels of Structure

It is clear that information entering the mind comes in different forms: from spatially arrayed retinal receptors, from frequency detectors of some sort in the ears, from pressure-sensitive receptors in the skin, and so forth. The information *leaving* the mind must ultimately be in the form of patterns of stimulation to muscle fibers, since it is through motion of the body that we act on the world. (This includes speech, of course—but not telekinesis, which, if it existed, would be direct action by the mind on the external world, parallel to the direct "grasping" of reality that we denied in chapter 1.)

It is also clear that none of these forms of information suffices to explain the way we understand the world in terms of objects, their motions, and our actions upon them. Rather, some form of internal code must be posited that permits integration of all the different input and output pathways into a unified form, so that we can, for instance, speak of localizing the same object through visual, auditory, or tactile cues. Hence, the mind must be able to transform information from one form to another, for instance from the form provided by the retinas, through a form suitable for visuomotor integration, thence into a form appropriate for motor output.

A number of terms are used to differentiate forms of information structure: Kosslyn (1980) uses the term "format," Marr (1982) "stage of representation," Anderson (1983) "representational type," and so forth. Here I will use the terms *level of mental information structure* and *level of representation* more or less interchangeably. I will also distinguish a gradation from "lower" or "more peripheral" levels of structure to "higher" or "more central" levels. The lowest levels of structure are, roughly, those that interface most directly with the physical world: the retinal array and the like on the input side, instructions to muscles on the output side. The highest-level ones, still more roughly, are those that represent the greatest degree of abstraction, integration, and generalization vis-à-vis sensory input; intuitively, we would like "thought" to consist of computations over a fairly central level of representation.

Let me be slightly more precise about what I mean by a level of representation: it consists of a structured repertoire of distinctions that can be encoded by the combinatorial organization of the computational mind. In the theories to be discussed here this structured repertoire is built up from a finite set of primitive distinctions, plus a finite set of principles of combination that make it possible to build primitives into larger information structures.

The notion of a level of information structure as a structured set of distinctions or oppositions has roots in the structuralist linguistics of the Prague Circle (Trubetzkoy 1939; Jakobson, Fant, and Halle 1952); there are also affinities to Spencer-Brown's (1969) approach to the foundations of mathematics. The essential idea is that one cannot notice or encode a distinction between two entities without having a means of representing the difference. One cannot encode similarity between two entities without defining a formal opposition between these two entities on the one hand and everything dissimilar on the other. Even to notice or recognize a single entity, one must be able to differentiate it from everything else; that is, it must be distinguished as the "figure" of a "figure-ground" opposition in the sense of Gestalt psychology. Thus, making distinctions and forming oppositions lie at the basis of a theory of mental representation; to say that an organism has certain information is in effect to say that it has encoded certain distinctions chosen from within its available repertoire.

As a simple illustration of a level of representation, consider the retinal array. Here the primitive distinctions might be (roughly) position, light intensity, and color. The principles of combination might be (1) identifying a position as encoding a particular intensity and color at a given time; (2) identifying the spatial relation of two adjacent positions (above, below, left of, and so on). From these primitives and principles of combination the state of the entire retinal field at a given time can be encoded. The total repertoire of distinctions that the retinal field can encode is the union of the possible states of individual positions. The *expressive power* of this level of representation—the range of information it can pass on to other parts of the computational mind—is defined by this repertoire of states.

This level, at least as I have described it, does not explicitly express *regularities* over the retinal array, such as the presence of edges or the like. If these regularities are made explicit—for example, encoded as a distinction "edge versus nonedge"—such encoding must belong with the distinctions of some other level of information structure. (Alternatively, it *does* belong at this level, and the preliminary theory of this level in the preceding paragraph is wrong.)

As soon as we raise such possibilities of different levels of representation, methodological issues begin to assail us. How can one tell what information is in what form? What evidence does one need in order to decide that two forms of information are distinct? Shouldn't one try to minimize the number of different levels, on general grounds of theoretical economy? Though I wholeheartedly agree that these are genuine and important questions, it is my feeling that if one demands answers to them as a precondition to research, one inevitably bogs down in sterile discussions of scientific methodology. Better that they should be answered tacitly for the most part, by sensitive scientific practice; they are most profitably brought into the open, it seems to me, only when one already has detailed theoretical options to confront. (Such a situation will arise in section 9.5, where we will discuss the debate over the proper form of representation for visual imagery and compare it with parallel issues in linguistics.)

We have seen, then, that there must be a number of distinct forms or levels of mental information structure, in order to account for the interaction of different input and output modalities. Consequently, the following questions emerge as crucial in the description of the computational mind: (1) How many different levels are there? (2) What are their distinctive characteristics—in particular, their primitives and principles of combination? (3) What is each one used for? (4) What are the formal relationships that permit information in one of these forms to be transformed into other forms? These questions are familiar in the study of language, where the separation of linguistic information into phonological (sound structure), syntactic (phrase structure), and semantic (meaning) levels is firmly entrenched in tradition. Accordingly, parts II and III, which survey the information structures of the computational mind, will begin with language, then move on to faculties where the separation of levels is less intuitively obvious.

In the course of this survey we will find that other faculties have the same general organization as language. Let me state the overall claims explicitly as the *Hypothesis of Levels*.

Hypothesis of Levels
1. Each faculty of mind has its own characteristic chain of levels of structure from lowest (most peripheral) to highest (most central).
2. These chains intersect at various points.
3. The levels of structure at the intersections of chains are responsible for the interactions among faculties.
4. The central levels at which "thought" takes place, largely independent of sense modality, are at the intersection of many distinct chains.

In short, the notion of level of information structure will play a central role in articulating the organization of the computational mind.

To finish this section, I should allay potential misunderstanding by mentioning some notions that must not be confused with that of levels of structure. One is the notion of "functional architecture," which is part of a theory of processing and which is described in terms of different memories such as iconic memory, auditory memory, short-term memory, episodic memory, and so forth. These are descriptions, not of levels of representation, but rather of receptacles in which information can be stored. Although it is important to find out what receptacles there are, it is also crucial to remember that in a computational device information must be stored *in some form* and that information must be sent from one receptacle to another *in some form*. So the question of what receptacles exist for information processing is logically independent of the question of the form(s) in which each receptacle is capable of storing information. (Empirically, of course, the questions are ultimately interwoven, as we will see in chapter 6.)

As an example of the confusions that may arise, consider the distinction between "episodic" and "semantic" long-term memory, proposed by Tulving (1972). The former is envisaged as storing information about particular events in one's life, and the latter as storing general time-independent knowledge such as word meanings. This distinction conceals two separate questions: (1) Are there different *forms* in which episodic and semantic information are encoded? and (2) Are there different *functional elements* of the mind in which such information is stored? The outcomes of the two questions may be independent. There could be a single form of information (that is, a single level of representation) for episodic and semantic information, stored in two distinct receptacles with different retrieval properties; or there could be two different levels of representation stored in a common facility. In short, one must keep separate the issues of what functional facilities there are and what forms of information these facilities store or process.

A slightly different notion of level appears in Craik and Lockhart's (1972) "levels of processing." Craik and Lockhart speak of different "stages" in the course of perceiving, understanding, and remembering, such that "earlier" stages are in a different form of representation from "later" stages. This conflates the issue of structure with the issue of processing, assuming that more peripheral forms necessarily are derived prior to more central forms. We will discuss this issue in some detail in sections 6.1 and 6.2. For the moment, notice only that, in speech *production*, the meaning of the utterance (a central level of representation) presumably exists prior to the peripheral information that drives the vocal tract to make sounds. Thus, it is improper to think of the progression from lower to higher levels in the sense intended here as necessarily connected to any sort of temporal order in processing.

A distinction of "level" also appears in descriptions of computer languages, where it is common practice for a "high-level" language such as LISP to be interpreted or translated into a "lower-level" language such as assembly language, which in turn is interpreted into machine language, the language that the computer actually executes. This distinction between high and low levels corresponds to the problem in psychology of specifying the mapping between abstract computational structures and neurological implementation, a problem orthogonal to that of specifying the levels of representation in the sense intended here. For example, there is no sense in which phonological structure is closer than syntactic structure to the neurological implementation of natural language. Both are equally "high-level codes" in the computer scientist's sense. However, in the sense used here phonology *is* a lower-level representation than syntax, in that it is formally more closely related to the acoustic signal and less closely related to meaning.

4.6 The Disunity of Awareness; *Theory IV*

The literature contains many allusions to the "unity of consciousness." By this term is meant the fact that, barring pathological conditions such as split personality, one understands all one's experiences and memories as happening to a single self. But I do not recall ever having come across mention of an equally obvious *dis*unity in consciousness. This disunity will prove to play an important role in relating the computational mind to the phenomenological.

What I have in mind is the fact that experience is sharply differentiated by modality. There is no mistaking visual awareness, for example, for auditory awareness, or either of these for tactile awareness. They are vividly differentiated in experience. To be sure, one may be able to determine by either sight or touch that some object is square, say—and at a later time one may not remember which. But in the experience itself there is no doubt whatsoever.

This observation seems almost so trivial as to be beneath notice; but it is far from logically necessary. Fortunately for my point, there is a contrasting example in taste and smell, whose phenomenological qualia intermingle indistinguishably. We can't tell which parts of something's "taste" are due to taste proper and which to smell. Why shouldn't the other senses be like that? Try to imagine what it would be like! (Another such case, spatial orientation, will be discussed briefly in section 10.2.)

Theory III, considered in the light of the Hypothesis of Levels, suggests an approach to this disunity in awareness. Theory III claims that particular privileged information structures of the computational mind cause/support/project the distinctions that are present in awareness. The Hypothesis of Levels has claimed, in advance of the evidence of parts II and III, that each faculty of the computational mind has its own proprietary levels of information structure, plus possibly one or more levels that are shared with other faculties. In turn, each level of structure is by definition a distinct structured repertoire of distinctions, with its own "alphabet" of primitives and its own principles of combination. Putting these pieces together, we can see that *the way to achieve a faculty-specific set of distinctions in awareness is to project it from a faculty-specific level of information structure.* For example, specifically visual distinctions in awareness can be produced by projecting them from a level of representation that deals in specifically visual computational distinctions.

The hypothesis that emerges from these considerations is that each modality of awareness comes from a different level or set of levels of representation. The disunity of awareness thus arises from the fact that each of the relevant levels involves its own special repertoire of distinctions. Such a hypothesis furthermore offers a straightforward way around the exceptional case of taste and smell: this particular modality of awareness may be projected from a level of representation in which information from the two senses has been combined into a relatively homogeneous repertoire of distinctions.

Though much remains to be fleshed out in formulating this position, let us state it roughly for now as Theory IV.

Theory IV
The distinctions present in conscious awareness are caused by/ supported by/projected from information structures in the computational mind that (1) are active, (2) are of privileged levels of representation, and (3) have other (as yet unspecified) privileged properties. In particular, each distinct modality of awareness is due to a distinct (set of) level(s) of representation.

As we will see in chapter 14, where we will have more evidence to back it up, Theory IV goes against the grain of the prevailing approaches to consciousness, which start with the premise that consciousness is unified and then try to locate a unique source for it. Theory IV claims that consciousness is fundamentally not unified and that one should seek multiple sources. (I have come across only one suggestion of such a position in the literature, in Churchland 1983.)

One last point bears mention. The distinctions made here among "modalities" of experience cut across the distinctions made in section 1.1 among "varieties" of experience. For example, just as one can experience perception, illusions, imagery, and hallucinations in the visual modality, so one can experience each of these in the auditory, tactile, or olfactory modalities. And in one's dreams one can hear, feel, and smell as well as see.

It is important to notice, moreover, that the modalities possible in imagery are exactly the same as those of perception: at least for a first approximation, the repertoire of distinctions in, say, visual imagery is exactly the same as (or perhaps a subset of) the repertoire of distinctions in visual perception, and similarly for the other modalities. This suggests that for each modality of awareness the *same* level of representation is responsible for all the varieties of experience. This point too requires fleshing out and clarification, though these are best put off until chapters 14 and 15.

We have now gone about as far as possible with the mind-mind problem, given our minimal degree of specificity about the character of the computational mind. In order to make any further progress, it is necessary to become a great deal more explicit about levels of representation and their interactions. Parts II and III are devoted to this task. After the rigors of examining three faculties in detail, we finally will emerge in part IV in a position to refine the theory of consciousness further.

PART II
The Language Faculty and What It Expresses

Chapter 5

Levels of Linguistic Structure

This chapter introduces the two levels of representation that have specifically to do with language: phonological and syntactic structure. I will discuss the sorts of evidence that lead linguists to believe that these levels are autonomous from the speech signal on the one hand and from meaning on the other, and I will give some hint of the richness of structure that has been discovered.

The usual introductory presentations of linguistic theory (such as Fromkin and Rodman 1974; Akmajian, Demers, and Harnish 1984; Lightfoot 1982) do not lend themselves entirely to being integrated with the rest of the computational mind. As my overall goal here is a large-scale integrated view, I have formulated my account somewhat differently from the standard treatments. This will be most noticeable in the discussion of the relationship between syntax and phonology and in the view of the lexicon (sections 5.6 and 5.7).

This chapter will also provide further grist for the distinction stressed in chapter 4 between theories of structure and theories of processing. Chapter 6 will put this evidence to work in developing aspects of a theory of processing in speech understanding and speech production. The issue of how language is formally connected to meaning is put off until chapter 7.

5.1 Phonological Structure

One of our strongest intuitive convictions about language is that the speech stream comes segmented into discrete units linearly ordered in time: words, and within them syllables, and within them individual speech sounds. It therefore comes as a shock to discover that such segmentation is hardly in evidence in the acoustic signal that constitutes the physical manifestation of speech. For a simple case, there is no acoustic difference between *attack* and *a tack* or between *an ash* and *a Nash*. Yet we "hear" different word boundaries, by virtue of our understanding of the context in which the expression appears.

For a more complex case, consider the boundaries between words in a pair like *Dick stops* versus *Dick's tops*. Acoustic recordings show, and careful

introspection reveals, that in speech at normal speed the distinction between these is not a space of silence before the *s* sound in one case and after
it in the other; the *s* follows immediately after the *k* sound of *Dick* in both
cases. Rather, the primary difference appears in the *t* that follows the *s*. Its
silent interval is maintained slightly longer and its release is slightly noisier
in *tops* than in *stops*. In other words, the acoustic cues for the word boundary are not at the word boundary itself but in the character of the end of a
consonant *following* the word boundary.

When we turn to the intuitively evident segmentation into individual
speech sounds, matters become even more puzzling. Consider the words
tap and *back*. Introspectively, these words are composed of three successive
speech sounds, and they share the same middle sound. Acoustically, however, the situation is quite otherwise: each word comes out as a smear of
formants (vocal tract resonances) that are continuously changing in frequency, and there are no identical parts that correspond to what is heard as
the identical vowel *a*. Rather, the acoustic character of the beginning of the
vowel is strongly affected by (and serves as a crucial perceptual cue for) the
character of the preceding consonant, and the end of the vowel is likewise
altered by the following consonant. These effects on the vowel are of
sufficiently great duration that no steady-state vowel *a* is present acoustically. Moreover, in many cases, such as the distinction between *pat* and *pap*,
the end effects on the vowel provide the only acoustic cue for the correct
choice of consonant. The acoustic signal may be roughly segmented into
temporal intervals that contain cues for $p + a$ and for $a + t$ but none that
consist of all the cues for *p* alone or *a* alone or *t* alone. (See Fodor, Bever,
and Garrett 1974, chapter 6, and Liberman and Studdert-Kennedy 1977 for
much discussion.)

The fundamental tenet behind the computational theory of mind is that
an organism can make no judgment or discrimination without having an
appropriate representation on which to base it. In the present case, the fact
that people segment the speech stream into discrete linear elements leads
us to posit a level of mental representation, *phonological structure*, in which
such segmentation does in fact exist. In phonological structure, then, a
speech stream is explicitly encoded as a linear sequence of discrete *words*,
which are themselves divided into discrete *phonological segments* (individual
speech sounds).

Among the more elementary observations about phonological structure
is that speech sounds fall into natural classes, the most obvious of which is
the distinction between consonants and vowels. Within these large classes
subclassifications appear, often based on articulatory distinctions. For instance, consonants differ with respect to factors such as those listed in (5.1),
and vowels differ with respect to dimensions listed in (5.2).

(5.1)   Complete obstruction of air flow (stop consonant)
        yes: *p, t*
        no: *f, s*
    Vocal cord vibration during production (voiced consonant)
        yes: *v, d*
        no: *f, t*
    Air flow through nasal passages (nasal consonant)
        yes: *m, n*
        no: *b, d*
    Point of major constriction:
        lips: *p, b, m, f*
        tongue tip on or behind upper teeth: *t, d, n, s*
        back of tongue on roof of mouth: *k, g*

(5.2)   Height of tongue and lower jaw
        high: vowels in *feed, food*
        low: vowels in *fat, spa*
    Body of tongue forward or retracted
        front: vowels in *feed, fat*
        back: vowels in *food, spa*
    Lips rounded
        yes: vowels in *food, foal*
        no: vowels in *feed, spa*

These categorizations of speech sounds play a role in stating principles of phonological structure. For instance, the syllables in (5.3a) are potential English words (in the sense of section 4.2), but those in (5.3b) are not.

(5.3)   a. stat   spack   skap
      b. sdat   sback   sgap

There is a simple generalization behind this difference: when a syllable begins with *s* followed by a stop consonant, the stop must be unvoiced (that is, *p, t,* or *k* but not *b, d,* or *g*). Notice that the combinations in (5.3b) are perfectly pronounceable. They may even occur in English if the *s* belongs to the preceding syllable (*misdate, misbrand, misguided*) or the preceding word (*this date, this back, this gap*). Thus, the distinction between (5.3a) and (5.3b) is a fact about the phonological structure of English, not an articulatory or acoustic problem. To be stated with proper generality, this distinction must make reference to the property of voicing.

Modern phonological theory posits, therefore, that speech segments are mentally encoded not as undifferentiated wholes but as explicit complexes of *phonological distinctive features*. Each feature of a phonological segment consists of a value (usually + or −) along one of the classificatory dimensions, and the collection of features is sufficient to completely specify the speech sound. Thus the phonological structure of the word *fat* would be roughly as shown in (5.4), a linear sequence of three phonological segments, each elaborated into a matrix of distinctive features.

(5.4)
$$
\begin{bmatrix}
+\,\text{consonant} \\
-\,\text{stop} \\
-\,\text{voiced} \\
-\,\text{nasal} \\
\text{labial articulation}
\end{bmatrix}
\begin{bmatrix}
-\,\text{consonant} \\
-\,\text{high} \\
+\,\text{front} \\
-\,\text{round}
\end{bmatrix}
\begin{bmatrix}
+\,\text{consonant} \\
+\,\text{stop} \\
-\,\text{voiced} \\
-\,\text{nasal} \\
\text{dental articulation}
\end{bmatrix}
$$

There is a certain amount of debate in the field on precisely what is the correct set of distinctive features—and I have considerably oversimplified here. But there is general agreement, going back to Jakobson, Fant, and Halle (1952), that distinctive feature analysis of the general form shown in (5.4) is an essential part of phonological structure. (I might mention also that the theory of phonological distinctive features, originally developed by Jakobson and Trubetzkoy in the 1930s, was a primary inspiration for the structuralism of Lévi-Strauss. It is not clear, though, whether the theory is as well suited for anthropological purposes as for phonological.)

The hypothesis of distinctive features again rests on the fundamental principle of the computational mind: distinctions and generalizations made by the organism must be explicitly supported by the information the organism processes. There can be no appeal to "implicit understanding" of similarity. We cannot, for example, just say that *t* and *p* are more alike then *t* and *a*, so naturally *t* and *p* appear in similar patterns and *t* and *a* do not. The purpose of distinctive features is to spell out exhaustively the distinctions, generalizations, and similarities to which human speakers are sensitive and that are therefore claimed to be "psychologically real." We return to this issue in the next section.

In addition to the linear sequence of segments, phonological structure must contain larger-scale segmentations of the speech stream, into syllables and words. The traditional theory (up to and including Chomsky and Halle 1968) was that this segmentation is marked by boundary symbols interpolated in the linear sequence of phonological segments. More recent practice (for instance, Selkirk 1984) treats the larger-scale segmentations as a labeled bracketing of the sequence of segments. For instance, (5.5) shows the bracketing of the phrase *eighteen men*. (For clarity, I omit representing the elaboration of segments into distinctive features, but it should be understood as mentally present. I do present examples in phonetic notation, though, to emphasize that we are dealing with spoken rather than written language.)

(5.5)   [Word[Syll ey] [Syll tin]] [Word[Syll men]]

Distinctive feature theory and the bracket notation together provide a uniform way of describing the phonological aspects of the speech stream in all human languages. Any particular language, of course, makes use of only a subset of the available sounds, and moreover only a subset of the possible combinations of those sounds. English, for example, does not permit the consonant clusters in (5.3b) at the beginning of a syllable. Other languages (such as Japanese) permit no consonant clusters at all at the beginning of a syllable, and still others (such as Russian) permit much more complex combinations than English. These constraints can be stated as partial templates for possible syllables, couched in distinctive feature notation. As argued in chapter 4, such constraints are part of one's tacit knowledge of one's language—even if it is not clear how they are employed in active language use.

A distinction is commonly made between *underlying* phonological structure and *surface* (or *phonetic*) structure. To make clear the basis for the distinction, I will present a well-known example. First consider the triplets of words in (5.6).

(5.6)   a. leap   lean   lee
        b. pipe   pied   pie
        c. lake   laid   lay

Each of these triplets contains words that share an initial consonant and a vowel but differ in the ending. By pronouncing the words in succession, you will be able to observe that the vowel has a shorter duration in the first member of each triplet than in the other two. Systematic investigation reveals that a stressed vowel preceding an *unvoiced* consonant is invariably of relatively shorter duration than one that precedes a voiced consonant or no consonant at all (within the same word).

Next consider the pairs in (5.7).

(5.7)   a. ride   rider
        b. write   writer

You will notice that in the second member of these pairs the *d* and *t* are not pronounced with their full value but are realized just as a light flap of the tongue tip against the roof of the mouth. (This is true only for American speakers—not British.) This variation too is systematic: *t* and *d* become flaps when they come between a stressed vowel and an unstressed one. As a result of this reduction to a flap, *t* and *d* often become indistinguishable: compare *latter* and *ladder*, for example.

Now carefully compare the casual pronunciations of *writer* and *rider*. Despite the spelling, the major difference between them is in the length of the vowel, not in the quality of the second consonant. How does this come about? What has happened, intuitively, is that although the *t* and *d* receive the same realization, as flaps, the former still "counts" as unvoiced and the latter as voiced for the purpose of determining the length of the vowel.

This intuition is expressed formally in phonological theory by positing two distinct phonological structures. In *underlying* phonological form *writer* has a *t* and *rider* a *d*, and there is no distinction of vowel length. This form expresses three generalizations. First, it shows a direct phonological relation between *write* and *writer* and between *ride* and *rider*. Second, it relates American to British dialects, since they are posited to have the same underlying form. Third, the omission of a distinction in vowel length corresponds to the generalization (to which this particular case is an exception) that vowel length is not distinctive in English—for example, there are no words *leep* and *leeep* that differ only in the length of the vowel (as there are in some languages).

On the other hand, in *surface* phonological form (or phonetic form) *writer* and *rider* both contain flaps, and the observed distinction in vowel length *is* represented. The surface phonological form is derived from underlying form by the application of two rules. First, vowel length is differentiated according to whether the vowel is followed by a voiced or an unvoiced consonant. Then, *t* and *d* preceded by a stressed vowel and followed by an unstressed vowel become flaps. (5.8) illustrates the derivation. (Again, elaboration into distinctive features is suppressed for convenience; the "neutral" vowel in the unstressed syllable is notated as ə, and the flapped sound as *D*.)

(5.8)	Underlying forms	raytər	raydər
	Differentiation of length (ā = long a)	raytər	rāydər
	Flapping	rayDər	rāyDər = surface forms

This derivation expresses the intuition that the flap in *writer* counts as unvoiced, whereas the flap in *rider* counts as voiced: they *are* unvoiced and voiced, respectively, in underlying form, and the length rule applies before both are changed into flaps. By contrast, in British English the flapping rule is absent, and the surface forms are the output of the length rule alone, preserving the *t-d* distinction.

This small set of examples illustrates in microcosm the standard conception of phonological information today. Underlying phonological structure represents regularities in the distribution of sounds in the language, and phonetic structure represents actual pronunciation. The two structures are related by an ordered sequence of rules that change the former step by step into the latter.

Although these rules "apply" in an "order," there is no implication that they are temporally ordered in active processing. Rather, rule ordering is

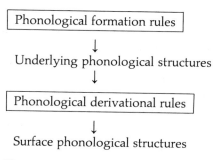

Figure 5.1
Organization of phonology

the formal device that determines the way rules interact; it proves to be the most general way of expressing the formal relationship between underlying and surface phonological structures. Like the templates for permissible syllable structures, the rules and their ordering express generalizations about the structure of the language, but their role in active language use is at present unknown. (To me, this is a surprising lacuna in psycholinguistics: there has been extensive treatment of the relationship between acoustic and phonetic form and of that between underlying and surface syntactic structure, but to my knowledge none on the role of phonological derivation in processing.)

Phonological structure is one of the clearest and least controversial examples of a level of mental representation. It consists of an analysis of an utterance quite distinct from the acoustic form. The elements of a phonological representation can be completely specified in terms of a set of *primitives* and *principles of combination*. The primitives are the distinctive features and the notions of phonological segment, syllable, and word. The principles of combination are (1) the simultaneous combination of a compatible set of distinctive features into a matrix for a single phonological segment; (2) the concatenation of segments; and (3) the bracketing of concatenations of segments into syllables and of syllables into words. Out of these primitives and principles of combination can be built both underlying and surface phonological representations of any utterance in any language. The additional principles that constrain available structures in any particular language are also stated in terms of the elements of phonological structure.

The overall system has a structure more or less as diagrammed in figure 5.1. I have exemplified formation rules here by the templates for possible English syllables, and derivational rules by the rules of length differentiation and flapping. Again, the arrows in figure 5.1 do not represent temporal relationships, only formal ones; the role of both kinds of rules in active processing is an open question. (And, as stressed in section 4.2, the fact that one may not immediately think of a way to implement them in active processing is not an argument against the rules' existence.)

This is the kind of organization we will typically find in levels of representation: a set of possible structures defined by a set of primitives and principles of combination and constrained by a set of formation rules. In some cases we will again encounter the distinction between underlying and surface representation, mediated by a set of derivational rules. (In linguistic terminology the underlying and surface forms are usually called distinct *levels*. However, I wish to reserve the term *level* for a structure with its own autonomous primitives and principles of combination, for example, phonology as opposed to syntax. Therefore, I will call underlying and surface phonological form *sublevels* of the level of phonological structure.)

5.2 The Psychological Reality of Formalism

A claim almost taken for granted in the practice of linguistic research, but invariably puzzling to those outside the field, is that the formalism in which the theory is stated is "psychologically real." Since I have already introduced enough formalism to discuss this claim, I will bring it up at this point to forestall misunderstanding later on.

What does it mean to say that phonological structures are "psychologically real"? It does not mean that they are necessarily available to conscious awareness (in fact, if they were, theoretical phonology would be a trivial introspective enterprise). Rather, they are to be considered as "data structures" of the computational mind that have indirect consequences for the organization of awareness and behavior. The primitives and principles of combination discovered by phonological research are claimed to be the elements out of which these data structures can be constructed.

What is the status of the formalism in which phonological theory is couched? It is not as though, for example, some neuron can be found that has a little label [+ voiced] on it (any more than if, when we use the symbol *e* to represent an electron in physics, we are implying that real electrons have little *e*'s written on them). Obviously, the labels used in the formalism are chosen arbitrarily for the theoretician's convenience.

What is significant, though, is the *organization* of the symbols. Their combinatorial properties reflect a system of distinctions and oppositions that *are* claimed to play a role in psychologically real data structures. For instance, the notational opposition of [+ voiced] to [− voiced] is meant to claim that there is a two-valued dimension in which speech segments can vary; this is distinguished from an independent dimension that is notated as the feature [± stop]; and each of these participates in the overall system in its own characteristic way. In other words, the notation of the theory is meant to represent the set of distinctions made by this part of the computational mind. This set of distinctions is encoded in the nervous system in as yet unknown fashion but along the lines suggested in section 3.1.

Thus, although there is a degree of arbitrariness in formal notation, we are not free to substitute alternative notations at whim: the algebraic structure of a notation makes a theoretical claim. Consider the change in the theory of chemistry when the atom was found to have internal structure in the electron orbits. This structure was used to explain in more principled fashion the interactions of substances and the natural classifications among them (such as the chemical similarities of the halogen elements). The change in the theory hence was not merely notational change; it reflected a difference in our conception of physical reality.

Chomsky and Halle (1965) make a similar point with respect to the choice of distinctive feature notation versus standard phonetic transcription. Though standard transcription (like simple symbols for chemical elements) is much less cumbersome, only distinctive feature notation permits one to express explicitly the natural classification of speech sounds revealed by a wide range of phonological phenomena (including those discussed in sections 4.2 and 5.1).

In the same vein, the previous section alluded to a change that has taken place in phonological formalism since 1968: the treatment of syllables. In structuralist phonology of the 1940s (for instance, Moulton 1947 and other papers reprinted in Joos 1957), syllable boundaries were treated as symbols interpolated among segments, as in (5.9a). Chomsky and Halle (1968) argued against the need for any representation of syllable boundaries at all, and more recent theory has represented syllables by bracketing, as in (5.9b).

(5.9) a. or + ga + ni + za + tion

b. [$_{Word}$[$_{Syll}$ or] [$_{Syll}$ ga] [$_{Syll}$ ni] [$_{Syll}$ za] [$_{Syll}$ tion]]

Again, why this more cumbersome notation? The difference is found in the potential algebraic structure provided by the notation. For instance, the bracketing notation provides the natural possibility of *hierarchical* structure, whereas the + notation is essentially linear in conception. Indeed, the bracket notation has been motivated by the need for hierarchical structure in the determination of stress (see section 5.6). (5.10) shows such structure applied to the word *organization*. It is unstatable in the + notation.

(5.10) [$_{Word}$[$_{Foot}$[$_{Syll}$ or] [$_{Syll}$ ga] [$_{Syll}$ ni]] [$_{Foot}$[$_{Syll}$ za] [$_{Syll}$ tion]]]

We see, then, how choice of a notation can make a theoretical claim about the organization of distinctions available to the computational mind.

One sometimes encounters statements to the effect that the psychological reality of linguistic theories cannot be established without recourse to experiments in a standard psychological paradigm, or to a complete theory of processing, or to a running computer program. Without satisfying such conditions, it is insinuated, linguistic theory remains at the level of mere formal conjecture (and can be disregarded by "real" scientists).

In fact, nothing could be further from the case. Phonological theory is motivated by a vast range of evidence from many languages of the world (references too numerous to cite), from speech errors, from language acquisition (as pioneered by Jakobson (1941)), and even from poetry (as studied by Halle and Keyser (1971), Kiparsky (1977), and many others). Thus there are diverse natural psychological phenomena that constrain the choice of theory before one even begins to do laboratory experiments. And just because one may believe that the formal theory is too complex, one is not entitled to disregard these phenomena. If one wants to reject generative phonology, one had better be prepared to appreciate and give a better account of the phenomena it aspires to explain.

It must of course be acknowledged, as in chapter 4, that a psychological theory is ultimately incomplete without theories of processing and of neurological implementation. The point is, though, that generative phonology provides, as prerequisite to such theories, an account of the information that must be processed and neurally encoded. Nor is experimental evidence unwelcome in phonological research. It is just not what phonologists generally rely on, given their other rich resources of data.

Finally, bear in mind that these arguments for psychological reality will apply to all the levels of structure we will discuss.

5.3 The Relation of Phonological Structure to Lower Levels

In claiming that there is a level of phonological structure distinct from the acoustic analysis presented by the ear, we thereby must take responsibility for an account of the relationship between the two analyses. The extensive literature on phonetic perception (see the review in Liberman and Studdert-Kennedy 1977) is concerned with elucidating this relationship. This literature typically does not explicitly distinguish between theories in structural and processing modes, but my impression is that the more satisfactory accounts make the distinction implicitly, asking first what principles of correspondence relate the two analyses and second what computational devices could implement such a correspondence in real time. The sorts of facts mentioned earlier—for instance, that cues for a stop consonant are present in the formant transitions of adjacent vowels—are elements in a description of the formal organization of the acoustics-phonology correspondence. Such principles are not part of phonological structure per se; rather, we must add to the box diagram of figure 5.1 another component that describes the relationship between the acoustic signal and phonological structure.

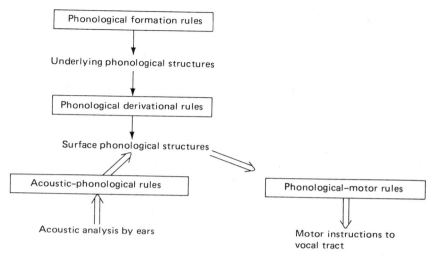

Figure 5.2
Relation of phonology to peripheral representations

This correspondence, of course, pertains only to speech *perception*. In speech *production* a different mapping is involved, from phonetic structure to motor instructions to the vocal tract. This too appears to require a great deal of temporal overlapping, as pointed out by Lashley (1951) and Lenneberg (1967), for example. Halle (1983) discusses some of the connections between phonological distinctive features and actual muscle activations. The interesting point here is that although distinctive features correspond fairly closely to idealized characteristics of vocal tract configurations, these in turn must be realized through the coordination of many muscles. A structural theory must include this correspondence as well as the acoustic-phonological one, resulting in a box diagram something like figure 5.2.

In figure 5.2 I have made a distinction between single and double arrows. The single arrows are taken to be aspects of the description that determine structure but are not necessarily involved in active processing. By contrast, the double arrows indicate relationships among structures that *must* be computed actively in the course of understanding or speaking a sentence. (I will justify this point in chapter 6.)

Figure 5.2 explicitly shows phonological structure as multipurpose: in the logical flow of information in the mind it can serve either as output of the acoustic-phonological rules or as input to the phonological-motor rules. Already, then, we are seeing an example of the abstraction and integration performed by more central representations vis-à-vis more peripheral ones.

5.4 Syntactic Structure

When we turn to syntactic structure, we find a set of fundamental notions familiar from traditional grammar and quite distinct from those in phonology. First, words are classified into parts of speech or *lexical categories* such as noun, verb, adjective, adverb, preposition, and conjunction. Second, words are combined into phrases, which are themselves classified into *phrasal categories* such as sentence, verb phrase, noun phrase, and prepositional phrase.

The syntactic structure of a sentence is best described in terms of the relation of *immediate constituency*. The constituents of a phrase are those segments of it that are either a word or a complete phrase. The *immediate constituents* of a phrase are the largest constituents that are not the entire phrase itself. For instance, the full set of constituents of the sentence *A boy hit the ball* is given in (5.11); its immediate constituents are the noun phrase *a boy* and the verb phrase *hit the ball*. On the other hand, sequences like *boy hit* and *hit a* are not constituents at all.

(5.11)   a boy hit the ball
          a boy
          a
          boy
          hit the ball
          hit
          the ball
          the
          ball

Constituency is customarily notated either by means of a labeled bracketing like the one in figure 5.3a, in which the labels identify the lexical or

a. [$_S$[$_{NP}$[$_{Art}$ a] [$_N$ boy]] [$_{VP}$[$_V$ hit] [$_{NP}$[$_{Art}$ the] [$_N$ ball]]]]]

b.

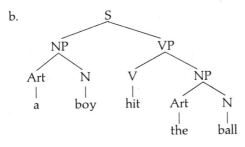

Figure 5.3
Two notations for syntactic structure

phrasal category of the bracketed constituent, or by means of a labeled tree structure like the one in figure 5.3b, in which labels at the nodes (or branch points) identify the lexical or phrasal category of the phrases they dominate. In the bracket notation, the immediate constituents of a phrase P are those whose brackets occur immediately inside P's brackets; in the tree notation, P's immediate constituents are those whose nodes occur directly under P.

It should be clear that in this case, unlike those discussed in section 5.2, the two notations are equivalent, in that they express precisely the same distinctions and relations. It would not make sense to dispute whether the computational mind makes use of one rather than the other: any notation that preserved the same distinctions and relations would be adequate. These two have the virtue of being easy to work with on paper, but what notation is easy to work with in a nervous system would likely be quite different in at present unimaginable but (one would hope) irrelevant ways.

It is useful to point out what these notations presuppose about syntactic structure, the better to be able to compare syntactic structure to other hierarchical structures we will encounter. First, every phrase is *exhaustively* segmented into immediate constitutents. There can be no interpolated bits and pieces that do not count as constituents, as might be suggested by the phrase dominated by E in figure 5.4a. Second, constituents always consist of *contiguous* parts. There can be no constituents like B in figure 5.4b, which consists of the nonadjacent constituents D and F. Third, every constituent (except the uppermost) is an immediate constituent of *exactly one* larger phrase. There cannot be a constituent like E in figure 5.4c, which is an immediate constituent of both B and C. Fourth, each constituent is labeled by a lexical or phrasal category; we will encounter hierarchies in which this kind of labeling does not occur.

The primitives of syntactic structure are thus the notion of constituent and the set of lexical and phrasal categories by which constituents can be labeled. There are two principles of combination: the relationship of immediate domination and the relationship of linear order. All syntactic trees can be described in these terms. (There are further possible syntactic rela-

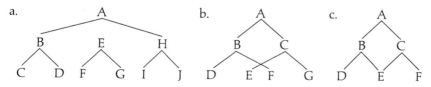

Figure 5.4
Impermissible syntactic structures

tions whose status is in dispute. For instance, certain cases of anaphora—the relation between a pronoun and its antecedent—are thought to be represented as part of syntactic structure. For the sake of manageability we will not trouble ourselves with such cases here.)

Particular languages need not make use of the entire available set of lexical and phrasal categories (just as no language makes use of all the possible speech sounds). Some languages—for instance, Warlpiri, Chinese, and Navajo—can arguably be said not to have adjectives, and very few languages have a syntactic category akin to the English modals such as *will*, *can*, and *must*. Thus, one's knowledge of a language must specify what subset of the universally available categories actually appears.

In addition, no language permits completely free combination of words into categories or of categories into other categories: the combinations are highly constrained. These constraints can be expressed by *phrase structure rules*. For instance, the phrase structure rule for the most common type of English noun phrase specifies an optional article, followed by optional adjectives, followed by a noun, followed by other optional constituents such as relative clauses. By contrast, the noun phrase rule for French specifies that most adjective types follow the noun. The phrase structure rules can be thought of as partial templates for syntactic structures: a syntactic structure in language L is well formed just in case each of its phrasal constituents breaks up in a fashion permitted by one of the phrase structure rules of L.

An important property of syntactic phrases is that they are *headed*. For instance, a noun phrase normally contains a privileged noun that serves as head, plus a number of modifiers—adjectives, articles, relative clauses, and so forth—grouped around it. Similarly, verb phrases are headed by verbs, adjective phrases (such as *less unusually handsome than Harry*) are headed by adjectives (here, *handsome*), and prepositional phrases (such as *rather far across the field*) are headed by prepositions (here, *across*). With two major exceptions, all types of syntactic constituents have this property. One exception is conjoined phrases, such as *Betty and Harry*, in which neither noun can be considered a modifier of the other. The other is the category Sentence; there is some dispute among linguists concerning whether it is headed and if so, what the head is.

Not only are phrases headed; there is also an intrinsic connection between the category of a phrase and the category of its head. One would not expect to find a language, for instance, in which noun phrases were normally headed by verbs, adjective phrases by nouns, and so forth. Rather, what makes something a noun phrase (normally) is having a noun as its head; and likewise for the other phrasal categories. Thus the phrase structure rules of a language are not free to break up constituents any way they please: there are fundamental constraints having to do with the relation between phrasal categories and the lexical categories that serve as heads. These constraints form part of the "X-bar" theory of phrase structure (Chomsky 1970; Jackendoff 1977a), an enrichment of the theory of phrase structure that incorporates a good deal of linguistic substance beyond the simple rewriting-rule models of the early 1960s, in particular making the head-modifier relation explicit.

As in phonological structure, a distinction between underlying and surface structure emerges prominently in syntax. For instance, consider the sentences in (5.12).

(5.12)   a. Which eggs did Freddy buy?
          b. Freddy bought some eggs.

These sentences are intuitively closely related, yet they differ drastically: (1) (5.12a) is a question, (5.12b) is a declarative. (2) Both have a noun phrase constituent X *eggs*, but (5.12a) has *which* where (5.12b) has *some*. (3) The noun phrase constituent in question is at the beginning in (5.12a), at the end in (5.12b). (4) (5.12a) has the auxiliary verb *did* preceding *Freddy*, whereas no such constituent appears in (5.12b). (5) (5.12a) has the infinitive form *buy* where (5.12b) has the past tense form *bought*.

The idea behind transformational generative grammar, introduced by Chomsky (1957), is that there is a sublevel of *underlying syntactic form* in which the close relation between these sentences appears much more explicitly. The differences between them are the result of a sequence of formal operations (transformations) that relate underlying form to the observed *surface syntactic form*. Roughly, the derivations proceed as shown in (5.13). (The bracketing is omitted for typographical convenience but is assumed to be mentally present.)

(5.13)
Underlying form (*past* = past tense marker)
a. Freddy past buy which eggs   b. Freddy past buy some eggs
Fronting of wh-*constituents*
   which eggs Freddy past buy   Freddy past buy some eggs
                                        (no change)
Inversion of tense in main clauses with fronted wh-*constituents*
   which eggs past Freddy buy   Freddy past buy some eggs
                                          (no change)
Attachment of tense to immediately following verb
   which eggs past Freddy buy   Freddy buy + past some eggs
   (no change: no immediately
   following verb)

Attachment of do *to unattached tense*
which eggs do + past Freddy buy   Freddy buy + past some eggs

Realization of tensed verb forms
which eggs did Freddy buy   Freddy bought some eggs
                                         = *Surface form*

In this derivation (5.12a, b) differ in only one respect in underlying form: *which* versus *some*. This syntactic difference is responsible for the difference in meaning, since *which* functions semantically as a marker of interrogativity. The other three surface syntactic differences between the two sentences follow from the obligatory operation of the sequence of transformations in (5.13), which collectively introduce severe distortions into (5.12a) while leaving (5.12b) virtually unchanged. (Note also that there is an alternative form of the question that does not undergo the same sequence of deformations: *Freddy bought WHICH eggs?*)

Each of the transformations can be stated formally, in terms of the syntactic primitives and principles of combination, as a regular conversion of one class of syntactic structures into another.[1] Like the phonological rules, they must be applied in a certain order for a derivation to be well formed. So a natural question arises: What is the status of the syntactic transformations in active processing?

5.5 Transformations and Processing

To answer this question, we must first determine the role of syntactic representation in an overall *structural* view of language—how syntax interacts with phonology and semantics. Among the major changes in linguistic theory over the last twenty years has been how these interactions are conceived.

Let us look first at the relation to phonology. In the "Standard Theory" (Chomsky 1965; Chomsky and Halle 1968) it was assumed that underlying phonological form was virtually identical to surface syntactic form, perhaps with the intervention of a few minor "readjustment rules." However, subsequent changes in phonological theory, to be discussed in the next two sections, have altered that view. According to the more recent views, the phonology-syntax connection is properly thought of as a relation of two independent structures, not as a near-identity. Still, since surface structure represents words in their proper order, it is clear that surface rather than underlying syntactic structure is relevant to phonology.

1. For linguists: All this discussion of the form and role of transformations applies equally to the movement rules of contemporary Government-Binding Theory (Chomsky 1981). In fact, the rules of Inversion and Tense Attachment used in (5.13), long neglected in the literature, have reemerged in modern dress in Chomsky 1986.

Now consider the relation of syntax to semantics. The Standard Theory claimed that *underlying* syntactic structure is the level germane to semantic interpretation. (This claim was developed explicitly by Katz and Postal (1964).) In this theory it is necessary that underlying syntactic structure be recovered in the course of active sentence perception and production, since it is a step in the logical mapping between meaning and pronunciation. It then becomes of interest to ask whether the formal transformations are actively involved or whether some other strategy is used instead. Some early results (Miller 1962; Miller and McKean 1964) suggested that the performance of transformations directly affects reaction time to sentences, but later work (discussed in Fodor, Bever, and Garrett 1974, chapter 5) cast doubt on these results. This seems to have led many psychologists to abandon transformational grammar as a framework for research: if transformations did not play an active role in processing, what sense could be made of a claim for their "psychological reality"? As should be clear from our previous discussion, such reactions are misguided, in that they fail to make the distinction between structural and processing descriptions.

In the meantime syntactic theory itself changed, with a number of different schools of thought all turning to surface syntactic structure as most directly related to semantic interpretation. The most direct current descendant of the Standard Theory, Chomsky's (1981) Government-Binding Theory, mediates between surface structure and meaning with a syntactic sublevel of *logical form* (LF), built of syntactic primitives and principles of combination. LF must be recovered in active processing, but underlying syntactic structure need not be: it is just an abstraction of certain regularities of form that cannot be expressed directly in surface structure.

One of the more prominent rivals to Government-Binding Theory is Bresnan's (1978, 1982) Lexical-Functional Theory, which does away with transformations but posits an additional level of *functional structure* intervening between syntactic structure and meaning. Functional structure has its own primitives and principles of combination, so it is a distinct level (as the term is being used here) rather than a sublevel of syntactic structure. In this theory, then, functional structure must be derived in active processing, but there is no underlying *syntactic* structure to recover.

In summary, current views of syntactic structure regard the phrase structure rules and transformational rules (if any) as together describing a set of structures that are related on the one hand to phonological structure and on the other to semantics. Neither kind of rule need be actively involved in processing: they simply constrain the set of available structures. This component can be summed up in the box diagram in figure 5.5, in which the single and double arrows have the same significance as in figure 5.2.

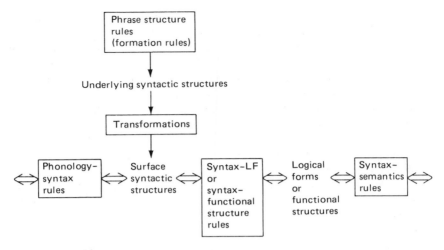

Figure 5.5
Organization of syntax and its relation to other structures

(However, since the double-arrow correspondences must be invoked in both perception and production, the arrows point both ways.)

Following the natural tripartite division of linguistic theory, the next logical step ought to be a discussion of semantics. However, I will put off semantics until chapter 7 and continue this chapter instead with some recent elaborations of phonological structure and their implications for the relation of phonology to syntax.

5.6 Phonological Segmentation: Intonation and Stress

Since about 1975 there has been considerable ferment in phonological theory about how the simple phonological representation described in section 5.1 must be enriched. This section will describe some of these trends.

In including syllables among the units specified in phonological structure, I have followed traditional grammar but not generative phonology of the 1960s. As mentioned in section 5.2, Chomsky and Halle (1968) eschewed use of a formal notion of syllable altogether. One reason for this is that segmentation into syllables is often at odds with another segmentation that is independently necessary: the segmentation into *morphemes*, or independently identifiable roots, stems, prefixes, and suffixes. For example, the word *organization* segments syllabically as in (5.14a) but morphemically as in (5.14b).

(5.14) a. [or] [ga] [ni] [za] [tion]   (syllabic)
        b. [organ] [iz] [ation]   (morphemic)

In particular, the *n* segments with the following vowel in the syllabic segmentation but is part of the morpheme *organ*; similarly for the *z*. Since Chomsky and Halle did not consider the possibility of independent phonological and syntactic structures, for various reasons the morphemic bracketing had to predominate.

However, Kahn (1976) shows the need to formally segment words into syllables in order to state rules of phonological derivation with proper generality. Thus, the two segmentations of a word illustrated in (5.14) must both be available in linguistic structure, and the morphological structure has been displaced from phonological representation by syllabic structure. What to do with it?

To my mind, the most satisfying answer has been offered by Selkirk (1982), who shows that the principles of morphological segmentation have the characteristics of syntactic phrase structure: they involve assigning lexical category labels to words, and each prefix or suffix has the power of changing the syntactic category of the resulting lexical item. So, for example, *organization* is not simply the concatenation of three morphemes shown in (5.14b) but is actually a tree structure of the form given in figure 5.6. In other words, the primitives and principles of combination in morphology are most directly compatible with those of syntax, not with those of phonology. Morphological structure thus represents the extension of syntactic structure downward to within words.

In addition, there is evidence of phonological structure in domains *larger* than the word. The most obvious case concerns the domain of intonation contours, the natural units of rise and fall in voice pitch. In "tone languages" such as Chinese the pitch is assigned essentially as part of each word. But it has long been observed that in English the segmentation of an utterance into intonation contours does not always respect even large-scale syntactic boundaries. An often-cited example is (5.15a), which has a syntactic segmentation given in part in (5.15b). In this syntactic structure *the cat*

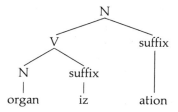

Figure 5.6
A morphological structure

that chased the rat that ate the cheese is direct object, and *the rat that ate the cheese* is direct object of the embedded relative clause. Yet the intonational segmentation, marked by pauses, is given in (5.15c), completely at odds with the syntactic segmentation and embedding.

(5.15) a. This is the cat that chased the rat that ate the cheese.

  b. This is [NP the cat [S that chased [NP the rat [S that ate the cheese]]]]

  c. [This is the cat] [that chased the rat] [that ate the cheese]

Selkirk (1984) points out a somewhat different case, in which the very same syntactic structure can correspond to two or more distinct intonation contours. An example is (5.16a, b), where the differences in pronunciation have been notated roughly by means of a pitch contour beneath the sentence.

(5.16) a. Abernathy gesticulated.   (one contour)

  b. Abernathy [*slight pause*] gesticulated.   (two contours)

In the more traditional approach pitch was taken to be represented as a feature of individual vowels. However, Liberman (1975) and Goldsmith (1976) (as well as earlier researchers such as Bolinger (1965) argue that intonation contours are represented as independent "melodies" assigned to utterances on the basis of a segmentation. In segments of different lengths the melody is realized at different speeds, but its contour is retained. (5.17a, b) illustrate this by altering the subject of (5.16b) to a very short segment and to a somewhat longer one. Notice how the contour preserves its down-up character, but the fall and rise are squashed or stretched to fit the length of the subject.

(5.17) a. Bob gesticulated.

  b. The man in the yellow hat gesticulated.

Thus the assignment of an intonation contour to a sentence depends on a segmentation into *intonational phrases*, units that correspond only partly to the syntactic units of the sentence. Intonation being a phonological property par excellence, this evidence suggests that phonological structure must be extended far beyond the domain of words, often producing a segmentation in conflict with syntactic structure. (This phenomenon has been studied experimentally by Gee and Grosjean (1983), with interesting results.)

Further enrichment of phonological structure has been revealed through the study of stress. To describe this enrichment requires a fairly extended discussion.

In traditional theories, including the theory of Chomsky and Halle (1968), stress is regarded as a feature of a vowel. So, for instance, the stresses of the word *organization* are indicated traditionally by accent marks as in (5.18a) or, following Chomsky and Halle's formalism, by numbers as in (5.18b) (0 indicates lack of stress; 1, primary stress; 2, secondary stress).

(5.18)   a. òrganizátion
         b. organization
             2   0 0 1 0

Liberman (1975) and Liberman and Prince (1977) point out a number of inadequacies in the traditional formalism, showing how it fails to capture certain basic characteristics of linguistic stress. Two can be mentioned in this nontechnical discussion.

First, stress is *patterned*: languages tend to have principles of stress that alternate stressed syllables with one or two unstressed syllables. This fact does not follow directly from the traditional theory of stress, which treats stress as a local attribute of individual vowels. Liberman and Prince suggest that an adequate theory of stress ought to treat stress patterns as larger units that can be specified as a whole.

Second, stress is not absolute, as suggested by the accent marks or numbers, but *relational*—determined in part by the context of surrounding stresses. For instance, the word *American* in isolation has a primary stress on the second syllable; but in *American history* it has secondary stress, and primary stress falls on the first syllable of *history*. Moreover, in *American history teacher* (in the sense "teacher of American history") it has tertiary stress; primary stress remains on *history*, and secondary stress falls on *teacher*. Chomsky and Halle develop complex conventions of stress subordination to account for this fact, but a more direct route would be desirable.

Liberman and Prince propose two interlocking formalisms to describe these characteristics of stress: *prosodic trees* and *metrical grids*. More recent research has attempted to make do with just one of these, thereby simplifying the representation. Halle and Vergnaud (1978) and Hayes (1982), for example, elaborate the prosodic tree and do not make use of metrical grids; Prince (1983) and Selkirk (1984) argue that the metrical grid alone is sufficient. At the moment there is no consensus. Since both devices have interesting analogues in music (see sections 11.4 and 12.4), I will briefly describe each of them.

The metrical grid is the simpler of the two. It is conceived of as an additional independent level of linguistic structure. Its sole primitive is an element called a *beat*, and its principles of combination are (1) concatenation of a temporal sequence of beats into a *layer* (the usual term is *level*, which I eschew to avoid confusion) and (2) stacking of layers into a *grid*. (5.19) presents some examples of grids. Each x represents a beat, and each horizontal row of x's represents a layer.

```
(5.19)  a. x   x   x      b. x      x       c.   x
           x x x x x         x  x  x             x       x
           xxxxxxxxx         xxxxxxxxx           x  x   x  x
                                                 xxxxxxxxx
```

The notion of stacking should be intuitively clear from these diagrams. Two layers are properly stacked if each beat of one of them coincides temporally with some beat of the other; there may be no alignments like (5.20a) in which each of two layers has beats not aligned with the other. I will call the layer with more beats the *smaller-scale* layer. In the smaller-scale layer I will call the beats that are aligned with those of a larger-scale layer *strong beats* of that layer and those that are not so aligned *weak beats* of that layer. In (5.19a), then, the smallest-scale layer alternates strong beats and weak beats, as does the middle layer. Since there is no still larger layer, the highest layer in (5.19a) does not have a distinction of strong and weak beats.

In addition to this absolute condition on proper stacking of layers, there is a condition that is not absolute but strongly preferred: strong beats in any layer should be separated by one or two weak beats. The grids in (5.19) satisfy this condition in various ways, but those in (5.20b, c) do not: (5.20b) has two adjacent strong beats in the smallest-scale layer, and (5.20c) has two adjacent strong beats in the middle layer. (These violations are indicated by dashed rectangles.)

```
(5.20)  a. x xx xx     b. x  x         c.  ┌x ¯ ¯x┐
           xx xx x         x ┌xx┐ x        x│x _ _x│x
           xx xx xxx        xx│xx│xxx       xxxxxxxxxx
```

(5.20a), then, is ill formed; (5.20b, c) are well formed but to be avoided.

The application of metrical grids to the description of stress is straightforward. Each syllable of an utterance is associated with a beat of the smallest-scale layer of a metrical grid. Syllables connected only to a beat of the smallest layer are unstressed, and the degree of stress of other syllables is a function of how many stacked x's in the grid they are connected to. For example, *organization* receives the following representation.

```
(5.21)  organization
                    x
           x        x
           x   x xx x
```

Primary stress goes with the maximal number of x's beneath the vowel, secondary stress with the next highest number, and so forth. The stress rules of a language, then, specify how layers of the grid other than the smallest-scale layer are to be aligned with syllables.

From this representation of stress follow the properties observed by Liberman and Prince. First, the pervasive patterns of alternating stressed and unstressed syllables are a result of the constraint that marks (5.20b, c) as highly nonpreferred grids. Second, the discrimination of more degrees of stress results from adding more large-scale layers to the metrical grid, while preserving small-scale layers intact. For instance, consider the grids in (5.22).

(5.22)   a. American   b. history   c. teacher
              x   x   x
          x   x x x   x x x   x   x
         d. American history   e. American history teacher
                  x   x
              x   x   x   x
          x   x x x   x x x   x   x   x
                                      x   x x x   x x x   x

It can readily be seen that the stress distinctions in *American history teacher* are derived from the representations of the individual words by the simple addition of a third and fourth layer of beats. Thus, the relational nature of stress emerges quite naturally from the grid theory.

Let us turn now to the other proposed formalism, prosodic trees. This formalism has two parts. First, the categories of phonological segmentation are enriched to include the notion of *foot* as an intermediate layer between *syllable* and *word*, and a binary branching structure is imposed on these categories. The resulting structures can be notated as labeled bracketings (as in (5.10)), but it is more convenient to use trees. *Organization* then has the tree structure in figure 5.7. Second, one member of each binary branch-

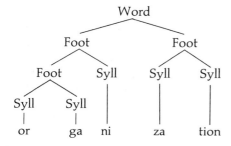

Figure 5.7
A prosodic tree

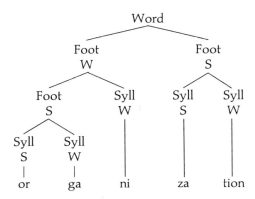

Figure 5.8
A prosodic tree with stress

ing is assigned the value S (strong), and the other member is assigned the value W (weak). This applies to *organization* as shown in figure 5.8. The Word node branches into two feet, one S and one W, and each Foot node branches into an S and a W.

Stress is read off the trees as follows: If a syllable is immediately dominated by W, it is unstressed. Relative stress of other syllables is determined by how far one has to trace up the tree before encountering a W. The highest stress is on the syllable that is dominated only by Ss, for example, *za* in figure 5.8. Thus, in this theory of stress, the stress rules of the language concern how the segmentation is imposed and how Ss and Ws are assigned to the resulting trees.

In this formalism the patterned nature of stress arises from the alternation of Ss and Ws imposed on the tree by virtue of its branching. The relational character of stress arises from the fact that it is represented as an opposition of S and W; as an utterance grows longer, more branchings and hence more S-W oppositions are added to the top of the tree, but lower branchings remain undisturbed.

These two accounts of stress are clearly quite similar in structure. The main difference between them lies in the enriched segmentation required by the prosodic tree theory. For instance, the tree theory claims that *organi* and *zation* each constitute a prosodic unit, so that the syllable *ni*, for instance, "belongs with" the syllable *or* in some sense. By contrast, the grid theory makes no such claim: *ni* is simply between the stressed syllables *or* and *za* but does not belong with one more than the other. So the dispute between the two theories has primarily concerned whether there is independent evidence for the extra segmentation. Since the issues are far from settled, I will not come down in either direction. Note, however, the significance of the dispute with respect to the notational issues discussed in section 5.2.

In either case the upshot of all this enrichment of phonological structure —syllabic segmentation, intonational phrasing, and grid or tree form for stress—is that phonological structure cannot be embedded directly into syntactic structure, as in the Standard Theory. Rather, phonological and syntactic structures are distinct and parallel representations of the entire utterance, each with its own characteristic principles of segmentation and hierarchical arrangement. As illustration, figure 5.9a presents the surface syntactic and morphological structure and figure 5.9b the phonological structure (including both representations of stress but not the decomposition into distinctive features) for the sentence *Harry disliked organization.* Both structures must be involved in perception and production of the sentence.

5.7 Correspondence Rules and the Lexicon

Given the disparity between syntactic and phonological structure, it is crucial to give attention to the principles that formally mediate between them. Unlike the rules of syntax itself or of phonology itself, these *correspondence rules* will have to invoke primitives and principles of combination from both levels. The typical form of a correspondence rule will hence be roughly "Fragment X of phonological structure corresponds to fragment Y of syntactic structure."

It is useful to divide the principles of correspondence into *lexical* principles, which deal with correspondences within words, and *supralexical* principles, which deal with the consequences of combining words into utterances. I will discuss the latter class first.

The supralexical correspondence rules are responsible for the matches and mismatches between syntactic and phonological phrasing. In the usual case each word of syntax (that is, each lexical category complete with all its prefixes and suffixes) corresponds to a word of phonology; this is a basic correspondence rule. However, mismatches can appear—for instance, through rules of *cliticization*, in which a syntactic unit loses its phonological independence. A simple example from English is the treatment of the articles *a* and *the*, which phonologically act as unstressed syllables appended to the next word. Similar is the behavior of monosyllabic prepositions such as *to* and *of* (though not bisyllabic prepositions such as *between* and *among*). In fact, both an article and a preposition can cliticize at the same time, resulting in correspondences like the ones in figure 5.10, which contain gross mismatches of phonological and syntactic constituency.

At a larger scale, correspondence rules must address the relation of Intonational Phrases to syntactic phrases. One fairly obvious rule of En-a.

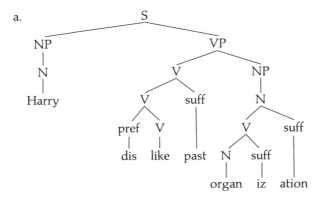

b.

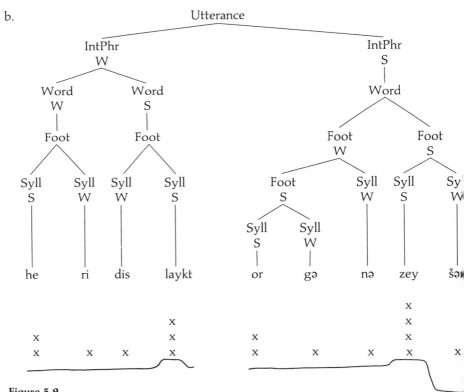

Figure 5.9
Corresponding syntactic and phonological structures for *Harry disliked organization*

(5.32)

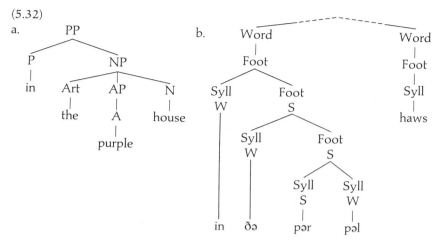

Figure 5.10
Mismatch of syntactic and phonological constituency

glish is that an appositive relative clause must constitute an Intonational Phrase. This is reflected in writing by its being set off with commas.

(5.23)   Harry, who has a pet rat, likes to read novels.
    a. Syntactic bracketing:
        [$_{NP}$ Harry [$_S$ who has a pet rat]] [$_{VP}$ likes to read novels]
    b. Phonological bracketing:
        [$_{IntPhr}$ Harry] [$_{IntPhr}$ who has a pet rat] [$_{IntPhr}$ likes to read novels]

Another principle that relates Intonational Phrases to syntactic structure accounts for the facts observed in (5.15)–(5.17). Its statement would take us too far afield for present purposes, so it has been relegated to appendix A.

Next let us turn to the *lexical* correspondence rules. Each word of the language can be thought of as a little correspondence rule that permits a phonological constituent to be mapped into a lexical category of the syntactic structure and into some chunk of semantic structure. Thus the small-scale correspondences among the levels of linguistic structure are specified by lexical entries, and the larger-scale correspondences are specified by the supralexical rules.

We could leave it at that if the lexical items of a language were just arbitrary matchings of phonological, syntactic, and semantic structure. But of course they are not. The lexicon is full of regularities and subregularities that are part of speakers' command of language. A simple case is the phonological realization of the morpheme *past tense* in English. This acts as an independent unit in the syntax (recall the derivations in (5.13)), but it appears phonologically in a number of guises. In the normal case it is realized as a suffix that changes phonological shape depending on the phonetic context: -*əd* after dental stops (*wanted, painted*), -*t* after other unvoiced sounds (*liked*, phonetically *laykt*), and -*d* everywhere else (*pinned*, phonetically *pind*). However, in other cases it is realized as a change in the vowel of the verb (*run-ran, forget-forgot*), as an irregular phonetic change (*teach-taught, buy-bought*), or as a complete change in phonological content (*go-went, is-was*). This mixture of partial regularity and wild irregularity is characteristic of relations among lexical items.

What is curious about such rules of lexical structure is that they need not be there. One could, in principle, learn all the lexical items in a language one by one; for example, every verb could have its own way of forming the past tense. Thus, although rules expressing lexical regularities may be used to aid learning, there is nothing to prevent a word's having an exceptional structure that the language learner must acquire individually.

By contrast, the salient characteristic of the supralexical correspondence rules is their constantly creative use: they must be invoked in every act of sentence perception and understanding, since one *cannot* memorize the full set of possible sentences. Thus they are by necessity regular. (In support of this point, languages such as Navajo use morphological (word-internal) structure much more productively and creatively than does English; and there is a corresponding increase in the regularity of morphological principles.)

I am suggesting, then, that principles of the same formal type can be used in two quite different roles, depending on whether or not they are supplemented by memorized information. Correspondence rules that involve freely invoked combinatorial processes must be used productively and must play a role in active processing. By contrast, correspondence rules that simply encode partial regularities among memorized lexical items are used primarily as an aid to learning, and it is not clear whether they are used in active processing or not.

Principles like the realization of the English past tense stand somewhere on the borderline between these two types. On the one hand, it seems odd to claim that one memorizes (stores in memory) the past tense form for every regular verb. On the other hand, one does have to memorize the exceptional cases like *ran, brought,* and *went*—and children's difficulties with these are well known. Yet most of these cases are subject to some partially general rule or another; *went* and *was* are the only completely irregular past tenses that come immediately to mind. Thus, there are a number of past tense rules—rules that all have the same formal composition —some of which are used productively and some of which are used only to group together memorized forms.

I bring up this case because it illustrates how the concerns of a structural theory of language cut across those of a processing theory. Structurally, there is a unified class of rules: realizations of English past tense. But the rules may be used quite differently in processing, depending on how they interact with memorized forms. (Alternatively, it may be that they are used in exactly the *same* way in processing, if we only come to conceive of processing in properly sophisticated terms.) Thus this case is yet another example of how a structural theory influences our ideas about what problems a processing theory must solve.

5.8 Summary

In this discussion of linguistic structure I have tried to convey a feel for what it means to develop a theory of mental structure in terms of levels of representation. In order to account for human language use, it is necessary to posit two independent levels of representation—phonology and syntax—plus their internal elaborations into intonation, metrical grid or prosodic tree, and possibly functional structure. Neither of these is a direct representation of either sound or meaning. Each has its own characteristic primitives and principles of combination; and in each of them a distinction must be made between underlying and surface form that must be described in terms of principles of derivation.

Since the different representations of a sentence are in many respects incommensurate structures, it is also necessary to posit a rich system of correspondence rules that describes how the levels are related. The complexity of the syntax-phonology correspondence is only appreciated in the context of the recent work on phonological structure that shows how richly organized the phonological level is.

Now, the leap. If it is the case that linguistic structure crucially involves not just sound and meaning but also these two idiosyncratic intermediate forms of information, there may be reason to believe that other psychological faculties involving input and output functions may be similarly organized. In vision, for example, one should not necessarily expect a direct translation from retinal image into conceptualization (or visual understanding); one ought to concede the possibility of a number of elaborate intermediate forms for visual information. Similarly, the theory of action may involve a number of complex structures that have no direct bearing on either the conceptualization of action or its execution in terms of motor commands but instead play only an indirect mediating role. One of the crucial problems for the theorist, then, is to discover whether such levels of representation exist, and if so, what their properties are. Part III will briefly summarize the outcome of such investigation in two other areas, vision and music, and their interactions with thought and language.

Before we turn to language processing, there is one more important topic we must take up.

5.9 Language Acquisition and Innateness

Perhaps the most controversial aspect of generative linguistics has been its stand on the acquisition of language by children. Common sense tells us that since children are born not knowing how to speak, and since they acquire the language of their social environment, language is entirely learned. Moreover, the lore of our culture suggests that language is somehow taught by the parents. Let me attack these beliefs in reverse order.

Two observations undermine the idea that parents teach language. First, it is well known that immigrant children acquire the indigenous language more rapidly and completely than their parents—and often from interaction with peers rather than from instruction in school. Second, anyone who has attempted to correct a two-year-old's language will know that it can't be done. Adults can provide instruction in vocabulary, perhaps, but little else; young children don't really respond to grammatical correction (Gleitman and Wanner 1982).

A further consideration emerges from the theory of language surveyed here. If one's ability to use language stems from a set of rules or principles, most of which are not available to conscious introspection, then *the acquisition of language must be the acquisition of this set of principles.* Since adults are not consciously aware of them, they certainly cannot explain them to children—if children could understand the explanations in any event. The most an adult can do is to supply evidence (in the form of grammatical sentences, judgments, or corrections) from which the child can induce the principles of the language. This is hardly teaching in the sense in which the term is usually intended—explicit instruction on the model of a high school French class.

Now, what about learning? Consider as a baseline the fact that hundreds of linguists have been studying the structure of English for decades and are far from a complete characterization. Debate continues about whether there are syntactic transformations, logical forms, functional structures, metrical grids, or prosodic trees; if so, what their properties are, and if not, how else to account for the observed organization of the language. Nonlinguists sometimes tend to view these debates as scholastic nattering ("If linguists are so smart, why can't they decide on a theory?"); but in fact they concern a properly explanatory account of real facts about real languages spoken by real speakers, and cannot be so lightly dismissed.

Yet children seem to have no such difficulties. If they did, none of us would have learned to speak English. So the question arises of how children—many of whom are not as smart as some linguists—manage to acquire a language by the age of ten or so. If all that were involved were simple context-free combinatorial patterns, they might make do with some sort of standard (though amazingly powerful) inductive device. But given that language involves a richly structured organization of distinctions along the lines sketched here, and given that linguists cannot consciously settle on the precise form of the grammar, using all the tricks of adult reasoning, it is hard to see how any sort of ordinary induction from the evidence present in the environment could lead an unaided child to the answers.

(Note that it does not help to say that the child does it unconsciously, whereas we have to do it consciously. Conscious or unconscious, the same information has to be processed, and the same distinctions have to be drawn. Unconscious learning is computationally no easier. It is just out of sight.)

The only way that anyone has thought of to resolve this apparent paradox is to grant the child a head start—to claim that the child does not have to ask all the questions that linguists have to ask. For example, children may not have to ask whether speech segments are analyzed into distinctive features, or whether there are syllables grouped hierarchically into feet, or whether syntactic constituents have heads, or whether there are syntactic transformations; they may just take the answers for granted, or simply not have a choice available. By contrast, linguists are attempting a conscious rational reconstruction of the unconscious principles behind language. Such rational reconstruction is not subject to the same constraints as naturally occurring language acquisition, so many more questions must be asked. Thus the linguist's job is far more difficult than the child's.

The claim, then, is that some aspects of our language capacity are not a result of learning from environmental evidence. Aside from divine intervention, the only other way we know of to get them into the mind is biologically: genetic information determining brain architecture, which in turn determines the form of possible computations. In other words, certain aspects of the structure of language are *inherited*.

This conclusion, which I will call the *Innateness Hypothesis*, provides a potential solution to the paradox of language acquisition by appealing to evolution. The child alone does not have enough time to acquire all the aspects of language that linguists are struggling to discover. But evolution has had more time at its disposal to develop this structure than linguists will ever have, even if it all has developed within the time since humans were differentiated from the great apes. In a moment we will see a strategy for lengthening the span even further.

For some reason the Innateness Hypothesis has provoked various degrees of astonishment, disbelief, and outrage since the time it was proposed in its modern form by Chomsky (1965). Let me try to defuse some of the more common reactions.

First, the hypothesis does not claim that the language capacity is necessarily present at birth. Like puberty and the eruption of teeth, development may well take place over some period after birth but according to a biologically determined (or guided) timetable. (Not that being present at birth or only later matters too much: if present at birth, it must in any event have developed prenatally, according to a biological timetable.)

Second, the biological development of the language capacity may well depend on the presence of exposure to language in the environment. Although one's bone structure is biologically determined, it will not develop properly without proper nourishment. Why should not the same be true of a brain structure, where "nourishment" includes a sufficient quantity and variety of incoming information? The necessity for environmental input is not incompatible with a biological endowment. (This argument is developed in Chomsky 1975; see Lorenz 1965 for a comparable argument with respect to various animal behaviors.)

Third, a biological "proof" of the Innateness Hypothesis would have to rest on two areas where we are almost completely ignorant at present: the way the genetic code determines the unfolding of biological structures, including the brain; and the way that brain structure determines the properties of the computational mind. But that should not be reason to reject the idea or minimize its importance. We certainly have faith that genetics *does* determine biological structure of all sorts, even if we don't know how; and we likewise have faith that brain structure determines computational properties. Moreover, the conjunction of these propositions—that cognitive characteristics can be inherited—is supported by a great deal of evidence, even if little of it is as detailed as linguists would like (see again Lorenz 1965 and also Lenneberg 1967).

For the moment, then, an argument for the innateness of specific aspects of language necessarily depends most heavily on evidence from within language itself. The Coordinate Structure Constraint, discussed in section 4.3, is one such kind of evidence. A responsible criticism of innateness must therefore confront the linguistic evidence and provide an alternative account of how the structure of language could be acquired.

There is a tendency in some quarters, however, to dismiss the notion of innateness as a "null hypothesis," a move of desperation to explain away embarrassing complexities. One can imagine critics of the theory of gravitation mounting a similar attack—it's an occult, invisible force that just restates the facts of the interaction of physical bodies. As I see it, the Innateness Hypothesis plays much the same role in linguistics as the hypothesis of gravitation in physics. It is a construct that serves to unify a large body of diverse facts from language structure, language universals, and language acquisition, and in turn it calls for eventual deeper explanation on biological principles.

Given the Innateness Hypothesis, the dialectic of theory construction in linguistics takes the following form.

(5.24)   Structure of Language $L =$ Innate part (Universal Grammar) + Learned part

One tries always to simplify the overall account of the structure of language L, consistent with the complexity of the facts of the language. At the same time one tries to properly parcel out the complexity of L between the innate and learned parts, according to three criteria. First, differences among languages must fall into the learned part, so that children may acquire any language to which they are exposed. Second, respects in which all languages are alike are likely to fall into the innate part—barring historical coincidence, which one can usually eliminate. Third, aspects of the language that appear unlearnable, given the data on which children must base their hypotheses, are candidates for the innate part of the language. This last criterion has been called the "poverty of the stimulus" argument; its use requires a certain amount of care, and in fact there is a running debate on what sorts of evidence children are capable of using (Gleitman and Wanner 1982; Baker and McCarthy 1981).

Thus, a claim that a certain aspect of language is innate is not a matter of desperation but a matter of delicate negotiation among the competing demands of cross-linguistic diversity, language universals, and theories of learning.

In turn, the innate part of language may be decomposed as shown in (5.25).

(5.25)   Innate part of language $=$ Part due to language-specific properties of the computational mind $+$ Part due to general properties of the computational mind

This decomposition has the effect of giving language acquisition an even longer head start in time. Only the part due to language-specific properties of the mind need have evolved within specifically human history; the part due to more general properties may have a much longer evolutionary history back into the primates or even the mammals.

Determination of the proper division in (5.25) will depend a great deal on evidence extrinsic to language. One important factor will be a comparison of the information structure of language—in all its complexity—with that of other cognitive capacities. (Superficial comparisons need not apply.) We will take up some facets of this issue in chapter 12, after we have looked at other cognitive capacities.

A second factor will be an examination of the capacities of other species and what cognitive precursors of human language can be teased out in them. My impression of the literature on sign language taught to apes (Linden 1976; Seidenberg and Pettito 1978; Ristau and Robbins 1982; plus popularizations too numerous to mention), for instance, is that the semantics is fairly good but that syntactic structure never really develops in any detail, if at all. This conclusion resonates with earlier nonlinguistic work on apes such as that of Köhler (1927). Such comparisons can provide interesting evidence toward establishing the proper division in (5.25).

Many people seem happy enough with innateness in language as long as none of it is specifically linguistic—that is, if it all follows from general properties of mind. (Such is the position taken by Anderson (1983), for instance.) As far as I can see, though, this is little but unfounded prejudice. Of course, scientific practice suggests that we should try to find theories that minimize differences among species. But again, the facts must be accounted for—including both the differences between human language learning and other kinds of learning and the differences between human language learning and animal language learning, such as it is. And again, evolution has after all had a couple of million years to make us different.

Most of these issues are not likely to be resolved in the immediate future. But for now we can set a plausible lower bound on the innate part of language, based on the material presented in this chapter and following an argument due to Fodor (1975). The premise is that the language learner's task is to determine which linguistic structures are acceptable in the language being learned. Since linguistic structures are built up from phonological and syntactic primitives and principles of combination, the learner's job is essentially a combinatorial problem.

However, we do not want to require the learner to learn the primitives and principles of combination themselves, that is, the space of dimensions along which linguistic information can vary. Such learning would be possible only if the linguistic primitives were themselves composite in some epistemologically prior "language" of the computational mind. Sooner or later, of course, the buck must stop at a set of primitives that are really primitive. But if we back up to something more primitive than the primitives of syntax and phonology, we are suggesting that the language learner must discover such essentials as phonological distinctive features, syllables, syntactic parts of speech, and the like. Given the apparent paradox of language learning, I submit that this is unlikely.

Rather, it seems plausible that the phonological and syntactic primitives and principles of combination are biologically determined organizations of data structure that follow from the computational properties of the human brain. This seems the minimum head start we can give the language learner on the linguist; far more is probably necessary. Life is hard enough for kids as it is.

Chapter 6
Language Processing

Having explored the formats in which linguistic information is encoded and the relationships among them, let us turn to some aspects of how this information is developed and processed in real time.

Our particular interest here stems from the problem of consciousness. Theory IV (section 4.6) restricted the information structures supporting consciousness to those that are *active*. So we will be asking, What information structures are being actively processed in the perception and production of language? Are any of these closer to conscious experience than others? But in order to deal with these immediate questions, we must consider more general issues in some depth.

6.1 The Logical Structure of Language Perception and Production

Let us begin by looking at what the organization of linguistic structure implies about processing. Although much of this has already been hinted at in chapter 5, it is useful to draw it together.

Figure 6.1 gives an overall view of the levels of linguistic representation, fragments of which appeared in more detail in figures 5.2 and 5.5. (I will motivate the semantic part in chapter 7, calling it there conceptual structure.) Each level of representation is defined by a set of formation rules: the primitives, principles of combination, and if there are sublevels, principles of derivation between them. Each double arrow in figure 6.1 stands for a set of correspondence rules: principles of translation between a pair of levels of representation.

If this is the form of linguistic information, consider what an act of perceiving and understanding an utterance must entail at minimum. The external stimulation on the organism is a sound wave, which is transduced by the ear into acoustic information. Understanding the utterance requires this acoustic information ultimately to be mapped into a semantic structure that encodes the meaning of the utterance. But what procedures are available to accomplish this mapping? The organization of linguistic structure dictates that the only possible way to translate consistently and productively from sound to meaning is to invoke the correspondence rules,

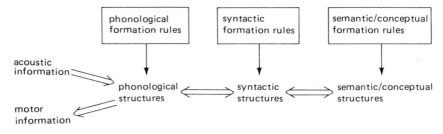

Figure 6.1
Overall organization of levels of linguistic representation

mapping acoustic information into phonological structure, then phonological structure into syntactic structure, then from syntax into meaning. There is no more direct route. (We are dealing here with spoken language, of course. We will consider written language in section 10.7.)

Language production provides the other side of the coin. The initial step in production is presumably the formulation of a semantic structure—an intended meaning. The final step is a sound wave, which is a physical consequence of motions of the vocal tract. The job of the computational mind in production is therefore to map from a semantic structure to a sequence of motor instructions to the vocal tract. Again, the logical organization of language requires that this mapping be accomplished in stages, mapping from semantic structure to syntax, thence to phonology, thence to motor information.

The argument, then, is that, given the organization of language, one cannot accomplish either speech understanding or speech production without making essential use of both phonological and syntactic information. I will codify this as the *Logical Structure of Language Processing*.

Logical Structure of Language Processing (LSLP)
Real-time mapping between meaning and the periphery (acoustic or motor) must proceed by way of the correspondences in figure 6.1, passing through translations into phonological and syntactic format.

As this claim has been widely disputed, it bears amplification. The problem lies in how to build it into a believable processing theory.

I can envision several ways of interpreting LSLP. The strongest interpretation can be stated as *Processing Hypothesis 1*.

Processing Hypothesis 1
In speech understanding each linguistic level is derived in its entirety from the next lower level before proceeding to the derivation of the next higher level. (Bottom-up sequential)

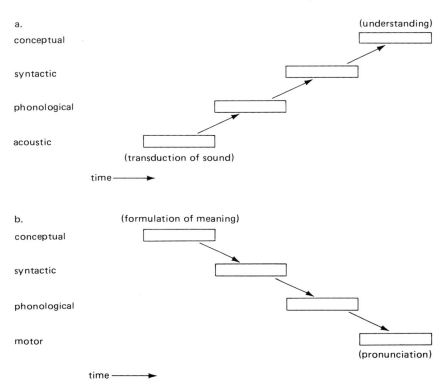

Figure 6.2
Processing Hypothesis 1

> In speech production each level is derived in its entirety from the next higher level before proceeding to the next lower level. (Top-down sequential)

The time course of speech perception according to this hypothesis should proceed as sketched in figure 6.2a; that of production should proceed as in figure 6.2b (time goes from left to right).

Processing Hypothesis 1 is patently false. In speech perception we do not wait until the end of an utterance before starting to interpret the intended meaning. In production we rarely have an entire sentence in mind before uttering the beginning; rather, we often have the impression of starting to utter a sentence without knowing exactly how we will end it, then completing it "on the fly." Thus this interpretation of LSLP is inadequate.

Processing Hypothesis 1 has seemed to many investigators the only possible interpretation of LSLP—and even of the prior claim that phonological and syntactic information are psychologically real and informationally independent of sound and meaning. Since Processing Hypothesis 1 is so obviously absurd, this has been taken as sufficient reason to reject all the conclusions (and data!) of generative grammar. The following are two representative quotations.

> Without [the competence versus performance (or structure versus processing) distinction], the attempt to construct a "theory of syntax" would have seemed quite problematic.... No one can seriously propose that people must, or even can, perform a complete syntactic analysis before they begin to decode the meaning of what they hear.... Can one formulate an adequate theory of language-processing behavior without first constructing a purely linguistic theory? Of course! (Schank and Birnbaum 1984, 210)
>
> ... the present results cast doubt upon the viability of using a transformational grammar as a basis for a psycholinguistic processing theory. According to the conventional interpretation of the implications of such a grammar for a performance system, the syntactic structure of an entire clause or sentence must be computed before a semantic representation can be assigned.... [Under] the more radical interpretation [of the present results], that semantic and syntactic analyses continuously interact as a sentence is heard,... there is no longer any clear requirement that an independent and purely syntactic level of representation would need to be computed in the first place. (Tyler and Marslen-Wilson) 1977, 690)

It is clear in these passages that theories of syntactic structure have been identified with Processing Hypothesis 1; then the baby has been thrown out with the bathwater, with no recognition of the phenomena that motivated the structural theory in the first place.

However, Processing Hypothesis 1 is not the only way to interpret LSLP. Another possibility is the following.

Processing Hypothesis 2
In speech understanding each part of each linguistic level is derived from information of the next lower level. (Bottom-up parallel)
In speech production each part of each level is derived from information of the next higher level. (Top-down parallel)

Figure 6.3a sketches a rough idea of the possible time course of speech perception under this hypothesis; figure 6.3b sketches production. (This is meant only to be suggestive; it makes the surely incorrect assumption that independent conceptual segments can be associated one to one with acoustic segments.)

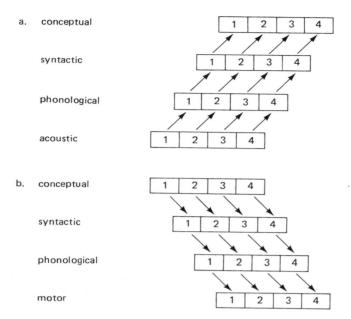

Figure 6.3
Processing Hypothesis 2

According to this picture, the hearer processes some segment of acoustic information, turning it into phonological structure. Then, while acoustic-to-phonological processing of a second segment is taking place, this first segment is being transformed into syntactic format, and so forth. The effect is that by the time the fourth acoustic segment is reached, conceptual information about the first segment is being derived. Similarly, in production, segments are handed down from one level to the next, so that by the time the fourth conceptual segment is being developed, the mapping of the first into motor information is being pronounced. Processing Hypothesis 2 is therefore consistent both with the logical organization of figure 6.1 and with the intuitions about processing that led to the rejection of Processing Hypothesis 1.

It is however possible—and desirable—to get even further away from Processing Hypothesis 1 while still retaining LSLP. To see why, we will for convenience separate speech perception from speech production, dealing with them in turn in the next sections.

6.2 Holistic and Top-Down Influences in Language Understanding

One of the most significant disputes in contemporary psycholinguistics has been over the extent to which language perception is "top-down" rather than "bottom-up." Although the distinction is rarely made explicit, questions of top-downness divide naturally into two categories. The first concerns influences within a particular level—for instance, how large-scale syntactic structures can affect local processing of syntax. I will call this distinction *localistic* versus *holistic* (intralevel) processing. The second category concerns influences among levels, such as how semantic exigencies can affect phonetic judgments. I will reserve the term *top-down* processing for such interlevel cases.

Processing Hypothesis 2 as it stands implies that language perception is entirely localistic and bottom-up. Conceptual segment 1 in figure 6.3a, for instance, is derived entirely from acoustic segment 1—to be sure, by way of phonological and syntactic segments, in accordance with LSLP. But there are no intersegment influences at any of the levels of structure; this is what makes Processing Hypothesis 2 *localistic* rather than *holistic*. And there are no influences from higher levels of structure that verify the correctness of lower-level structures or suggest possible structures; this is what makes Processing Hypothesis 2 *strictly bottom-up*. Two different questions arise: Is strictly localistic bottom-up processing possible? And even if it is possible, is this the way people do it?

In fact, there is substantial evidence, much of it rather obvious, to the effect that human language perception has both holistic and top-down aspects. This section will present a small sampling of this evidence. We will then see how such processing can still conform to LSLP instead of becoming an unstructured free-for-all.

Consider first holistic effects within individual levels. Early information-theoretic approaches to language perception (such as Shannon and Weaver 1949) proposed strictly local "Markov process" models, in which perception was to be guided by a knowledge of "transition probabilities"—the likelihood that such-and-such a word would occur after such-and-such another word or string of words. The death knell for such word-based theories was sounded by Chomsky (1957), who showed that the kinds of grammatical dependencies that occur in human languages cannot be stated in such localistic terms. For instance, in English the inflection of a present tense verb depends on whether its subject is singular or plural (*The boy eats spaghetti* versus *The boys eat spaghetti*); but the head noun of the subject can be separated from the verb by an indefinitely large number of modifiers (as in *The boys from Cincinnati whose mother you met on the train to Timbuktu eat spaghetti*). Since sentence perception must include recognition of the relation of subjects to verbs and the accompanying grammatical dependencies, no theory that depends only on the preceding n words (for any fixed number n) can account for the facts of English. Rather, the operative constraints must be stated structurally, that is, in terms of syntactic constituents larger than individual words, and of potentially indefinite length.

Similar objections on the semantic level had already been raised by Lashley (1951). Lashley points out that the significance attached to a particular sequence of phones (say, the sequence spelled variously as *right*, *write*, or *rite*) depends heavily on its role with respect to context—including material that follows rather than precedes the sequence of phones. For instance, if example (6.1) is presented orally, the hearer is liable to construe the second word as *writing* until the end of the sentence strongly suggests another interpretation.

(6.1)   Rapid righting with his uninjured hand saved from damage the contents of the capsized canoe.

In such a case the interpretation of the beginning of the sentence cannot be fixed for sure until the end. Hence, interpretation cannot be a purely localistic process as suggested in figure 6.3.

Nonetheless, sentence perception cannot be purely holistic either: as already noted, we obviously do not wait until a sentence is over before assigning at least tentative syntactic and conceptual structures. This point is driven home by "garden path" sentences such as (6.2), which many people initially find incomprehensible.

(6.2)   The horse raced past the barn fell.

Evidently, one is too attached to the initial localistic hypothesis that *raced* is the main verb (as in *The horse raced past the barn*) to be able to reconsider later on and treat *raced* as a past participle (as in *The horse that was raced past the barn fell*). Yet only the latter interpretation provides a grammatical reading. Examples such as this show that holistic considerations can sometimes be overwhelmed by localistic ones, to the detriment of understanding.

So the issue comes down to what combination of localistic and holistic processes is actually used in sentence perception. Many variants have appeared in the literature. In the augmented transition network (ATN) model of Wanner and Maratsos (1978) a single local analysis is computed; if subsequent evidence conflicts with this analysis, processing must either go back and start over from the point where the mistake was made or else tinker with the already posited analysis. Frazier and Fodor (1978) and Marcus (1980), however, avoid making a complete commitment to an analysis by leaving indeterminate certain parts of the structure until their correct role in the sentence can be ascertained more globally. (Their proposals for what is held off and for how long are, however, quite different.)

Woods (1982) and Arbib (1982a) propose models in which many distinct partial analyses are maintained at once, their relative probabilities being constantly reweighted by successive segments of input.

Let us turn now to the issue of top-down interlevel influences. The hypothesis of many computational theories of perception (see, for example, Neisser 1967 and Craik and Lockhart 1972) has been that lower-level representations are computed first, autonomously, to be followed by the next level of representation, and so on up to the highest-level conceptual structures. But rather ordinary facts militate against such a treatment of language perception.

In the following sentences, for instance, the phonological structure cannot be computed definitively without feedback from syntax and/or semantics.

(6.3)   a. Bill sat on a tack.
        b. The planes set out to attack.
        c. The planes went out on attack.
        d. Bill pointed to a tack.

The last two syllables of (6.3a–d) are acoustically identical. Yet, as the orthography reveals, they differ phonologically: (6.3a, d) have a word boundary between the two syllables and (6.3b, c) do not. There is nothing in phonological structure per se that predicts these results. The difference can come only from consideration of the well-formedness or ill-formedness of associated syntactic and/or conceptual structures.

(6.4)   a. *Bill sat on attack.
        b. *The planes set out to a tack.
        c. ?*The planes went out on a tack. (bizarre pragmatics)
        d. *Bill pointed to attack. (only possibly good with intonation different from that of (6.3d))

These examples show furthermore that the top-down influences need not be particularly local. It is not just the choice of *on* or *to* immediately preceding the phrase in question that determines its phonological structure but at least the choice of verb as well. (Attempts at computer understanding of natural language circumvent this particular problem by starting with written language, which encodes word boundaries as spaces. Similarly, much experimentation on verbal learning starts with written presentation, so the problem has not been noticed there either. On the other hand, as mentioned in section 5.1, acoustic phonetics reveals this problem immediately, and we human speakers deal with it effortlessly all the time.)

In (6.3) higher-level influences have apparently determined a two-way choice among phonological alternatives: whether or not there is a word boundary between the two syllables. But such influences may go further and actually help *fill in* relatively indeterminate parts of phonological structure. Consider, for example, speech perception with noisy or defective input—say, in the presence of an operating jet airplane or over a bad telephone connection. In such circumstances one evidently uses one's knowledge of the language as a whole, plus possibly one's guesses about the speaker's intentions, in order to perceive the sentence. What one constructs, moreover, is not just an intended meaning but a phonological structure as well: one "hears" more than the signal actually conveys. One is generally not conscious of performing this reconstruction—only of its being hard to hear what is being said. (On this "phoneme restoration effect," see Warren 1970.)

For a different case, consider how hard it is to take dictation in a language one does not understand. In addition to the impossibility of placing word boundaries on phonetic grounds alone, it is often extremely difficult even to judge what speech sounds one has heard. This suggests that, in ordinary use of one's native language, a certain amount of what passes for phonetic perception is actually facilitated by knowledge of the language—including syntactic and semantic knowledge. In other words, phonetic information is "filled in" from higher-level structures as well as from the acoustic signal; and though there is a difference in how it is derived, there is no qualitative difference in the completed structure itself.

The realization that there are higher-level cognitive effects on perception, of which those just presented are almost trivial examples, led to a rejection of the bottom-up view of processing by "New Look" psychologists such as Bruner (1957) and the later Neisser (1976). According to their view, all aspects of perception are guided by higher-level expectancies, including world knowledge.

But surely there are limitations on top-down influences. For instance, Fodor (1983) points out that knowing about visual illusions such as the Müller-Lyer illusion (figure 6.4) does not dispel them: the aspect of visual processing that is responsible for producing them is evidently sealed off from the relevant world knowledge. Similarly, in language, violations of the Coordinate Structure Constraint (section 4.3) are not mitigated by studying linguistics. Numerous examples like these show that there must be aspects of perceptual organization that are not influenced by conceptual

Figure 6.4
The Müller-Lyer illusion. The two horizontal lines are actually the same length.

schemata. Thus, as usual, the issue does not concern a categorical choice between two extreme positions but only what interaction of high-level and low-level influences are operative in determining any particular level of structure.

One of the principal constraints on a solution is the fact that, as Fodor (1983, 68) puts it, "the perception of novelty depends on bottom-to-top perceptual mechanisms." To perceive something as novel depends on having constructed a representation of it (at some level) that is different from stored representations; this requires a sensitivity to the input that goes beyond fitting it into existing schemata.

With this in mind, consider what is necessary for the phoneme restoration effect. Preliminary attempts at phonological representation must be based on the acoustic information transduced by the ear—that is, from the bottom up. The conceptual information necessary to complete the phonological structure cannot be available until after these initial hypotheses are formed and after potential choices of lexical items, based on these hypotheses, are retrieved. Semantic information cannot be fed back into the phonology until still later. In other words, there are inherent time delays in the use of top-down processes, and they tend to function as a "second resort" when bottom-up processing has failed to arrive at a fully determined structure.

Granted that there are top-down influences on perception, two questions arise: (1) What kind of higher-level information can serve in a top-down process? (2) What lower levels can be affected? Our observations about visual illusions and the Coordinate Structure Constraint suggest that conscious beliefs in propositional form are not potential input for top-down processes; on the other hand, the semantics of the language and expectancies about the topic of conversation do seem to have influence. Thus the borderline in question 1 is somewhere between these cases. In answer to question 2, the phoneme restoration effect suggests that top-down influences extend all the way to phonological structure at least—contra Fodor (1983), who would like to claim that language perception is pretty much strictly bottom-up to at least syntax. On the other hand, to my knowledge there is no evidence to suggest that acoustic information is also filled in from above, so perhaps acoustic-to-phonetic processing is a strictly bottom-up module in Fodor's sense.

Such a mixture of bottom-up and top-down processing is not inconsistent with LSLP, as might first be thought. For instance, LSLP does not forbid top-down influences on phonological structure from conceptual structure (including context encoded in this form). It requires only that such influences take place via the intermediate step of syntactic structure. Such a position can be developed as *Processing Hypothesis 3*.

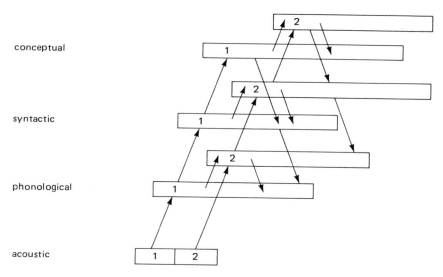

Figure 6.5
Processing Hypothesis 3 for perception

Processing Hypothesis 3
In speech understanding, each part of each level of representation from phonology up is derived by virtue of correspondences with neighboring levels. (Interactive parallel)

Figure 6.5 sketches the potential time course of processing along these lines. It includes both intralevel (holistic) and interlevel (top-down) effects. For comprehensibility, the sketch is limited to an utterance with two segments.

One of the virtues of autonomous levels of representation between sound and meaning emerges from this view of processing. Given that the mapping from sound to meaning is complex, tortuous, and in many cases not fully determined by the input, the intermediate levels provide way stations where the outputs of bottom-up and top-down processes can be compared and integrated. Moreover, the various processes that relate levels do not have to affect each other directly. They can run autonomously, while further processes, informationally localized at the individual levels, can be busy correlating the results. (This advantage of autonomous levels in processing is pointed out by Marr (1982) with respect to visual processing; it applies equally here.)

In other words, we can refine the large-scale monolithic language perception module envisioned by Fodor (1983), decomposing it into a number of highly specialized "minimodules," the sum of whose effects produces the comprehension of spoken language. (I discuss Fodor's position in more detail in chaper 12, showing a number of grounds on which the present view is more satisfactory.) (6.5)–(6.7) give a decomposition into mini-modules motivated by Processing Hypothesis 3.

(6.5)   Bottom-up processors
    a. Transduction of sound wave into acoustic information
    b. Mapping of available acoustic information into phonological format
    c. Mapping of available phonological structure into syntactic format
    d. Mapping of available syntactic structure into conceptual format

(6.6)   Top-down processors
    a. Mapping of available syntactic structure into phonological format
    b. Mapping of available conceptual structure into syntactic format

(6.7)   Integrative processors
    a. Integration of newly available phonological information into unified phonological structure
    b. Integration of newly available syntactic information into unified syntactic structure
    c. Integration of newly available conceptual information into unified conceptual structure

(6.5b) is the processor most directly addressed by acoustic phonetics; (6.7b) is the processor most directly addressed by standard theories of parsing.

This view of processing is consistent both with the position defended most forcefully by Forster (1979), that there is autonomous syntactic processing, and with the position argued by Tyler and Marslen-Wilson (1977), that semantic effects do influence syntactic parsing. Forster admits semantic effects but argues that they lag behind syntactic analysis in time. He concludes that they are an effect of a separate "general problem solver" whose job is to disambiguate sentences and on whose structure he provides no speculations. The present account makes no such appeal to a cognitive wild card and is therefore more constrained. At the same time it predicts the timing results as a consequence of LSLP.

A further decomposition of the minimodules is not unlikely. For instance, since phonological structure contains not only segmental phonology but also intonational and prosodic structure (tree and/or grid), there may well be separate processing components for each of these structures and for their relationships, governed by the correspondence rules between them. However, the experimental literature is so far from testing such conjectures that at the moment they had better remain just that.

The overall picture that emerges is of a highly interactive system made up of specialized processes. We see, then, that although language comprehension as a whole may seem to wildly intermix bottom-up and top-down processes, it may still on closer inspection prove to be highly regimented both in its use of information and in its time course.

6.3 Lexical Access during Speech Perception

The decomposition of speech perception in (6.5)–(6.7) does not include one aspect of language processing that has been an important topic of research in psycholinguistics: retrieving material from the lexicon. Let us briefly see how this process fits in with LSLP and Processing Hypothesis 3.

Acoustic information transduced by the ear is mapped by processor (6.5b) into a sequence of speech sounds. For simplicity, let us suppose that this sequence is determinate, so that no phoneme restoration is necessary from top-down sources. The integrative phonological processor (6.7a) can segment this sequence of sounds into syllables, a purely phonological procedure. But it cannot in general mark word boundaries. For this it must refer to the lexicon, asking in effect, Do any of these syllables or syllable sequences form a word?

Remember that at this point the processor has no conceptual information about the sentence yet: according to LSLP, such information is available only via phonological and syntactic information. Thus, when the lexicon is asked this question, it has no basis for picking and choosing candidate words other than the phonological specifications it has been provided. It therefore has no choice but to deliver up all possible words that meet those specifications (possibly in order of frequency, but that is a further refinement). So, for instance, it should deliver up both *a tack* and *attack* in response to (6.3a–d).

Each candidate word that is delivered to the phonological processor also brings with it corresponding fragments of syntactic and conceptual structure. In order to tell which is the correct choice of word in the sentence currently being processed, the syntactic and conceptual structures must be fit into overall well-formed structures at both levels. Thus each candidate word must be passed up to the higher levels via the bottom-up processors (6.5c) and (6.5d) and used by the integrative processors for syntactic and conceptual structure—in some cases even before definitive word boundaries can be established in phonological structure.

The general picture of lexical access during speech perception, then, is that it initially can discriminate only on phonological grounds. Only somewhat later in processing, after the syntactic and conceptual processors have gotten access to the list of possible candidates, can the ultimate choice of word be determined.

Widely cited experimental work confirms this picture. Swinney (1979, 1982) and Tanenhaus, Leiman, and Seidenberg (1979) demonstrate that for a brief time after presentation all senses of a word are active, regardless of preceding semantic and syntactic context. During this period all senses, of whatever part of speech, are capable of priming (speeding up recognition of) semantically related words. For example, subjects in an experiment by Onifer and Swinney (1981) heard either (6.8a) or (6.8b).

(6.8) a. All the cash that was kept in the safe at the bank was stolen last week when two masked men broke in.
  b. A large piece of driftwood that had been washed up onto the bank by the last storm stood as a reminder of how high the water had actually risen.

Immediately after hearing the word *bank*, and while auditory presentation of the sentence continued, subjects saw *money, study, river, twelve*, or a nonsense syllable flash on a screen and had to decide whether it was a word or not. Either (6.8a) or (6.8b) sped up recognition of both *money* and *river*, showing that both senses of *bank* were active at that point. However, if the words were flashed several syllables after *bank* was heard, only the contextually appropriate sense was primed—that is, *money* in (6.8a) and *river* in (6.8b). In other words, lexical items are retrieved initially on the basis of phonological structure alone, and refinement to the syntactically and conceptually proper structure comes only after integration into the rest of the sentence.

David Swinney (personal communication) informs me that this priming even takes place on initial syllables of words before they are complete: a word primes not only all its own senses but also the senses of its initial syllable. This confirms the view argued here that lexical retrieval is driven by phonological structure and that even the setting of word boundaries may require higher-level integrative processing.

This experimental evidence, then, lends support to our general approach to processing motivated by LSLP. In turn, LSLP is a consequence of a theory of the organization of the *structure* of language in terms of discrete levels of representation. These results thus provide a good illustration of the interaction of theories of structure and theories of processing, one of our major methodological concerns here.

6.4 The Time Course of Language Production

Evidence about the course of processing in speech production is less extensive than in speech perception, but it tends to indicate processing along similar lines.

One important kind of evidence is based on the distribution of spontaneous speech errors or "slips of the tongue." Recall Fromkin's (1971) observation, noted in section 4.2, that slips of the tongue are invariably subject to well-formedness constraints on syllable structure. This suggests the existence of an autonomous component dedicated to integrating and maintaining well-formed phonological structures in production, even in the face of erroneous input from higher-level structures.

More telling is an argument due to Lashley (1951), which demonstrates the existence of some degree of holistic processing in the course of phonological production. Certain errors (including "spoonerisms") involve the insertion of material at an earlier point in the sentence than intended. For instance, in (6.9a) sn has been exchanged with sh; in (6.9b) aw replaces the intended i sound.

(6.9)   a. So while you do the cooking, Bill *sn*ovels *sh*ow, does
            he?   (intended: shovels snow)
        b. The straight l*aw*n drawn through . . .   (intended: straight line)

Lashley observes that the word or sound that appears ahead of its intended place must already have been chosen soon enough to appear early. This means that the production of a phonological structure cannot take place one word at a time but must involve a span of material that is at least as long as the span encompassed by the erroneous anticipation.

Garrett (1975), who provides the examples in (6.9), takes this argument one step further. In analyzing a large corpus of speech errors collected by himself and others, he finds that anticipatory errors fall into a number of types. In one type individual sounds are anticipated or interchanged; the errors in (6.9) belong to this type. In another type entire morphemes are interchanged, but their suffixes are preserved in their original position, as in (6.10).

(6.10)   a. McGovern favors *push*ing *bust*ers.   (intended: busting pushers)
         b. It just *sound*ed to *start*.   (intended: started to sound)

In a third type entire words are shifted in position, as in (6.11).

(6.11)   a. although *murder* is a form of *suicide* . . .   (intended: suicide is a
             form of murder)
         b. I've got something *all* to tell you.   (intended: something to tell
             you all)

Garrett finds that the maximum spans of these three types of errors—the amount of material over which a shift or exchange can take place—are different. Roughly, the word shifts like (6.11) have the longest possible span, followed by the morpheme exchanges like (6.10); and the phoneme exchanges and shifts like (6.9) have the shortest span. Garrett interprets this pattern to mean that choice of words, on the basis of the intended meaning of the utterance, must take place farther in advance of actual speech than placement of the words into morphological frames (a syntactic function); still later comes formulation of phonological structure.

This evidence thus suggests to Garrett a theory of speech production that conforms to LSLP, in that information flow proceeds from each level down to the adjacent level, but in which there are also holistic integrative functions at each level.

Might production also make use of *bottom-up* feedback in the formulation of higher-level structures? The sort of phenomenon that might suggest lower-level feedback in production is as follows. Recall the Coordinate Structure Constraint (section 4.3), a constraint on syntactic form that forbids understanding a *wh*-word outside a coordinate construction as having a grammatical function within the coordinate construction. A related constraint, called the *Complex NP Constraint*, forbids understanding a *wh*-word outside a relative clause as having a grammatical function within the relative clause. For instance, in sentence (6.12a) *who likes Bill* is a relative clause. One could follow (6.12a) in discourse with (6.12b). But then suppose that the hearer wishes to find out who the someone else in (6.12b) is. He cannot frame his request in the form (6.12c), because the *wh*-phrase *who else* is understood as the object of *like*, which is within the relative clause.

(6.12)   a. I have a friend who likes Bill.
         b. I have a friend who likes someone else.
         c. *Who else do you have a friend who likes?

As in the discussion of the Coordinate Structure Constraint, I have built up this example so as to show that one knows what such a sentence means— it is conceptually acceptable. However, because of a property of syntactic structure, one cannot express the thought this way.

Now consider the familiar experience of starting to utter a sentence something like (6.13) and sensing in mid-course that something is about to go wrong.

(6.13)   What movies do you know lots of people who....

What has gone wrong is that the speaker has constructed a sentence in which the *wh*-phrase *what movies* must be understood as having a function within the relative clause that has just begun with *who*. In other words, the speaker is about to utter the ungrammatical (6.14a), which like (6.12c) violates the Complex NP Constraint. One way to recover from this blunder, though lamely, is to insert a pronoun in the gap, as in (6.14b). This is at least comprehensible, though still not grammatical English.

(6.14)   a. *What movies do you know lots of people who like?
          b. *What movies do you know lots of people who like them?

A better recovery, though, is to start over and reformulate the sentence as (6.15).

(6.15)   What movies are liked by lots of people you know?

(6.15) retains the general sense of (6.14a, b). However, it reverses the dependency relations between the two clauses: *people like movies* is the subordinate clause in (6.14) and the main clause in (6.15), whereas *you know people* is the main clause in (6.14) and the subordinate clause in (6.15). Thus, the grammatical function of *what movies* has been shifted into the main clause in (6.15), avoiding violation of the Complex NP Constraint.

This recasting of syntactic structure entails a reformulation of conceptual structure as well, since the syntactic dependency relations among clauses have semantic repercussions. In other words, recovery from an impending Complex NP Constraint violation in syntax requires the speaker to formulate a roughly equivalent conceptual structure that can be mapped into an expressible syntactic form. Thus syntactic exigencies have had a feedback effect on conceptual structure in the course of production.

Something else is going on in this particular example. From a syntactic point of view the most direct reformulation of (6.14) would be (6.16).

(6.16)   What movies do lots of people you know like?

(6.16) is more direct than (6.15) because its main clause is active rather than passive. But it doesn't sound very good, evidently for prosodic reasons. The only way to pronounce (6.16) comprehensibly is to pause after *know* and start a new intonational phrase consisting only of *like*. But there is a strong prejudice against sentences that end with a long intonational phrase plus a very short one: a well-known case contrasts (6.17a) with the synonymous but less felicitous (6.17b), which ends with the short intonational phrase *up*.

(6.17)   a. I called up the man who likes peanut butter and jelly sandwiches.
          b. I called the man who likes peanut butter and jelly sandwiches up.

(6.15) avoids the prosodic problem of (6.16) by placing the long phrase *lots of people you know* at the end, better balancing the length of the intonational phrases.

But what are the implications of being able to make this choice? Clearly, constraints of *phonological* structure have resulted in drastic reordering of *syntactic* structure into a more complex form. We thus have further evidence that speech production involves feedback from lower-level to higher-level structures.

This example is in itself hardly conclusive. However, I know of no research on the extent to which lower-level structure affects choices of higher-level structure in the course of sentence production; this example is indicative of the sort of evidence that would seem germane.

There is, of course, an additional source of feedback in production: hearing oneself speak. Here information passes out to the vocal tract, is transduced into a sound wave, is transduced by the ear back into acoustic format, and thence feeds into the language perception process. Without going into details, I will only mention one well-known effect: if, by clever manipulation with a tape recorder and headphones, this auditory feedback is delayed by 200 milliseconds or so (about the duration of a syllable), production can be severely disrupted in many speakers, producing uncontrollable stuttering (Black 1951; MacNeilage and Ladefoged 1976; Howell and Archer 1984). Thus auditory feedback must play a role in production.

All of this evidence tends to point toward a production equivalent of Processing Hypothesis 3, which does not specify anything about direction of derivation.

Processing Hypothesis 3
In speech production, each part of each level of representation from syntax down is derived by virtue of correspondences with neighboring levels.

Figure 6.6 is a sketch of the time course of production, paralleling figure 6.5 for perception.

6.5 Bidirectionality in the Language Processor

Comparing the modular organization of language comprehension with that of language production, we stumble on an interesting conjecture: that much of the language processing device may be inherently *bidirectional*. To substantiate this possibility, I will go through the components posited for language comprehension in (6.5)–(6.7).

Consider component (6.7a), which integrates newly available phonological information into a unified phonological structure. In comprehension such information may come via the mapping from acoustic information (bottom-up), or it may come as top-down feedback from the syntax, producing the phoneme restoration effect. The source doesn't matter: once the information is in phonological format, component (6.7a) integrates it with whatever was present before. But this means that this component can serve equally well in a situation where its primary source of information is the syntax, that is, in production. In short, there is no bar in principle to using it for both perception and production.

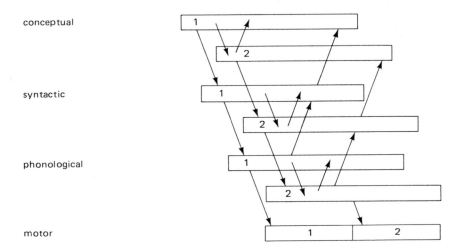

Figure 6.6
Processing Hypothesis 3 for production

A similar argument applies to component (6.7b), which is devoted to integrating newly available syntactic information into a unified syntactic structure. It need not care whether its primary source is via the mapping from phonology, and information from meaning is providing top-down feedback, or whether its primary source is meaning, and phonology is providing feedback.

Moreover, the mappings between levels observe exactly the same principles of correspondence, whether they are used in perception or production. For example, component (6.5c), which maps phonological structure into syntactic format, can in principle be used either as a primary source of syntactic information in perception or as a feedback function in production. The transformation of information is identical in the two processes. The same applies to component (6.6a) (syntax to phonology), (6.5d) (syntax to conceptual structure), and (6.6b) (conceptual structure to syntax). Each of these can be seen as taking whatever new information has been provided at the input level and translating it, compulsively, to the output level. The interaction of such systems will result in the sort of processing sketched in figures 6.5 and 6.6.

The only inherently directional parts of the system, then, will be at its ends. At the periphery the acoustic-to-phonological mapping serves only perception, and the phonological-to-motor mapping serves only production. At the most central level, conceptual structure, perception will feed processes of inference, whereas production will be fed by them. (In addition, production is presumably subject to general constraints on initiation of action, such as the presence of a computational equivalent of a "will to act," whatever that may prove to be.)

For the purposes of my larger argument it does not matter too much whether these facilities of comprehension and production are completely shared. More important is that comprehension and production make use of common information structures—the same levels of representation from conceptual down to phonetic. Beyond the feasibility argument just given, however, there is a certain amount of empirical evidence for shared processes or facilities. For one thing, both must invoke a common lexicon, stored in long-term memory. According to Garrett (1982), current experimental results indicate a common mechanism of lexical retrieval in perception and production as well as a common retrieved structure. In addition, it is now widely acknowledged that Broca's and Wernicke's aphasias, two of the most important varieties of language impairment due to stroke or brain injury, involve parallel deficits in perception and production, pointing again to common facilities and/or mechanisms. (See Bradley, Garrett, and Zurif 1980 and papers in Arbib, Caplan, and Marshall 1982.)[1]

6.6 Levels of Representation in Short-Term Linguistic Memory

We now move from the concerns of psycholinguistics proper to notions of processing more characteristic of standard-practice cognitive psychology.

The commonsense ("folk psychology") notion of memory sees it as a sort of filing cabinet—a receptacle in which information is passively stored in some organized fashion so it can be retrieved in time of need. The application of the term *memory* to a component of the computer derives from and reinforces this conception: computer memories are indeed passive storage devices, from which information must be removed before it is available for computation.

---

1. I have not said anything about one of the hot issues of psycholinguistics: the status of the linguist's principles of structure—the grammar—in the organization of the processor. There are two main possibilities. Under one view the rules of grammar are nowhere explicitly present; they are only implicit in the organization of the language processors. Alternatively, the rules of grammar, like the lexicon, could be stored separately from the processor as a sort of "microprogram"; as the repository of possible structures, they would be referred to constantly in the course of processing. (For much discussion, see Berwick and Weinberg 1984 and references there.)

One small argument in favor of the latter view comes from bilingualism. On the former view someone who speaks two languages—or even two dialects of the same language—must have two distinct sets of language processors, one per language. On the latter view one set of language processors suffices, making reference to either of two sets of possible structures (grammars) and lexicons. From a pure engineering point of view this alternative seems more parsimonious and on the face of it more easily able to account for switching of languages back and forth in midsentence. But then, nature *is* curious in her ways.

Whether this is an accurate assessment of memory in the mind, though, may be another question. It does not account, for instance, for such phenomena as the spontaneous reorganization of memories over time (as discussed by Bartlett (1932), for instance) and the absence of a known anatomical locus for "thought" (recall the discussion of decentralization in section 3.2). It is difficult to articulate alternatives with existing terminology, but it would seem desirable to break down the strict distinction between storing information and reprocessing it.

For the memory facilities usually thought to be involved in language perception, at least, the issues can be set on fairly firm ground. There seems to be some (though not total) consensus on two distinct types of perceptual memory. (It does not matter whether they are neurologically integrated into localized areas of the brain or somehow distributed throughout the brain's volume: the *functional* differentiation is what is important.) Following Neisser's (1967) terminology, one of these is called *iconic* memory in the visual system and *echoic* memory in the auditory system. This is thought to be a facility that holds very low-level representations of stimuli for a very brief time, at most about two seconds. There is also thought to be a facility called *short-term* memory or *immediate* memory or *active* memory or *working* memory, in which perceptual information is already integrated or "chunked" to some extent. Here information is stored during further temporal integration and compared with information retrieved from long-term memory for purposes of interpretation. Information to be stored is transferred from short-term to long-term memory.

But in what form? It is tempting to think of the transfer of information from one memory to another as like sending an electrical signal down a wire—as if the bit configuration from one computer register were copied into another. But if memory is simply a storage device, this creates a logical problem. Suppose, for purposes of argument, that echoic memory stores phonetic representations. Then some facility must be responsible for transforming acoustic information from the ear into phonetic format. This facility must be either echoic memory itself or the conduit from the ear to echoic memory. Similarly, if the information in short-term memory is at some higher level of representation (say, syntactic structure), echoic memory cannot just send phonetic information down the wire to short-term memory; it must be translated by one of the memories or by the conduit. In short, the logical structure of linguistic processing dictates that a theory of memory must posit not just facilities for storage and transfer of information but also facilities for transforming information from one level of representation to another.

Accordingly, we will view echoic memory, for instance, as not just a termporary holding facility for information on its way to short-term memory but as a processor that transforms acoustic information into phonetic structure. In this view one cannot ask, as Neisser (1976) does, about *the* form of the icon (the information stored in iconic memory): there is no such thing as the icon per se. Rather, iconic and echoic memory are to be conceived of (grossly) as two registers or receptacles, one in the format of the transducer (retina or ear) and one in the format of the next higher level of representation, plus a processor that translates the information from one form into the other. (Ultimately, I suspect that the strict distinction between storage facilities, conduits, and processors is a convenient fiction, reinforced by the computer analogy, and that it should be abandoned without reluctance when the right sort of evidence from neurophysiology comes along. In the meantime this idealization is a way to continue discourse in the absence of a more highly articulated theory.)

With all these provisos in mind, let us think about what might be going on in short-term or active memory during language perception. The role of short-term memory in perception, roughly speaking, is to integrate and categorize incoming information for potential delivery to long-term memory. So we can ask, in what form is linguistic information delivered?

Obviously, the usual goal of language perception is to deliver up information in conceptual structure (meaning) format. Sometimes it is taken that this is the *only* format in which long-term memory operates, since people tend to remember only the gist of things they have been told, not the particular syntactic and phonological forms in which communication has been couched (Sachs 1967; Bransford and Franks 1971; Anderson and Bower 1973). But in fact one *can* remember syntactic and phonological form if, at the time of learning, it is known that the memory task specifically demands it—think of memorizing lines of a play, for example. Moreover, one can remember phonological structure in the absence of syntactic and semantic information, as in memorizing strings of nonsense syllables. For a more true-to-life case, a depressingly large part of my religious education as a child consisted of memorizing prayers in Hebrew, through which I was able to assimilate phonological and morphological structure but achieved at best only a fragmentary understanding of the syntax and semantics. From such examples it appears that long-term memory must be capable of encoding linguistic information at all levels from phonological structure on up. One cannot identify long-term memory with "semantic memory" alone. (If one's memory for words of one's language is not a separate facility from ordinary long-term memory, the lexicon provides an obvious confirmation of this claim, since a lexical item requires information at all linguistic levels.)

There is no question that information may be easier to memorize or recall in one format than in another. Remembering the gist of a telephone conversation, for instance, is vastly easier than remembering exactly what was said and by whom. Similarly, section 4.2 demonstrated a gradation in

learning and recall, from easy cases that presented maximal linguistic structure to inordinately difficult cases that appeared only as a sequence of
uninterpretable symbols. In fact, as Neisser (1967) is at pains to point out,
the imposition of practically *any* sort of structure will aid memorization and
recall; he cites as an example the facilitating effect of simple rhythmic
segmentation on the learning of random digit strings (125−847−634 is
easier than 125847634, for instance). But the ease or difficulty of encoding
different structures, though it cries out for explanation, must not obscure
the fact that such encoding does in fact take place.

We conclude that, under appropriate task demands, information from
any of the levels of linguistic structure can be delivered to long-term
memory. Since short-term memory is the immediate source of such information, it too must have the capacity to encode linguistic information at all
levels of representation from the phonological level up. This conclusion is
supported by three points. (1) There must be *some* facility that effects the
translation of information from phonological through syntactic to conceptual form. (2) This facility probably is not echoic memory, which is
thought to deal only in low-level representations. (3) A level as high as
conceptual structure must be available in short-term memory to account for
active processes of interpretation.

6.7 The Function of Short-Term Linguistic Memory

Let us integrate our discussion of the time course of language processing
with that of the contents of short-term linguistic memory (STLM). An
overall picture emerges of the function of STLM; there are three salient
parts, which we take up in turn.

1. STLM is an active processing device that creates all levels of
linguistic representation that can be computed on the basis of incoming information.
2. STLM maintains these levels of representation in registration with
each other.
3. If more than one set of matched representations is present, STLM
designates (or tries to designate) one as most salient (*the* current
interpretation of the input).

Function 1 attributes to STLM all the bidirectional functions discussed in
sections 6.2 and 6.5. In speech comprehension the input is such phonetic
structure as can be gleaned from the acoustic signal. On the basis of this
structure plus knowledge of the language and possibly broader contextual
information, short-term memory constructs full phonological structure,
syntactic structure, and meaning (if possible). In speech production the
input to STLM is a conceptual structure (an intended meaning), in response

to which the processor creates corresponding syntactic and phonological structures. The surface phonological structure is in turn sent off to some lower-level processor to be transformed into motor instructions to the vocal tract. In short, the goal of this facility is to fill in representations at all levels that correspond to an input at either end of the chain.

I deliberately have said that STLM *fills in* representations, in order to suggest that representations are not automatically discarded once their role in the perception or production chain is over. In speaking, for instance, we do not (always) forget what we intended to say as soon as an appropriate phonological form has been computed. Similarly, in speech perception we still have short-term access to phonological representation after we have understood a sentence. Thus, short-term processing ought to be thought of as having the goal not just of translating information from one format into the others but of constructing and maintaining all formats possible at once.

Next let us consider function 2. There is reason to believe that the multiple levels are maintained *in registration with each other*; that is, STLM contains in explicit form the links between respective constituents of different levels—for instance, which parts of the phonological structure correspond to which parts of syntactic structure and so on. There are several reasons why such overt registration is plausible.

First, the process of deriving the three levels must in any event establish the correspondence between them. Once all three levels are derived from an input representation, there are two possibilities: either the correlations used to derive the representations may be retained, or else they may be thrown away. The idea that the levels are maintained in registration with each other essentially amounts to the claim that the correspondences are retained. By contrast, a view that did not incorporate registration of levels would therefore be not so much parsimonious as wasteful.

Moreover, consider what is involved in the use of higher-level information to help fill in defective or inconclusive input (as in deriving a full phonological structure despite a bad phone connection). Suppose that once a piece of syntactic structure were derived from a piece of phonological structure, the processor were to lose the information that these pieces are corresponding parts of their respective structures. Then it would be impossible to use the syntactic structure to help complete the phonological structure, except by recomputing the connection: the processor could not tell what part of the phonology to fix without knowing what part of the syntax justified fixing it. By contrast, if short-term memory retains the registration of the structures as they are gradually established, top-down feedback is a simple matter of looking up a correspondence link that is already present. Thus, in speech perception the existence of higher-level feedback provides a strong rationale for the registration of levels.

Similarly, in speech production the development of a conceptual structure leads to a correlated syntactic structure and in turn a correlated phonological structure. If, as shown in section 6.4, there is lower-level feedback to the higher-level structures, then, as in perception, such processing would be greatly facilitated by not only maintaining all the levels of structure in short-term memory but also retaining the correspondence links between them. Otherwise, such connections would have to be recomputed for feedback to occur. Hence, registration of levels is useful in speech production as well as perception.

Something much like the notion of registration has in fact appeared in artificial intelligence systems that compute multiple levels of representation. (See, for instance, Arbib 1982a and Woods 1982; in Arbib's theory the parallel to my notion of short-term information appears as a multilevel "blackboard" in which the levels are linked by "knowledge structures.") Furthermore, Arbib (1982b) argues that simultaneous computation of multiple levels, in which each level helps to refine and differentiate the others, is characteristic of neurological processes. If so, the proposal here is, to use Arbib's term, very much "in the style of the brain."

Summing up our progress to this point, we have justified the claim that all levels of linguistic representation are constructed in the course of sentence perception and production. Whatever the time course of construction, they are all fully specified by the time processing is complete. In addition, to the extent that there are feedback effects (top-down in perception, bottom-up in production), this shows that the levels must be kept in registration with each other throughout their construction and might as well be in the end product. I know of no evidence that weighs *against* registration of the levels—only a desire for theoretical parsimony, which is probably misguided in this case.

6.8 The Selection Function of Short-Term Linguistic Memory

There remains function 3 of STLM, which I will call the *selection function*: if more than one set of matched representations is present in STLM, it designates (or tries to designate) one as most salient.

One of the most common observations about awareness and/or attention is that at a particular moment one can only be aware of a single interpretation of the presented field. Standard examples in visual perception include the Necker cube (figure 6.7a) and the vase-faces illusion (figure 6.7b). Though the two interpretations may alternate freely, they are not simultaneously present to awareness. It is the alternation of interpretations over time, not the presence of both at once, that leads to the judgment that these figures are ambiguous.

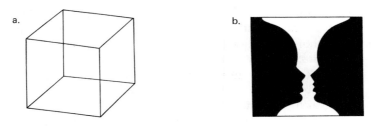

Figure 6.7
Ambiguous figures: the Necker cube and the vase-faces illusion

The same is true, I believe, of language perception. When I consider examples like (6.18a) or the less hackneyed (6.18b), the phenomenology seems to be of only one interpretation at a time.

(6.18)   a. Visiting relatives can be boring.
          b. She left the table covered with flowers.

It is the successive apprehension of different interpretations, not the simultaneous experience of them, that leads to the judgment of ambiguity. (What makes this cloudier than the visual ambiguities is that one must repeat the sentences to oneself over time, and this seems to interfere with experiencing a precise and striking moment when the interpretation switches. Puns are perhaps the limiting case, where the ambiguity is intended. Here my sense is still of rapidly alternating interpretations—though I feel myself verging on Wundt-like speculation by this point.)

The phenomenon of selection is sometimes attributed to the function of consciousness itself—Marcel (1983), if I read him correctly, makes this claim explicit. Alternatively, it is attributed to limitations on capacity of short-term memory or attention. The assumption seems to be that selection is extrinsic to language processing—that language processing hands its results over to some "higher cognitive function" that is responsible for selection.

Yet there are at least precursors of the selection function in language processing, in the resolution of local ambiguity. Recall the experiments on lexical access discussed in section 6.3, which showed that all possible senses of a word are temporarily active, then one is designated as contextually most appropriate and the others are suppressed. Suppose, however, that more than one sense is contextually appropriate, so the sentence presented is in fact ambiguous. Investigating such a case, Hudson and Tanenhaus (1984) find that when ambiguous words are introduced in this experimental paradigm without prior biasing context, the multiple senses continue to prime lexical decision tasks for a longer period of time than when a unique sense can be picked out from preceding context. But by the time a clause boundary is reached, several words later, only one sense is left capable of priming. (The sense chosen is usually the one that is more salient when the word is presented in isolation (David Swinney, personal communication).) Hence, selection of a single word sense has taken place even when there is no contextual basis for it. This suggests that a process very much akin to the selection function has taken place within the language processor, over the local domain of individual words.

In syntactic structure a similar process is at work in the symptoms of the "garden path" sentences such as (6.2) mentioned earlier.

(6.2)   The horse raced past the barn fell.

This sentence has its striking effect because, by the time one has heard *barn*, the past tense sense of *raced* has been chosen uniquely and *the horse raced past the barn* has been interpreted as a main clause. Is this choice made immediately upon hearing *raced*, or are multiple structures considered from which the past tense reading is chosen? Consider (6.19).

(6.19)   a. The horse led a long way down the road fell.
           b. The horse led a long line of wagons down the road.

Neither (6.19a) nor (6.19b) has the phenomenological shock value of (6.2), yet the proper structure for *led* cannot be determined until the choice between *way* and *line* has been evaluated, three syllables later. This suggests that for at least this long, in this case, multiple readings are under consideration and one is selected by subsequent context. (Unfortunately, I know of no experimental literature parallel to that on lexical access that can show more definitively the presence of multiple syntactic structures.)

Turning back to (6.2), then, we see that the garden path effect must be a result of a choice between multiple structures independent of context—so that when the determining context (*fell*) finally arrives, the right choice is no longer available. The evidence thus points to something like the selection function operating in the domain of syntactic structure as well.

Another piece of circumstantial evidence arises from an experiment of Lackner and Tuller (1976), in which subjects heard repeated sequences of four English monosyllables such as (6.20a, b).

(6.20)   a. the see I sun the see I sun the see I sun...
           b. I like to fish I like to fish I like to fish...

After a period of time listening to such sequences, subjects experienced spontaneous regrouping akin to the reversal of the Necker cube. (6.20a, b) were heard as (6.21a, b), respectively.

(6.21)   a. ice on the sea ice on the sea ice on the sea...
           b. to fish, I like; to fish, I like; to fish, I like;...

What is significant here is that all listeners reported stress and intonation changes accompanying syntactic regroupings. When the list (6.20a) was regrouped as the syntactic phrase (6.21a), "perceived stress and intonation immediately changed so that 'sea' was stressed, and a pause was heard between 'on' and 'the.' No pause was heard between 'sun' and 'the' in the original sequence form, nor was any pause actually present" (Lackner and Tuller 1976, 305).

The punctuation in (6.21b) is meant to indicate the perceived intonation in this interpretation of the sequence. "As the experimenters themselves experienced, when one voluntarily switches between these segmentations, the changes in stress and intonation are so startling it is difficult to believe that the acoustic signal has not been changed. Moreover, in the latter segmentation, a considerable pause is heard after 'fish' ...; no pause is actually present in the signal" (p. 305).

This experiment shows that multiple interpretations are not limited to the conceptual or syntactic level but extend down even to the level of phonological structure, including intonation. This confirms the claim that STLM is computing all levels in registration with each other and that the selection function is choosing not just a high-level conceptual structure but the syntactic and phonological structures in registration with it. It would thus seem to dispel any notion that the selection function is performed by a "higher-level cognitive device" that deals exclusively with central levels of representation such as meaning or even syntax.

In short, although the evidence is hardly definitive, it suggests a selection function at work in language perception, involving all levels of representation and operating without benefit of awareness or attention. If the language processor is doing this all the time in local domains, there seems no reason for it not to do the same job in the case of globally ambiguous examples like (6.18).

What intuitions motivate the belief that the selection of a single reading *is* a function of awareness or attention? These seem to be (1) that one can consciously reflect on the ambiguity and (2) that one can willfully switch interpretations over time. But notice: conscious reflection and conscious switching cannot take place unless one has already consciously experienced each interpretation in succession. For example, if you have not yet noticed that (6.18b) actually has *three* interpretations, you will be unable to "find" the third and pay attention to it at will. You can consciously "look for" the third reading, but its finally popping into awareness is more an "aha-experience" than a conscious act. This seems to be the case with the classic ambiguous visual figures as well.

My interpretation of the phenomenology, in light of the rest of language processing, is that the language processor itself performs the selection of a single set of linguistic structures (one of each level), and the selected set is all that is passed on to whatever mysterious mechanisms are responsible for awareness. With a fully ambiguous sentence, the selection process cannot settle on a single most salient structure but, as in the lexical access case, chooses one more or less arbitrarily. It may, however, change its choice over time.

How then does willful choice of interpretation arise? This might be seen as the voluntary creation of an internal biasing context. This context tips the scales of the selection process in favor of the desired interpretation and thereby causes the selection process to present the new interpretation to attention and/or awareness. Thus, this view of the selection function is not inconsistent with the phenomenology. (However, it *is* strictly speaking inconsistent with Pylyshyn's (1984) doctrine of "cognitive impenetrability," especially as Fodor (1983) applies it to language perception: even phonological structure may be changed willfully under the right conditions. In the present theory, comparable and, I think, more realistic constraints follow from the logical structure of language processing, as observed earlier in this chapter.)

This leaves open what happens to nonselected sets of structures in STLM. They may in most cases be discarded. On the other hand, they may still be unconsciously present, particularly in the case of fully ambiguous sentences. Full or partial alternative structures may also have cognitive effects, even if not open to awareness. The multiple structures of puns and poetry presumably exploit these possibilities. But we have done enough for our purposes, and leave the subject here.

6.9 Summary; *Theory V-A*

Let us sum up this chapter in terms of the refinements it permits to the theory of consciousness. During speech understanding and production information structures of all linguistic levels are active in short-term linguistic memory. Moreover, the correspondence links that keep the levels in registration with each other are active as well. Thus at any moment STLM contains one or more matched sets of representations, each of which consists of a full or partial phonological structure matched with a full or partial syntactic structure and a full or partial conceptual structure.

By a certain point in time, which depends on the available evidence, the selection function of STLM chooses one of these matched sets as the most salient analysis of the sentence. Only the information structures of this most salient analysis are available to awareness. (It may consciously be known *that* the other structures exist, perhaps because one has previously experienced them—but they are not at the moment directly experienced.)

We can therefore refine Theory IV of section 4.6 for the case of awareness of language. We will call the new version *Theory V-A*; parallel versions for other modalities will be developed and further refined in chapter 14.

Theory V-A

The distinctions present in conscious awareness of language are caused by/supported by/projected from information structures of the computational mind that (1) are in phonological, syntactic, and/or conceptual format, (2) are part of the matched set of representations chosen as most salient by the selection function of STLM, and (3) have other (as yet unspecified) properties. In particular, linguistic awareness is due to specifically linguistic levels of representation.

Chapter 7
Boundary Conditions on Conceptual Structure

Beyond phonology and syntax is the third broad area of inquiry into the structure of language: the study of meaning, the information that language conveys. It is in the interests of conveying this information—turning it into a form transmittable as an acoustic signal—that phonology and syntax serve as way stations.

In philosophical and linguistic circles the study of meaning is often divided into two major subareas. *Semantics* is the study of aspects of meaning that are due purely to linguistic form; *pragmatics* is the study of aspects of meaning that arise from the interaction of language with one's nonlinguistic perceptions, with one's knowledge of the social circumstances in which a sentence is uttered, and with one's general knowledge of the world. On the other hand, psychologists have tended to lump the two areas together under the term *knowledge representation*. For reasons to be suggested at the end of section 8.1, I side with the psychologists on this issue (though with strong reservations about most proposals in the psychological literature). For now we will assume without argument the absence of a principled division.

The issue to be posed in the present chapter is this: What must a theory of meaning look like in order to be integrated into the computational theory of mind? We will examine traditional requirements on semantic theory and see how some of them must be modified or even abandoned under the constraints imposed by a computational theory; and we will add some new requirements of our own. The next chapter will lay out some of the important elements of a theory, "Conceptual Semantics," that meets these requirements. The theory is developed in greater detail in my *Semantics and Cognition* (henceforth *S&C*).

7.1 Meaning as a Component of the Computational Mind

The fundamental premise of an approach to meaning within the computational theory of mind might be called the *Mentalist Postulate.*

Mentalist Postulate
Meaning in natural language is an information structure that is mentally encoded by human beings.

According to the Mentalist Postulate, the utterances of a language must receive systematic descriptions not only in terms of phonological and syntactic structure but also in terms of an independent level of representation that may be called *semantic* or *conceptual structure*. As with syntax and phonology, the theory of conceptual structure can be divided into two parts: the theory of the structure itself (the formal nature of the representation and its formal correspondence to other information structures) and theory of conceptual processing (how conceptual structures are retrieved in real time from acoustic inputs, how they are stored in and retrieved from memory, how they are used in reasoning, and so forth). Here, as in chapter 5, we will concentrate on the theory of structure.

A mentalist theory of conceptual structure, like the mentalist theories of syntax and phonology, must specify a set of primitives and principles of combination out of which all possible structures at this level can be constructed. The set of possible conceptual structures must in principle be rich enough to encompass all the distinctions of meaning available to speakers of a language: if one can think of a difference in meaning between two words or phrases, this difference must appear as a difference in the conceptual structures associated with these words or phrases. In particular, if a word or phrase is ambiguous, the distinct meanings must appear as distinct conceptual structures. This requirement of *expressivity* is absolutely formidable, and at the moment only a very small portion of the conceptual structure of English can be said to have been explored, much less understood. Moreover, it is as yet very much an open question whether conceptual structure can in fact be reduced to structured combinations of primitives after the fashion of phonology and syntax. Nevertheless, candidates have been suggested for conceptual primitives and principles of combination, some of which will appear in chapter 8.

Another requirement on a theory of conceptual structure is that it provide an account of *perceived relations of meaning* among sentences, for instance, the judgment that sentence (b) can be inferred from sentence (a) in cases like (7.1)–(7.4).

(7.1)   a. Sue walked slowly across the room.
       b. Sue walked across the room.

(7.2)   a. If John is a genius, then I'm an idiot.
       b. If I'm not an idiot, then John isn't a genius.

(7.3)   a. Not everyone in this room speaks English.
       b. Someone in this room doesn't speak English.

(7.4)   a. Sue forced Harry to leave the meeting.
       b. Harry left the meeting.

Crucial to the computational theory of meaning is that the validity of these inferences must be explicated by virtue of *the form of their conceptual structures alone*. That is, the human capacity for interpreting sentences and drawing inferences must ultimately be traced to a set of formal manipulations performed on mental representations. There can be no further step of appealing to what the representations *mean*, that is, interpreting them in terms of some deeper tacit understanding. The buck stops here: expressions at the level of conceptual structure simply *are* the meanings of utterances. (Chapter 10 will suggest that there are one or more further levels of representation over which inference-like operations may be defined. But such operations are still formal manipulations of internal symbols.)

Principles of inference and reasoning within a mentalist theory of conceptual structure are stated as rules that license mapping one conceptual structure into another on the basis of form. (7.5) illustrates their general shape.

(7.5)   If one supposes/believes sentence *a*, whose conceptual structure is of form *A*, then one is entitled to suppose/believe any sentence whose conceptual structure is *B*, where *B* is formally related to *A* by the following principles:
       [list of principles]

For instance, we can state the rule of inference involved in (7.4) very informally as (7.6).

(7.6)   If one suppose/believes a sentence whose conceptual structure is that someone or something caused some event *E* to take place, then one is entitled to suppose/believe any sentence that asserts that *E* took place.

In order to use this inference rule in (7.4), we will have to specify that the verb *force* has a conceptual structure in which someone (or something) causes an event to take place, that the someone or something is specified by the grammatical subject of *force*, and that the event is specified by the subordinate clause after *force* (in (7.4), *Harry leaves the meeting*). The problem, of course, is to find a way to provide such specifications in a systematic and enlightening fashion, so that inference rules are of sufficient generality. In turn, this reflects back on one's hypotheses about primitives and principles of combination, so the problems of expressivity and of inference are intimately interwoven. (There are some—for example, Wason and Johnson-Laird (1972) and Johnson-Laird (1983)—who have pointed out that people do not perform nearly as well as logicians say they should on tests of ability at logical inference. The inference in (7.2) is representative of the problematic cases. The phenomenon is genuine and should be taken into account in a theory of conceptual structure. I leave open however, whether these difficulties are just a consequence of the way conceptual structures are *processed*, as many have responded in the face of these observations, or whether they indicate something significant about the character of the conceptual structures and inference rules themselves, as Wason and Johnson-Laird claim.)

In addition to expressivity and inference, any formal semantics of natural language must provide an account of *compositionality*: how the meaning of an utterance is built up from the meanings of its constituent words plus its syntactic structure. Such an account will take the form of a set of correspondence rules; just as there are correspondence rules establishing the relation of phonological and syntactic structures, so there will have to be correspondence rules establishing the relation of syntactic and conceptual structures.

In discussing the inference in (7.4), we have implicitly made use of correspondence rules, in that we have specified that the person doing the causing (a conceptual notion) is expressed by the grammatical subject of *force* (a syntactic notion) and that the event being caused (a conceptual notion) is expressed by the subordinate clause after *force* (a syntactic notion). As in the syntax-phonology correspondence, we can divide the rules of correspondence into *lexical* principles (the meanings of words) and *supralexical* principles (the contribution of syntactic structure to the organization of meaning).

7.2 Connections to Other Faculties

All of the considerations so far have been addressed to conceptual structure as a vehicle for the understanding of sentences. Many approaches to semantics stop at this point, and perhaps wisely, since this stage alone poses many lifetimes worth of problem. However, a full computational theory of mind must address an additional set of issues, summed up by the title of a 1978 paper by John Macnamara: "How Do We Talk about What We See?" In order for us to be able to talk about what we see and hear and smell, there must a way to translate information generated by the visual and auditory and olfactory systems into a form suitable for linguistic expression. Evidently, the appropriate form is conceptual structure: it does not make sense for other faculties to directly derive a syntactic or phonological form.

Similarly, from the fact that one can carry out verbal instructions, it follows that there must be a way to translate linguistic information into a form appropriate for execution by the motor system. Again, the appropri-

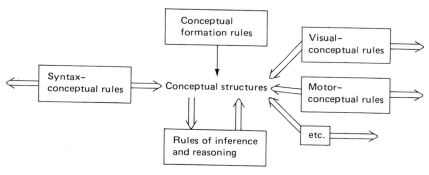

Figure 7.1
Organization of the theory of conceptual structure

ate locus of linguistic structure is the meaning: one must *understand* an instruction, not just parse it into syntactic structure, in order to be able to carry it out.

Thus, the theory of conceptual structure must incorporate additional sets of correspondence rules that specify the connection of linguistic meaning to the forms of information characteristic of sensory and motor modalities. The overall organization of the theory of conceptual structure can be diagrammed as shown in Figure 7.1. On the linguistic side it will connect with the diagram of syntax and phonology given in figure 6.1; chapter 10 will develop the important nonlinguistic connection to visual cognition.

It should be emphasized that the existence of these types of rules follows by *logical necessity* from the computational theory of mind. As chapters 4 and 6 emphasized, whenever one speaks of information processing in the mind, it is crucial to ask, Information *in what form?* If information in one form is to be compatible with (that is, comparable with or integrated with) information in another form, there must be principles for translating information from one form to the other. One cannot blithely assert, for instance, that the visual system "sends its information to the speech center"; there must be a means of converting visual information into linguistic format. Similarly, if one is to be able to compare the number of letters on a page, say, with the number of notes played by a trumpeter, there must be a modality-independent way of counting, so that the two kinds of input data may be compared. Conceptual structure may be thought of as one such lingua franca of the computational mind, a meeting ground for information from many sources; another, spatial structure, will appear in chapters 9 and 10. The many sets of correspondence rules in figure 7.1, then, describe the principles by which various kinds of modality-specific information are brought together.

7.3 Approaches Ruled Out by the Mentalist Postulate

Now let us return to the Mentalist Postulate, the first principle of a computational theory of meaning. From the stipulation that meanings are mentally represented, there follow two immediate constraints on the theory. First, meanings must be finitely representable and stored in a brain of finite (albeit large) capacity. This rules out any sort of "extensional" theory of meaning in which, for instance, the meaning of *dog* is taken to be the set of all dogs: there are no dogs in the mind, only at best dog-representations. Extensional theories can be ruled out on grounds of expressivity in any event; the move made by many logicians to repair the problems (see, for example, Montague 1970 and Lewis 1972) is to speak of extension in "all possible worlds," one of which happens to be the real world. But the set of all dogs in all possible worlds, if even a coherent notion, surely cannot be crammed into a brain either. Rather, the best one can hope for is a finite schema (or rule system) whereby the language user *internally represents* the dogs in all possible worlds.

The fact that meaning must be internally represented also eliminates any sort of Platonic theory, in which meanings are abstract objects existing independently of minds (such a view has been revived recently by Katz (1981)). Similarly, this constraint rules out the simplest construal of "situation semantics" (Barwise and Perry 1983), in which meaning is taken to reside in the world and is somehow grasped by humans. It is the *internal representation of what is grasped* that is of interest to us here. (See Jackendoff 1985a for more extended remarks on situation semantics, and Barwise and Perry 1985 for a reply.)

We may reject for the same reason a theory like Putnam's (1975) doctrine of the "division of linguistic labor," in which only experts are said to possess the meanings of words (for instance, only a chemist who knows the chemical tests for gold is said to "really" know the meaning of the word *gold*). Rather, since we are concerned with the mental encoding of word meanings, we will take the position that people differ in how highly specified their meanings are and that it is a matter of sociology that people often look to an authority when faced with uncertainty.

This view raises a potentially dangerous objection: if we do not all have the same internal representations for word meanings, how can we manage to communicate with each other? There are two parts to a potential answer. The first is that in the process of learning a language the possibilities of associating a word with different meanings are very narrowly constrained by the interaction between the language the child hears and the means the child has for internally representing the situation in which the language is presented. In other words, the variation among speakers cannot be terribly great because of the conditions (both inside and outside the language learner's mind) under which language is acquired. (See Gleitman and Wanner 1982, Carey 1978, 1982, Landau and Gleitman 1985 for discussion of this issue.) Second, when we reach fine details of meaning, we often find that speakers do disagree—sometimes, for example, in discussion of politics, art, or semantic theory, to the point of being mutually unintelligible. Thus, a certain amount of interspeaker variation must be countenanced in any event.

In other words, when we speak of what a word means, we are regarding it, for a first approximation, as represented identically by all speakers. Putnam's observations argue that there must be a further step of characterizing the range of interspeaker variation in representation and of explaining how such variation can occur much more freely with some words than with others. For now, though, it will be convenient to stay at the level of first approximation, with the understanding that it is hardly a rigid assumption.

7.4 Reference and Intentionality

A more subtle but profound consequence of the Mentalist Postulate is what it entails about the *reference* of linguistic expressions—roughly speaking, the entities that language conveys information *about*. The bottom line of the computational theory of mind, as it applies to meaning, is that *people have things to talk about only by virtue of having mentally represented them.* If some entity E in the real world is not represented in the mind of some person P, E does not exist for P. Nor does it even explicitly *fail* to exist for P—it is simply unavailable to P. In other words, without a mental representation of E, P cannot refer to E in an utterance. Thus, the real existence of E is not a sufficient condition for P's being able to refer to it.

Nor is it a necessary condition. There are many entities to which speakers refer for which there are no appropriate real-world counterparts, such as the entities in mental images, dreams, and hallucinations. (We cannot consider the brain-events involved in these phenomena as the real-world reference. One is speaking about brain-events no more when discussing one's dreams than when discussing one's perceptions.) Similarly, linguistic entities such as phonological segments, noun phrases, and metrical grids can only in some very attenuated sense be said to exist independently in the real world. These are kinds of entities that we are able to speak about only because of the way we organize the signals that impinge on us from the real world. (Sections 8.4 and 9.1 will moreover argue that much the same is true even of visually perceived entities, where our gut feelings are that what we speak of is really out there.)

In short, the correspondence between the entities we refer to in our utterances and the entities in the physical world is not at all as simple as one might be tempted to assume. In general, it seems much more apt to treat reference as a relationship that obtains between linguistic expressions and speakers' *construals* of the external world, where one's construal is the result of an interaction between external input and the internal means available to represent it. If our constitution is such that we construe the world as containing phonological segments or noun phrases or mental images or the people in our dreams, then we are capable of referring to them.

In chapter 2 a similar point was made about consciousness: one can be *conscious* of things only insofar as they have been mentally represented. In fact, all the entities just mentioned as candidates for reference are equally candidates for experience—whatever their real-world status. (In other cases, of course, consciousness and reference tease apart: we are sometimes conscious of things we cannot report, and we certainly can talk about things we cannot experience. The point is that mental representation is a necessary condition in either case.)

This brings us back to the discussion in section 2.3 on the *intentionality* of mental states—their being "about something." The question asked there was, What are mental states about? I argued there that Searle (1980) is overly simplistic in finding intentionality in the relation between mental states and the real world; rather, the relevant relation is that between mental states and the world *as experienced*. We have now come round to a parallel conception of the intentionality of linguistic expressions (that is, the ability of language to refer to things): language is about entities in *the world as construed by the language user/perceiver.* (I want to distinguish this view from one more common in the literature that invokes the language user's *beliefs.* The term *belief*, particularly in philosophical usage, carries overtones of sentence-like information (propositions) and of conscious reflection. I do not want to presuppose that conceptual structures are sentence-like, even if sentences are the means we have for expressing them. Nor need they be conscious, of course. I choose the term *construal of the world* in order to distance myself from such connotations.)

7.5 Truth

Chapters 3 and 4 differentiated the description of the computational mind from neuroscience, artificial intelligence, and common-practice cognitive psychology. Now, alas, the time has come to part company with the enterprise of semantics as it is generally conceived of in the philosophical tradition.

According to this approach, a semantic theory of a natural language must include an account of how the language maps into the world. In particular, following the lead of Tarski (1956), the goal has been to flesh out semantic theory in terms of a theory of truth, where truth is taken to be an objective relation between sentences and the objective world. The canonical form of statements of semantic theory is to be something like (7.7), where $C_1, \ldots, C_n$, the *truth-conditions of S*, are conditions on the world.

(7.7)   Sentence S (of language L) is true if and only if
         $C_1, \ldots, C_n$.

By contrast, the Mentalist Postulate locates meanings in the computational mind, as expressions built out of conceptual primitives and principles of combination. David Lewis (1972) is widely accepted as having demolished any approach that, in his words, "conceive[s] of semantic interpretation as the assignment to sentences and their constituents of compounds of 'semantic markers' or the like." As this includes the present approach, it will be useful to have a little dialogue with Lewis. (All quotations are from Lewis 1972, 169–170.)

> Semantic markers are *symbols*: items in the vocabulary of an artificial language we may call *Semantic Markerese*. Semantic interpretation by means of them amounts merely to a translation algorithm from the object language to the auxiliary language Markerese.

So far, so good, except for the gratuitous "artificial," "auxiliary," and "merely."

> But we can know the Markerese translation of an English sentence without knowing the first thing about the meaning of the English sentence: namely, the conditions under which it would be true.

As we will see, this sentence is the crucial one. The rest consists mostly of insults.

> Semantics with no treatment of truth conditions is not semantics. Translation into Markerese is at best a substitute for real semantics, relying either on our tacit competence (at some future date) as speakers of Markerese or on our ability to do real semantics at least for the one language Markerese. Translation into Latin might serve as well, except insofar as the designers may choose to build into it useful features—freedom from ambiguity, grammar based on symbolic logic—that might make it easier to do real semantics for Markerese than for Latin.

Here and elsewhere in his paper Lewis betrays an attitude common among philosophers: that one is free to choose a theory of language according to convenience or taste. Our discussions in chapter 5 of the significance of formalism and of the psychological reality of representations are diametrically opposed to this attitude. We take our notations as empirical hypotheses, to be chosen on the basis of facts and generalizations, not convenience or taste. If there is any "designer of Markerese," it is evolution, in terms of which the "convenience" of a feature amounts to the feature's ecological usefulness to the organism—an issue of somewhat more interest than a theoretician's personal preferences.

> The Markerese method is attractive in part just because it deals with nothing but symbols: finite combinations of entities of a familiar sort out of a finite set of elements by finitely many applications of finitely many rules. There is no risk of alarming the ontologically parsimonious.

Ontological parsimony is not the issue: the problem is rather, how else can we get the *grasp* of meaning into a finite brain?

> But it is just this pleasing finitude that prevents Markerese semantics from dealing with the relations between symbols and the world of non-symbols—that is, with genuinely semantic relations. Accordingly, we should be prepared to find that in a more adequate method, meanings may turn out to be complicated, infinite entities built up out of elements belonging to various ontological categories.

This is Lewis's argument in its entirety: essentially, if you don't relate language to the "world of non-symbols," it ain't real, genuine semantics. I suppose one could simply reply, Well, the study of conceptual structure isn't semantics—maybe something else, let's call it psychology. But it is worth resisting Lewis's terminological imperialism at least long enough to see what is at stake. Accordingly, let us grant him his terminology, but capitalize it as Real Semantics; we will contrast it with Conceptual Semantics, the approach that follows from the Mentalist Postulate.

Consider the truth-conditions of sentences such as (7.8a–g).

(7.8) a. $\begin{Bmatrix} \text{I am} \\ \text{Fred is} \end{Bmatrix}$ now vividly imagining a purple cow.

b. In $\begin{Bmatrix} \text{my} \\ \text{Louise's} \end{Bmatrix}$ dream, a unicorn bit Harry.

c. $\begin{Bmatrix} \text{I} \\ \text{Harry} \end{Bmatrix}$ saw a menacing figure in the road, but it turned out (just) to be the shadow of a tree.

d. When you said "banana" just now, you said it with a "p" instead of a "b."

e. The subject of the previous sentence is "you."

f. The rhythm of the word "banana" is "da-DA-da."

g. David's semantic theory is untestable.

Each of these sentences refers to entities of a sort that can only be said to exist by virtue of our construal of the world: mental images, dreams, hallucinations, theories, and various linguistic units. In order to encompass these cases, the truth-conditions of Real Semantics must include such entities within their purview. ((7.8a–c) fall in with expressions of "propositional attitude"; for discussion of their treatment in Conceptual Semantics and the inadequacy of standard approaches, see *S&C*, chapter 11, and also Fauconnier 1984.)

Consider also sentences whose subject matter deals with social or cultural institutions—say, ownership, marriage, tenure, or baseball. The truth-conditions of such sentences depend on underlying social compacts created by a culture or subculture, which in effect define these institutions. Yet our sense of truth or falsity for sentences like (7.9a,b) is not terribly different from the sense we have for sentences dealing with physical events like (7.9c) or natural kinds like (7.9d).

(7.9)   a. The husband's property also belongs to the wife (in culture *C* or according to the laws of state *S*).
         b. A foul ball counts as a strike unless the batter already has two strikes.
         c. A warthog walked into my bedroom.
         d. An ostrich is a bird that, unlike other birds, doesn't fly.

That is, marriages and foul balls are as real for us, as much "in the world," as ostriches are, even if they are only a product of social organization.

These sorts of examples—and you can certainly supply many more—show that if we are to explicate the relation of sentences to the "world of non-symbols," we must among other things determine what there is in the world as construed for sentences to be true of. Which brings us back to the necessity of a theory of mental representation that describes the organization of the world as construed, that is, the theory of Conceptual Semantics.

The argument may be pushed further: truth as a part of objective reality is itself suspect. Consider that something is a *sentence* only if it has syntactic structure, a mentally imposed organization. This means that the entities that are to be characterized as true by Tarskian truth-conditions exist only by virtue of our construal of the world. Now if "true" is a predicate over entities of the world as construed, and if the conditions on truth also involve such entities, it is odd to assume that truth somehow at the same time has an objective status independent of mind. Put differently, if both the "symbols" and the "world of non-symbols" are constrained by the nature of the mind and its construal of reality, it is hard to see the relation between them as not being similarly constrained. Truth too must be regarded as a characteristic of the world as construed.

Suppose one tried to avoid this argument by removing from truth any notion of mentality: truth is to be a property of the world as it is in reality, independent of how it is perceived or construed. Such a view would have a number of unpleasant consequences. First, sentences like (7.8a–g) could not have truth-values, since they refer to entities of dubious real-world status. More damaging, truth would no longer be a potential property of *sentences*—it would pertain only to the world. Tarskian statements of the form (7.7) would be part of a different theory, one of how sentences come to correspond to The Truth; all my previous arguments would then apply to this new theory. In particular, one would still need a psychological theory of how humans grasp The Truth and of how they ascertain whether sentences correspond to The Truth. But this returns us again to the problem set by Conceptual Semantics: what is the form in which humans internally represent Reality?

One might attempt to meet this criticism by adopting the "promiscuous realism" of Barwise and Perry (1985), which admits into Reality anything one may happen to need, including sentences, states of mind, mental images, theories, and so forth. Even so, one must still ask what constrains and structures this menagerie, such that humans can mentally represent and organize it. And if states of mind are included, then what constrains and structures *their* possibilities? Yet again, we have to do Conceptual Semantics.

Let us now go back to Lewis's statement "But we can know the Markerese translation of an English sentence without knowing the first thing about the meaning of the English sentence: namely, the conditions under which it would be true." We have seen here that before knowing "the first thing about the meaning of an English sentence," one must determine the terms in which truth-conditions are to be stated. The evidence points to the proper terms being delineated by a theory of conceptual structure and moreover to the notion "true" as being itself an element of conceptual structure. Conceptual Semantics is thus a prerequisite to Real Semantics: the first thing one must know about an English sentence is its translation into conceptual structure. Its truth-conditions should then follow from its conceptual structure plus rules of inference, which are stated as well in terms of conceptual structure.

How then can a mind relate its internal symbol systems, including conceptual structure, to the "world of non-symbols," fulfilling Lewis's program? Presumably, through the information about the world garnered by the senses, encoded in symbol systems specialized to particular sense modalities, then translated into expressions of conceptual structure. In other words, the connection our language has to Real Reality is explicated by psychological theories, not by mappings of language into some arbitrary set-theoretic construct such as Lewis adopts. So the way in which

Real Semantics purports to go beyond Conceptual Semantics proves to be subsumed under other parts of psychology, not to be a "higher part" of semantics. (We will return to this issue in chapter 10.)

This approach to truth seems to me the only possible view that is consonant with the approach of generative linguistics. The fundamental tenet of generative linguistics is that language is mentally represented and that the structure of language is not "out in the world" but rather a consequence of the mental organization of language users. From this tenet follow all the conclusions of chapter 5 about the necessity of rules, the problem of language acquisition, and the biological foundations of the language capacity. In particular, statements of the form "Sentence S in Language L is *grammatical* if and only if $C_1, \ldots, C_n$" are explicated in terms of the speaker's internalized syntactic and phonological structure. The argument here is that "true" is a predicate entirely on a par with "grammatical": a predicate over sentences for which language users can produce judgments. The only difference is that "true" is explicated in terms of conceptual rather than syntactic or phonological structure. (We will return to this issue in section 16.1.)

It is useful, if perhaps tendentious, to compare the shift in the foundations of the theory here to the shift that motivated the Special Theory of Relativity. There the basic notions of absolute position and velocity were replaced not only by position and velocity relative to an observer's frame of reference but in fact by position and velocity *as the observer is constrained to measure them*. Similarly, we are replacing the notion of absolute satisfaction of truth-conditions with the judgment of satisfaction of truth-conditions *as the observer is constrained to internally represent them*. As in the case of Newtonian versus relativistic mechanics, we should expect similar predictions in many ordinary cases but divergences in more exotic circumstances; the next chapter will uncover a number of such instances, substantiating our approach. (And as in the case of the two theories of physics, we should not be surprised if the languages of discourse are not mutually comprehensible; there seems to be a strong risk of incommensurability in the Kuhnian sense.)

Chapter 8
Some Elements of Conceptual Structure

Having considered some of the general boundary conditions on a satisfactory theory of conceptual structure, we now turn to issues that are somewhat more particular. We will work out a number of the basic primitives and principles of combination in conceptual structure, following the treatment in S&C. Each of these is chosen not only for its descriptive interest but also for the light it sheds on the distinction between Conceptual Semantics and Real Semantics.

8.1 Categorization

An essential (perhaps *the* essential) aspect of cognition is the ability to categorize: to judge that a particular thing is or is not an instance of a particular category. A categorization judgment is expressed most simply in English by a predicative sentence such as *Rover is a dog*. But categorization judgments need not involve the use of language at all: they are fundamental to any sort of discrimination task performed by dogs or rats or babies. The ability to categorize is what makes it possible to use previous experience to guide the interpretation of new experience, for without categorization, memory is virtually useless. Thus, an account of the organism's capacity for categorization is not just a matter of the semantics of predicative sentences; it is central to all of cognitive psychology.

Following the discussion of the previous chapter, we take a theory of categorization to concern, not whether a particular categorization (say, of Rover as a dog) is true, but rather what information and processing must be ascribed to an organism to account for its categorization judgments—what is involved in grasping Rover's dogginess. Since there can be no judgment without representation, categorization cannot be treated simply as the organism's comparison of some component of reality (say, Rover) to a preexisting category of dogs: the comparison must be made between the internal representations of Rover and of the category of dogs. In short, a categorization judgment is the outcome of the juxtaposition and comparison of two information structures.

In order to be compared, these information structures must be in compatible formats: there is no way to compare, say, a low-level visual representation with a high-level linguistic representation. What is the appropriate format? Since categorization takes place in nonlinguistic organisms, the format in question cannot be a strictly linguistic level of representation. On the other hand, categorization can be expressed linguistically or even through a combination of linguistic and nonlinguistic modalities, as in (8.1).

(8.1)   That [*pointing*] is a dog.

In interpreting (8.1), the hearer must use both knowledge of the language (the meanings of the words) and an appreciation of the visual field (what is being pointed at) to judge whether (8.1) expresses a correct categorization.

The evidence thus points to the level of conceptual structure as the locus of categorization judgments, for it is at this level that the kinds of information derived from linguistic and nonlinguistic modalities are available in comparable form.

The primary distinction that must appear in conceptual structure in order to be able to encode categorization is between the individual things (*tokens*) being categorized and the categories (*types*) to which the tokens do or do not belong. I therefore introduce as a first putative conceptual primitive the opposition of [TOKEN] concepts and [TYPE] concepts; we can think of TOKEN versus TYPE as a feature opposition like voiced-unvoiced in phonology. The individual objects that the organism sees or remembers at any moment will be mapped into [TOKEN] concepts in conceptual structure; the *kinds* of objects that the organism has found useful in categorizing the world will appear as its collection of [TYPE] concepts. In language, proper names like *Rover*, which designate individuals, will map into [TOKEN] concepts; common nouns like *dog* will map into conceptual [TYPES]. (*S&C*, chapter 5, develops details and justification of the mapping.)

We will represent the conceptual structure in which a [TOKEN] and a [TYPE] are juxtaposed and compared by means of the notation IS-AN-INSTANCE-OF; we will distinguish different [TOKENS] and [TYPES] from each other by means of subscripts (for instance, if *Rover* corresponds to [TOKEN]$_i$, *Bill* must correspond to [TOKEN]$_j$, $i \neq j$). Then the basic form of a categorization judgment can be notated as (8.2), where the ellipses (...) stand for all further and as yet unspecified information in the two concepts.

$$(8.2) \quad \begin{bmatrix} \text{TOKEN} \\ \cdots \end{bmatrix}_i \text{IS-AN-INSTANCE-OF} \begin{bmatrix} \text{TYPE} \\ \cdots \end{bmatrix}_k$$

What is the form of the rest of the information in the concepts, such that one can arrive at judgment (8.2)? The standard set-theoretic account of categorization, as adopted in many theories of Real Semantics, is that a category consists of the set of its instances (in the world or in all possible worlds). This would make the relation IS-AN-INSTANCE-OF simply a lookup function: (8.2) would be judged true just in case [TOKEN]$_i$ were found in the list of members of [TYPE]$_k$. However, in a mentalistic theory such an account is impossible. An essential characteristic of categorization is its *creativity*—one's ability to categorize novel tokens as instances of a known type. If a [TYPE] concept is to be used creatively, its internal structure cannot consist merely of a list of the [TOKENS] one has encountered that instantiate it: one could not apply it to a newly encountered [TOKEN]. Nor can it be a list of *all* (possible) [TOKENS] that instantiate it, both because of the finiteness of the brain and because [TYPE] concepts must be learnable through a finite amount of experience. Hence, the creativity of categorization judgments suggests that a [TYPE] concept consists of a set of principles or rules—in the same way that the creativity of sentence perception and production argues that phonology and syntax must be encoded as sets of rules, as shown in chapter 5.

Alternatively, one might consider the possibility that each [TOKEN] is specified by the list of types it belongs to—its exhaustive set of properties. (This is the approach taken by Montague (1973), in effect.) Then IS-AN-INSTANCE-OF could again be a lookup function, being judged true if [TYPE]$_k$ were found among the list of properties of [TOKEN]$_i$. But this too is impossible, for one can create new [TYPE] concepts at will. One of the simplest ways to do this is to construct, for an arbitrary [TOKEN]$_i$, a [TYPE] of THINGS LIKE [TOKEN]$_i$, where likeness can be determined along any arbitrary class of dimensions. For each of the indefinitely many [TOKENS] one can construct in response to environmental stimulation, there are any number of such [TYPES]. These in turn can be used to categorize arbitrary new [TOKENS]: is [TOKEN]$_j$ or is it not an instance of the [TYPE] consisting of THINGS LIKE [TOKEN]$_i$? Thus, the creativity of [TYPE]-formation shows that a [TOKEN] concept cannot consist merely of a list of all the [TYPES] it is an instance of, since there may be indefinitely many such. Some [TYPE]-inclusions may well be explicitly encoded (as a processing shortcut, perhaps), but by no means all.

The creativity of categorization also gives us reason to reject Fodor's (1975) theory that all possible [TYPES] (or even just all possible [TYPES] that are encoded as single lexical items) are innately given as unanalyzed monads with no internal structure. Such [TYPES] could not be computationally compared with novel [TOKENS] to yield categorization judgments, so creative categorization would be impossible. Moreover, Fodor's theory entails that there is only a finite number of possible monadic [TYPES], since there is only a finite space in the brain for storing them all. But since one can generate new [TYPES] at will on the basis of given [TOKENS] (and invent words for them, if that is crucial to Fodor), then either the set of possible monadic [TYPES] must be infinite—and hence cannot be innate—or else the set of possible [TOKENS] must be finite and innate, a totally implausible conclusion.

Similar objections can be raised to *semantic network* theories (Collins and Quillian 1969; Simmons 1973; Smith 1978), in which both [TOKEN] and [TYPE] concepts are represented as nodes in a finite network, connected by a finite number of predicative links. In effect, this theory says that (8.2) is judged true just in case the network contains the right sort of link or sequence of links from $[TOKEN]_i$ to $[TYPE]_k$. Hence, the relation IS-AN-INSTANCE-OF reduces to a finite lookup function, this time searching for the right pathway of network links. Research within this paradigm has been largely concerned with how to make this finite lookup function computationally manageable. However, such an account is *observationally*, not just computationally, problematic: there is no way to deal with [TOKENS] that have never been encountered before and that therefore are not already in the network. Nor is there a way to generate new [TYPES], enter them into the network, and compare them to previously known [TOKENS]. Again some more creative mechanism is necessary.

For a more adequate mentalistic theory of [TYPES], one must treat a [TYPE] concept as a finite set of rules or conditions that can be used in categorizing novel [TOKENS]. Since [TYPE] concepts can be constructed creatively, the total set of possible [TYPES] is indefinitely large and cannot be encoded in the finite brain. Rather, the set of possible [TYPES] must itself be characterized by the finite set of *conceptual formation rules* of figure 7.1. The process of concept acquisition can then be thought of as using environmental evidence to help select or construct a [TYPE] concept from the possibilities provided by the conceptual formation rules. The conceptual formation rules thus play a role in this theory reminiscent of that of Universal Grammar in syntactic theory: they are the innate basis for acquisition of environment-particular knowledge.

This approach to the structure of [TYPE] concepts is, I believe, the only viable way to deal with the creativity of categorization within the constraints of the Mentalist Postulate. In turn, this approach requires that the [TYPE] concepts (or predicates) expressed by natural language be assembled from a finite innate set of primitives and principles of combination—in other words, a *decompositional* view of word meanings. Among the primitives will of course be the TOKEN-TYPE distinction; sections 8.4 and 8.5 will motivate further fundamental oppositions. Sections 8.2 and 8.3 will discuss some basic aspects of the principles of combination, by which clusters of distinctions are combined into [TYPE] concepts.

Returning briefly to the characterization of the information structure embodied in the relation IS-AN-INSTANCE-OF, we have just seen that it cannot be any simple sort of lookup function in which either the [TOKEN] or the [TYPE] acts as an unstructured primitive. Rather, the categorization function must involve a comparison of the internal structures (or decompositions) of the two concepts being related. This makes the theory of categorization a more complex matter than often supposed, one that must be seen in terms of the organism's construal of the world—the distinctions it makes—rather than in terms of purely logical or set-theoretical analysis. This will become more evident in the succeeding sections.

One of the major arguments of *S&C* (especially chapters 5 and 6) is that any conceptual theory expressive enough to include an adequate account of categorization will automatically include rich enough machinery to account as well for a great deal of linguistic inference, one of the primary desiderata of more traditional semantic theories. The argument is too long to reproduce in detail, but I will sketch the essentials.

The description of many forms of linguistic inference can be reduced conceptually to relations of [TYPE]-inclusion, that is, conceptual structures of the form (8.3).

(8.3) $\begin{bmatrix} \text{TYPE} \\ \cdots \end{bmatrix}_k$ IS-INCLUDED-IN $\begin{bmatrix} \text{TYPE} \\ \cdots \end{bmatrix}_m$

This structure is most transparent in "generic categorization sentences" such as *A poodle is a dog*. But it is also apt for semantic relations such as those involved in the inference from (7.1a) (*Sue walked slowly across the room*) to (7.1b) (*Sue walked across the room*): the type of action describable as *walking slowly* is included in the type of action describable as *walking*. (Whether it extends to cases with quantification such as (7.3) is as yet an open question.) *S&C* (section 6.1) shows that when we examine the relation IS-INCLUDED-IN, its characteristics turn out to be very similar, possibly even identical, to those of IS-AN-INSTANCE-OF. Thus, any theory that adequately accounts for ordinary categorization will easily extend to an account of (8.3) as well and, with it, an account of much of linguistic inference.

This means that the goal of accounting for linguistic and nonlinguistic categorization is not at all independent of the traditional goal of accounting for inference, as one might initially think. Rather, the former subsumes at least much of the latter. This reaffirms the centrality of categorization to semantic theory and further justifies my obsession with the computational character of such an elementary structure as (8.2) and with its implications for the theory of the mind.

8.2 The Noncategorical Nature of Categorization

So far, then, we have established that the structure of concepts must be decomposable, and we have found one basic conceptual primitive, the type-token opposition. Now I want to discuss the overall character one should expect in decomposition, establishing an important principle of combination in conceptual structure.

The most prevalent among decompositional theories has been one in which the conditions making up a word meaning (or concept) are taken to be collectively necessary and sufficient to determine categorization. For instance, the meaning of *dog* supposedly contains a checklist of defining conditions; anything meeting all of these conditions is a dog, anything that fails one or more of them is not. This theory is a close cousin of Tarskian truth-conditions (7.7), which are likewise to be necessary and sufficient for the truth of a sentence.

Such a theory nicely satisfies the commonsense intuition that words have definite and precise meanings. This probably accounts for the theory's great popularity and antiquity and for the fact that it has so frequently been offered without seeming to need a defense. However, as Putnam (1975, 192–193) cautions,

> The amazing thing about the theory of meaning is how long the subject has been in the grip of philosophical misconceptions, and how strong these misconceptions are. Meaning has been identified with a necessary and sufficient condition by philosopher after philosopher.... On the other side, it is amazing how weak the grip of the facts has been.

Fodor et al. (1980) confirm Putnam's suspicion by pointing out that the number of convincing decompositions into necessary and sufficient conditions in the literature is vanishingly small, and these are restricted primarily to kinship terms (*bachelor, uncle*), axiomatized systems (*triangle*), and jargon terms (*ketch, highball*). The rest of the vocabulary of English has so far firmly resisted formal analysis of the requisite sort.

There are at least two prominent difficulties with necessary and sufficient conditions. The first lies within single conditions. At what point in a smooth transition of hue from focal red to focal orange does the color cease being red and begin being orange? If an intermediate color, red-orange, is inroduced, where is the border between it and red? A theory of necessary and sufficient conditions predicts a sharp border between colors, whereas, in fact, actual judgments grade from "That's definitely red" through "I'm not sure" to "That's definitely not red."

Similarly, at what height does a man qualify as tall? For a spatial case, at precisely what point does a fly crawling down your neck come to be on your shoulder? Or, to use the well-known case studied by Labov (1973), at what ratio of height to width does one draw the line between cups and bowls? The object in figure 8.1a is likely a cup, and the one in figure 8.1b is likely a bowl, but the one in figure 8.1c is not clearly either. In each of these

Figure 8.1
A cup, a bowl, and something in between

cases there is a gradation of judgment parallel to that between red and orange.

For the processing-minded, there are performance concomitants of these gradations of judgment. In the unclear cases people are more prone to variation of judgment (both inter- and intrapersonal), to distortions of memory toward clearer cases, and to sensitivity to context (for example, which of the clear cases was presented most recently). They also take longer to make judgments in unclear cases than in either clear positive or clear negative cases.

Notice how odd it is to attribute these gradations in judgment to the judger's lack of knowledge of the concept in question: it is absurd to think there is a real borderline between red and orange that just has not been discovered. It is sometimes necessary or expedient to *stipulate* a borderline—perhaps for instance in a height regulation for prospective police officers—but such stipulation can hardly be taken as an explication of the ordinary-language concept expressed by *tall*.

In the same vein, it seems equally odd to insist that a sentence like (8.4) must be strictly true or false.

(8.4)   The object pictured in figure 8.1c is a cup.

And it makes still less sense to try to get off the hook by saying that it *is* true or false, but we don't know which, or that it has some probabilistic degree of truth—or any such move that tries to retain truth as a reality-based rather than observer-based notion. In such cases it seems absolutely clear (to me at least) (1) that the category "cup" is an observer-imposed (and culturally sanctioned) bifurcation of a potentially continuous range of objects, (2) that this bifurcation sometimes yields uncertain results, (3) that the notion of the truth of (8.4) is dependent on properties of the categorization, and hence (4) that truth itself must be defined in observer-dependent terms for this case.

These are the simple cases where necessary and sufficient conditions fail—where the gradation of judgment occurs along a single dimension. In certain of the cases, such as color, one can specify central values for the categories in question; the category of a particular hue is then (in part) a function of its relative distance from the nearest focal hues. Uncertain cases arise when the disparity of relative distances is not too great. In other cases, such as *tall*, there is no focal value; rather, distance away from focal value ("normal height") is criterial.

A second and more serious difficulty with necessary and sufficient conditions concerns the interaction of conditions. The best-known citation of this problem is Wittgenstein's (1953, 31–32) discussion of the word *game*, in which he challenges the reader to find any condition common to all games but not to nongames. He suggests that there are no such common conditions but only a set of relationships and similarities that he characterizes as "family resemblances." It is clear from the context of the passage that Wittgenstein considers this not an isolated counterexample but a typical instance of how words are understood.

More generally, Wittgenstein's problem concerns the possibility of discrete exceptions to defining conditions. If it is a necessary part of being human to have two legs or high intelligence, then are one-legged people and imbeciles not human? If having stripes is criterial for tigers, are albino tigers tigers? And so forth. (Such difficulties are not confined to nouns. Coleman and Kay (1981) find similar problems in the verb *lie* ("tell a lie"); *S&C* (section 8.6) in the verb *see*; Jackendoff (1985b) in the verb *climb*; and Brugman (1981) in the preposition *over*.)

There have been various reactions to Wittgenstein's argument. One popular move (halfheartedly advocated even by Putnam (1975) and Fodor (1975), and more enthusiastically embraced by many others) is to claim that categories are mentally represented by prototypical instances and that categorization is a process of comparing a given token to the prototype. So, for instance, one's concept of a tiger is mentally represented by a prototypical tiger, and an albino tiger is enough like it to qualify.

The first question we should ask of this proposal is, Since you can't have a *real* prototypical tiger in your head, in what form is the prototype represented? In particular, in what form is it represented such that it can be *computationally* compared with the mental representation of the token being categorized? This question is typically left unasked by the advocates of prototypes; we will come back to it in sections 9.4 and 10.4.

The second question we should ask is, How do we represent categories for which there is no single prototype, for example, *animal* or *furniture* or *game*? (Wittgenstein: "Think of board-games, card-games, Olympic games, and so forth.") One might try introducing a disjunctive class of prototypes (it's like this, or this, or this), but then what remains of the notion of family resemblance that Wittgenstein has been so careful to point out? Such a solution is equivalent to saying there is no single concept "game," just a multiplicity of unrelated concepts, each with its own prototype. Thus, the notion that a category can be mentally represented by a rigid unanalyzed prototype is inadequate.

Falling back into decompositional theories, there have been a number of suggestions for how decomposition into necessary and sufficient conditions could be weakened to deal with the problem of family resemblances. Searle (1958) suggests that the totality of conditions in a word's definition need not be fulfilled—only a sufficiently large number of them. As we will see in section 8.3, "a sufficiently large number" may sometimes be *one*; a great deal depends on the particulars of the case at hand. So this solution, though on the right track, will not do either.

A related suggestion appears in the work of Smith, Shoben, and Rips (1974), who place on each condition a degree of "definingness." Conditions of lesser degree are permitted to have exceptions, and in cases of doubt the more highly defining conditions are to be relied upon. However, Smith, Shoben, and Rips assume there is a central core of most essential conditions that serve as "dictionary" definitions. Since this is just what Wittgenstein denies, they have not solved the problem either. The same difficulty appears in Katz's (1977) attempt to separate out "dictionary" definitions of necessary and sufficient conditions from an "encyclopedia" entry that is subject to exceptions.

By contrast, Rosch and Mervis (1975) and Mervis and Pani (1980) develop a theory of categories in which family resemblance phenomena play an essential part. They show experimentally how artificial categories of objects can be learned whose defining conditions are subject to exceptions. Those instances that satisfy all or most defining conditions are perceived as more central instances and are more easily learned and remembered. This confirms Wittgenstein's argument that concepts can have a family resemblance nature and extends the argument beyond word meanings to perceptual concepts. (For an answer to widely cited objections to Rosch's work posed by Armstrong, Gleitman, and Gleitman (1983), see *S&C*, p. 255, n. 6.)

Thus, semantic theory must include the possibility of conditions that play an essential role in defining categories but are nevertheless subject to exceptions. Though such a notion goes against the grain of traditional philosophical thinking, it seems altogether justified on psychological grounds.

8.3 Preference Rule Systems

The apparent difficulty with conditions that are subject to exceptions is the slippery slope argument: if each of the conditions in a category is subject to exceptions, what is to prevent calling a token that fails *all* of them a member of the category? The essential properties of a mechanism to solve

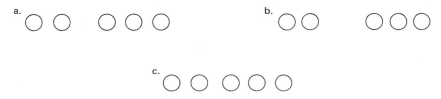

Figure 8.2
Evidence for the rule of proximity

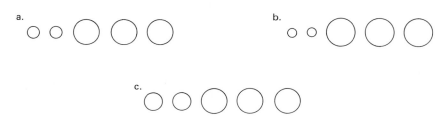

Figure 8.3
Evidence for the rule of similarity

this problem were discovered by Wertheimer (1923). The mechanism has been dubbed by Lerdahl and Jackendoff (1983) a *preference rule system*; it plays a fundamental role in our analysis of musical cognition (see section 11.4).

For a simple illustration of a preference rule system, consider two of the well-known Gestalt principles for spatial grouping: proximity and similarity. Each of these in isolation is a condition of graded strength that is sufficient to produce a grouping judgment. For instance, the configuration in figure 8.2a is naturally seen as grouped into 2 + 3 by virtue of the relative proximity of the two left-hand circles and that of the three right-hand circles, in contrast to the relative distance of the second and third circles. If the disparity of spacing increases, as in figure 8.2b, the judgment is stronger (harder to overcome by act of will); if the disparity decreases, as in figure 8.2c, the judgment is weaker. Similarly, in figure 8.3 the grouping is 2 + 3 by virtue of similarity of size; the judgment is stronger (figure 8.3b) or weaker (figure 8.3c), depending on the relative disparity in size.

So far, these conditions behave like the graded conditions for hue or height discussed earlier. The interest of the system arises, however, in situations where both principles apply. In figure 8.4a both proximity and similarity analyze the configuration as 2 + 3, so a still stronger grouping judgment applies. But proximity analyzes figure 8.4b as 2 + 3, while similarity analyzes it as 3 + 2. The outcome is a vague or ambiguous judgment

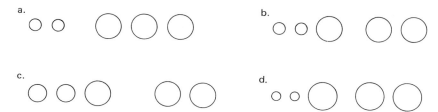

Figure 8.4
Proximity and similarity in reinforcement and in conflict

that may even switch interpretations spontaneously, in Necker-cube fashion. In figures 8.4c and 8.4d the two principles are also in conflict; but proximity prevails in figure 8.4c and similarity in figure 8.4d, by virtue of their relative strengths of application.

The consequence of this interaction in conflicting situations is that neither proximity nor similarity can be viewed as a sufficient condition for grouping: both are subject to exceptions. Moreover, neither is necessary, since figures 8.3a and 8.4d are grouped without appropriate proximity, and figures 8.2a and 8.4c are grouped without appropriate similarity. Still, both principles clearly play a role in grouping judgments; neither can be dispensed with.

The conditions of proximity and similarity and their interaction in grouping judgments constitute a simple case of a preference rule system. More generally, such a system is a means of producing a judgment or analysis based on a number of conditions. In any given field of input to which the system applies, each individual condition may contribute a preferred analysis, with an intrinsic strength or weight of application. The overall analysis arrived at by the system is the one that receives the greatest weight from individual conditions. In a field in which a number of the preference rules reinforce each other and there is no conflict from competing conditions, a highly stable judgment results. On the other hand, in case two or more competing analyses receive approximately equal weight, an ambiguous judgment (as in figure 8.4b) results.

Once the basic nature of preference rule systems has been isolated, it is possible to recognize them everywhere in psychology. The content of the preference rules varies widely from one domain to the next, but the characteristic computational interaction appears in every case. Section 12.3 will develop this point further, arguing that the principles of preference rule systems can be regarded as a fundamental building block of the computational mind.

In particular, the interaction of preference rules has just the characteristics appropriate to conditions in word meanings that are subject to exceptions. To see this, let us look very briefly at how the notion of a preference rule system may account for the intuitions behind prototype theories of categorization, while dealing more adequately with the problems inherent in such theories.

First, by claiming that a [TYPE] concept may be mentally filled out by a system of conditions working together as a preference rule system, we have allowed for an explicitly decompositional account of [TYPE] concepts, as required by the creativity arguments of section 8.1. Unlike a holistic prototype theory, its decompositional properties make possible a computational comparison of the [TYPE] with novel [TOKENS].

Second, since preference rules admit exceptions under the proper conditions, one can specify, for instance, stripedness as a characteristic of tigers without thereby throwing albino tigers out of the category. On the other hand, "the proper conditions" for exceptionality are crucial: there must be enough countervailing evidence from other preference rules to overrule the exception to the stripedness condition. Thus, the slippery slope argument is avoided, since not all preference rules can be violated at once.

Third, within a preference rule system there need be no core of "defining" conditions that are together necessary and sufficient, as Katz and Smith, Shoben, and Rips postulate. From this follows the impossibility of definitions of the traditional sort, as observed by Fodor et al. (1980).

Fourth, tokens that satisfy greater numbers of preference rules are judged more typical instances of the category, whereas those that satisfy fewer preference rules or have alternative conflicting analyses as members of other categories are judged less typical instances. In general, prototypical instances will satisfy all preference rules to the greatest degree possible. Thus, the notion of prototype, although not directly specified by the preference rule system, emerges as a natural consequence of the way the rules interact.

Fifth, it is possible for a concept to contain two or more preference rules that inherently conflict—so that an instance of the concept may only satisfy one of them at a time. This leads to the possibility of a quasi-disjunctive concept for which there is no single prototype, a plausible account of Wittgenstein's observations about games.

Sixth, even a token that satisfies all or most of the preference rules for a particular [TYPE] may be subject to unclear judgments if, fortuitously, there is another mutually exclusive [TYPE] that it also strongly satisfies. The sort of case I have in mind is a new gadget described in a recent airline magazine: a screwdriver with a flashlight in its handle (or is it a flashlight with a screwdriver blade on the rear end?). It seems that a dispute arose with customs officials about whether to charge for the importation of such devices at the rate for screwdrivers or the rate for flashlights. The interest of the example lies in the fact that these devices pretty well satisfy all the defining conditions for *either* category, yet the demands of the task require one to decide which of the categories they belong to. In the theory of preference rules, which claims that a categorization judgment is a function of relative satisfaction of conditions among competing categories, the uncertainty of this case is a natural consequence. By contrast, Searle's theory of satisfaction of "enough" conditions and Smith, Shoben, and Rips's theory of satisfaction of "essential" conditions do not make any satisfactory prediction of how this case should come out.

We also see again from this case that categorization of a token is a matter not so much of "objective" truth or falsity as of how one's mentally represented categories interact with each other. If one were to stipulate a new category of "flashdrivers," the range of categorization judgments for artifacts in this general field would readjust, just as, for instance, color categorization changes if one introduces "red-orange" between red and orange. We also see that the nature of the task in which the token is to be used is relevant. For customs evaluation it must belong to only one of the two categories; but for driving screws it's a screwdriver and for finding one's way in the dark it's a flashlight.

All this, of course, reinforces our conclusion that the theory of categorization should deal in mental representations of the world rather than in the real world itself. It makes little sense to think of the categories out there in the world competing for members; but it makes a great deal of sense to think of the mind as presenting competing alternatives and selecting among them. So the "family resemblance/prototype" problem provides another test case in favor of an observer-based theory of reference and truth.

In closing this section, a caution (or challenge!) is in order. The combinatorial and logical properties of systems of necessary and sufficient conditions have been intensively studied and are well understood. By contrast, the combinatorial properties of preference rule systems are at present a mystery. Consider an example given by Armstrong, Gleitman, and Gleitman (1983), a phrase like *foolish boy*. If both *foolish* and *boy* are defined by necessary and sufficient conditions, the phrase is defined by the conjunction of the two sets of conditions. But if they are defined by systems of preference rules, each component of which has an intrinsic weight, it is quite unclear how the components are to be combined into a preference rule system for the entire phrase. (One approach that has been suggested is "fuzzy logic" (Zadeh 1965), which treats categorization as graded rather than all-or-none. But this is inadequate as a theory of categorization (*S&C*, section 7.3) and turns out not to solve the combinatorial problem in any event (Osherson and Smith 1981, 1982).)

Minsky and Papert (1969) develop a mathematical theory of "perceptrons," computing devices with properties similar to preference rule systems. (More recent "connectionist" approaches to artificial intelligence,
such as that of Feldman and Ballard (1982), have a similar flavor. Rumelhart
and Zipser (1985) make the relationship explicit.) Minsky and Papert are
sometimes cited as having shown that the combinatorial problem for a
system of perceptrons is essentially insoluble. If this were true, the outlook
for preference rule systems would be rather dismal. However, my (ad-
mittedly superficial) reading of what they actually say is that many predicates of psychological interest cannot be computed by a system that
consists *only* of an unstructured network of perceptrons. Once one admits
prior (that is, innate) structure and various other computing devices, the
story need not be so gloomy.

My assessment is that at the moment we have too few actual analyses in
terms of preference rules to be able to attack the combinatorial problem
intelligently, but that it must be a priority of the near future. In the
meantime the importance of preference rule systems throughout psychology has been sufficiently established that there can be no objection to
using them in a mentalistic semantic theory.

8.4 Ontological Claims: Some Major Categories of Concepts

Let us next consider the ontological presuppositions of natural language—
what sorts of entities inhabit the world as construed and are capable of
being referred to by linguistic expressions.

One circumstance under which a speaker clearly construes there to be an
entity in the world is when he refers to it by means of an expression like
(8.1) (*That* [pointing] *is a dog*). In (8.1) the use of the demonstrative pronoun
is accompanied by a gesture that serves as an invitation to the hearer to
locate the entity in his own visual field. If the hearer cannot identify an
entity of the appropriate sort, perhaps because he has his eyes shut, or the
conversation is taking place over the telephone, or the speaker is pointing
to something in a blurry photograph, the intended referent is unavailable to
the hearer, and discourse cannot proceed. A demonstrative pronoun used in
this fashion has been called a "pragmatic anaphor"; it takes its reference
from nonlinguistic context.

So far this should be fairly unsurprising. The interest arises when we
observe, as pointed out by Hankamer and Sag (1976), that pragmatic
anaphora is possible not only to designated *objects*, as in (8.1), but also to
entities best classified as *places* (8.5a), *paths* or *trajectories* (8.5b), *actions*
(8.5c), *events* (8.5d), *sounds* (8.5e), *manners* (8.5f), *amounts* (8.5g), and *numbers*
(8.5h).

(8.5)   a. Your hat is here [*pointing*] and your coat is there [*pointing*].
        b. He went thataway [*pointing*].
        c. Can you do that [*pointing*]?
           Can you do this [*demonstrating*]?
        d. That [*pointing*] had better not happen in *my* house!
        e. That [*gesturing*] sounds like Brahms.
        f. You shuffle cards $\left\{ \begin{array}{l} \text{like this} \\ \text{thus} \\ \text{this way} \end{array} \right\}$ [*demonstrating*].
        g. The fish that got away was $\left\{ \begin{array}{l} \text{this} \\ \text{that} \\ \text{yay} \end{array} \right\}$ [*demonstrating*] long.
        h. Please bring back this many cookies [*holding up some number of fingers*].

The conditions on the interpretation of *that* in (8.1) also obtain with the pragmatic anaphors in (8.5). For instance, if the hearer is unable to see or figure out what goings-on the speaker is pointing at in (8.5d), he will not fully understand the utterance—he will not have received all the information he is intended to receive, and discourse cannot properly continue.

If, as seems uncontroversial, the pragmatic anaphor in (8.1) refers to a thing (or physical object), those in (8.5) must also refer, but to entities quite distinct from physical objects—namely, a place, a path, an action, an event, a sound, a manner, an amount, and a number, respectively. Thus, the world as construed must include such entities—a variety rarely recognized in extant semantic theories.

Other grammatical constructions also support this range of entities. One is the expression of identity and individuation with *same* and *different*. (More appear in *S&C*, section 3.4.) Compare (8.6), which expresses identity and individuation of physical objects, with (8.7a–f), which express identity and individuation of other entity types. (In some cases such sentences assert only that two distinct individuals belong to a common type—for instance, *Bill ate the same sandwich he always eats*, on the normal, nonregurgitation interpretation. But even these cases presuppose the existence of distinct individuals to be categorized.)

(8.6) $\left\{ \begin{array}{l} \text{Bill picked up the same things } \left\{ \begin{array}{l} \text{that} \\ \text{as} \end{array} \right\} \text{ Jack did.} \\ \text{Bill picked up something different than Jack did.} \end{array} \right\}$ [Object]

(8.7)   a. Bill ate at $\left\{ \begin{array}{l} \text{the same place as} \\ \text{a different place than} \end{array} \right\}$ Jack did.   [Place]
        b. Bill went off $\left\{ \begin{array}{l} \text{the same way as} \\ \text{a different way than} \end{array} \right\}$ Jack did.   [Path]

c. Bill did $\left\{\begin{array}{l}\text{the same thing as} \\ \text{a different thing than}\end{array}\right\}$ Jack did.   [Action]

d. $\left\{\begin{array}{l}\text{The same thing} \\ \text{A different thing}\end{array}\right\}$ happened today $\left\{\begin{array}{l}\text{as} \\ \text{than}\end{array}\right\}$ happened yester-
day.   [Event]

e. Bill heard $\left\{\begin{array}{l}\text{the same noise as} \\ \text{a different noise than}\end{array}\right\}$ Jack did.   [Sound]

f. Bill   cooks   meat $\left\{\begin{array}{l}\text{the same way (as)} \\ \text{a different way than}\end{array}\right\}$ he   cooks   eggs.
[Manner]

Amounts and numbers are identified and individuated by different expressions than the other entities, but the semantic parallelism is clear.

g. $\left\{\begin{array}{l}\text{Bill is as tall as Jack is.} \\ \text{Bill is taller than Jack is.}\end{array}\right\}$ [Amount]

h. The trumpeter played $\left\{\begin{array}{l}\text{as many notes as} \\ \text{more notes than}\end{array}\right\}$ there were marks on
the page.   [Number]

In order for these sentences to say what they do, there must be entities of the requisite sort for the sentences to talk about, and conceptual structure must be capable of distinguishing among them. Accordingly, we introduce into conceptual structure a set of *ontological category features*, including at least [OBJECT], [PLACE], [PATH], [ACTION], [EVENT], [SOUND], [MANNER], [AMOUNT], and [NUMBER], as well as possible others such as [PROPERTY], [SMELL], and [TIME]. These can be thought of as elements that serve as primitive "parts of speech" of conceptual structure. Just as each syntactic constituent must be of a unique syntactic category, so a conceptual unit must be of a unique ontological category.

Each of these category features may be associated with either the [TOKEN] or the [TYPE] feature. For instance, a perceived object will be represented as an [OBJECT TOKEN], and a category of objects as an [OBJECT TYPE]. Similarly, a perceived event will be represented as an [EVENT TOKEN], and a category of events as an [EVENT TYPE].

Now consider how the ontological categories are expressed in language. Traditional grammar implies that the correspondence between syntactic categories and ontological categories is fairly obvious: a noun names a person, place, or thing; a verb names an action or state of being; and so on. Actually, the only simple case is [OBJECT], which seems always to be expressed by a noun. Otherwise, the situation is more complex. The standard expression of [EVENT] is as a Sentence; but [EVENT] can also be expressed by a noun (*earthquake*). The standard expression of [PROPERTY] is as an adjective (*red, tall*), but there are also idiomatic noun phrases (*a gas, a bummer*) and prepositional phrases (*out of luck*) that express [PROPERTIES]. And so on. This divergence shows the potential complexity of the correspondence rules between syntactic and conceptual structure. It is also important in showing that syntactic structure cannot be based entirely on semantics, as is sometimes assumed. (See *S&C*, chapter 4, Grimshaw 1979, and Jackendoff 1985b for discussion.)

Let us look next at nonlinguistic connections to conceptual structure. In order for the pragmatic anaphors in (8.5) to be interpreted, the visual system must deliver information that corresponds to the visibly distinguishable ontological categories in conceptual structure. For instance, to distinguish (8.8a) from (8.8b), the visual system must fill in the pragmatic anaphors with objects in one case and locations in the other.

(8.8)   a. This is your coat, and that is your hat.
          b. Here is your coat, and there is your hat.

To interpret (8.5e), the auditory system must deliver information that appears in conceptual structure as [SOUNDS]. In order to verify (8.7h), both the visual and the auditory systems must deliver information that appears in conceptual structure as [NUMBER].

Although perception of entities other than objects has not been prominent in the literature, the work I have encountered (for example, Michotte 1954 on causation; Jenkins, Wald, and Pittenger 1978 and Cutting 1981 on event-perception; remarks in Köhler 1929 on temporal grouping; Piaget 1952 and Gelman and Gallistel 1978 on amounts and numbers) reveals characteristics entirely parallel to the perception of physical objects, such as the Gestalt properties of proximity, closure, "good form," and the like. There seems no bar in principle to the perceptual systems delivering information about diverse ontological categories, using mechanisms similar to those for the perception of objects, if we think to look for it. (We will return to some aspects of this problem in sections 10.3 and 10.5.)

Besides giving evidence for an important class of primitives in conceptual structure, this section reinforces the arguments of chapter 7 on the priority of Conceptual Semantics over Real Semantics. Even if we can refer to this variety of entities, and even if truth-conditions must involve them, we do not want to have to justify them as objective elements of physical reality. For instance, the continuous flow of matter in the physical world does not come neatly segmented into events, as language seems to imply; nor does it seem plausible that the Real World contains manners segregated from the actions whose manners they are; nor does it contain numbers except in some curious Platonic sense. The characteristics of these entities seem much less paradoxical if we regard them in terms of how humans structure the world—what is real *for us*. This in turn is determined by our capacity for mental representation, in particular, the properties of the ontological categories available in conceptual structure. Thus, the nature of the internal system of symbols that support meaning must be a primary focus of semantic inquiry.

8.5 Generalization of Spatial Concepts to Abstract Domains

We end our foray into conceptual structure with some further evidence from language that bears on the organization of conceptual primitives. (This material derives from the analysis in Gruber 1965 and is developed in greater detail in Jackendoff 1976, 1983, chapters 9–10.)

Consider the English verbs of spatial position. These can be divided into three important classes, which I will call *GO verbs*, *BE verbs*, and *STAY verbs*. The sentences in (8.9) exemplify the class of GO verbs.

(8.9)   a. The dog ran from the door to the table.
       b. A meteor hurtled toward the earth.
       c. The hawk flew over the prairie.

These sentences all express concepts that pick out types of physical motion. Following Gruber's (1965) terminology, I will refer to the object in motion as the *theme* of the sentence. In each sentence the theme travels along a path, which may, as in the first example, be further differentiated into a source, or initial point, and a goal, or final point. The semantic similarity between these sentences can be described by saying that the concepts they express are all specialized forms of the general concept [GO (X,P)], which represents the motion of some object X (the theme) along some path P. This concept belongs to the ontological category [EVENT]: it is something that happens over time. In turn, the variables X and P belong to the ontological categories [OBJECT] and [PATH], respectively. So the concept is more fully expressed as shown in (8.10). (In this and subsequent examples I will notate ontological category as a subscript.)

(8.10) $[_{\text{Event}} \text{GO} ([_{\text{Object}} x], [_{\text{Path}} p])]$

In turn, the expressions of path in (8.9) are composite. Each contains one or more *reference objects* (*the door, the table, the earth, the prairie*) plus a *path-function* that determines how the path is related to the reference object. The path-function expressed by the preposition *from* designates a path that begins at the reference object; that expressed by *to*, a path that ends at the reference object; that expressed by *toward*, a path that if extended would end at the reference object; that expressed by *over*, a path that passes through a point (or region) vertically above the reference object. Thus, the general form of these path-concepts is (8.11).

(8.11)   [$_{Path}$ PATH-FUNCTION ([$_{Object}$ y])]

Combining (8.10) and (8.11), we get (8.12) as the general form of the conceptual structures expressed by the sentences of (8.9). ((8.9a) has two path-functions and reference objects in its path.)

(8.12)   [$_{Event}$ GO ([$_{Object}$ x], [$_{Path}$ PATH-FUNCTION ([$_{Object}$ y])])]

BE verbs are exemplified in (8.13).

(8.13)   a. Max was in Africa.
         b. The cushion lay on the couch.
         c. The statue stands in the woods.

These describe not motion but the location of an object. Thus, they express forms of a general concept [BE (X,L)], where X is the theme (the object being located) and L is a location. The ontological category of this concept is not [EVENT]: these are not things that happen but rather states of affairs. We will adopt the notation [STATE] for the requisite ontological category. The locations are of the ontological category [PLACE]; like paths, they can be decomposed into a *place-function* expressed by the preposition and a reference object expressed by the object of the preposition. Thus, the general form of the concepts expressed by (8.13) is (8.14).

(8.14)   [$_{State}$ BE ([$_{Object}$ x], [$_{Place}$ PLACE-FUNCTION ([$_{Object}$ y])])]

In addition to the verbs of location illustrated in (8.13), there is a second, smaller class of location verbs with rather different semantic properties, which I will call *STAY verbs*.

(8.15)   a. The bacteria stayed in his body.
         b. Stanley remained in Africa.

Like BE verbs, these express the location of an object in a place. But unlike them, they involve the maintenance of this location over a period of time; they cannot be attributed to a point in time such as *at six o'clock*.

(8.16)   a. The bacteria $\left\{\begin{array}{c}\text{were}\\ \text{*stayed}\end{array}\right\}$ in his body at six o'clock.
         b. The cushion $\left\{\begin{array}{c}\text{lay}\\ \text{*remained}\end{array}\right\}$ on the couch at six o'clock.

Because of their temporal structure, they turn out to belong to the ontological category of [EVENTS]. Thus, like the GO verbs and unlike the BE verbs, they can occur after the phrase *what happened was*.

(8.17)   What happened was

$$\begin{cases} \text{the dog ran to the table.} \\ \text{the hawk flew over the prairie.} \end{cases} \text{GO}$$
$$\begin{cases} \text{Stanley remained in Africa.} \\ \text{the bacteria stayed in his body.} \end{cases} \text{STAY}$$
$$\begin{cases} *\text{Max was in Siberia.} \\ *\text{the statue stood in the woods.} \end{cases} \text{BE}$$

The general conceptual form of (8.15) will therefore be decomposed as in (8.18).

(8.18) $[_{\text{Event}} \text{STAY} ([_{\text{Object}} x], [_{\text{Place}} \text{PLACE-FUNCTION} ([_{\text{Object}} y])])]$

Given these three subfields of verbs of spatial position, let us consider another semantic field, verbs of possession. These can again be divided into three subfields, exemplified in (8.19), (8.20), and (8.21).

(8.19)   a. Harry gave the book to Betty.
          b. Charlie bought the lamp from Max.
          c. Will inherited a million dollars.

(8.20)   a. The book belonged to the library.
          b. Max owned an iguana.
          c. Bill had no money.

(8.21)   a. The library kept the book.
          b. The iguana stayed in Max's possession.
          c. The leopard retained its spots.

The (8.19) the things described by the direct object of the sentence undergo a change in possession. The sentences in (8.20), however, express states of possession. The sentences in (8.21) also express a single unchanging possessor, but *at six o'clock* may be added only to (8.20), not to (8.21), and *what happened was* may be prefixed to (8.21) but not to (8.20).

Thus there is an important parallel between (8.19)–(8.21) on the one hand and (8.9), (8.13), and (8.15) on the other. Gruber (1965) represents this parallel by claiming that the verbs in (8.19) are also instances of [GO (X,P)], the verbs in (8.20) are instances of [BE (X,L)], and the verbs in (8.21) are instances of [STAY (X,L)]. The difference between (8.19)–(8.21) and (8.9), (8.13), and (8.15) is then expressed by a modifier on GO, BE, and STAY, picking out the proper semantic field. For physical motion and location, the field modifier is *Positional*; for possession, it is *Possessional*. For example, (8.9a) expresses something like (8.22a), (8.19a) something like (8.22b).

(8.22)   a. $[_{\text{Event}} \text{GO}_{\text{Posit}} ([_{\text{Object}} \text{DOG}], [_{\text{Path}} \text{FROM} ([_{\text{Object}} \text{DOOR}]) \text{ TO} ([_{\text{Object}} \text{TABLE}])])]$
          b. $[_{\text{Event}} \text{GO}_{\text{Poss}} ([_{\text{Object}} \text{BOOK}], [_{\text{Path}} \text{FROM} ([_{\text{Object}} \text{HARRY}]) \text{ TO} ([_{\text{Object}} \text{BETTY}])])]$

This now gives us a principle with which to organize a third important semantic field, verbs of predication or ascription. These verbs are used to describe properties of things. The same three-way division into subfields obtains.

(8.23) a. The coach changed from a handsome young man into a pumpkin.
        b. The metal turned red.
        c. The ice became mushy.

(8.24) a. The coach was a turkey.
        b. The metal was vermilion.
        c. The pumpkin seemed tasty.

(8.25) a. The poor coach remained a pumpkin.
        b. The metal stayed red.

The sentences of (8.23) describe changes of state; those of (8.24) describe a state; those of (8.25) describe persistence of a state. Of the two latter cases, (8.24) and (8.25), *at six o'clock* may be added only to (8.24) and *what happened was* may be prefixed only to (8.25). Thus, these three sets of verbs are further instances of the concepts GO, BE, and STAY, respectively. We will call the field modifier this time *Identificational*; locations and paths in this field make claims about what the theme is, rather than where it is, as in the Positional field, or whose it is, as in the Possessional field.

Let us look a little more closely at sentences that express Identificational concepts. The theme as usual is a noun phrase, but the phrase expressing the reference object may typically be either a "predicate nominal," as in (8.23a), (8.24a), and (8.25a), or an adjective phrase, as in the rest of the examples. The latter express [PROPERTIES]; what about the former? In Positional sentences the reference objects are particular (that is, token) objects; similarly in Possessional sentences. But Identificational sentences speak of category membership. This suggests that predicate nominals differ from ordinary noun phrases in that they express [TYPE] concepts rather than [TOKEN] concepts, a distinction we have so far ignored in this section. (This suggestion is worked out and defended in *S&C*, section 5.3.) For example, (8.23a) expresses something like (8.26a); (8.23b) expresses (8.26b). (I am assuming that the events and paths are particular (that is, TOKENS) here. For PROPERTIES the type-token distinction is harder to justify and may be absent altogether; I leave the feature blank in (8.26b).)

(8.26)

a.
$$\left[\begin{array}{l} \text{TOKEN} \\ \text{GO}_{\text{Ident}} \left(\begin{bmatrix} \text{TOKEN} \\ \text{COACH} \end{bmatrix}_{\text{Object}}, \begin{bmatrix} \text{TOKEN} \\ \text{FROM} \left(\begin{bmatrix} \text{TYPE} \\ \text{MAN} \end{bmatrix}_{\text{Object}}\right) \text{TO} \left(\begin{bmatrix} \text{TYPE} \\ \text{PUMPKIN} \end{bmatrix}_{\text{Object}}\right) \end{bmatrix}_{\text{Path}}\right) \end{array}\right]_{\text{Event}}$$

b.
$$\begin{bmatrix} \text{TOKEN} \\ \text{GO}_{\text{Ident}} \left(\begin{bmatrix} \text{TOKEN} \\ _{\text{Object}} \text{METAL} \end{bmatrix}, \begin{bmatrix} \text{TOKEN} \\ _{\text{Path}} \text{TO} \left([_{\text{Property}} \text{RED}] \right) \end{bmatrix} \right) \\ _{\text{Event}} \end{bmatrix}$$

Thus, the three major concepts GO, BE, and STAY apply to three semantic fields that a priori have nothing to do with each other. This illustrates a phenomenon that might be called *cross-field generalization*. A basic notion of what it is to be "in a place" differs from one field to another. In the Positional field a location is a spatial position; in the Possessional field it is to be owned by someone; in the Identification field it is to have a property or be in a category. From any of these notions of location an entire field of verbs is elaborated out of instances of the three basic concepts GO, BE, and STAY, understood as they apply to that particular type of location.

As evidence that cross-field generalization is of genuine grammatical significance, observe that it is common for particular verbs to function in more than one semantic field, while still preserving their classification as GO, BE, or STAY verbs. Consider the examples in (8.27).

(8.27) a. The coach turned into a driveway.   (Positional)
            The coach turned into a pumpkin.   (Identificational)
        b. The train went to Texas.   (Positional)
            The inheritance went to Philip.   (Possessional)
        c. Max is in Africa.   (Positional)
            Max is a dog.   (Identificational)
        d. Bill kept the book on the shelf.   (Positional)
            Bill kept the book.   (Possessional)
        e. The coach remained in the driveway.   (Positional)
            The coach remained a pumpkin.   (Identificational)

In each pair the same verb is used in two different semantic fields. Since these uses are not a priori related, it is a significant generalization that a sizable number of verbs exhibit such behavior. The hypothesis proposed here claims that the relation between these uses is simple and nonaccidental: the verb stays fundamentally the same, changing only its semantic field via a cross-field generalization. One way in which words can extend their meanings, then, is by keeping all semantic structure intact except the part that picks out the semantic field.

In particular, the fundamental semantic function of categorization, called in section 8.1 IS-AN-INSTANCE-OF, is now subsumed by the function BE_{Ident}. It is now seen to be, not a primitive function sui generis, but a composite formed from the intersection of the family of BE concepts and the family of Identificational concepts. This enables us to unify various uses of the verb *be* under a more general function; we do not have to say that in its use with expressions of location it means one thing, and in its use in categorization sentences it means something entirely different. As this generalization appears in many languages of the world besides English, we would like to ascribe it to something more than coincidence. The hypothesis of cross-field generalization makes possible a more enlightening approach. But it also removes categorization from the purely logical domain, in that it has come to be formally connected with concrete representations of spatial relations.

We are proposing, then, that among the set of conceptual primitives is a three-way opposition between GO, STAY, and BE and that the former two are associated with the ontological category EVENT and the third with the category STATE. However, the units cannot appear in isolation: they must co-occur with a field modifier in order to be realized as a well-formed concept. The class of field modifiers (the three given here plus at least a few others discussed in *S&C*) constitute a feature opposition that operates independently of the choice of GO/STAY/BE, of EVENT/STATE, and of TYPE/TOKEN. Thus, we have uncovered four fundamental oppositions in conceptual structure; these operate in many respects like phonological distinctive features—particularly in that they must be bundled together for a well-formed concept to be produced. For instance, the feature EVENT alone is meaningless, just like the feature [+ voiced].

The usual polemic applies to the pair of oppositions introduced in this section. There seems to be nothing intrinsic to the real world that requires possession and ascription of properties to be mentally represented in an algebraic system that parallels the representation of spatial events and states. Rather, the most appealing explanation of this parallelism (to me, at least) is that it is a reflection of the way human beings are constrained to construe the world. It is not that this is a true or false representation of the world—it is just the way we have. Again we are led to the necessity of an observer-based treatment of reference and truth, rather than one that depends on a preestablished Reality.

Similar cross-field generalizations having to do with notions of causality are hinted at by Jackendoff (1977b) and developed in splendid detail by Talmy (1985). As it turns out, the conception of physical force and causation, as well as that of the resistance or acquiescence of one object to force applied by another object, find parallels in such domains as social coercion and resistance and in logical and moral necessity. The most abstract of these domains, that of logical relations, has often been regarded as a field isolated from human conceptualization, to be studied by purely mathematical techniques. On the other hand, analysis through cross-field generalization reveals that this domain, like categorization, has formal parallels to a very concrete semantic field having to do with pushing objects around in space. Although radically at variance with the philosophical tradition, this result makes a great deal of sense in the context of a theory of meaning as conceptualization. One can begin to see the principles of logic as abstractions away from the general algebraic form implicit in our understanding of the physical world, and through this one can begin to envision the evolutionary channels by which they might have developed in the computational mind.

(A personal note: it was the existence of cross-field generalizations that first led me to believe that linguistic evidence could motivate powerful hypotheses about the structure of thought. From them emerged the germ of all my present thinking on conceptual structure, the observer's construal of the world, and the observer-based notions of reference and truth. I mention this, not just as an anecdote about my own intellectual development (or degeneration, as the case may be), but primarily because these facts have played absolutely no role in more standard theories of semantics. It seems to me that they cry out for explanation and that, if taken seriously, they lead inescapably to a wholly mentalistic semantics of at least approximately the form proposed here.)

8.6   Final remarks

This chapter and the last have explored the consequences of assuming that there is a level of mental representation that simultaneously (1) encodes the meaning of linguistic expressions, (2) permits a formal account of linguistic inference, and (3) serves as an interface between language and other mental faculties. As these consequences are not widely appreciated, I have had to spend most of chapter 7 clearing away the debris left by other theories popular in the literature. Moreover, as a satisfactory theory is very much in its infancy, I have been able only to suggest a few of the most fundamental distinctions it must express. Still, the role of this level in the system as a whole has been made fairly clear.

You will probably have noticed that the arguments from intuition to theory, even at this elementary level, are far more convoluted and fraught with peril than those in phonology and syntax. I think there is a principled reason for this: the units of decomposition in syntax and phonology are far more open to successful introspection than those in semantics. The relative ease of introspection is aided no doubt by the fact that our writing system is couched in terms of phonological and syntactic units. On the other hand, this fact is probably a symptom of the phenomenon in question: if we are inventing a writing system, it will be based on word-, syllable-, or phoneme-shaped units, not semantic ones, because the former are much more accessible to introspection. For now this is just to be taken as a methodological observation on why semantics is so hard, but I will make more of it in part IV.

Having repeatedly attacked the notions of reference and truth vis-à-vis the objective real world, I will not go after them again. Instead, let me close this chapter by pointing out the liberating effect of the observer-based theory of reference and truth. On the face of it, the idea that one speaks of the world as one construes it—that one can understand only what one is *constrained* to understand—sounds as though it puts the mind in a conceptual straitjacket, stressing its limitations. But in fact, its effect is quite the opposite. Even in the tiny domain we have explored we have seen that it vastly enriches our notion of the information in terms of which the world can be interpreted, and it opens new avenues toward an account of human understanding with a depth and subtlety unparalleled by any of the "Realist" approaches.

PART III
Nonlinguistic Faculties

Chapter 9
Levels of Visual Structure

As observed in chapter 4, the idea of treating a cognitive capacity in terms of levels of representation is an old one in linguistics, and the intuitions behind such a treatment of phonology and syntax are relatively robust. In this and the next two chapters we turn to other faculties for which explicit levels of representation have been recently proposed: vision and music. We will see that although the content of the levels is quite different from that in language, the overall organization of the theories is not dissimilar. On the basis of these three faculties, we will be able to formulate some broad hypotheses about the organization of the computational mind.

9.1 The Problem of Vision

The problem posed by vision may be harder to appreciate than that posed by language. We are all aware of the differences among languages and the need for children to learn language, but vision seems to come to us without any conscious effort. What we so easily take for granted might be illustrated in the breach by a recent children's television program on science. It goes into some detail about the optics of the eye: the focusing of the lens, the crossing of the light rays, and finally the emergence of an upside-down image on the retina. From there it shows a lightning-like arrow carrying the image up into the brain, given with the assurance that we don't see things upside-down because the brain knows to turn the image over!

Well, it can't be that simple, of course. How do the independent activations of some millions of retinal receptors add up to visual perception? For perhaps the simplest instance: where there is a homogeneous region in the visual field (say, the surface of a blackboard), how is the activation of some huge number of retinal receptors that respond to light from this region bonded together into the *perception* of a region? It can't just be that these receptors are physically next to each other: an individual receptor alone can't convey information about its location, such as whether it is related to other receptors that together form a coherent and continuous boundary. Rather, to derive such information, computations must be performed over the information conveyed by complexes of retinal receptors.

So, as in the case of language, we can ask, In what form is the mental information used in visual perception, and what formal properties permit this information to be derived from retinal input?

Here are some well-known boundary conditions on possible answers. First, one can see objects as remaining the same despite different retinal projections and different surrounding contexts. As I walk around my desk, its projection on my retinas changes drastically in size, shape, and location, but the desk still looks like the same object to me. It would still look like the same object if, in my absence, someone screwed it to the ceiling or threw it out the window so it stuck out of the grass at a funny angle.

On the other hand, the very same retinal projection can result in quite different perceptions—for instance, in the well-known Necker cube and vase-faces illusions (figure 6.7). Thus, the information provided by the retina is not in one-to-one correspondence with the information provided by visual perception, as implied by the children's television program. Identity of retinal information is neither necessary nor sufficient for visual identity. (It may be that different eye movements normally occur in the alternative perceptual conditions of ambiguous figures, so the retinal projections are not actually the same. But if so, behind the choices of eye movements lie higher-level distinctions, which in turn cannot be determined from raw retinal information alone. In any event, one can still get Necker-cube reversals in afterimages, which are fixed on the retina, so the issue of eye movements is not relevant here (Gregory 1970, 40).)

Consider further my perception of my desk. I see it as retaining a rectangular shape as I walk around it, even though its projection on my retina is never rectangular—it is at best (when all of it is in my visual field) a near-parallelogram. It produces a rectangular projection only when viewed directly from above, a point of view I have never been privileged to adopt. And even if I happened on some occasion to adopt the view that produces a rectangular retinal projection, how would I know that *that* was the privileged position?

Recall the case of phonology, where a variable and not clearly segmented acoustic signal results in a differentiated perceptual constant, say, the sound "p." We argued there that a constant mental representation must underlie a constant of phonetic perception. Similarly, the computational theory of mind here must take the view that behind a shape constancy in vision lies a representation in which the constant rectangular shape is explicit and that this representation is correlated with a variable input by computational processes. Thus, within this framework rectangularity is to be regarded as an abstract attribute in mental representation, not an immediate attribute to be found in the information provided by the sense organ.

This general account is characteristic of all the so-called perceptual constancies, including for instance size and color as well as shape. In each case visual understanding must use variable and continually changing retinal input as a basis for judgments of constancy in the attributes of perceived objects. Let us look briefly at one such aspect of visual perception, for the light it sheds on the structure of a formal theory.

The perception of depth, or distance of surfaces from the observer, can be derived from a variety of cues. One is the degree of accommodation the lens must make to focus the object sharply. Another is the disparity in the angle at which the eyes must point to focus on the object (if it is closer, the angular disparity is greater). Another is stereopsis, the disparity in the view of the object as seen from the two eyes (if it is closer, the views are less alike). Another is texture gradient: if texture elements (say, polka dots or stripes) are smaller and closer together in one part of a surface, that part is seen as farther away. In viewing pictures, only the last kind of cue is available, since actual distance, necessary for accommodation and stereopsis cues, is constant. Yet texture gradient alone can be responsible for a sensation of depth.

In addition, mere judged occlusion can produce a sensation of depth. For instance, the vase-faces illusion presents none of the preceding four kinds of cues. But when the figure is seen as faces, the white background is seen as behind the faces; when it is seen as a vase, the black background is seen as behind the vase.

In real viewing situations all these factors and others may contribute to perceived depth of different parts of the viewed scene, their effects overlapping in some areas and separate in others, depending on the configurations of the areas in question. Evidently, these factors operate together as a preference rule system (in the sense of section 8.3), together bearing on the judgment of depth of elements in the visual field.

Consider more closely one of these factors, stereopsis. The information-processing problem that must be solved by stereopsis is that of taking two slightly different images (one from each eye), neither differentiated for depth, and combining them into a single perceived image that contains depth information. There is a straightforward trigonometric solution to the problem of deriving depth from disparity, but it depends on one crucial factor: one cannot measure the difference between two images unless one also knows which parts of the images count as the same.

One's immediate tendency is to overlook this requirement, since it seems so trivial. If we had to do the matching *consciously*, we would locate the objects in the two images, then compare corresponding parts for disparity of shape. Nothing would seem simpler. The potential pitfall of such an account appears if we ask whether stereopsis might be used to *discriminate* objects, that is, if it might be a process that logically

Figure 9.1
A random-dot stereogram. (Reprinted, by permission, from B. Julesz (1971). *Foundations of cyclopean perception*, fig. 2.4−1. Chicago: University of Chicago Press. Copyright 1971 by University of Chicago Press.)

precedes the identification of objects in the visual field. Can we always assume that the information "corresponding parts of objects in the two images" is available to stereopsis, or does stereopsis itself sometimes make available the information that there are two objects to be discriminated?

That this is not just a hypothetical question is dramatically demonstrated by Julesz's (1971) "random-dot stereograms." Figure 9.1 is one of Julesz's figures. It consists of two arrays of 100 × 100 little squares or *pixels*, with black and white distributed randomly. No higher-order organization at all is apparent in these arrays on ordinary viewing. However, if they are viewed stereoscopically, one array presented to each eye, a vivid perception arises: the viewer sees a square region in the middle of the array floating above the rest of the page. (Julesz 1971 presents these examples in a format that can be viewed with red-green 3D glasses.) The design of the arrays that gives rise to this perception is as follows: the two arrays are identical, except that a square region in the middle of the left-hand array has been shifted one pixel to the left in creating the right-hand array, and the column left blank as a result has been filled in with new random pixels. As a result, the two eyes are presented with just the appropriate sort of cue for stereoptic depth perception—a left-right disparity in the relative positions of parts of the retinal arrays. Therefore, the system is "fooled" into imputing depth to the array, and this depth is part of what the viewer sees.

Notice, though, that the central square is perceived as a unit (or achieves "objecthood") only as a result of the functioning of stereopsis. It is not present in the array viewed monocularly. This means that at least for some cases the discrimination of objects must take place at a later stage of visual processing than stereopsis and must be logically dependent on stereopsis. Therefore, the commonsense hypothesis that stereopsis depends on locating corresponding parts of objects in the field is inadequate; rather, stereopsis must be based (at least partly) on detection of purely local pattern correspondences.

Suddenly the problem becomes a great deal less tractable and more frightening. Without the comfortable notions of objects to work with, we suddenly confront the real task of vision: finding the objects at all in a retinal array of vast variability and potential vagueness. Leaving Julesz's examples and confronting real life, consider what might be involved in discerning a house through the trees: unifying many separate patches of irregular shape into the perception of a single object. (If this seems reminiscent of the problem of finding phonological segments in an acoustic signal, you are thinking along the right track: the qualitative character of the problems that vision and language perception must solve appear quite similar, even if the content is quite different.)

From confronting problems of this sort, there has arisen a widespread consensus that one's perception of a three-dimensional visual world full of objects is informationally underdetermined by two-dimensional retinal arrays and that visual processing must involve a great deal of reconstruction of the probable physical source of the optical input. The first prominent statement of this thesis is due to Helmholtz (1867), who speaks of the "unconscious inferences" made in visual perception; similar views occur throughout the Gestalt school (Wertheimer 1923; Köhler 1929; Koffka 1935) and into modern times (Neisser 1967, 1976; Gregory 1970; Hochberg 1978). Views differ on the relative contributions of retinally derived and high-level cognitive information (for example, Neisser makes a dramatic shift in favor of high-level information between 1967 and 1976), but the overall hypothesis is on the whole unquestioned by now. (An important and influential exception is Gibson (1966, 1979), who considers everything to be derivable from retinal information alone. See Shepard 1984 and Marr 1982, 29–31, for sympathetic rebuttals and Fodor and Pylyshyn 1981 for an unsympathetic one.)

However, what most of these approaches leave unspecified, despite much talk about "perceptual" versus "cognitive" or "low-level" versus "high-level" information, is any serious notion of what the *form* of the information is. To understand the computations involved in any information-processing task, it is essential to characterize the structure of the information being processed. The work of David Marr provides the beginning of a theory of the form of visual information, and we now turn to that work.

9.2 The Form of Marr's Inquiry into Vision

Marr's *Vision* (two good introductions to which are Marr and Nishihara 1978 and Pinker 1984b) starts by making a distinction between three kinds of theoretical description. The first is what he calls a *computational* theory, which he explicitly compares to Chomsky's notion of competence in linguistic theory and which is parallel to what I have called here a theory of information structure. In this theory "the performance of the device is characterized as a mapping from one kind of information to another, the abstract properties of this mapping are defined precisely, and its appropriateness and adequacy for the task are demonstrated" (Marr 1982, 24).

Next is what he calls an *algorithmic* theory, closely parallel to what I have called a processing theory: How can the computational theory be implemented, so that it can actually be run as a processing device? As Marr observes, distinct processes can be proposed to implement the very same computational theory, with different predictions about the relative difficulty of certain cases of the computational theory. As an example he cites changes in his own algorithmic theory of stereopsis on the basis of psychophysical evidence, while holding the computational theory constant. This parallels the discussion in chapter 6 of different theories of syntactic processing, based on essentially the same conception of syntactic structure, which make different predictions about processing complexity of various sentences. Marr specifically cites one of these (Marcus 1980) as an example in linguistics of what he means by an algorithmic theory, so the intended parallel is quite clear.

Marr's third sort of description is that of *hardware implementation*: How can neurons (or computers) physically realize these representations and algorithms? The relationship of this description to the others is precisely that between brain and the computational mind, the latter including both structure and process. In the study of vision, more than in language, there has been both considerable success at this sort of description (most notably in the work of Hubel and Wiesel 1962, 1968) and also considerable unwarranted expectation that this might prove to be all that is necessary. Speaking to the latter point, Marr observes that the understanding of how a cash register works, for instance, requires more than an understanding of its parts and how they causally affect each other. There must be an understanding that its operation is a realization of certain principles of arithmetic, that is, a computational theory. Similarly for vision: calling a particular neuron an "edge detector," say, implicitly attributes to it a function in an unstated computational theory. One must specify how the information to which this neuron is sensitive contributes to the global problem of seeing objects.

To make his problem manageable, Marr restricts himself to what he considers the "quintessential fact of human vision—that it tells about shape and spatial arrangement...its purpose [is] building a description of the shapes and positions of things from [retinal] images" (1982, 36). By "description" here Marr does not mean a description in the form of sentences; rather, he means an explicit representation, in its own characteristic terms, of the spatial forms revealed by vision. He takes notice of other aspects of vision such as brightness and color and texture and motion but makes a methodological choice to treat them as secondary (just as someone studying syntax may choose to disregard intonation, for instance). Similarly, he says little or nothing about the role of eye movements or attention. This does not absolve a visual theory from eventual responsibility for these facts—and when they interact with the primary explicanda of the moment, their influence must be taken into account. But, as always, the success of the methodology depends on a guess that the idealization is a theoretically revealing one.

Note, for instance, an idealization that Marr does not adopt: the reduction of the visual field to the form of a line drawing, such as the "blocks world" of Waltz (1975). His discussion of the reasons not to do so (1982, 344–345) reveals why: real-world scenes are full of fuzzy, incomplete, and even nonphysically existent boundaries. Two examples of the latter are the boundary of the square seen in the random-dot stereogram in figure 9.1 and the boundary of the "virtual circle" seen in the center of figure 9.2. In the general case, then, boundaries are not given to the visual system as the "blocks world" idealization assumes; they must be *found* or constructed.

For the next step in motivating the theory, it is easiest to quote Marr himself (1982, 36–37).

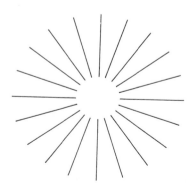

Figure 9.2
A virtual circle

Desirable as it may be to have vision deliver a completely invariant shape description from an image . . . , it is almost certainly impossible in only one step . . . . Thus we arrived at the idea of a sequence of representations, starting with descriptions that could be obtained straight from [a retinal] image but that are carefully designed to facilitate the subsequent recovery of gradually more objective, physical properties about an object's shape. The main stepping stone toward this goal is describing the geometry of the visible surfaces, since the information encoded in images, for example by stereopsis, shading, texture, contours, or visual motion, is due to a shape's local surface properties. The objective of many early [that is, peripheral] computations is to extract this information.

However, this description of the visible surfaces turns out to be unsuitable for recognition tasks. There are several reasons why, perhaps the most prominent being that like all early visual processes, it depends critically on the vantage point. The final step therefore consists of transforming the viewer-centered surface description into a representation of the three-dimensional shape and spatial arrangement of an object that does not depend upon the direction from which the object is being viewed. This final description is object-centered rather than viewer-centered.

The theory therefore is worked out in terms of a sequence of discrete levels of representation, like phonology, syntax, and semantics in language, each with its own characteristic primitives and principles of combination, and each linked to the next in the sequence by a set of correspondence rules. The most peripheral level is the retinal image, which represents simply the light intensity at each point in the image at each moment (remember we are abstracting away from wavelength or color). The most central level is the object-centered three-dimensional description, to which we will return presently by way of the intermediate levels.

9.3 The Primal Sketch and 2½D Sketch

The level derived most directly from the retinal image is the *primal sketch*. The primal sketch expresses the local organization of the visual field but not yet the segmentation of the field into distinct regions. The basic principle behind the primal sketch is that perception of form depends first of all on the detection of discontinuities of intensity in the retinal image. These signal the presence of parts of boundaries between one region and the next. Accordingly, some of the primal sketch primitives are local markers or boundaries: small *segments* of edges with positions, length, and orientations, markers of *termination* of an edge, and markers of *discontinuity* of orientation (or corners) in an edge. Another primitive, the *blob*, is a small region of specified position, length, width, and orientation surrounded by a boundary. The *bar* likewise has position, length, width, and orientation, but only its sides are boundaries; its ends are considered open, possibly connecting to other bars. Thus, for instance, a narrow stripe can be built up in the primal sketch from a sequence of bars, bounded on the ends by terminations.

In addition to positional and orientational information, motion of a primitive element may be specified in a limited way by means of an associated vector. This vector indicates direction of motion and possibly speed—not in the world, but in the retinal field.

Marr shows in some detail how these primitives can be derived formally from the retinal image. He takes pains to show that these are the correct sorts of primitives for human vision and that his way of deriving them corresponds to the way that human vision accomplishes the task—down to neurological detail, in some cases. Though we need not go into any specifics here (and some of his solutions are, I gather, disputed), we can see that this part of the theory constitutes a description of the correspondence rules between the retinal image and the primal sketch, more or less parallel in function to the principles by which phonetic representations are derived from acoustic signals.

The full field of primitive elements derived from the retinal image constitutes what Marr calls the *raw primal sketch*. These elements are then subjected to computations that group them recursively into large-scale elements to form the *full primal sketch*. The larger-scale elements are of the same types as the primitive elements—edges, terminations, discontinuities, blobs, and bars—but they represent the geometrical organization of collections of smaller-scale primal sketch elements rather than that of retinal image elements. For instance, the raw primal sketch for figure 9.3a consists of a lot of small blobs; the next layer of organization consists of oriented bars built up from the configurations of blobs, corresponding to the perception of areas filled with or made up of dots. The raw primal sketch for figure 9.3b consists of a lot of oriented bars, with orientation discontinuities; in the next layer or organization the linear arrangement of the

Figure 9.3
Evidence for hierarchical organization of primal sketch elements

discontinuities is detected and encoded as an edge. In figure 9.2 the raw primal sketch encodes a lot of bars and their terminations; in the full primal sketch the terminations are grouped into a sequence of oriented segments, which eventually give rise (at a higher level of representation) to the perception of the "virtual circle" in the center.

Marr sees this grouping process as continuing recursively: the second layer of primitives can be further grouped into a third layer, and so on.

> Thus if the image [is] a close-up view of a cat, the raw primal sketch might yield descriptions mostly at the scale of the cat's hairs. At the next level the markings on its coat may appear ... and at a yet higher level there is the parallel-stripe structure of these markings.... At each step the primitives used are qualitatively similar symbols ... but they refer to increasingly abstract properties of the image. (Marr 1982, 91)

Thus the primal sketch is a hierarchical structure, already quite unlike the unstructured retinal intensity array, though still far from a full visual interpretation. In particular, there is no notion yet of "physical object."

However, the primal sketch does provide the kind to information that makes possible a derivation of the next level of visual representation, the 2½D *sketch*. This level represents the geometry of the surfaces visible to the observer—including their contours, depth, and orientation—so it is more than a flat, two-dimensional image (a "picture in the head"). But since it represents only visible surfaces, not volumes, it is less than a full three-dimensional representation—hence its curious name.

Marr conceives of the 2½D sketch as (in part) another map of the visual field, in which depth and orientation are represented at each point. For example, if figure 9.4 is the contour of a flat circular disk, points *a*, *b*, and *c* will be encoded as equidistant from the viewer and oriented parallel to the picture plane; they will all be encoded as closer than point *d*, which is part

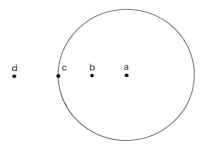

Figure 9.4
A disk or a sphere, depending on distance and orientation of points *a*, *b* and *c*

of the background. On the other hand, if figure 9.4 is the contour of a sphere, point *a* will be closest to the viewer and oriented parallel to the picture plane, point *b* will be farther away and oriented obliquely, point *c* will be farther away still and oriented perpendicular to the picture plane, and point *d* will again be background and hence farthest away of all.

The importance of this representation from the point of view of visual processing is that it provides a unified locus at which several relatively autonomous computations can converge. Stereopsis, motion, shading, surface contours, and texture gradients all depend on information present in the primal sketch, and all yield information relevant to determining depth and orientation of visible surfaces—but through computations of quite disparate sorts. Marr points out that postulating this level of representation permits the theories of these computations to be formulated quite independently, so that the full theory of the correspondence between the primal sketch and the 2½D sketch is strongly modular in construction. Thus he sees a formal organization like figure 9.5 for this part of visual theory.

Some of the principles of correspondence are worked out in detail by Marr, in particular stereopsis and contour-from-motion (in the latter case he draws heavily on work by Ullman, especially Ullman 1979). Others, such as the role of linear surface contours in determining perceived surface geometry, are far less well specified. But the general program is clear.

As for the formation rules for the 2½D sketch, Marr includes in his list of

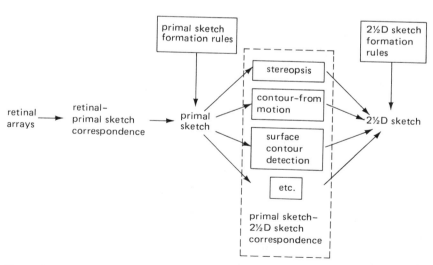

Figure 9.5
The paths of information up to the 2½D sketch

primitives (1982, 37) the following: local surface orientation, distance from viewer, discontinuities in depth, and discontinuities in surface orientation. Although some of his diagrams explicitly include the latter two, in fact only the first two are discussed in any detail, and there is no discussion of combining primitives into larger units. Thus, the 2½D sketch as presented by Marr has little in the way of hierarchical structure. Appendix B suggests some enrichment of its formal vocabulary.

Whatever the formal character of the 2½D sketch, it still represents only surfaces, not objects, and it does not account for the shape and size constancies necessary in a full treatment of visual perception. For these purposes we need another level of representation.

9.4 The 3D Model

Marr's most central level of visual representation is the *3D model representation*. This level is conceived of as *volumetric*: objects are represented as occupying volume in space, by contrast with the surface representations of the lower levels. In addition, it is *object-centered* rather than viewer-centered: it makes explicit the shape and size constancy of objects, regardless of the viewer's position. It is therefore the level most appropriate for encoding an object's shape in long-term memory, so that it may be recognized on subsequent occasions. (Recall from section 9.1 that the viewer is unlikely to see it from exactly the same position again.) Marr develops 3D structure in detail only for single objects, not for the complete configuration in the visual field; we will consider some extensions in the next chapter.

What is particularly interesting about the 3D structure of an object is that it is *hierarchical*: it represents the three-dimensional structure of objects not just in terms of holistic shape (it is not a "statue in the head") but rather in terms of a hierarchical decomposition of the object into parts and parts of parts.

For example, consider figure 9.6 (from Marr and Nishihara 1978), which suggests the organization of the 3D structure for a human figure. At the coarsest layer of description the figure is represented simply by a cylinder, itself defined by a vertical axis down the middle and a cross section. At the next layer of description the cylinder is elaborated into a torso, a head, and four limbs, each of which is a cylinder defined by its own axis. The points of attachment of the head and limbs to the torso, and the angles that they form, are specified in terms of the coordinate system defined by the axis of the torso. In turn, each of the parts is subject to elaboration at finer levels of detail. For instance, the arm cylinder can be elaborated as two connected cylinders corresponding to the upper and lower arm; the lower arm can be elaborated into lower arm and hand; the hand can be elaborated into palm

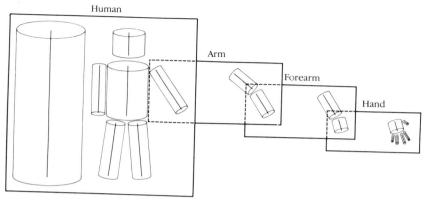

Figure 9.6
3D structure for a human figure. (Reprinted, by permission, from D. Marr and H. K. Nishihara (1978). Representation and recognition of the spatial organization of three-dimensional shapes. *Proc. R. Soc. Lond.* B 200, 269–294.)

and fingers; the fingers can be elaborated into joints. Thus, the 3D model is a sort of tree structure.

In each case of elaboration the configuration of parts is specified in terms of the coordinate system defined by the axis of the main part in the configuration. The positions of the fingers, for instance, are specified most directly in terms of their configurations within the hand. Their position with respect to the body as a whole is specified only indirectly, through the hand's position on the arm and the arm's on the torso.

This, then, is what Marr means by saying the description is object-centered: through recursive elaboration, the position of the parts of an object are specified ultimately with respect to the main axes of the object as a whole and can therefore be specified without mention of the viewer's position. Of course, in integrating the object as a whole into the scene, its position with respect to the viewer must be specified. But this can be determined entirely by specifying the position of the object's main axis, and the positions of the parts will fall into place automatically.

Though the formal characteristics of the 3D model representation are at present far from well understood, the general outlines are fairly clear. The primitive units of the representation are the coordinate axes and the means for generating simple shapes such as the cylinders of figure 9.6 around them. Marr describes only the class of "generalized cone" primitives—shapes generated by rotating a fixed contour around an axis. But clearly other primitives are necessary, as many have pointed out. The problem is to determine empirically what other primitives would be most productive.

The principles of 3D combination provide the means to combine simple shapes into more complex shapes. From figure 9.6 we can see that the principles of combination essentially provide a way to elaborate a description of an object from a coarse description to the next higher degree of specificity—for example, from a single cylinder to a torso plus head and limbs. Further layers of description will be possible simply by applying the principles of combination recursively.

Note that the principles are *not* of the form "such-and-such a part is connected to such-and-such a part." Rather, the dispositions of the parts are specified in relation to the coordinate axes of the next coarser layer of description: "(the axis of) such-and-such a part at layer of description L_i is disposed in such-and-such a configuration with respect to the axes of such-and-such an element of layer L_{i-1}." Principles of this form are a great deal like the phrase structure rules of syntax, in which, for example, a relative clause is understood as an expansion not of the head noun but of the next larger unit, the noun phrase.

It is moreover possible to discern a notion of "head" not unlike that found in syntax. Just as one talks of the head noun—the principal element of a noun phrase, the one that determines the noun phrase's categorical status—one can in many cases speak of the head constituent of a 3D model elaboration: that subsidiary element in an elaboration whose axes and volumetric form are identical to (or most similar to) the coarser-layer element being elaborated. In the human figure, for instance, the torso is the head of the initial elaboration; the palm is the head of the hand. In other cases, though, such as the elaboration of the arm into upper and lower arm, the presence of a head constituent is less obvious. Perhaps there is an analogy here to coordination in language (as in the noun phrase *my father and my brother*), in which neither of the two conjuncts plays the role of head.

Now consider the task of identifying an object that can change its shape, for example, a human or animal. The long-term memory 3D model of such an object, to which its presented appearance can be compared, need not represent just a single pose of this object. Rather, the parameters specifying angle of attachment of the various parts in a decomposition like figure 9.6 can give a range of possible values, corresponding to the possible configurations of the joints. On the other hand, certain aspects will be kept rigid, for example, the point of attachment. (If somehow the shoulder joint could slide up and down the torso, the way the carriage slides across a typewriter, that too could be specified by a variable.) Thus, the object-centered decomposition of objects makes possible a description of an object's possible *variations in shape*.

Similarly, the 3D model permits an intuitively attractive account of the representation of the *action of moving figures*, as Marr and Vaina (1982) point out. For instance, in describing the action of walking, the 3D model can specify the angular changes in each of the joints and relate these changes in a temporal framework. Moreover, a rather natural segmentation of actions arises at points in time when joints start or stop changing in angle or when angular change reverses direction. For instance, the swing of a leg in walking is bounded at its beginning and end by points of stasis in the change of angle at the hip joint. (This corresponds nicely to observations of Cutting (1981) on the segmentation of events.) Such specifications can be made only in an object-centered framework, since it is the angular change measured "objectively" at the hip that is significant, not the angular change in the visual field. Thus, not only for object identification but also for the description of action, an object-centered description along the lines of Marr's seems a necessity.

A further move of abstraction permits the 3D level to encode *variations in form among individuals of a common type*. For instance, consider how a long-term representation might encode what horses look like. By allowing a range of permissible sizes, both overall and constituent by constituent, and by specifying ranges of proportions of size among parts, one can arrive at a geometrically parametrized encoding that can be matched with a class of presented objects more variable than a specific individual.

Notice how this conception differs from the widespread hypothesis that one stores a mental image of a stereotypical instance of a category. As often conceived, such an image is of a particular individual—a comparatively rigid template against which putative instances are matched by some unspecified computational process of "judging similarity." By comparison, the 3D model is decompositional and hierarchical and thus capable of greater generality than a rigid template, in that the elaboration of the object into parts can specify proportions and tolerances rather than a single fixed value for the size, shape, and disposition of the parts. (The phenomenon of an experienced *image* of a prototypical instance probably arises in part through fixing typical or focal values for the variable parameters; see the next section and also section 14.5.) Moreover, the 3D model representation is not an arbitrary stipulated representation but one motivated and developed on the grounds of its general adequacy for visual form recognition tasks.

The mention of stereotypes brings us into territory familiar from discussions of linguistic meaning, so we will defer further discussion of this issue to the next chapter.

Turning from the 3D model itself to the correspondence rules, a certain amount of 3D structure can be derived on purely geometric grounds from a fully specified 2½D sketch, since the latter's depth and distance information can readily be translated into object-centered shape information. Much of this is worked out by Ullman (1979). However, many problems remain:

how to infer the shape of hidden portions, how to derive coordinate axes from external shape information, and so on. The important problem of how to decompose complex shapes into parts has been addressed by Hoffman (1983a, b), Hoffman and Richards (1984), and Brady and Asada (1984).

More complex problems arise when the 2½D sketch information is incomplete. One of the best-known illustrations of the difficulties involved is a startling experiment by Johansson (1975). Movies are made in total darkness of people walking or dancing; in these movies the only things visible are small lights placed at the people's joints. Individual frames of these movies look like merely a random collection of white spots against a dark surround. But when viewed in motion, the movies are immediately and convincingly seen as portraying human figures. Evidently the character of the lights' motion is sufficient to induce full three-dimensional form perception, although hardly any local distance and depth information is present in the 2½D sketch. The principles underlying such startlingly good performance by the visual system have been the subject of intensive research; Ullman 1979 is one of the most prominent pieces of work.

To sum up, it should be clear that Marr's theory is at this point far from a complete theory of visual perception, and many details and even basic hypotheses are likely to change with further research. However, Marr's basic insight is that it is crucial to ask what sort of information the visual system delivers before attending to the real-time details of how the information is processed and stored. From this it follows that visual perception must be studied in terms of the formal properties of its levels of representation and the principles of correspondence among them; this methodology is the reason his approach can be integrated into the present study.

For our subsequent purposes, therefore, I will assume that Marr's theory is approximately correct: that there are three levels of visual representation, namely, an encoding of local boundary elements (the primal sketch), a viewer-centered representation of visible surfaces (the 2½D sketch), and an object-centered representation of shape and decomposition into parts (the 3D model). In so assuming, I am not necessarily committing myself to all the precise details of any current formulation. What is important for our purposes is the overall conception of what each level encodes, how the levels interact with each other formally, and how they are to be justified through their usefulness in the overall visual task of form recognition. To reject Marr's theory because of its failure in particular details, as some have done, is analogous to rejecting generative grammar because there is still no completely satisfying account of the passive or because its practitioners are not unanimously in agreement. I should hope that the field could outgrow that sort of dialectic.

9.5 Visual Imagery and the Imagery Debate

One of the most fascinating and controversial lines of experimentation in recent psychology concerns the production and manipulation of visual images, such as one might have in response to an instruction like "Imagine a triangle twisting its way across your visual field." This section will briefly describe some of these results and the debate surrounding a proper account of them; we will then integrate them into the treatment of levels of representation in the visual faculty.

What is surprising (and to some, unsettling) about imagery research is that subjects are given a task that explicitly or implicitly requires them to make use of visual imagery, the subjects indeed report the presence of visual imagery, and their performance on the task varies in a way that strongly correlates with what they say is happening to their image. By lending credence to the commonsense intuition that visual imagery is psychologically significant, this research flies in the face of the bad reputation imagery has had since the turn of the century, when the behaviorists banished talk of introspected images from scientific respectability.

The first and most widely cited of these experiments was conducted by Shepard and Metzler (1971). Subjects were presented with a pair of perspective views of three-dimensional objects and asked to determine whether the objects were identical or mirror images. Figure 9.7 gives a sample of the stimuli. Figure 9.7a depicts two objects that differ by a rotation in the picture plane; the objects in figure 9.7b differ by a rotation in depth (axis parallel to the picture plane); the objects in figure 9.7c are mirror images.

The striking result of this experiment was that subjects' reaction times for "same" judgments varied linearly with the angular difference between the portrayed orientations of the two objects. This linear relation obtained (though with different slopes) for both the picture-plane and the depth rotations. Subjects reported that they were carrying out the task by "mentally rotating" images of the objects in an attempt to bring them into congruence. And in fact the reaction times support the subjects' reports. More particularly, they support the theory that subjects mentally rotate the figures *at constant angular velocity*: the greater the degree of mental rotation necessary to match the figures, the longer the time it takes to judge that a match has been obtained.

A sizable series of experiments, reports of many of which have been collected by Shepard and Cooper (1982), have confirmed these results on mental rotation. For example, Cooper (1976) presented subjects with a figure and instructed them to start mentally rotating it. After a certain time they were presented with another figure to match against their mental image. If the second figure was at an orientation close to that at which

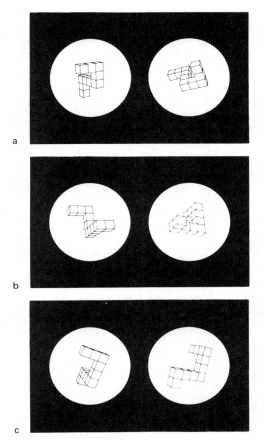

Figure 9.7
Pairs of objects that differ (a) by a rotation in the picture plane, (b) by a rotation in depth, and (c) by a mirror-image reflection as well as a rotation. (Reprinted, by permission, from R. N. Shepard and J. Metzler (1971). Mental rotations of three-dimensional objects. *Science* 171, 701–703. Copyright 1971 by the American Association for the Advancement of Science.)

(according to the theory) the mentally rotating figure should have been at that precise moment, matching was faster than if the orientation of the external figure and the predicted orientation of the internalized figure differed. Adding these results to the hypothesis suggested by Shepard and Metzler's experiment—that comparing figures requires matching in orientation, and that matching in orientation requires time proportional to angular difference—Cooper's experiment shows that reaction times can be affected in exactly the predicted way by *explicitly* instructing subjects to perform mental rotation.

Another series of experiments, performed by Kosslyn and associates and summarized by Kosslyn (1980), concerns the scanning of visual images. Subjects are asked to imagine some object or a previously memorized diagram and to focus on one part of it (for example, they are asked to imagine a dog seen from the side and to focus on its tail). They are then asked to report a property of some other part of the image (for example, are the dog's ears pointed?) or in some cases simply to shift focus to a different part. Over a wide range of different experimental conditions Kosslyn finds that reaction time is linearly related to distance between successive loci of attention in the image. In the example just given, for instance, it would take longer to answer whether the dog's ears are pointed than whether its tail is bushy.

The argument drawn from these experimental results is that there is a type of mental information structure that is roughly *geometric* in character, in terms of which visual images are internally encoded and over which such operations as rotation and scanning can be formally defined. This structure exists as a level independent of the *algebraic* structure in which linguistic meaning is most directly encoded. (Shepard and Cooper call the opposition "analog versus propositional" and Kosslyn calls it "depictive versus descriptive." I deliberately want to avoid the term "propositional" because of the traditional connotations of truth-value it calls up; my reasons should be clear from chapters 7 and 8. Similarly, for many people "analog" seems to call up connotations of noncomputational theories or even computational chaos. So I drop these terms in favor of more neutral terminology.)

In a geometric representation objects are necessarily represented in terms of their shapes and apparent sizes. By contrast, algebraic representations like logic, associative nets, or the conceptual structure of chapter 8 represent an object by means of an arbitrary symbol that has no bearing on its physical appearance. In a geometric representation multiple objects under simultaneous consideration are necessarily spatially related in distance and orientation. But in an algebraic representation x *is to the left of y* is altogether parallel in formal character to, say, x *possesses y* or x *has a desire for y*: it is a formal relation between a pair of symbols. Finally, in a geometric representation one can define a uniform notion of distance that can be measured directly *between any two points*; hence, an indefinitely large number of distances can be read off the representation (disregarding for the moment the graininess of the representation). By contrast, in an algebraic representation one can only list some finite number of stipulated distances ("Point A is x units from point B") or compute new ones by trigonometric principles such as the Pythagorean theorem.

Shepard et al. sum up these characteristics by saying that the geometric representation stands in a "functional isomorphism" to Euclidean space. It is not that images take up physical space in the head in the way objects take up physical space in the world; rather, the representations of distance and relative location in images are structurally parallel to those in the representations of visually perceived configurations of objects.

Kosslyn goes beyond this claim to explore the properties of the mental medium in which visual images can subsist. He supposes that there is an "image buffer," a part of working memory in which images are constructed. Since this buffer must be limited to a finite number of neurons, it must represent only a finite amount of information. Hence, images can be neither indefinitely large in apparent size nor indefinitely fine in detail. In a series of experiments that ask subjects to expand and shrink visual images, he shows that images can "overflow" the visual buffer ("Imagine walking closer and closer to an elephant. How close are you before you cannot see the whole thing anymore?") and that the visual field available for images subtends a measurable visual angle. He also finds that it is more difficult, and takes longer, to discern very small details of images than large ones. This suggests that there is a grain of resolution, smaller than which discriminable representation is impossible. Moreover, he finds that the grain is finer near the center of the image buffer than toward the periphery, paralleling the resolution of the visual field in perception. Since such properties could not follow from an algebraic representation but are a *consequence* of assuming a neurally instantiated geometric representation, Kosslyn argues that these results are strong evidence for his theory of imagery.

A number of objections have arisen to the hypothesis that a geometric representation underlies the computations of visual imagery. Perhaps its most persistent opponent has been Pylyshyn (1973, 1981, 1984). Most of his objections stem from the question, Why posit two distinct representations, if the algebraic one is independently necessary and in fact can do all the computational work required of the geometric one? In particular, (1) the algebraic representation is required to express one's conceptual understanding of images (see chapter 10). Moreover, (2) in manipulating images of physical objects, one makes use of one's tacit knowledge of how physical objects behave, knowledge that Pylyshyn presupposes to be conceptual (or propositional in his terms). Finally, (3) the manipulation of images must be performed computationally, and indeed Kosslyn's computer model of image rotation reverts to a series of tiny discrete digital steps. But if image representation is ultimately discrete, why can't image representation be just a fine-grained version of conceptual representation? In short, Pylyshyn claims that all characteristics of images can be described propositionally, so there is no argument for a separate representation. Among other important critics, Dennett (1969) presents a variety of arguments along the general lines of argument (1), and Anderson (1978) presents an argument that elaborates Pylyshyn's argument (3).

Since part of my goal is to clarify the methodology behind a theory of levels of representation, it is enlightening to compare these arguments with a dispute that raged in linguistics during the late 1960s and early 1970s. The issue was whether syntactic structure and semantic structure are to be considered distinct levels of representation. Postal (1972), representing the "generative semantics" school, argues that the best theory is the one with the fewest components; therefore, on a priori grounds a single level of representation combining syntax and semantics is preferable to two levels that make these phenomena distinct. Chomsky (1972), representing "interpretive semantics," concedes that indeed one can take any semantic phenomenon and simulate it in the syntax—just as Anderson (1978) shows that one can simulate any image phenomenon propositionally. But, Chomsky continues, the crucial scientific issue is not how to describe the bare facts with the most parsimonious machinery but how to describe *the generalizations and the restrictions* on the facts with the most parsimonious machinery—that is, to explain why the facts come out as they do and not some other conceivable way. Thus, if the facts cluster into two distinct types, each of which can be described by a rather restrictive theory, and if a single-component theory that subsumes them both predicts a wide range of additional possibilities that in fact do not exist, the two-component theory is to be preferred.

Just as Chomsky argues on explanatory grounds for the separation of levels of syntax and semantics, Shepard, Cooper, and Kosslyn effectively argue for the distinction between algebraic and geometric levels. The main point is that although one can, through a variety of strategems, derive reaction time data from a purely propositional theory, they are a natural consequence—a prediction—of the two-level theory. Kosslyn even demonstrates a clear split in reaction time paradigms, depending on whether or not imagery is used to answer a question: one branch of the split conforms to the image-scanning time results, the other conforms to the usual propositional association-strength results. Thus, there seem to be two quite distinct phenomena, each with characteristic properties. A purely propositional theory that does not distinguish them will have to include as well too many other nonexistent possibilities to be of much empirical force. (In fact, Anderson (1983) begins to realize this and admits into his theory a distinct form for image representations.)

A second answer to these objections, suggested by Shepard and Judd (1976), Waltz (1979), Pinker (1984b), Finke (1986) and (to a lesser extent than one might expect) Kosslyn (1980), is that the machinery for the representation of visual imagery is independently necessary for visual perception. In order for us to talk about what we see, there has to be a way for retinal arrays to be translated ultimately into conceptual form, and along the way geometric levels of representation are pretty much a necessity. In fact, the content of Kosslyn's image buffer bears a strong resemblance to Marr's 2½D sketch; and, although Kosslyn never works in three dimensions, his form for long-term storage of image information— particularly its decomposition into parts—bears a strong resemblance to the hierarchical organization of Marr's 3D model.

In support of this interpretation of Kosslyn, consider the rotations in depth of Shepard et al. (for instance, figure 9.7b). In the course of these rotations, the shapes of the figures and their parts in the images change radically. To explain the understood shape constancy of the images, there-fore, it seems necessary to posit a three-dimensional shape-invariant repre-sentation on which rotations are performed and from which the "visible" surfaces are derived. Again this corresponds nicely with Marr's distinction between 2½D and 3D structures in visual perception.

Shepard and Judd (1976) argue furthermore that the rotational trans-formations performed on images are precisely those that are involved in the phenomenon of *apparent rotational motion* in perception. For instance, if the two shapes in figure 9.7b are presented in alternation, with the proper time interval between them, the result is seen as a rigid object rocking back and forth. The proper time interval, in turn, depends on the angular differ-ence between the two orientations, in direct correlation with the image-rotation results. Thus, the very same computation appears to be used both in perception and in imagery. More generally, image operations such as rotation, scanning, and zooming may be seen as "visual inference rules"— principles for deriving (or anticipating) one visual representation from another.

This sort of consideration completely undermines any sort of argument from parsimony. It also undermines arguments from tacit knowledge and the use of conceptual structure. For on the one hand, the 3D model contains more structure than either Pylyshyn or Kosslyn is wont to attri-bute to it: the formation rules for this level in effect encode a great deal of our tacit knowledge of space and how objects behave in space. And on the other hand, to the extent that conceptual (algebraic) knowledge plays a role in visual understanding, it obviously can play the same role in imagery. Thus, the argument is turned on its head: in order to argue against a geometric representation for imagery, one must argue that there is no geometric representation in perception either—an argument unlikely to be persuasive.

The view of visual imagery that emerges from these considerations is that it can be regarded as a sort of analogue of language production. In visual perception the visual system is activated by external input at its lower end, producing a sequence of representations that include a primal sketch, a 2½D sketch, and a 3D model. In imagery, on the other hand, the visual system is activated from the upper end, by input from conceptual structure or the 3D model, and it produces at least a 2½D sketch and possibly lower representations. The difference between vision and language is that for language we have an organ that can externalize low-level representation: the vocal tract. However, "visual production" is arrested somewhere down the line from the 2½D sketch for lack of an output device. If we had, say, little TV screens on our foreheads, so we could communicate visual thinking, the parallel with language would be complete. (Lacking that, we do sometimes use drawing or gesturing to partly make up the deficit.)

To sum up our discussion of visual information structure, we have seen that the visual faculty resembles the language faculty in its organization. Marr's theory claims that the information structure for visual form recognition is a chain of three levels of representation beyond the retinal array, each with its own characteristic primitives and principles of combination, and each linked with the next level up by a set of correspondence rules. Only at the highest level, the 3D model, does the notion of "physical object" play a role. Like the levels of linguistic structure, the visual levels are (at least down to the 2½D sketch) bidirectional: they function either in perception or in imagery, which is a partial analogue of language production.

9.6 Remarks on Visual Processing

The parallel in the overall organization of visual and linguistic information structures leads us to look for parallels as well in the general organization of their processing. Because the content of the information in the two faculties is so vastly different, we should probably not expect very detailed similarities, but it is worth pursuing similarities that arise specifically from the division into levels of representation. This section will lay out the issues and provide some evidence; I leave it to others better versed than I in experimental literature to fill in the many gaps (or enlarge them, as the case may be).

The general layout of the levels of representation in visual perception and

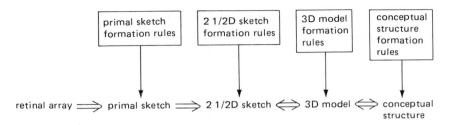

Figure 9.8
Overall organization of levels of visual representation

visual understanding is sketched in figure 9.8; this parallels figure 6.1, the diagram of linguistic levels. Each double arrow stands for a set of correspondence rules between a pair of levels; the two on the right are double-headed to indicate their use in imagery as well as perception. Each of these sets of rules may decompose further into logically separate components, as suggested for the primal-to-2½D mapping sketched in figure 9.5. The connection to conceptual structure, already alluded to a number of times, will be discussed in some detail in the next chapter; for now let us take it for granted.

As in the language faculty, this organization has a strong implication for the possible flow of information in the course of processing:

Logical Structure of Visual Processing (LSVP)
Translation of visual information from one level to another must follow the correspondences in figure 9.8, involving intermediate levels of translation where necessary.

Because of this logical decomposition of visual processing, it is possible to divide the functions of visual processing into autonomous processors as we did in the language faculty (see (6.5)–(6.7)).

(9.1)   Bottom-up processors
  a. Transduction of light into retinal information
  b. Mapping of available retinal information into primal sketch format
  c. Mapping of available primal sketch information into 2½D format (decomposes further as in figure 9.5)
  d. Mapping of available 2½D information into 3D format
  e. Mapping of available 3D information into conceptual format

(9.2)   Top-down processors
  a. Mapping of available conceptual information into 3D format
  b. Mapping of available 3D information into 2½D format

(9.3)   Integrative processors

    a. Integration of newly available primal sketch information into unified primal sketch

    b. Integration of newly available 2½D sketch information into unified 2½D sketch

    c. Integration of newly available 3D information into unified 3D model

    d. Integration of newly available conceptual infomation into unified conceptual structure (= component (6.7c))

The crucial components here, as in the language faculty, are the integrative processors: they make it possible for different processors to provide information to a single level of representation. For instance, information from the primal sketch is translated into 2½D sketch format by a number of autonomous processors dealing with stereopsis, texture gradients, structure from motion, and so on, as sketched in figure 9.5. It is the integrative processor for the 2½D level (9.3b) that puts all this heterogeneous information together into a unified structure. Moreover, during visual imagery the very same component receives information in 2½D format that has been translated from 3D structure by component (9.2b).

Similar bidirectionality emerges at the 3D model level. In visual perception information is translated into this level by component (9.1d) and is integrated by component (9.3c). If one then wishes to talk about what one sees, this 3D information can be passed on to conceptual structure via component (9.1e) and from there to the language faculty. On the other hand, when one produces visual imagery in response to spoken instructions, conceptual information derived from the language faculty is translated into 3D format by component (9.2a) and maintained and integrated by (9.3c). In short, the integrative processors do not care where they get their information, as long as it is already in the right format; they take whatever comes and make out of it as coherent a representation as they can.

Again as in the language faculty, this arrangement of processors allows for the possibility of feedback. In perception top-down information from the 3D level, translated by processor (9.2b), can play a role in formation of the 2½D sketch; the 2½D integrative processor can combine this with information that has come up from the primal sketch. Similarly, conceptual information can play a top-down role in formation of the 3D model, via processor (9.2a); this information might even be passed further down to the 2½D sketch via processor (9.2b). Such top-down effects would parallel the effects of semantics on phonological structure in language perception.

It is generally acknowledged that top-down effects of *some* sort exist in visual perception: what we see is in part affected by what we know about the world and what we expect to see. For instance, an auto mechanic sees more than I do under the hood of a car—more separate parts and more relationships among them. (And the experience is of *seeing*, not of thinking about linguistic descriptions of the visual field.) Just as in the case of language, the empirical problem is to find the general extent of top-down effects: what kind of higher-level information can contribute to visual perception, how novelty can be perceived in the face of expectations, and so forth. For now this is not my problem.

In the lore Marr is often criticized for adopting a strictly bottom-up approach to visual perception, excluding the kinds of top-down processes advocated here. My reading, though, is that he is trying to find how much information can be derived by bottom-up processes before appeal must be made to top-down information. This is partly in reaction to excessively top-down approaches to computer vision ("If it's a black blob at about desk level, it's likely to be a telephone") and in response to phenomena like Julesz's stereograms, which cannot appeal to "higher-level" knowledge. In point of fact, Marr clearly acknowledges the need for top-down information (see Marr 1982, 100–101, 287, 351), and he sees the 2½D sketch as "the end of pure autonomous [that is, bottom-up] perception..." (p. 351). The present approach follows Marr's view: in the course of processing, higher-level information can pass down into the 2½D sketch and be integrated there, but it is passed down no further. (This still ignores, of course, the effects of eye movements, which, like auditory feedback in speech production, provide a kind of feedback at even the very lowest levels.)

Given this treatment of feedback in perception, it follows that the same processors ought to be used for visual perception and imagery. As mentioned in the last section, Shepard and Judd (1976) show that at least similar if not the same processes are used for rotation of images and apparent rotation in perception. In addition, Farah (1984) cites neurological evidence that various defects in imagery due to brain damage are accompanied by parallel deficits in perception. So preliminary results on the bidirectionality of the processors are encouraging.

All of this leads to a position on short-term visual memory (STVM) similar to that for short-term linguistic memory. Paralleling the arguments of sections 6.6–6.8, STVM should be seen as a device that creates and maintains several levels of visually relevant representation—at least 2½D sketch, 3D model, and conceptual structure. STVM can be activated by input from lower levels in the case of perception, or by conceptual input in the case of imagery; whichever the source of activation, a full set of levels is created.

Moreover, these levels are kept *in registration* with each other, in the same sense that the linguistic levels are. In the case of perception this is suggested by the perceptual stability of the world in the face of constant eye movements. Eye movements have the effect of shifting everything across the retina and thus across the primal sketch and $2\frac{1}{2}$D sketch as well. Yet the 3D model remains stable and connected to the $2\frac{1}{2}$D sketch—we do not have to reidentify objects after we have shifted our gaze. This would be easiest to accomplish computationally if the instructions directing eye movements were correlated with the registration between the $2\frac{1}{2}$D sketch and the 3D model, so that translation of the eye would be accompanied by compensatory alteration of the registration function. Without registration everything would have to be computed all over again.

In imagery a more direct case can be presented for registration. Recall that during the in-depth rotation of Shepard and Metzler's figures in figure 9.7b, various faces of the figures disappear and others appear over time. If the rotation were carried out on the $2\frac{1}{2}$D sketch alone, there would be no source for the newly visible faces. Only by maintaining the $2\frac{1}{2}$D sketch in registration with a full 3D model can the newly visible faces be immediately available. Kosslyn (1980) points out a similar problem with the motion of large images that overflow the field ("Imagine an elephant walking by you from left to right at a distance of two feet"). Only part of the figure is present in the image buffer at any one time, and new parts keep appearing on the left while other parts go out of view on the right. There has to be an underlying source for the newly visible parts, which Kosslyn attributes to the long-term memory representation (here, the 3D model). He explicitly includes in his model a registration function called the "inverse mapping function" (Kosslyn 1980, section 2.3) that keeps the image and the underlying representation in step.

An important part of short-term linguistic memory was the selection function (section 6.8), which in the case of ambiguous representations selected one as most salient. Recall that the preliminary motivation for the selection function came from ambiguous visual figures, which present only one interpretation to awareness at a time. It was argued that the selection function for language is not carried out by a "higher cognitive capacity" such as consciousness or attention but instead is part of the language processor itself. Can the same be said of the visual selection function?

The evidence in language concerned the fact that selection in local environments and on low-level information goes on all the time in language perception. Selection in the case of a globally ambiguous sentence is therefore just the limiting case where no extrinsic evidence is available for choosing between alternative structures.

The same appears to be the case in vision. Figure 9.9 shows an example of a type common in the literature of Gestalt theory. Figure 9.9a is most likely seen either as six horizontal rows of circles arranged diagonally or as three diagonal rows of circles arranged horizontally. Figure 9.9b is most likely seen either as six vertical rows of circles arranged diagonally or as

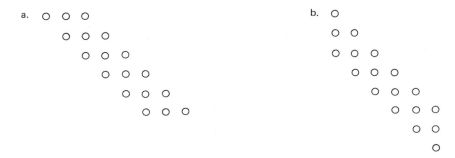

Figure 9.9
Two configurations that differ only in the placement of two circles at the extremities, but are seen as having quite different organization

three diagonal rows of circles arranged vertically. But the middle portions of both figures are identical—only the leftmost and rightmost circles in figure 9.9a need be moved to change the figure into figure 9.9b. Thus, a selection function has operated on the fully ambiguous interiors of the figures to make their interpretations consistent with the borders. Marr (1982, 141–144) discusses a similar effect produced in random-dot stereograms by Julesz and Chang (1976); here the selection evidently involves the mapping from primal sketch to 2½D sketch—hardly a "higher-level cognitive function." Thus, local selection must be going on in STVM in order to make perception globally consistent.

And even in the switching of fully ambiguous figures, the lower levels and their registration with upper levels must be implicated. For instance, in the vase-faces illusion the choice between "vase" and "faces," a conceptual distinction, correlates with a difference in the orientation of boundaries in the 2½D sketch (see appendix B). If there is a "higher cognitive function" that carries out selection, then it must be a function that has access to the details of lower-level representations and their registration with higher levels. It makes more sense to attribute selection to the capacity specifically devoted to these representations, namely, short-term visual memory itself—particularly since STVM is performing precursors of selection in any event.

The only role left for "higher cognitive functions," then, is that of willfully creating internal contexts that bias the selection function toward one interpretation or the other. Such actions will have the feel of "consciously switching" from one interpretation to the other on demand, but the actual computational work that needs to be performed on visual representations outside of STVM is minimal.

To sum up, the description of the visual capacity in terms of levels of representation has led to a view of visual processing similar to that of language processing. Insofar as evidence is available, it supports a bidirectional, highly modular, interactive system. At the same time the theory leaves enough room for empirically determined limitations on processing, such as the ultimate extent of top-down effects in perception, and for incorporating additional effects such as eye movements. Correlating the predictions of this approach with the vast literature on visual perception, however, is a job I hope someone else will take on.

Chapter 10

The Connection between Language and Vision

10.1 Preliminary Correspondences

As mentioned in section 7.2, one of the fundamental problems for a theory of natural language appears as the title of John Macnamara's (1978) paper: "How Do We Talk about What We See?" In order to approach this problem, a point of connection must be found between the theory of language and the theory of vision. Following Marr, we have so far spoken of the 3D model primarily as the culmination of visual processing and the locus of visual form recognition, only hinting at its connection to conceptual structure and thence to language. This chapter develops the relationship between language and vision more explicitly and shows that their connection not only helps answer Macnamara's question but also solves certain outstanding problems in both areas.

Within an information-processing theory of mind it is not enough to say that we talk about what we see by transferring information (or representations) from visual memory into linguistic memory. The heart of the problem, as Macnamara recognized, is one of *translation*: in order for us to talk about what we see, information provided by the visual system must be translated into a form compatible with the information used by the language system. The essential questions are these: (1) What form(s) of information does the visual system derive? (2) What form of information serves as input to speech? (3) How can the former be translated into the latter?

The importance of establishing a formal translation between visual and linguistic information cannot be overestimated: it makes possible for the first time a theory whose levels of representation extend all the way from the retinal image through the core of thought out to the vocal tract. The levels of linguistic representation therefore need not back up indefinitely into murkier and murkier central representations, nor does linguistic theory have to appeal to a mysterious direct connection of "intentionality" with the external world. Rather, the computational theory will itself provide all the necessary links for describing how we talk about what we see. It will thus be able to relate mental representations to an important part of the "world of non-symbols," in the sense discussed in chapter 7.

Within the present framework the translation between language and vision should be specified by a set of correspondence rules between one or more visual levels and one or more linguistic levels. Ideally, the two faculties should interact via those representations whose units come into closest correspondence and whose functions are most closely related.

Under this basic criterion the most appropriate levels to link appear to be conceptual structure and the 3D model. Of all the levels we have examined, it is only these two that encode the notion of *physical object*—though in quite different fashions, to be sure. In linking these levels, our first principle of correspondence can therefore relate 3D constituents that encode objects to conceptual constituents that encode objects; there is no other pair of levels over which this essential relation could be stated.

Another important correspondence that can be established immediately is in the encoding of the conceptual relation of *part-whole* or *inalienable possession*. This relation has always been one of the staples of linguistic semantics; Marr's hierarchical theory of the 3D model allows it to be spelled out explicitly in spatial terms (recall the discussion of the human body shown in figure 9.6). Basically, for physical objects X and Y, X IS A PART OF Y obtains in conceptual structure just in case the 3D model corresponding to X is an elaboration within the hierarchical 3D model corresponding to Y.

A third basic correspondence arises in the functions that Marr considers central to the 3D model: object identification (that thing before me is a known individual, say, Rover) and object categorization (that thing before me is of a known type, say, a dog). As discussed in section 8.1, the linguistic level that performs similar functions is conceptual structure. Again a good first hypothesis is that, in order to capture the relationship of visual and conceptual categorization, the 3D model and conceptual structure are the right levels to link. We return to these functions in section 10.3.

10.2 The 3D Model as a Central Representation

Before exploring the connection between the 3D model and conceptual structure, let us establish the overall role of the 3D model in the computational mind by briefly noting some other uses to which it might be put.

First, one can identify the shapes of objects not only by looking at them but also by handling them—so-called *haptic* perception. This suggests that the 3D model notions of physical object, shape, and contour are shared between the visual and haptic modalities. However, the haptic route to the 3D model is informationally distinct from the visual route. It certainly does not make use of anything like the primal sketch, which encodes local boundary segments in the retinal field. And although haptic perception is likely to involve some integrated representation of "touchable" surfaces, such a representation must be adapted to the shape and mobility of the hand rather than to the eye-centered coordinate system of the 2½D sketch. Thus, the primal and 2½D sketches, concerned with the recovery of shape information from a retinal image, are proprietary to the visual system and are not part of the haptic system. The parallel haptic levels will have to deal with recovering shape information from touch and pressure sensors in the skin. Through faculty-specific correspondence rules, both systems converge on a common representation of shape, the 3D model; this is what enables one to identify the same object by sight or by touch.

Next consider what is probably the most important use of information derived from the visual system: to help us find our way around in the world. From an evolutionary point of view this use is prior to the linguistic connection, since it is shared by nonlinguistic organisms. The eventual scope of the 3D model envisioned by Marr includes not just individual objects but the full spatial layout of the perceived world; we will be pursuing suitable extensions in section 10.5. Given such extensions, it is easy to imagine using the 3D model as an *input level for the capacity for physical action*: this level encodes what there is in the environment for the organism to approach or avoid, as the case may be.

Among the objects in the environment, of course, is one's own body. In order to compute what to do with one's body in order to act in the environment, one must have information about the spatial layout and motion of one's limbs and a sense of one's position and motion as a whole with respect to other objects in the environment. The 3D decomposition in figure 9.6 of the human body provides a natural way of encoding this information.

However, in the case of this particular object one has a privileged set of sensory cues that exist for no other object in the environment. Touch and pressure cues from the skin provide evidence about the direction and magnitude of forces (including gravity and acceleration) on the body; the semicircular canals in the ears provide evidence about rotation of the head in various directions; sensors in the muscles and joints provide information about the position of the limbs. In addition, one has visual cues from observation of the visible parts of the body.

Despite this plethora of sensory cues there is in awareness an essentially unified sense of one's spatial position and motion—one cannot consciously dissociate the sources of one's position sense. A series of experiments by James Lackner and associates (Lackner and Levine 1978; Lackner and Graybiel 1983, 1984; Lackner and DiZio 1984; Lackner and Taublieb 1984; Lackner 1981, 1984, 1985) has shown that all these sources play a role in the position sense and that they interact strongly with each other. For instance, one can elicit in a subject an illusory sensation of arm movement by mechanically vibrating the biceps muscle while the arm is restrained. A subject watching his arm under such conditions visually experiences it as being in motion. However, watching the arm turns out to reduce the magnitude of illusory experienced motion, indicating that the visual and proprioceptive cues partially cancel each other out when there is a conflict. Lackner et al. find similar interactions between all combinations of cues for position sense.

In addition, a part of position sense that we more or less take for granted is the sense of the *size* and *shape* of our bodies. Lackner et al. have created illusions of change of size and shape as well as position. For instance, if a finger is placed on the nose and then the arm is subjected to illusory extension as above, one senses one's nose growing longer! Under various other conditions the legs seem to grow longer, the finger seems to be detached from the hand, or one seems to have multiple arms. Evidently the cues from position and motion must be integrated into a unified and consistent representation of the body. Under illusory conditions there is give and take among the various sources of information, resulting in a more or less self-consistent but anomalous perception of the body, with no conscious sensation regarding which sensory modality is providing which cues.

The usual story applies here. In order for information from a variety of sources to interact, there must be a common format into which all the sources of information are translated. The appropriate integrative level for the position sense would seem to be the 3D model, whose primitives of size, shape, and relative position of parts are well suited for the purpose. Thus, it is possible to envision a whole series of mappings from the different sensory sources to the 3D model of one's own body—a part of this level of representation that is specialized in terms of sources of information but that differs not at all in its formal structure as such.

More speculatively, notice that organisms such as bats and dolphins that use echolocation (sonar) to find their way around may have still another connection to the 3D structure, through that modality. Again, the lower levels of information structure that lead up to the 3D model in echolocation will be distinct from those for vision and touch. (Alternatively, this capacity might merge with vision at the $2\frac{1}{2}$D sketch, since it does provide a viewer-centered image of sorts. I don't know at this point how one could tell the difference, but in principle it should be an empirically decidable question.)

The overall hypothesis that emerges from these considerations is that the 3D model, like conceptual structure, is one of the central interface languages of the computational mind. It is a general-purpose representation for all tasks involving spatial cognition, and language, vision, touch, action, and the body senses can all influence it and make use of it.

It is interesting to consider some consequences of such a hypothesis. For one thing, it says that the spatial information encoded by the blind, at its most central level of representation, is of the same nature—uses the same primitives and principles of combination—as spatial information available to the sighted. Furthermore, the way this information is put to use in finding one's way about in the world is the same. This is not to say that the same wealth of spatial information is available at any moment or even in toto to the blind, because of the inherent limitations of the haptic channel of input. But all such notions as object, distance, angle, trajectory, and so forth that play a role in spatial perception will be useable and derivable—not via the route of primal and 2½D sketches but via as yet unknown lower levels of representations specialized to the haptic capacity. (See Landau, Spelke, and Gleitman 1984 for confirming evidence.)

Of course, not all aspects of the 3D model need be equally available to all the capacities with which it exchanges information. For instance, color information is brought into the 3D model via the visual system, and it is available to conceptual structure. However, it obviously plays no role in the haptic or action systems; their correspondence rules are entirely silent on the translation of color information. (If we could somehow discern colors by touch, the story would be different.)

This raises a converse question: Is there spatial information supplied by touch that is unavailable to vision? Two candidates might be temperature and weight. How such properties might be formally integrated into a spatial representation remains open, though they need not present any more inherent difficulties than color.

It has sometimes been suggested to me that instead of Marr's 3D model serving general spatial cognition, one might reserve the 3D model specifically for visual cognition and introduce a separate amodal representation for space, fed by the 3D model and all the other sensory faculties. Note, however, that this would not change in any way the overall hypothesis of a level of spatial representation as a central level of cognition; it would only add an extra way station in the visual system.

In fact, at the moment I see no justification for the move. The essential primitives of the 3D model involve shape, contour, and motion; the essential principles of combination involve building up objects from parts. These are likewise essential for the haptic sense, for the body position sense, and, for that matter, for echolocation. What different primitives might be justifiably introduced for the supposed new level is altogether obscure. Even if each of these faculties contributes a subset of proprietary vocabulary in the 3D model (for example, color or weight), that does not negate their fundamental unity of formal structure. So for now there seems no point in an extra level.

10.3 Visual Identification and Categorization

We now come back to the central topic of the chapter, the interplay between the 3D model and conceptual structure.

Recall that Marr designed the 3D model level to encode long-term memory information suitable for either object *identification* or object *categorization*. But now let us ask, How is the long-term memory for a known individual distinguished from that for a known category? So far the two are not distinguished in formal structure—they are both 3D models—so what makes the difference?

One's first impulse is to claim that memories of individuals and memories of categories differ in vagueness or generality, individuals being much more specific. But this will not do. One may be vague about the appearance of a slightly known individual—say, the car that hit mine and sped off into the night—and therefore encode it rather imprecisely in memory; on the other hand, one may be very knowledgeable about the appearance of an extremely delimited category—say, IBM PC keyboards—and therefore encode it in great detail and specificity.

Further reflection suggests that in fact there are *no* features of the 3D model, which is purely geometric in conception, that can distinguish representations of individuals from representations of categories. For example, the 3D models for the individual "my dog Rover" and for the category "dogs that look just like Rover" are necessarily identical, because of the way the category is defined. What is needed to distinguish the two kinds of representations is in fact the binary [TYPE/TOKEN] feature of *conceptual* structure, an *algebraic* form of representation. Only an algebraic structure can provide the proper sort of distinct two-way opposition.

Let me be more precise. The claim is that visual memory contains not just 3D representations but matched pairs of representations: a 3D model for how the thing looks and a conceptual structure that "annotates" the visual representation, specifying at least whether this is taken as a representation of a token or a type. The visual forms given by *perception* are automatically linked to the [TOKEN] feature in conceptual structure: that is, what one directly sees consists of particular individuals. On the other hand, what one *learns* and stores in memory can be linked either with [TOKEN] (if one is remembering an individual) or with [TYPE] (if one has learned a category).

Now consider the relation between the individual being perceived and the remembered individual or category. The two 3D model representations must be juxtaposed and compared, and the outcome of the matching process must be recorded. (This is the "Höffding step" of classical perception theory; see Neisser 1967.) But the outcome of a match cannot be represented visually: it is basically of the form "successful match" or "un-

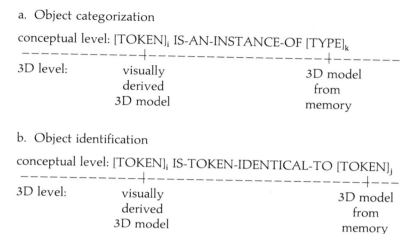

a. Object categorization

conceptual level: [TOKEN]$_i$ IS-AN-INSTANCE-OF [TYPE]$_k$

———————————+——————————————————+———————

3D level: visually   3D model

                                   derived   from

                            3D model   memory

b. Object identification

conceptual level: [TOKEN]$_i$ IS-TOKEN-IDENTICAL-TO [TOKEN]$_j$

———————————+————————————————————————+———

3D level: visually   3D model

                                   derived   from

                            3D model   memory

Figure 10.1

The roles of conceptual structure and the 3D model in (a) object categorization and (b) object identification

successful match." It can, however, be encoded in conceptual structure. A successful match in object categorization is encoded conceptually by our old friend IS-AN-INSTANCE-OF (section 8.1), an algebraic relation between a [TOKEN] and a [TYPE]. Object identification is encoded by a different relation, which may be called IS-TOKEN-IDENTICAL-TO, a relation between two [TOKEN] concepts. The overall form of the two relations is given in figure 10.1; the vertical lines indicate associations or linkages between representations at the two levels. Note that the 3D model part of the judgment is exactly the same in both cases: the comparison of a structure derived from vision with one from memory. The only difference between identification and categorization, then, lies in the conceptual level.

The notion of paired 3D and conceptual structures helps solve another, more often recognized problem concerning the visual encoding of categories of *actions*. The need for such categories has cropped up occasionally in the literature. For instance, Marr and Vaina (1982) discuss how a few "basic action types" such as throwing, saluting, and walking can be defined in terms of sequences of motions of body parts in the 3D model. Peterson (1985) suggests that there is a class of "natural actions" described by verbs like *throw* and *push*, analogous to "natural kinds" like *dog* and *banana*. Like natural kinds, natural actions are learned by ostension ("This is what it looks like") more than by definition. Moreover, section 8.4 observed that we can point to actions ("Can you do *that*?"), concluding that action information must be provided by the visual system.

How are action categories to be encoded? The problem goes back in its essence at least to the British empiricists. The visual representation of the action of walking, for example, requires by its very nature a walking *figure*—say, a generalized human. But then, what is to make it clear that this is a representation of *walking* rather than of *human*? The requisite distinction is simply not available in the geometric representation. However, it *is* available in conceptual structure, where we have the algebraically structured features that distinguish major ontological categories (section 8.4). By linking the 3D figure in motion to an [ACTION TYPE] concept rather than an [OBJECT TYPE] concept, we can encode the fact that the motion of the figure rather than its shape is taken as the significant information in the 3D model. Thus, a linkage of 3D and conceptual structures again provides the right range of distinctions.

10.4 The Use of 3D Models in Word Meanings

We have just seen that the visual system must make use of the level of conceptual structure in encoding long-term memories of individuals and categories. In this section we will see that language likely makes use of the 3D model in encoding distinctions among word meanings. This will reinforce the view of conceptual structure and the 3D model as partners in central representation.

First, there are distinctions of meaning among words that appear to be spelled out far more naturally in terms of spatial structure than in terms of conceptual structure. A good example (brought to my attention by Thomas Kuhn) is distinguishing among ducks, geese, and swans. In conceptual structure it is quite natural to make a taxonomy of these types, such that they are distinct from one another and together form a larger type "waterfowl," itself a subtype of birds. But how are the differences among these types to be expressed? Clearly, one of the most salient differences, and the one by which an individual is normally classified into one or the other of these categories, is how ducks, geese, and swans *look*—their relative sizes and the proportions and shapes of their respective parts.

Now the idea that these differences are represented in conceptual structure by features like [±LONG NECK] is implausible, because the features seem so ad hoc. Yet these have been the sorts of features to which descriptive semanticists have had to resort, for lack of anything better. (One suspects, in fact, that the evident need for such bizarre features is one of the major factors contributing to the suspicion with which lexical semantics has often been regarded.) However, notice that descriptions of size, proportion, and shape of parts, being purely geometric notions, are quite naturally expressed in the 3D model, which must include them in any event in order to accomplish object recognition. This suggests that conceptual structure may be divested of a large family of ad hoc descriptive features by encoding such information in 3D model format, where it is not ad hoc at all but precisely what this level of representation is designed to do.

An immediate implication is that *the representation of a word in long-term memory need not be just a triple of partial phonological, syntactic, and conceptual structures but may contain a partial 3D model structure as well*. From a different angle, a word for a spatial concept may be thought of as appending syntactic and phonological structures to a language-independent spatial concept, itself built from a linkup of conceptual and 3D structures.

This conclusion reflects the intuition that knowing the meaning of a word that denotes a physical object involves in part knowing what such an object looks like. It is the present theory's counterpart of the view that one's lexical entry may contain an image of a stereotypical instance. However, as observed in section 9.4, the 3D model provides a much more coherent account of what lies behind such an intuition than does a rigid "picture-in-the-head" notion of stereotype, allowing it to play a more interesting role in a formal lexical semantics.

Not only nouns benefit from 3D model representations. For instance, a group of verbs such as *walk, run, jog, lope,* and *sprint* differ from each other in much the same way as *duck, goose,* and *swan*. It is embarrassing even to consider a set of binary algebraic features that will distinguish them. However, since the 3D model level can encode actions, it can naturally provide the relevant distinctions in gait and speed as a part of the verbs' lexical entries.

Going further afield, consider *functional* definitions, which pick out objects that one can use in a certain way. For instance, an important component of the concept of *chair* is that it is something to sit in. How can this be encoded? Sitting is a "natural action," specifiable by an [ACTION TYPE] linked to a 3D model of what sitting looks like. The chair, in turn, can be specified as an auxiliary character in the action: it is the surface upon which the acting figure comes to rest. In the 3D model its appearance can be specified very coarsely, giving only its approximate size and the crucial horizontal surface that the figure makes contact with. Thus, as Vaina (1983) points out, a functional definition can be encoded by linking a particular object in a 3D action description with an [OBJECT TYPE] in conceptual structure—the 3D model encodes what one does with the object, plus only enough of the object's appearance to show how one does it.

Although the formal niceties of such word meanings are yet to be worked out, I think it is possible to see the germ of an important descriptive advance here. By using linkages of 3D models with conceptual structure, one can begin to circumvent the limitations of the purely algebraic systems to which semantics has been largely confined and at the same time begin to see how language can make contact with the world as perceived.

This is not to say that *all* elements of linguistic meaning are conveyed by 3D models. Far from it. The essential algebraic features described in chapter 8 have been shown to be necessary even for *visual* memory, much less language. Moreover, such aspects of meaning as negation and quantification are fundamentally conceptual and cannot be translated into a 3D model. And of course there are plenty of words that express auditory, social, and theoretical concepts, for which no 3D counterpart should be expected. The point is only that when language has an opportunity to exploit the expressive power of the 3D model, it does so, and hence that one should expect words for spatial concepts to exhibit characteristically geometric distinctions as well as algebraic.

10.5 Enriching the Conceptual-3D Connection

If the 3D model is to be the component of the visual system most directly responsible for our ability to talk about what we see, it must be rich enough in expressive power to provide *all the visual distinctions that we can express in language*. (It may of course be even richer—there may be further 3D model distinctions that are not expressible in language but that play a demonstrable role in spatial cognition or the capacity for action.)

This section will use evidence from language to suggest some natural enrichments of Marr's theory. These will help extend the 3D model beyond the description of individual objects and actions to a description of the full spatial array. The evidence comes from the sorts of sentences concerning spatial location and motion discussed in section 8.5.

It has often been noted (Gruber 1965; Clark and Chase 1972; Miller and Johnson-Laird 1976; Jackendoff 1976; Talmy 1983; Langacker 1986) that spatial relationships between two objects are pretty much never expressed symmetrically in language. Rather, the language usually distinguishes two roles: a landmark or reference object, which often appears as the object of a preposition, and a figural object or theme, which often appears as grammatical subject. For instance, in (10.1a) *the table* is the reference object and *the book* is figural. And it is intuitively clear that there is a distinct difference between (10.1a) and (10.1b), where the roles of reference object and figure have been exchanged.

(10.1)   a. The book is on the table.
         b. The table is under the book.

The usual examples illustrating sentences of spatial relation, like (10.1), use only the neutral verb *be*. However, the asymmetry between the figural and reference objects is clearer in sentences of location that use more specific verbs, as in (10.2).

(10.2)   The book is $\left\{ \begin{array}{l} \text{standing} \\ \text{lying} \\ \text{leaning} \\ \text{resting} \end{array} \right\}$ on the table.

Here the lexical distinctions among the verbs encode object-internal information about the figural object, the book—in particular, the spatial disposition of its major coordinate axis. In other words, whereas the neutral verb of location *be* gives only the very coarsest description of the subject, more specific verbs of motion and location elaborate some internal details of its 3D model. In turn, this supports the asymmetry of the relation between the figural object and the reference object.

The proper treatment of this asymmetry in conceptual structure (Jackendoff 1978; 1983, chapter 9; Talmy 1983; Herskovits 1985) is to make use of the formalism of section 8.5, in particular the conceptual category Place. As seen there, locational sentences like (10.1) and (10.2) assert, not a spatial relation between two objects, but the place at which the figural object is located. In turn, the place is specified as a function of the reference object, each choice of preposition specifying a different function and hence determining a different place. The conceptual structure of such sentences is therefore organized as in (10.3), paralleling (8.14).

(10.3)   [$_{\text{State}}$ BE ([$_{\text{Object}}$ BOOK], [$_{\text{Place}}$ ON ([$_{\text{Object}}$ TABLE])])]

If indeed conceptual structure is set in correspondence with a 3D model structure, the notion of Place ought to play a role in the latter level of representation. And in fact it seems quite natural to encode in the 3D model the notion of regions of space related to an object, determined in terms of the object's 3D representation. For example, the preposition *in* expresses a function that (for a first approximation) maps an object into the region consisting of its interior. *On* maps an object into the region consisting of its surface (in many cases, its upper surface). *Near* maps an object into a region exterior to but contiguous with the object. *Beside* is like *near* but restricts the region to roughly horizontal contiguity (a cloud above a mountaintop may be *near* it; it cannot be *beside* it).

More interesting are the prepositions that make use of the reference object's own intrinsic coordinate axes. For instance, one can be either *beside* or *along* a road, but one can only be *beside*, not *along*, a field or a tree (unless the tree has been felled). Evidently the domain of the function expressed by *along* is (roughly) objects of significant extension in one horizontal dimension only; this function maps such an object into an exterior contiguous region.

Another well-known class of examples of this sort consists of prepositions such as *in front of*, *behind*, *on top of*, and *to the right of*. These are used in two ways. Suppose the reference object is a person or a house. Then it has its own intrinsic axes, used in the 3D model to determine the internal layout of its parts. For instance, the head of a person and the roof of a house go on top, as specified by the directed up-down axis; the face and the front door go on the front, as specified by the directed front-back axis. These axes, independently necessary to establish the form of the object, may simply be extended beyond the surface of the object to determine regions that can be referred to by prepositional phrases such as *in front of the house*, *behind the man*, and so on.

On the other hand, some objects such as featureless spheres have no intrinsic axes. In such cases the position of the speaker (or hearer) extrinsically imposes a set of coordinate axes on the reference object: the front is the side facing me (or you), so that *behind the sphere* picks out a region contiguous to the sphere and on the side of it not facing us.

As has frequently been noted (Talmy 1983; Clark 1973; Olson and Bialystok 1983), ambiguities arise in the use of such prepositions in cases where two possible sets of coordinate axes are available and in conflict. For instance, in the situation depicted in figure 10.2, *The ball is behind the house* may be read as describing the ball at either position X (house's intrinsic axes) or position Y (speaker-imposed axes). Similarly, if Fred is lying down, *Fred's hat is on top of his head* can describe a configuration where the hat is in its normal position relative to his head (*on top of* is in terms of Fred's intrinsic axes) or one where it is covering his face (*on top of* is in terms of gravitational axes).

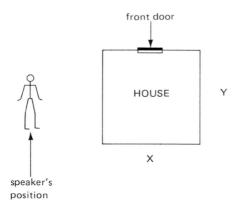

Figure 10.2
The sentence *The ball is behind the house* is ambiguous for a speaker at the position shown.

One of the points made by Olson and Bialystok (1983) is that such conflict between coordinate systems may occur even in purely spatial tasks, where language is not involved. This suggests, at the very least, that extending object-internal coordinate axes to the space exterior to an object plays a role in spatial understanding and that linguistic expressions of location are simply encoding information that is present for independent purposes. (See Shepard and Hurwitz 1984 for development of this point with respect to the preposition *up* and for further discussion of spatial axis systems.)

Let us turn next to the linguistic description of the motion of objects. This often divides rather nicely into two parts, which may be called *object-internal* and *object-external* aspects. (Lasher (1981) makes a similar distinction between "contour motion" and "locomotion.") Object-internal motion is in many cases expressed by lexical distinctions among verbs of motion; object-external motion, by the structure of accompanying prepositional phrases. Consider the possibilities in (10.4), for instance.

$$(10.4) \quad \text{John} \begin{Bmatrix} \text{walked} \\ \text{ran} \\ \text{squirmed} \\ \text{crawled} \\ \text{soared} \end{Bmatrix} \begin{Bmatrix} \text{under the bridge.} \\ \text{into the room.} \\ \text{through the tunnel.} \\ \text{over the rug.} \\ \text{along the road.} \end{Bmatrix}$$

As in the location sentences (10.2), the differences among the verbs reflect the internal dispositions and motions of the parts of John's body; they express the object-centered description of John himself. As observed in the previous section, these differences are not easily characterized in terms of conceptual features. They are, however, rather naturally differentiated in terms of 3D action descriptions.

On the other hand, the differences among the prepositional phrases in (10.4) reflect the motion of John as a whole. For this part of the description John can be regarded as a very coarsely described object (a point or an undifferentiated lump) traveling along some externally specified trajectory. Thus, the total description can be seen as hierarchical: the outer layer, expressed by the prepositional phrase, is the external trajectory of the object; the inner layer, expressed by the verb, is an object-centered elaboration of the object-internal motion. (There are verbs in English that themselves express object-external motion, as in *John circled the tree* or *The fly spiraled down to the table*, so the conceptual division is not always reflected grammatically. The semantic intuitions are clear, however, and it is these that we are concerned with.)

Talmy (1980) points out that in some languages (such as French and Spanish) this bifurcation of motion description is even clearer, in that one cannot say "John squirmed through the tunnel" but must say, literally,

"John went through the tunnel squirming." Here the main clause expresses the object-external motion, while the dependent clause *squirming* expresses the object-internal motion. A similar constraint exists in Japanese (Mitsuaki Yoneyama, personal communication).

Object-external motion is encoded in conceptual structure as an Event constituent of the sort in (8.12).

(10.5)   [$_{Event}$ GO ([$_{Object}$ JOHN], [$_{Path}$ TO ([$_{Place}$ IN ([$_{Object}$ ROOM])])])]

In particular, the Path constituent corresponds to the trajectory of motion, and the preposition expresses the function that maps the reference object (here, the room) into the Path (here, a trajectory that begins outside the room and ends inside it).

Some of the prepositions that express such functions treat the reference object at the coarsest layer of description. *To*, for instance, treats its object essentially as a point (which may be elaborated, of course, by the object's own description). Many other prepositions of path, however, exploit the reference object's geometry to some degree or another. For instance, *into* and *through* describe paths traversing the interior of the reference object, and *onto* encodes a path that terminates on the reference object's surface.

One of the more complex cases is *across*. As pointed out by Talmy (1983), the kinds of objects one can go across usually have one horizontal axis longer than the other and edges roughly parallel to the long axis. Going across such an object involves traversing a path from one of these parallel edges to the other. For instance, one can go across a road or a river, and across the short dimension of a swimming pool, but not across the long dimension of a swimming pool—in fact, there happens to be no appropriate English preposition for this case. (There are exceptions to these conditions, due to the presence of a preference rule system as described in section 8.3, but I think the basic principles stand. This description may be thought of as "stereotypical *across*.")

Marr's theory as it stands does not include any notion of "trajectory traversed by an object". However, it is not difficult to imagine extending the 3D model to include such information as Paths. Just as with Places, the geometrical properties of the reference object that are referred to by Path-functions seem most often to be information that is independently necessary for a Marr-type description of the object itself—for instance, its major coordinate axes. Hence, the extension of the 3D model to include Paths seems quite natural, and yet another correspondence can be established between constituents of conceptual structure and 3D model structure.

There is nonlinguistic motivation as well for a notion of Path in spatial understanding. If an organism is to use something like a 3D model derived from vision to direct its action—to find its way around in the world—it will necessarily have to compute trajectories, both those of moving objects, to see where they will end up, and those that it plans to traverse in its own future action. Thus, the enrichment proposed in order to adequately account for motion expressions in language in fact serves an independent purpose. The language is just capitalizing on what is already present in spatial understanding.

10.6 Summary

From this very preliminary investigation of the correspondence between conceptual structure and 3D model structure, a number of points emerge. First, the two structures can indeed be brought into contact, and much of spatial thinking depends on aspects of both. Thus, these two levels of representation constitute a central core accessed by a number of different peripheral faculties, including visual perception, language, haptic perception, body perception and action.

Second, the theory of Conceptual Semantics developed in *S&C* and summarized in chapter 8 contains many of the right sorts of elements to interface with spatial understanding. This is evidence that it is on the right track toward a properly mentalistic theory of the semantics of natural language, and in particular toward an answer to the question of how we talk about what we see.

Third, language can provide evidence for the constitution of the 3D model level, in that it motivates elements such as Places and Paths that are not immediately apparent in intuitions about the theory of vision per se. Such enrichment is expressed naturally in terms of elements that are already made available by Marr's theory and that turn out on reflection to be supported by the organism's performance at nonlinguistic tasks. Moreover, these enrichments lead the theory toward an adequate description of the full spatial field, in that they encode relations among objects.

Fourth, the 3D model level, thus enriched, does not conform to one's intuitive stereotype of what information the visual system delivers. The "visual world" is not simply a collection of holistic objects—"statues in the head." Rather, the 3D representation is teeming with elements that one does not "see," such as the hierarchical part-whole structure and the coordinate axis systems proposed by Marr, and now regions determined by the axes of objects and trajectories being traversed by objects in motion. In other words, the information necessary to encode spatial understanding includes a great deal that, although still purely geometric rather than conceptual, is not part of visual appearance as such.

Some (though I hope not all) readers may question this idea: How can a theory of perception countenance the presence of abstract visual information that one does not see? From the vantage point of linguistic theory, though, such a situation seems entirely as it should be. A major thrust of generative linguistic theory is that there are elements of hierarchical and abstract structure that one cannot hear and that one does not speak but that must play a role in explicating one's understanding of language. Moreover, there is nothing inherently suspect in investigating such entities: one can ask meaningful empirical questions about them and choose intelligently between alternative hypotheses. This is exactly the situation we have arrived at here in visual theory, paralleling language. If it calls for new methodology and new forms of argumentation, so be it; the flowering of linguistic theory in the last quarter century has been a direct result of giving up the expectation of overly concrete solutions.

10.7 Special-Purpose Capacities That Draw on Vision

To give a broader idea of the role of the 3D model in cognition, I conclude this chapter with extremely brief discussions of three special-purpose capacities that draw on it.

10.7.1 Face Recognition

Some research (Carey 1978; Carey and Diamond 1980, and references cited there) suggests that there is a specialized human capacity for face recognition and memory for faces. Like language, this capacity seems to have a characteristic developmental course (major growth between 6 and 10 years of age) and a brain localization (right posterior), damage to which produces deficits in face recognition but not in vision in general. Memories for faces are remarkably differentiated and long-lasting: people remember many thousands of faces and often can recognize casual acquaintances they have not seen for many years—even despite changes due to aging. And this capacity is informationally not very well linked to language: try describing your mother's face so someone else could pick her out in a crowd, and compare that to how easy it is pick her out in a crowd yourself.

Where might this capacity fit into a computational theory? It would be silly to suppose that it is entirely separate from the visual system. Rather, it would seem most plausible to assume that it is a specialization within the visual system: most of the work of face recognition is done by the standard devices of vision, but at some point an additional component takes over the information and performs face-specific analysis on it. That is, we would ideally like face recognition to be "parasitic" on independently necessary characteristics of ordinary object recognition.

So the standard question arises: What is the form in which faces are encoded by this special-purpose capacity, and to which of the already known levels is this most closely related? Since face recognition is a specialized form of object recognition, the appropriate jumping-off point appears to be the 3D model representation. Like ordinary objects, faces are recognized, not at a particular single orientation or distance, but from a variety of orientations (though not upside down) and at any distance that permits adequate resolution of facial features. Thus, memory for faces should be encoded in a normalized form and in some sort of object-centered coordinate frame, altogether parallel to the ordinary 3D model.

This suggests that facial representation involves a set of primitives and principles of combination of the general form of those for the 3D model level, but very specific and refined for the task of differentiating human faces. Since faces are, after all, spatially integrated with bodies and with the rest of the world, these representations must be related to the more general 3D model structure via correspondence rules. In addition, there might well be some specialized correspondence rules that are designed to pick facial features more effectively out of the $2\frac{1}{2}$D sketch. But since research on this capacity has primarily been directed at showing that it exists, and not at the structure of the information it processes, it is hard to go beyond speculation at this point.

It is worth mentioning, though, that this capacity is not specific to humans. Along with voice recognition, emotion recognition (from visual and/or auditory cues), and possibly other specialized capacities, it subserves an elaborate system of *social cognition* in many mammals and especially primates. Though it has long been recognized that animals have an elaborate social existence, little attention has been paid to the substantial computational capacities that social cognition presupposes. However, Cheney and Seyfarth (1985) observe that vervet monkeys deal routinely with complex problems in the social domain—say, three-term transitivity problems over the social dominance hierarchy—even though they are quite inept at problems of comparable logical structure in the nonsocial domain, the sort presented by the usual laboratory tests of animal intelligence. Cheney and Seyfarth go so far as to speculate that human intelligence might have arisen as a generalization of social cognition.

In any event, one of the essential foundations of social cognition is the ability to sharply distinguish individuals of one's species from one another. Thus, face recognition is not just a pleasant quirk in the system but an essential part of the biological capacity to play a role in society.

10.7.2 Reading

What forms of representation are involved in reading? Obviously some levels of the visual system must encode information from the page, and obviously the information provided by the visual system must eventually end up at some level in the language system. So the question is, Which levels?

Within the visual system it is clear that letters can be recognized and read regardless of their apparent size and, to a certain extent, regardless of orientation with respect to the reader. There are also tolerances with respect to letter shape, as seen by the effortless reading of new type fonts (within reason—German script, for instance, is relatively opaque to someone accustomed only to ordinary Roman letters). Above all, reading involves a recognition process—whether one is recognizing individual letters or larger units. These considerations suggest that the visual part of reading is a function of the 3D model level, where size and shape invariances can be specified. From the point of view of vision, then, letter and word recognition is a learned object discrimination task, not unlike, say, "automobile recognition": telling a B from an R is qualitatively similar to telling a Ford from a Buick.

The difference, of course, is that the objects discriminated in reading are translated into linguistic information. Again: At what level? This depends on the orthography. If it is an alphabetic script, like the Roman and Cyrillic alphabets, symbols of the orthography correspond more or less to phonological segments (there are plenty of exceptions, of course: x is phonetically ks, th is a single sound, often e stands for no sound at all; but segment-by-segment correspondence is the norm). In scripts like Hebrew and Arabic all consonants are represented in the orthography but vowels are omitted. In the Japanese kana script each symbol stands for a syllable. Whatever the differences among these scripts, they share the property of characterizing the *phonological* information of the language—how words are pronounced. By contrast, in Chinese orthography (much of which has been borrowed into Japanese as *kanji* script) and in ancient Egyptian hieroglyphics, for the most part each symbol corresponds to a morpheme, regardless of its pronunciation. Here, then, the orthography is an indication of the *syntactic* or *semantic* level of representation.

This means that in learning to read, one must be establishing two things: a set of visual concepts that permit one to recognize elements of the orthography, and a set of correspondence rules between the orthography and the level of representation that the orthography symbolizes. In the case of morphemic scripts the correspondence is between the written symbol and the appropriate lexical item (perhaps at all of its levels), since one must learn such an orthography essentially one word at a time. In the case of a phonological script one may associate spellings with phonological representations in the lexicon (especially for idiosyncratic orthographies like that of English), but in addition there are general default principles for associating orthographic symbols with elements of the sound system, so that one can read ("sound out") words one does not know.

Thus, all levels of the visual system are implicated in the general information structure of the faculty of reading. Then, from the 3D level, information is translated into the appropriate level of the linguistic system, whence it proceeds upward to the conceptual level. (I am not inclined to think there are any *new* levels of representation specialized for reading: how could one develop them?)

In processing, of course, information need not pass unidirectionally along this tortured route through the levels of representation. There can be the usual amount of top-down influence in perception—where this time "top-down" means down the informational path from conceptual structure through the linguistic system, thence into the visual system going down to at least the 2½D sketch. Think, for instance, of trying to read a messy handwriting, where one's identification of the letters is so strongly aided, even consciously, by one's knowledge of the language and one's guesses about what the writer must mean. And having read the scrawl, its segmentation into letters is visually obvious—the equivalent in reading of the phoneme restoration effect.

Interestingly, there is some neurological evidence for the distinction between phonological and morphological scripts. Tzeng and Wang (1983) report a number of studies in which reading and writing of phonological scripts is impaired by temporal lobe lesions, whereas reading and writing of morphological scripts is impaired by posterior, occipital-parietal lesions. Especially interesting is the case of Japanese, which intermixes the two kinds of script freely. According to Sasanuma (1974), deficits in reading and writing the two kinds of script can be independent of each other, each being associated with a different sort of aphasia. Here, then, is neurological evidence that the translation of visual symbols into linguistic forms varies with the kind of orthography, circumstantially supporting my claim that the two types invoke different types of correspondence rules.

10.7.3 Sign Language

American Sign Language (ASL) is the primary language of the deaf community in North America. It is a language independent of English ("signed English" imposes English word order and grammatical conventions on ASL vocabulary and is quite distinct), fully as expressive as any spoken language.

The acquisition of ASL by children is governed by principles similar to those for the acquisition of spoken languages. In particular, it is typically not taught to deaf children by (hearing) parents or teachers. Rather, until recently its use was actively discouraged by educators; the language is most often "picked up" from peers in the dormitories of schools for the deaf (Klima and Bellugi 1979, chapter 3). Moreover, sign language aphasias appear quite comparable to those in spoken language (Bellugi, Poizner, and Klima 1983).

Although it seems once to have been fashionable to claim that ASL has no grammatical structure, recent investigation (for example, Klima and Bellugi 1979; Padden 1983; Supalla 1982; Gee and Kegl 1982; Newport 1982) has revealed a rich syntactic and morphological structure altogether comparable to that of natural languages; Elissa Newport (personal communication) finds its grammar not unlike that of Navajo. The difference, of course, is that instead of having a phonological structure that leads to the auditory and vocal modalities, ASL connects to the visual and gestural systems.

Again we can ask what levels are involved in this mixture of modalities. The evidence at the moment points to ASL certainly having a level of syntactic structure. Since we are regarding morphology as the word-interior aspect of syntax, the existence of ASL morphology fits in well here. On the other hand, there is no evidence for much beyond a rudimentary phonological level: there are words, and there are aspects that correspond to the suprasegmental information of stress and rhythm, but there is certainly no syllabic and segmental organization. Rather, at this point the information slips over into the visual-gestural modality, in which the usual criteria (object-centered descriptions, categorial recognition) implicate the 3D model representation. In ASL perception the 3D model will be derived via the lower visual levels; in production the 3D model will serve as input to the production of gesture, via whatever levels of representation are appropriate for that. One might hope, in fact, that the rich and yet contained system of action made use of by sign language could provide interesting evidence toward a theory of motor representation and of temporal segmentation in both vision and action.

The point of bringing up these specialized capacities, even if much too briefly and speculatively, is to suggest how accounts of them are to mesh with the primary theoretical construct of the present theory, the notion of levels of representation. To the extent that their information demands can be framed in terms of independently justified levels, this confirms the overall form of the theory. To the extent that such capacities can provide evidence for refinement of the theories of various levels, or suggest new sorts of connections among levels, or even suggest new levels, this too is useful. The overall goal, of course, is to keep the number of independent forms of representation small, not to have to invoke brand new levels for each task, and yet to recognize distinctions among levels when necessary.

Chapter 11
Levels of Musical Structure

11.1 What Is Musical Cognition?

Music presents an interesting contrast to the faculties we have discussed so far. For one thing, there is no obvious ecological pressure for the species to have a musical faculty, as there is for vision and language. Although there may be a certain cultural advantage in having some rudimentary form of music to help synchronize collective rhythmic activity or to serve some ceremonial aspect of social life, no particular reason is evident for the efflorescence of musical complexity that appears in so many cultures.

Music also differs from language and vision in the vast disparity of musical ability among individuals, from Mozart to the tone-deaf. In our society, at least, this leads to a bifurcation between producers of music and mere consumers. Moreover, producers of music (both composers and performers) in most cases have undergone substantial conscious instruction and endless practice to hone their skills. Thus, music tends to be regarded as one of those specialized learned skills like chess or tennis or mathematics.

Nevertheless, average "unmusical" folk know a great deal more about music than they might give themselves credit for. They can probably hum, or at least recognize, hundreds of nursery rhymes, folk songs, and popular tunes. They can probably spontaneously clap or tap their feet in time to pieces of music they have never heard before. They can probably distinguish between a competent and an inept performance of a piece, though they may not be able to explain what makes the difference. And they can make aesthetic judgments about what pieces they like better than others.

Like linguistic and visual ability, such musical abilities seem on the whole trivial and self-evident. From the example of the other faculties, though, we should be alert against concluding that things are just as they seem. Beneath effortless performance may lie a completely unconscious system of formidable complexity.

So let us couch the problem of musical cognition in a manner familiar from the other capacities: What kinds of mental information must a person be able to construct, process, and store in order to exhibit ordinary musical abilities of the sort just cited? In particular, what mental capacity is necessary beyond perceiving and recording a succession of notes? What deeper organization does the listener impose that makes a sequence of notes cohere into a piece of music?

As in the case of language, the problem is complicated by the fact that knowledge of music is culture-dependent. Just as we find thousands of languages across the world, themselves differentiated into dialects and even more finely into speech styles, so there are numerous "musical idioms" among the world's cultures, and within them more specialized styles. And just as one "picks up" the language(s) spoken in one's environment, so one "picks up" an acquaintance with indigenous musical styles without any necessary formal training.

What does it mean to be acquainted with or experienced in a musical idiom, as opposed to being acquainted with a particular piece of music? It has to do with one's ability to apply what one knows to new pieces. For instance, one is likely to demonstrate better recognition and recall memory for pieces in a familiar idiom than in an unfamiliar idiom, given equal exposure, and to hum along sooner and more accurately. If one plays an instrument, one is more likely to be able to sight-read a piece in a familiar idiom than in an unfamiliar one (Sloboda 1982) and even to unconsciously rectify errors in the printed music (Wolf 1976; Sloboda 1984). And, more generally, one experiences a piece in a familiar idiom as "making more sense" than one in an unfamiliar idiom. For instance, if you are an average American consumer of music, imagine how coherent a random Sousa march sounds in comparison to a random Indian raga.

Again, our general methodology leads us to ask how the forms of musical information differ from idiom to idiom—and what listeners have learned that permits them to perform these tasks in a familiar idiom and not in an unfamiliar one. Beyond this question is the deeper one of what listeners must know in advance in order to be able to learn the principles of a musical idiom to which they are exposed. Is there an inborn capacity for music, just as there is for language, which enables listeners to construct for themselves the principles of a musical idiom on the basis of sufficient exposure? Or are the principles of music just a subset of more general principles of associative memory?

In *A Generative Theory of Tonal Music* (henceforth *GTTM*) Fred Lerdahl and I address the formal organization that experienced listeners unconsciously attribute to a piece of music and the principles by which they determine this organization. Taking the experienced listener as an idealization parallel to the "ideal speaker-hearer" of linguistic theory, we seek a theory of the listener's understanding of musical *structure*—parallel to linguistic competence—rather than a theory of musical processing.

In the *GTTM* theory the listener's knowledge of a musical idiom is expressed in terms of a musical *grammar*, or set of rules, that collectively describe the abstract musical structures the listener has available and the principles by which appropriate structures are matched with any given piece in the idiom. Our musical grammar does not, however, conform to certain preconceptions of what a generative music theory should be like: it does not compose, or "generate," pieces of music, nor does it mark pieces "grammatical" or "ungrammatical." Rather, we take the grammar to be a set of principles that match pieces with their proper structures.

In developing this grammar, *GTTM* makes no presumption that it resembles the grammar of language in any particular way: it is motivated on grounds of musical intuition, not on theoretical notions borrowed from language. There is, for example, no attempt to find musical counterparts of parts of speech, meaning, movement transformations, or distinctive features. Rather, such notions as pitch, scale, consonance, dissonance, meter, ornament, tension, and relaxation, which have no strict parallel in language, play the central roles in musical grammar.

Although *GTTM* is concerned primarily with constructing the grammar of one particular musical idiom, Western tonal music of the eighteenth and nineteenth centuries, it also addresses the question of how familiarity with a musical idiom could be acquired. Following the overall scheme for answering this question in linguistic theory (see (5.24)–(5.25)), we see an account of a musical idiom dividing up as in (11.1).

(11.1)   Structure of Musical Idiom I = Innate part (Universal Musical Grammar) + Learned part (Idiom-specific elements)

In turn, the innate part of music may be decomposed as in (11.2).

(11.2)   Innate part of music = Part due to music-specific properties of the computational mind + Part due to general properties of the computational mind

Those who would see music as a consequence of completely general capacities try to eliminate or at least minimize the contribution of the first term of the sum in (11.2). However, as argued for language, such a move cannot be made on grounds of a priori plausibility: it can only be made in the context of the overall range of facts for which a theory of musical cognition must be responsible. As I will show, some aspects of musical grammar do seem to be explicable as specializations of more general capacities, and others do not. We will thus see that music yields interesting evidence on the proper division between specialized and general-purpose machinery in the computational mind.

As a consequence of the differences between music and other faculties, one more criterion for a satisfactory theory bears mention. Though there is a vast disparity among individuals—and cultures—in musical achievement, there seems to be no sharp discontinuity between simple and complex musical styles, between experienced and inexperienced listeners, and between musically talented and untalented people. We would like the theory, insofar as possible, to show a similar lack of discontinuity. Such is the case in the *GTTM* theory: simple forms of tonal music such as folk songs and nursery rhymes are constructed along exactly the same lines as a Mozart or Beethoven symphony, and most of the principles underlying the music of Mozart and Beethoven can be revealed by relatively simple examples. The folk music and the art music differ primarily in the complexity and ambiguity of the structures built up from the common primitives, not in the principles of grammar themselves. Since practically everyone can learn to sing and appreciate folk songs and nursery rhymes, it is conceivable that differences in musical talent are a function largely of something like a computational capacity to deal with large, multiply ambiguous structures. This remains to be seen, of course, but if true, it means that musical expertise is essentially a more refined and highly articulated version of an ability that we all share.

The next four sections will outline the *GTTM* theory of musical structure, which involves five levels of representation. The rest of the chapter will explore some of the implications of the theory for musical performance, musical affect, and music processing.

11.2 Tonal Systems

The most obvious elements out of which music is constructed are notes of a given pitch, intensity, and duration, played in sequence or simultaneously. As is well known, it is not the absolute pitches of notes that are significant for musical purposes but the relations of pitches to each other. For instance, a melody may begin on any pitch and still be perceived as the same, as long as the correct intervals (frequency ratios) among notes are preserved.

As essential part of a musical idiom is a system of pitch relationships out of which pieces of music can be constructed and in terms of which many aspects of musical coherence in the idiom can be defined. It is well to discuss such systems as a prelude to presenting the hierarchical levels of musical representation. (*GTTM*, section 11.5, is somewhat more detailed.)

The most basic element of a pitch system is its *pitch collection*, the set of available pitches. It seems universal that these pitches are discrete. In drum musics the pitch collection may be specified primarily in terms of timbre; in Indonesian gamelan music the pitch collection is arrayed from low to high without too detailed specification of the exact pitch intervals. But for music more specific about pitch (in other words, most idioms) the pitch collection specifies a number of discrete pitches and the intervals between them. Even in the numerous idioms that make use of portamento (gliding pitch) it is the beginning or end point of the glide that is significant, not the range of pitches traversed.

In some systems, such as Western tonal music, the pitch collection is extended indefinitely upward and downward by octave equivalence: each pitch in the collection is available in any octave. In many musical systems a number of different pitch collections are available; in Western music these are the collections for the familiar major and minor scales.

Most musical idioms (much twentieth century "classical" music excepted —see remarks in *GTTM*, section 11.6, on atonal systems) impose on the pitch collection a system of stability relations. One member of the pitch collection, called the *tonic*, is heard as inherently most stable; typically, it is the pitch on which pieces end. The other pitches of a piece are heard in relation to the tonic, and each member of the pitch collection bears a distinctive stability relative to the tonic. In many idioms there is a next most stable pitch called the *dominant* or secondary pitch, which also plays an important role in organizing pitch relations; it is often a point on which intermediate phrases end. In Western tonal music the dominant is the interval of a fifth above the tonic, but other idioms present other possibilities. In Western music it is possible in the course of a piece to change which pitch serves as tonic (and change pitch collection accordingly), but most idioms maintain the same tonic and pitch collection throughout a piece.

In addition, an idiom may specify relations of stability among pairs of nontonic pitches: particular intervals may count as more consonant or dissonant than others. The relative consonance of a pair of pitches may differ depending on whether the pitches are sounded sequentially (as part of a melody) or simultaneously (as part of a harmony). Such is the case in Western tonal music, where, for instance, the interval of a step (two adjacent pitches in the pitch collection) is highly stable as part of a melody but harmonically counts as a dissonance.

This system of relationships as a whole specifies the tonal system of an idiom; it is in the details of the tonal system that we find the most salient differences among the grammars of musical idioms. (The work of Krumhansl and her associates has succeeded in evoking the properties of the tonal system from subjects' responses in experimental settings, confirming many traditional insights of music theory (see Krumhansl 1983 and references therein). Castellano, Bharucha, and Krumhansl (1984) extend this paradigm across idioms, comparing the responses of experienced and inexperienced listeners to the tonal system of Indian ragas.)

11.3 The Musical Surface

The tonal system, however, is not itself a level of musical representation. Rather, it is simply a set of relationships among elements that are present in levels of representation. It might be comparable to the system of available phonemes in a language and their relationships to each other, or in vision to the relationships among colors specified by the color solid. These relationships among available elements play an important role in determining the structure of a given input, but they are not the structure itself.

GTTM deals with five distinct levels of mental representation for music. The first, the *musical surface*, encodes the music as discrete pitch-events (notes and chords), each with a specific duration and pitch (or combination of pitches, if a chord). Standard musical notation represents the pitch-events of the musical surface by means of symbols for discrete pitch and durations; thus, it is easy to overlook the fact that the musical surface, like the sequence of discrete phonological segments in language, comes to our perception only after a substantial amount of processing.

Both pitch and duration are derived in this processing. First consider pitch. As has been known since Helmholtz, we normally hear overtones, not as discrete pitches, but indirectly as contributions to timbre (or tone quality). On the other hand, we are capable of sorting different instruments out of a musical texture. So the acoustic signal must undergo processing that determines which acoustic frequencies are heard as distinct pitches of the musical surface and which are just part of the timbral envelope of other pitches.

In addition, the duration of a note is hardly clear in the acoustic signal. Different instruments have different characteristic onsets in their tone production, none of which are instantaneous; yet we hear notes as having instantaneous beginnings, and we can hear various instruments as beginning simultaneously despite quite different attack envelopes. After the attack we hear the note as sustained in amplitude, whether (as in the case of the organ) it is in fact sustained or (as in the case of the piano or harpsichord) it is not. The ends of notes, particularly in the case of nonsustaining instruments, may be acoustically indistinct, and performers can and do get away with much less precision in releases of notes than in attacks. Finally, all this is overlaid by the acoustic properties of the environment in which the music is being performed; reverberation further obscures the attacks and releases and adds its own components to the signal.

Just how much processing is involved in making the acoustic signal into a coherent musical surface might be suggested by the experience of listening to a recording played backward. Instead of a sequence of discrete pitch-events, one typically hears an incoherent mélange in which most distinctions of duration and contour and even many distinctions of timbre and intensity are lost. The auditory system, which is adapted to the asymmetry of attack, release, and reverberation, cannot make much sense out of a signal in which all the usual relationships are reversed. (Some of these problems are discussed by Vos and Rasch (1982) and Piszcalski and Galler (1982).)

Hence, a full psychological theory of music must account for the derivation of the musical surface from the acoustic signal. The musical surface, however, is the lowest level of representation that has musical significance. For convenience, I will use traditional musical notation as a representation of the information encoded at this level.

11.4 Grouping and Metrical Structure

The other four levels of musical structure discussed in *GTTM* are derived ultimately from the musical surface. Unlike the musical surface, they are hierarchical rather than just sequential. The first of these is *grouping structure*, the segmentation of the musical surface into motives, phrases, and sections. Grouping structure is notated by means of slurs beneath the musical surface. For example, figure 11.1 gives ·the intuitively correct grouping structure for the opening motive of Mozart's G minor symphony, K. 550. At the smallest scale, groups are made up of notes 1–3, 4–6, 7–10, 11–13, 14–16, and 17–20. At the next layer, 1–3 and 4–6 group together, as do 11–13 and 14–16. The four groups of this layer pair up into 1–10 and 11–20. Finally the whole passage forms a group, which is in turn paired with the next phrase.

That these are not gratuitous formal impositions on the music is demonstrated by figure 11.2, which illustrates two incorrect ways of grouping the passage. One clearly cannot hear the passage as broken up in the fashion indicated in figure 11.2a. Although figure 11.2b segments the passage correctly into smallest-scale groups, the aggregation of small groups into larger ones is strongly in violation of musical intuition. In other words, our unconscious understanding of music enables us intuitively to choose a hierarchical segmentation, and therefore there must be means for mentally representing it. (This should not, of course, exclude the possibility of cases in which the grouping is intuitively unclear or ambiguous, as happens frequently in music; these too must be accounted for as an integral part of the theory.)

The set of possible grouping structures is described by formation rules

Figure 11.1
Grouping structure in the opening of Mozart, K. 550

Figure 11.2
Two well-formed but intuitively deviant grouping structures for the opening of Mozart, K. 550

that create hierarchical nested structures. Included in the formation rules are principles of overlap and elision, which describe a class of musical situations in which a pitch-event serves as both the last event of one group and the first event of the next group. The rules of grouping also include a set of correspondence rules that describe the association of a grouping structure with a musical surface. Figures 11.1 and 11.2 exhibit well-formed grouping structures in the hierarchical sense; the correspondence rules must pick out which of them is most highly favored.

Wertheimer (1923) points out the close parallel between principles of musical grouping and principles of visual grouping. He shows how the principles of proximity and similarity have close musical analogues and how these principles operate in characteristic fashion: no single rule is a necessary condition for grouping, no single rule is under all conditions sufficient for grouping, and rules may reinforce each other or conflict with one another depending on the configuration of the presented field. The notion of a preference rule system discussed briefly in section 8.3 is in fact precisely appropriate to the purposes of musical cognition; most of the correspondence rules between the musical surface and grouping structure are stated in preference rule format. Among these rules are the principles of proximity and similarity, in a form specialized to musical purposes. Other rules deal with symmetry, parallelism, cues for the placement of larger-scale group boundaries, and optimal correspondence to the other hierarchical structures.[1]

1. For readers familiar with *GTTM*, the division made here between formation rules and correspondence rules is not the same as that made there between well-formedness rules and preference rules. The latter distinction has to do with whether rules are necessary or only preferred; we are concerned here with whether the rule defines grouping structure per se or the correspondence between grouping structure and other levels. Thus, the formation rules include GWFRs 2–5 and GPRs 1 and 5, plus the rules of Overlap and Elision. The correspondence rules to the musical surface include GWFR 1, which requires groups to correspond to contiguous stretches of the musical surface, plus GPRs 2, 3, 4, and 6; GPR 7 is a correspondence rule connecting grouping structure with higher levels.

Figure 11.3
Metrical grids for the openings of Mozart, K. 331 and K. 550

As far as we can determine, it appears that the principles of grouping structure—both the formation rules and the correspondence rules—are universal among musical idioms. In fact, on the whole they do not seem specific to music at all but are rather specialized forms of principles involved in any sort of temporal pattern perception. If musical grouping achieves greater richness and complexity than patterns from ordinary life, it is likely because music is a human artifact, part of whose point is to exploit the possibilities inherent in our capacity for imposing regularities on the environment. (Deutsch 1982b and references therein present experimental evidence bearing on principles of grouping; Deliege 1985 reports an experimental investigation specifically of the *GTTM* grammar of grouping.)

The second hierarchical structure is *metrical structure*, the organization of strong and weak beats that listeners impose on music. The notation for metrical structure is a *metrical grid*, identical in overall form to the metrical grid in phonology (see section 5.6; we will reflect on this parallelism in the next chapter). Figure 11.3 presents two examples of metrical grids, one associated with the opening of the Mozart A major sonata, K. 331, and one with the Mozart G minor symphony again.

Each dot in the grid represents a *beat*—a point in time at the onset of the note under which the dot appears. Each horizontal row of dots indicates a particular temporal regularity in the music, a sequence of beats equally spaced in time. For each row it is natural to tap or clap along with the music at the points marked by the beats of that level of the grid.

The topmost row indicates the most fine-grained metrical regularity; as one moves to lower rows, the metrical regularities are at successively larger scales. The beats present at larger scales are relatively *strong* beats; those present only at small scales are relatively *weak* beats.

One important temporal asymmetry of music emerges from the way beats are associated with the musical surface. Beats are marked at the attack points of notes, not at their releases or somewhere in the middle. Thus, if a recording is played backward—even if the pitches are perfectly sustained and there are no reverberation effects—the metrical structure is not reversed. Rather, beats must be associated with what were originally the *ends* of notes. In other words, a physical reversal leads to something other than a reversal in the structure imposed by the listener.

Unlike grouping structure, metrical structure does not extend hierarchically to the very largest scale of an entire piece. Rather, perceptions of metrical regularity tend to fade out when the time interval between beats is more than a few seconds. Thus, in terms of the organization of pieces of music that may be several minutes long, metrical structure tends to be a relatively small- to medium-scale phenomenon.

The relationships among the layers of the grid are specified by formation rules for metrical structure. In Western classical music and in most European and American folk music, each metrical layer is uniform in spacing, and its spacing is either two or three times as large as the next smaller layer. (A ternary regularity occurs for instance in waltzes and in figure 11.3a.) In other idioms more complex metrical patterns can occur. For instance, much Greek folk music has a metrical pattern with a regularity of 7 beats, subdivided into 2 + 2 + 3; Macedonian and Bulgarian music often involves more intricate patterns along similar lines (Singer 1974); much African music involves the superimposition of multiple metrical patterns. So the formation rules for metrical structure, like the principles of the tonal system, are an area where musical idioms can differ. This means that part of becoming experienced in a musical idiom is learning what class of metrical patterns is possible in that idiom and learning to identify a piece as having one pattern or another. It also means that at least the idiom-particular part of the metrical formation rules is specific to music, so that unlike grouping we cannot completely attribute this sort of structure to a general-purpose temporal patterning device. (More on this in section 12.4.)

The correspondence rules for metrical structure relate it primarily to the musical surface. Before I sketch them, a remark is in order on standard musical notation. This notation represents certain aspects of metrical structure by means of the notated meter (2/4 versus 3/4 versus 6/8, for instance), the bar lines, and the beams joining eighth and sixteenth notes. However, these aspects of meter are *not* present in the musical surface, which consists only of the sequence of pitches with their durations and intensities. Rather, the listener must reconstruct the intended meter from the musical surface. Musical notation can therefore be regarded as providing the performer not just with the musical surface but also with some aspects of the metrical structure the composer intends. The performer in turn must translate these hints into operationally detectable differences in the signal that will aid the listener in inferring the intended metrical structure.

It is often presumed that the cues for metrical structure in the musical surface consist primarily of degrees of relative stress or accent, that is, that one invariably finds heavier stress on stronger beats. (Martin (1972) makes this mistake, for example.) However, music actually performed this way sounds clumsy and ridiculous. Heavy stress *may* be an indication of a strong beat, but cross-accentuation, in which accents occur in weak metrical position, is quite common in Western tonal music and altogether the norm in jazz. Moreover, there are musical styles in which differentiations of stress can arguably be said not to occur (European sacred choral music of the Renaissance may be one such). Yet such styles undeniably produce intuitions of metrical structure.

It turns out that relative stress is but one of a number of conditions within a preference rule system that determines the most stable metrical structure for a piece. Other factors include the relative duration of notes, of harmonic patterns, and of patterns of articulation (longer implies metrically stronger in each case). A role is also played by considerations of parallelism, a preference for binary regularity, and, in Western tonal music, a number of principles specific to melodic and harmonic patterns of the idiom. In addition, there is a strong tendency to continue the same metrical pattern uniformly throughout, which enables the listener to preserve the sense of meter in the face of local disruptions.

Like stress, some of these factors are open to manipulation by the performer. Sloboda (1984, section 3.2.3, 1985) shows experimentally how experienced pianists instinctively vary stress, length, and articulation to communicate metrical structure, whereas less experienced players tend not to have these parameters under control. (We return to this in section 11.7)

There are also correspondence rules between grouping and meter. Most prominently, there is a tendency for metrical structure to line up with grouping structure, strong beats coinciding with the beginnings of groups. However, this is only a weak preference, and all sorts of other cues can override it. Consider figure 11.4, which notates both grouping structure and metrical structure for the two examples in figure. 11.3. The two grouping structures are essentially the same. However, the relationships between grouping and meter are quite different. In figure 11.4a they are maximally in phase: strong beats occur at the beginning of each group, and stronger beats are correlated with the inception of larger-level groups. In figure 11.4b, however, the two structures are decidedly out of phase, in that the strongest beat in each group is toward the end of the group. This sort of situation is perceptually less stable and less common in the literature of music but hardly incomprehensible or rare. It is just an ever so slightly more exotic case along a long continuum.

Figure 11.4
Correlation of grouping and meter in Mozart, K. 331 (in phase) and K. 550 (out of phase)

Figure 11.5
Opening of *Pastoral* Symphony finale and a variation

11.5 Time-Span and Prolongational Reductions

Grouping and metrical structure together constitute the basic rhythmic articulation of a piece of music, the temporal framework in which the notes of the piece are heard. These structures, however, do not address the organization of pitch in the music: one could to a certain degree substitute any pitches whatsoever into the same rhythmic framework without altering grouping and metrical structure. So these levels of representation do not exhaust the listener's comprehension of music. In particular, they say nothing about what makes a sequence of notes into a melody or a sequence of chords into a progression. This is the function of two further levels of representation, *time-span reduction* and *prolongational reduction*.

The basic musical intuition behind these levels is that some passages of music can be heard as *ornamentations* or *elaborations* of others. For instance, the passage in figure 11.5a is the opening theme from the finale of

Beethoven's *Pastoral* Symphony; the passage in figure 11.5b is the form in which it returns later in the movement. Despite the differences in rhythm and melodic contour, one has no difficulty hearing the latter as a variation of the former.

Music theorists have been aware of principles of ornamentation and elaboration for centuries. However, it was the insight of the early twentieth century theorist Heinrich Schenker that the organization of an entire piece of music may be conceived of in terms of such principles and that such organization provides explanations of many of the deeper and more abstract properties of tonal music. *GTTM* summarizes this insight as the *Reduction Hypothesis*.

Reduction Hypothesis

The pitch-events of a piece are heard in a hierarchy of relative importance; structurally less important events are heard as ornamentations or elaborations of events of greater importance.

A representation of the relative structural importance of the events in a piece has come to be known as a *reduction* of the piece, for reasons that will become obvious in a moment. By contrast with traditional Schenkerian theory, *GTTM* claims that musical representation contains two distinct forms of reduction, differing in what sorts of relationships obtain between more important and less important events and over what temporal domains ornamentation or elaboration can take place.

In the *time-span reduction* the domains of harmonic and melodic elaboration are defined by the rhythmic framework of grouping and metrical structure. Its organization is best explained through an example. Figure 11.6 presents the beginning of the Mozart A major sonata again. Above the musical text is a tree diagram, the formal notation for the time-span reduction of the passage. Below the passage is an informal musical interpretation of the tree. Each successive line in the example results from a deletion of the relatively least important events remaining in the next line above. Line (a) presents the most important events in each of the eight-note domains; only the few sixteenth notes are eliminated. Line (b) gives the most important events for each half-measure domain; line (c) for each measure; line (d) for each group consisting of a pair of measures; line (e) for the group consisting of the whole passage.

The best way to understand figure 11.6 is to attempt to hear the successive musical lines in rhythm. If the analysis is correct, each line should sound like a natural simplification of the previous one. Thus, each line represents a step in *reducing* a piece from its musical surface to a skeleton of relatively important events.

As in the case of grouping, it is useful to present an example of an incorrect reduction, in order to show that real musical intuitions are at

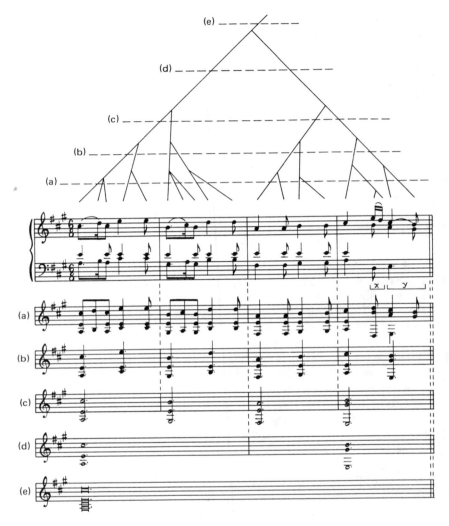

Figure 11.6
Time-span reduction of the opening of Mozart, K. 331

stake. Figure 11.7 presents two fragments of figure 11.6, contrasting the correct reduction for the domains bracketed as x and y with an incorrect one. It should be intuitively clear that the incorrect reduction sounds "less like the piece."

Now turn to the tree diagram in figure 11.6. Each pitch-event in the musical surface is at the bottom of a branch of the tree. With the exception of the branch connected to the first event of the piece, each branch terminates at its upper end on another branch. Typical situations are illustrated in figure 11.8. When a branch connected to event x terminates on a branch connected to event y, this signifies that x is structurally less important than y and is heard as an ornament to or elaboration of y. This is the case shown in figure 11.8a. In reducing the passage consisting of x and y, then, y is the event retained; its branch continues upward in the tree. We will call y the *head* of the passage x–y. Figure 11.8b, on the other hand, represents a situation in which x is more important than y and hence is the event retained in a reduction. Figure 11.8c illustrates the recursion of this process. In the domain w–x, w is the most important; in the domain y–z, z is the most important; in the larger domain w–x–y–z, z is the most important.

One can think of each line of music in figure 11.6 as representing a horizontal slice across the tree, showing only the events whose branches appear in that slice. The dotted lines across the tree in the figure show this correspondence. Note, however, that the tree conveys more information than the musical notation, in that the branching explicitly shows to which more important event each event is related.

Having gone this far, we can already see an important application of time-span reduction in musical understanding. Consider what makes a set of variations on a theme "like" the theme—what constancy underlies the judgment that the variations are in some sense "the same piece." The time-span reduction provides an answer: the theme and the variations share a common structural skeleton in the time-span reduction. The structurally more important events of the theme stay the same, whereas the relatively less important elaborations are varied. In jazz, for example, a tune is often reduced to the skeletal form of a set of chord changes, upon which performers improvise new elaborations. In order to perceive the constancy of the theme, then, the listener must be able (unconsciously) to abstract out the relevant structural layer in time-span reduction where the theme and variations are identical.

The formation rules for time-span reduction have already been intimated: the primitives are the notions of domain, head, and elaboration. The principles of combination are (1) the hierarchical embedding of domains and (2) the specification of one element of each domain as head and the rest as elaborations, recursively from small to large domains, in the manner of figure 11.6. (For Western tonal music there are a number of more spe-

Figure 11.7
Comparison of alternative time-span reductions in measure 8 of Mozart, K. 331

(11.10)

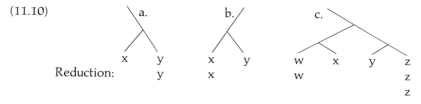

Reduction:

Figure 11.8
Schematic situations in time-span reduction trees

cialized principles of combination as well, with which we will not concern ourselves. See *GTTM*, chapter 7, for details.)

The correspondence rules for time-span reduction relate this level of representation to the previous three. They come in two parts. The first part derives the domains of time-span reduction from grouping and metrical structure, starting with the smallest metrical units and working up to the largest domains defined by grouping. The second part is the set of rules that determines which element of each domain is heard as the head. Again this consists of a preference rule system.

One factor in choice of head is metrical position: a metrically stronger element is preferable as head, other things being equal. But many other factors can interfere with this preference, so that metrically weak elements often come to appear as heads. (The two domains x and y in figure 11.7 are examples.) These other factors grow out of the properties of the tonal system sketched in section 11.2. Most important is the harmonic consonance of a pitch-event—both in relation to the tonic pitch and, in the case of a chord, its own intrinsic consonance: relatively consonant events are preferred as heads. In addition, reductions are favored in which each layer of reduction follows stable melodic contours, as defined by the principles of melodic consonance and dissonance in the tonal system. Finally, the tonal system may prescribe a number of *cadential formulas*—specified sequences of melodic and/or harmonic material—that are used to articulate phrase endings. Because of their importance as surface cues for large-scale segmentation of the piece, cadential formulas invariably assume importance in time-span reduction. All of these factors, then, interact to determine a maximally coherent time-span reduction for the piece.

The time-span reduction thus organizes the pitch-events of music into a rhythmically governed hierarchy. What it cannot encode, though, is the sense of musical flow *across* phrases, the building and releasing of musical tension. This is the function of *prolongational reduction*, the fourth hierarchical level of musical structure. Although this is probably the structure of greatest interest to music theorists, because of its close relationship to

Schenker's theory, it is hard to describe the elementary intuitions behind it to readers not conversant in music theory, so I will be brief and informal.

The prolongational reduction is another tree structure that expresses the relative importance of all the pitch-events of a piece in hierarchical fashion. Its primitives are again the notions of domain, head, and elaboration; its principles of combination again consist of the recursive embedding of domains and the specification of one element per domain as head. However, unlike time-span reduction, prolongational reduction recognizes three distinct sorts of elaboration, corresponding to different patterns of tension and relaxation.

First, if the head and elaboration are the same note or chord, the connection between them is one of *strong prolongation*, a connection that signifies no net change in tension in passing from one event to the other. If such an elaboration follows the head, it is heard as a *repetition* of the head; if it precedes the head, it is heard as *anticipation* of the head. Second, if the elaboration is a different note or chord from the head, the connection between them is a *progression*, which signifies a net change in tension in passing from one event to the other. When such an elaboration follows the head, there is an increase in tension, and the elaboration is heard as a *departure*. When such an elaboration precedes the head, there is a relaxation, and the elaboration is heard as *leading into* the head. Third, if the elaboration is the same chord as the head but in a less stable form (for instance, inversion rather than root position), the connection is a *weak prolongation*; its effects are intermediate between the two other types of connection. Figure 11.9 gives the prolongational tree structure corresponding to the time-span reduction in figure 11.6. Strong prolongations are notated by open circles at the branch-points, progressions by ordinary branches, weak prolongations by filled circles at the branch-points. The temporal domains for prolongational reduction, notated explicitly in figure 11.9, are actually implicit in the tree: each domain corresponds to a cluster of branches elaborating a head.

From the definitions of the three kinds of elaboration, it can be seen that moving through the music from a head to a following elaboration always maintains or raises the degree of tension, and moving from an elaboration to a following head always maintains or lowers it. Thus, the head of a domain is always at the lowest degree of tension (or greatest degree of repose) in the domain. Since the prolongational structure is hierarchical, the overall prolongational organization of a piece is an arrangement of embedded waves, each of which consists of a tensing followed by a relaxing of tension. In Western tonal music (and I believe this is likely true for most musical idioms) the point of maximal repose in a piece, and hence the head of the piece's entire prolongational structure, is at the end. (In figure 11.9,

Figure 11.9
Prolongational reduction of opening of Mozart, K. 331

which is only the beginning of a piece—as is readily audible—the end is not maximally relaxed.)

In order for listeners to be able to sense the patterns of tension and relaxation in a piece of music, they must be able to derive the prolongational reduction from the musical signal, via correspondence rules that relate this level to lower levels of musical structure. The main correspondence rules relate the prolongational reduction to time-span reduction. Essentially, the events that are structurally important in time-span reduction must also be important in prolongational reduction. In musical terms this means that the events most important in articulating the rhythmic phrasing of a piece are also most important as axes around which patterns of tension and relation are organized.

However, these events need not be connected to each other in head-elaboration dyads in at all the same way in the two structures. Compare figures 11.6 and 11.9, where major structural differences occur in the second half of the passage. In the time-span reduction (figure 11.6) the domains are laid out symmetrically in accordance with the symmetrical grouping structure and regular metrical structure. By contrast, the domains in prolongational reduction tend to be fundamentally asymmetrical, even for pieces that in their rhythmic and motivic form are rigidly symmetrical. In Western tonal music the overall prolongational form tends to be one of a gradual overall increase in tension throughout most of a piece or phrase, followed by a rapid decrease in tension to the final repose at the end. This is evident in figure 11.9, where the first three measures plus the first event of the fourth constitute a prolongation, increasing overall tension only minimally; the point of maximum tension is reached in the second event of the fourth measure, followed by a rapid relaxation to the end of the phrase. Thus, there is a counterpoint between the relatively uniform and symmetrical articulation of rhythmic structure in time-span reduction and the asymmetrical, elastic articulation of prolongational structure.

A distinguishing feature of Western "classical" music is the recursive elaboration of this asymmetrical prolongational shape through many layers, all the way from individual phrases, through major sections, to the organization of entire movements lasting many minutes. It thus turns out that the musical complexity of Bach, Mozart, and Beethoven—what makes their music so structurally coherent—is not a cognitively unfamiliar *kind* of complexity but rather an unusually rich and rigorous use of the complexities found in a common four-measure phrase. This is the sense in which musical sophistication is more an extension of ordinary musical competence than a totally novel capacity.

To sum up the levels of musical structure, the overall organization of the levels can be charted as shown in figure 11.10, following the conventions used in previous chapters.

11.6 Musical Understanding versus Linguistic and Visual Understanding

The central claim of *GTTM* is that the experienced listener's understanding of a piece of music involves, among other things, the derivation of the four hierarchical levels of musical structure from the musical surface. Musical perception, like visual and linguistic perception, is not just a passive taking in of information from the environment: it requires an active structuring of information in forms not explicitly present in the external signal.

There is a respect in which musical perception differs from the other two faculties we have examined. In both language and vision one's understanding depends on the derivation of the most central levels of representation: the conceptual and 3D levels. The lower levels—syntax, phonology, the

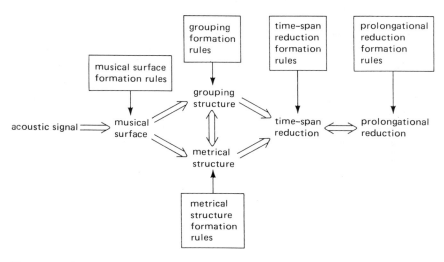

Figure 11.10
Organization of levels of musical representation

primal and $2\frac{1}{2}$D sketches—serve essentially as way stations for translating peripheral information into the central formats, over which are defined all the conceptually interesting and "intelligent" operations such as recognition, categorization, and inference. By contrast, musical understanding crucially involves *all* the levels of musical representation, not just the most central (prolongational reduction). Much of the effect of music depends on appreciating the interaction through time of grouping, meter, and the two reductions.

Moreover, different genres of music, and different pieces within genres, may exploit the possibilities of different levels of representation in developing their own characteristic richness and complexity. Some styles, such as jazz, Balkan music, some African genres, and much of Stravinsky, make extensive use of different sorts of metrical complexity. Contrapuntal styles like that of the fugue make use of complexity in grouping: each voice to a degree has its own grouping structure. The highly organized harmonic system of Western classical music permits complexities in the reductions not available in more purely melodic idioms. Such examples confirm the notion that musical understanding and appreciation in general require all levels of representation, not just the central one(s).

This would seem to make music the odd man out among the faculties we have looked at. A little more reflection suggests it is odd in a further way: it is a cognitive capacity used only for artistic purposes. I would like to suggest that its artistic use is responsible for the difference in the nature of musical understanding. Notice what happens when language is used for artistic purposes, as in poetry. All of a sudden the phonological and syntactic levels become of crucial significance. One counts syllables; one matches phonological segmentations in rhyme and alliteration; one makes use of calculated deviations from normal word order. Thus, the understanding of poetry, like the understanding of music, makes use of all the relevant levels of representation. Similarly, visual art involves the manipulation of textural and configurational properties of the surface, extrinsic to the literal objects being depicted. This suggests that again lower-level representations are invoked (see Arnheim 1974 and a tiny hint in Marr 1982, 356). The generalization appears to be that artistic activity and artistic appreciation in any faculty may make use of formal properties of all levels of representation in that faculty. Music is thereby no anomaly in this respect.

11.7 Musical Understanding and Musical Performance

In activities that involve the coordination of musical information with other capacities, more levels of representation come into play. In perceiving singing, for instance, the incoming information must be processed both as music and as (temporally and intonationally distorted) language. In *performing* music, the motor system must be deployed in the service of manipulating the voice or the musical instrument. If the music is being read, visual representations too must play a role. For the same reasons as in the reading of language (see section 10.7.2), this probably involves all the visual levels up to and including the 3D model.

One could imagine hooking a computer up with a visual pattern recognizer and an electric organ in such a way that it performed printed music without invoking any knowledge at all of the tonal system. I would like to show, however, that humans are not like that—that human musical performance is more than a simple visual-motor transfer and that it must invoke the specifically musical representations.

It is of course undeniable that a great deal of learning a musical instrument involves learning appropriate motor patterns, and performers often speak of "getting a piece in the fingers." Indeed, Sudnow (1978) talks of his own experience of learning jazz piano as if the hands were doing all the work. Yet that simply can't be all there is. For instance, besides playing a piece on one's instrument, one can usually sing it (within the limitations of one's vocal technique). Likewise, if one plays more than one instrument, knowing a piece on one instrument facilitates learning it on another. This suggests that performance of music invokes some nonmotor encoding that is independent of the instrument on which the music is performed— namely, the musical surface. Moreover, the use of the musical surface is obviously necessary for describing what happens when one plays "by ear," imitating a heard piece of music instead of playing it from the printed page.

In reading music, then, information is likely translated from the visual system into a musical representation, then retranslated into whatever specialization of the motor system is appropriate for the instrument at hand. In fact, in my experience as a performer I have found that good players are often playing "by ear" even when using the printed page, in the sense that they have auditory images of what they are about to play. Such auditory images are strong aids in hitting the correct pitch, particularly on "analog" instruments such as the violin, the trombone, and the voice, but on other instruments as well. Thus, phenomenologically, the musical surface is invoked in translating from printed notation to performance.

All this goes without saying, of course, for a musical style in which improvisation plays a role, such as jazz. Here the performer must keep in mind not (only) the musical surface of a piece but (also) its abstract structure in order to improvise variations on it. A successful improvisation must bear the proper sort of relationship to the original tune, while injecting a distinctive character of its own. It is clear that this must involve more than the production of a musical surface, bringing into play deeper levels of understanding.

Still, one may wonder, is there anything involved in the performance of "classical" music beyond playing out the notes exactly? Does one need all the machinery of GTTM? A hint may come from the kind of remark one often hears in disparagement of the latest wunderkind: "Well, he played all the notes, but . . ." The implication is that musical understanding is absent. The difference between a mechanical performance and a musically gratifying one lies in the performer's understanding of the role of the individual notes not just as elements in a sequence but in building integrated structures.

To elaborate on this point: expressive musical performance is not the mystical grafting of some emotional response onto a sequence of notes; it is the communication of one's musical *understanding*—including the hierarchical structures. Of course, the only means available to performers for projecting their understanding is the manipulation of elements of the musical surface, and in fact a great deal of "musical interpretation" involves minute subliminal details of how the notes are produced. The way individual notes are begun and ended, the way notes are connected, the lengthening and shortening of durations, the shape of the amplitude and timbral envelopes, and even deviations from exact intonation—all these are highly controlled by the great performers, and they can make the difference between an ordinary and a striking performance. What happens to each individual note, in turn, is not an arbitrary expressive caprice but depends crucially on the note's role in the larger musical structure. This is very explicit in the teaching of such musicians as Szigeti (1969) and Casals (Blum 1977); to a degree it has been confirmed experimentally in studies by Sternberg, Knoll, and Zukofsky (1982) on timing, by Makeig (1982) on intonational modulation, and by Sloboda (1984, 1985) and Todd (1985) on timing and articulation.

One last piece of experimental evidence: Sloboda (1984) discusses the eye movements of experienced pianists during sight-reading. He finds that the eyes track the musical sense on the printed page. In particular, in contrapuntal music they follow individual lines ahead for a way, then go back and pick up another line, all in advance of playing both lines. The eyes are also found to reach ahead to the end of a phrase and rest there momentarily before going on to the next phrase—again, all ahead of the steady temporal flow of playing. Now notice that the presence of phrase boundaries is not marked explicitly in the printed music; in fact, phrase boundaries are determined by grouping and time-span reduction, so they are not even encoded in the musical surface. This means that experienced players seeing a piece of printed music for the first time must be able to derive the musical structure, in real time, in advance of actually producing the notes on the instrument.

We conclude, then, that good musical performance, with or without the printed music, requires musical understanding. It thus must make use of all levels of musical representation, not just the musical surface.

11.8 Musical Affect; Toward a Level of Body Representation

Having nearly reached the end of the chapter, you may be feeling a mild discontent: still nothing has been said about why one's favorite melody makes one weep. Surely *this* is the essence of musical understanding! Though perhaps true, such a statement should not be used as a justification for rejecting a theory of musical structure. It is clearly not the acoustic signal or the musical surface that makes one weep. So the question is, as always, What forms of information lead to musical affect? The lesson we learn from language and vision is that, even if the response seems altogether direct and unmediated, vast amounts of information processing may be taking place, hidden to consciousness, that are necessary preconditions to its appearance. An aesthetic response to a poem or a painting depends on the computation of the full set of linguistic and visual levels. Why should the same not be true of music?

At the very least, the perception of one's favorite melody requires the presence of grouping structure. Without grouping the musical surface is an undifferentiated stream of pitch-events, and one could not even tell where the theme begins and ends. In addition, the organization of the theme requires a metrical structure: try singing your favorite waltz as a march or vice versa and its coherence vanishes. In order to perceive one part of the theme as a variation or intensification of another part, in order to get an overall sense of the theme's contour, and in order to sense its patterns of tension and relaxation, one must make use of the reductions, which permit one to strip away the surface detail and perceive the essential musical skeleton beneath. In short, the hierarchical levels are intimately involved in hearing the theme *as the theme*. They are thus necessary precursors of the affective response.

One may still be skeptical, in that musical responses are somehow felt as more direct, more primal, than linguistic or visual responses. The reason for this, I think, is that musical representations do not lead ultimately to the construction of conceptual structures. Since it is the presence of conceptual structures that makes verbalization possible, the musical response in large part simply cannot be verbalized. Having less verbal access to it and to the steps in its derivation, we find it less describable yet phenomenologically more immediate and intuitive.

In turn, this difference between musical and linguistic experience tends to invoke certain all-too-common cultural prejudices. The ability to verbalize and explain an experience is often taken as a necessary condition for accepting it as rational or even real. Whatever cannot be verbalized, especially if it involves emotion, is mysterious, irrational, threatening, and perhaps does not exist. Or, to take the opposite side of the dialectic, it is mysterious, wonderful, holistic, sacred, and what makes us humans instead of machines. Whichever side we fall on, such a distinction does not encourage scientific investigation of the musical response.

However, from what we have seen of language and vision, it should be clear that we have only the slimmest verbal access to what these faculties are doing as well. It is only the availability to verbalization of a tiny bit of their end products that leads to the drastic experiential difference between them and music. Thus, the computational theory of mind bids us ask, Granted that all the levels of musical representation are necessary for the understanding of music, and granted that none of these levels translates into conceptual structure, what *do* they translate into that accounts for the affective response to music? Let me sketch out one possible approach to this question.

From an evolutionary point of view, there is no reason to think that musical structure came into being in splendid isolation, as a structure sui generis that somehow came to be linked to affective response by brand-new pathways. More plausible is that musical perception, a highly specialized cognitive activity, is linked to some phylogenetically older cognitive representation that in turn has preestablished links to the affective response.

Searching for circumstantial leads, we observe that, among human activities, one that is closely related to music both in its structure and its affective response is *dance*. Dance is almost invariably performed to music, and its rhythmic characteristics parallel those of the music. Moreover, going beyond crude rhythmic correspondences, we have undeniable and detailed intuitions concerning whether the character of dance movements suit or fail to suit the music. Such intuitions are patently not the result of deliberate training, though they can be sharpened by training.

This suggests that behind the control and appreciation of dance movements lies a cognitive structure that can be placed into a close correspondence with musical structure. So far the only structure we have discussed that might encode dance movements is the purely spatial 3D model. But this seems inappropriate for representing how dance *feels*, which is the information we are trying to get at.

An appealing alternative might be a further level of mental representation, provisionally called *body representation*—essentially a body-specific encoding of the internal sense of the states of the muscles, limbs, and joints. Such a structure, in addition to representing the position of the body, would represent the dynamic forces present within the body, such as whether a position is being held in a state of relaxation or in a state of balanced tension. This level, then, could encode not just what motions are involved in a dance but the bodily sensations attendant upon the movements.

There is every reason to believe that such a representation is independently necessary for everyday tasks. It would, for example, be a crucial link between spatial perception and the control of action. To choose a fairly obvious example, consider the problem of controlling how hard to jump in order to get across a stream (or for monkeys and squirrels, to get from one branch to another, a life-and-death matter). The spatial judgment of distance must be translated into a judgment of muscular force in the leap. Another example: one can imitate someone else's facial expression by sensing how it "feels" in the face. These kinds of patently nonspatial information about how actions feel in the body are what body representation is to encode.

Recall the discussion in section 10.2 of the sense of one's own body position and how it is encoded in the 3D model level. It was pointed out there that many nonvisual sensory pathways contribute to this sense, including touch and pressure cues, the vestibular organs in the ears, and the sensors of the muscles and joints. At least some of these would likely feed information to the 3D model through the body representation. Thus, in carrying out actions there would be a constant interaction between the two representations.

Suppose then that there is such a structure, used for the perception and control of one's muscular states. It would likely be involved as well in correspondences between emotional and muscular states—for instance, one carries oneself differently in states of joy, anger, depression, elation, or fear. So a putative level of body representation appears to have some appropriate links to affect.

The hypothesis, then, is that musical structures are placed most directly in correspondence with the level of body representation rather than with conceptual structure. By virtue of invoking or entraining temporal patterns in body representation, music can be placed in detailed correspondence with dance. In turn, body representation, whether or not it is further translated into lower-level motor instructions, evokes the affective response characteristic of music. (Suggestive evidence for this linkup of representations comes from the work of Clynes and associates (Clynes and Nettheim 1982; Clynes and Walker 1982), who find highly specific temporal patterns of muscular tension and relaxation that seem to be biologically associated with specific emotional responses; these can be invoked and identified in the visual and musical modalities as well as through one's own bodily awareness.)

Such a hypothesis accords with the sense of traditional music theory that notions like gesture, tension, and relaxation are germane to musical expression—that the use of these kinesthetic terms is not an arbitrary metaphor. The *GTTM* theory builds on this intuition in claiming that prolongational reduction is a representation of hierarchical temporal patterns of tension and relaxation.

All this, of course, is sketchy and highly speculative. But there is no doubt that the organism requires some form of information about the state of its body. The great variety of interactions such information has with other capacities points to it as a potentially exciting locus for further research in the computational theory of mind.

11.9 Remarks on Musical Processing

There has been little experimental work that bears on how listeners actively use the acoustic input from a piece of music to derive the musical structures developed in *GTTM*. Such work as there is concerns primarily the imposition of grouping structure (Deliege 1985; Deutsch 1982b), elementary inference of metrical structure (Povel and Essens 1985), the integration of a sequence of tones into either one melody or two interleaved melodies (Bregman and Campbell 1971; Dowling 1973), and the perception of harmonic relations among elements of a musical sequence (Krumhansl 1983; see also references there). As far as I can determine, this work verifies that the factors Lerdahl and I have claimed as significant to music cognition are indeed recoverable through experimental procedures. Unlike at least some of the work in language processing, however, they do not yet help us take a snapshot of processing in progress. (Krumhansl and Kessler (1982) provide a notable exception.) Thus, theories of the course of active musical processing are at the moment based more on considerations of plausibility than on empirical evidence.

An important theory of how musical affect is derived from musical processing is the "implication-realization" theory of Meyer (1956; 1973) and Narmour (1977). The idea behind this theory is that listeners continually form hypotheses about the expected continuation of the music they are currently hearing and that musical affect arises from suspense about the actual continuation and from satisfaction or surprise when the expectation is fulfilled or violated. This theory in its outlines simply echoes a common intuition about musical perception. However, Meyer shows that "musical implications" are not just superficial associations to past experience but rather the product of musical cognition—the construction of abstract musical structures by the listener on the basis of a multitude of learned and innate principles of musical form. Thus, the general outlines of this theory seem congenial to the present approach to musical understanding (even if Meyer's and Narmour's notions of musical structure are relatively impoverished compared to that of GTTM; see GTTM, pp. 26–27, and also Keiler 1978).

However, there is a fundamental difficulty with the usual formulation of the implication-realization theory. If one is listening to a piece that one knows very well, one should not have to "form hypotheses" about the expected continuation. One should know for sure what will happen next, and so there should be none of the element of surprise that is supposed to trigger affect. Hence, the affect of a piece of music should diminish with increasing acquaintance. In fact, just the opposite is the case, at least for the masterpieces: our enjoyment increases the better we get to know them. This seems to undermine the theory entirely. Nonetheless, let us keep the theory in mind as we develop a somewhat deeper account of processing than Meyer's. We will come to see the sense in which it captures an important insight.

Let us consider the consequences of the GTTM theory for processing. As in the language and visual faculties, the organization of levels of representation puts strong constraints on the flow of information in processing.

Logical Structure of Musical Processing (LSMP)
Translation of musical information from one level to another must follow the correspondences in figure 11.10, involving intermediate levels of translation where necessary.

In particular, as noted previously, one cannot get from an acoustic signal to musical affect, a derivative of the reductions, without passing through the intervening levels of grouping and metrical structure.

Again as in the other faculties, the logical structure of processing permits the functions of processing to be divided among a number of autonomous processors. For each level of representation in figure 11.10 there is an integrative processor that takes all information available in its format, from whatever source, and attempts to construct a unified structure. For each set of correspondence rules in figure 11.10 there is a processor that translates between the two formats related by the correspondence rules (possibly one in each direction, where bidirectionality is necessary).

Within the constraints imposed by LSMP a general view of processing entirely parallel to that for language develops. I will work this out essentially point by point in correspondence with the discussion of language processing in chapter 6.

In musical perception one clearly cannot derive each level of representation in its entirety before going on to process the next level up, since that would require listening to the entire piece before even beginning to derive grouping, not to mention the reductions. Obviously a certain amount of parallel processing must be going on. It seems likely that all the processors are active at once, trying to attach as much structure as possible to whatever portion of the piece has been heard up to that point.

In addition, musical processing cannot be strictly localistic bottom-up. Each level of musical structure imposes holistic constraints, in the form of overarching structural schemas—for example, the preference for symmetry in grouping, a strong preference for constant meter throughout a piece, preferred voice-leading in time-span reduction, and a "normative phrase structure" of tension and relaxation in prolongational reduction. These schemas are important in fixing the role of individual pitch-events in their musical context and in determining global properties of perceived musical structure for which there is little local evidence.

Moreover, there are top-down effects that fill in lower-level representations. For instance, grouping boundaries are often signaled by abstract harmonic patterns such as cadences, which can be detected only once a preliminary time-span reduction has been derived. Thus, at least from the musical surface up, it is necessary to posit a certain degree of holistic interactive parallel processing.

On the other hand, LSMP constrains the time course of such processing. It is impossible to engage the higher-level processors until they have received some information from lower-level ones. For instance, provisional grouping and metrical structures must be derived for any point in the music before hypotheses can be formed about the role of that point in the reductions. Thus, the derivation of reductions should be expected to lag in time behind the derivation of the lower-level structures. In turn, this means that top-down effects on grouping and meter are constrained to occurring after bottom-up effects. (This parallels the claim that top-down effects on phonological perception must occur after bottom-up effects.)

The holistic constraints on musical structure at each level are the source of "musical implications" in Meyer's sense. When a fragment of the music engages any of these schemas, hypotheses are formed about subsequent structure in the music that is necessary to complete the schema. (This parallels the situation in linguistic parsing, where for example the perception of a definite article engages the schema for Noun Phrase, and hypotheses are formed about what elements of syntactic structure will occur subsequently.) Such *prospective* hearing is of course largely unconscious: these implications need not present themselves to awareness.

There is also a phenomenon of *retrospective* hearing, in which one suddenly experiences a restructuring of what one has heard on the basis of its relationship to new input. This often happens when the music fails to fulfill a structural expectation: an anticipated phrase ending, say, turns out to be something else—which in turn means that the structural schema that implied a phrase ending must itself be reevaluated. Such occasions produce a sense of surprise. In a multitude of less striking cases the musical structure at some point is simply indeterminate among a number of possibilities, until subsequent input confirms one analysis or another. For example, at the beginning of a piece the meter and the key are often not completely clear to the listener until a measure or two have been heard, and it is only at that time that the very first events of the piece are experienced in retrospect as properly comprehended. (Some composers, such as Haydn and Schumann, frequently exploit the uncertainty of such situations for artistic effect.)

What kind of processing system is necessary in order for the phenomenon of retrospective hearing to take place? To focus the question a little more closely, let us see what the processing system must have available in short-term musical memory (STMM) from moment to moment.

First, recall the discussion of section 11.6. Unlike language and vision, where comprehension is based on the central representations alone, musical understanding depends on the rhythmic interaction of all levels of musical structure. This means that in order for musical comprehension to take place, all the levels must be present in STMM simultaneously, and they must all be maintained *in registration with one another* so their counterpoint can be detected and appreciated. This parallels the goal of short-term linguistic and visual processing—and it is in fact more easily motivated because of the nature of musical understanding.

In addition, the logistics of musical processing demand a device that develops and compares multiple possible analyses in parallel. For instance, to determine the key or meter of the beginning of a piece, one must rely not on isolated local details but rather on the accumulation of evidence in real time over a sequence of events. This means that a parser cannot choose to pursue a single most likely analysis, then go back and start over if it later finds it has made a mistake: the music continues on inexorably and must be monitored in real time. Nor can the meter or key be left entirely open until the clinching evidence arrives: its role as clinching evidence is only apparent in the context of alternative possibilities that are available to be compared. Thus, the processor must keep track of these alternative analyses and see how each successive new event contributes to their relative salience. In short, of the theories of language processing mentioned in chapter 6, the processing theory necessary for musical perception more closely resembles multiple-analysis theories such as those of Woods (1982) and Swinney (1979) than it does the majority of models such as those of Wanner and Maratsos (1978), Frazier and Fodor (1978), and Marcus (1980), which try to compute a single best analysis.

The presence in STMM of multiple analyses being computed in parallel implies the existence of a *selection function* that compares current possibilities and designates one as most salient. Moreover, it is implausible to consider the selection function an autonomous "higher cognitive process," somehow concerned with the production of awareness: in order to make its decisions, the selection function must delve into intimate low-level details of musical structure and hence must have access to all the musical representations. Thus, the selection function is best treated as one of the essential components of STMM itself, paralleling the situation in language and vision.

Given this organization of STTM, here are three representative situations that can arise in the course of processing:

1. Multiple possible analyses are present, but there is insufficient evidence for the selection function to decide among them. The phenomenology will be of ambiguity or vagueness in the music. Then suppose the evidence for deciding arrives, so that the selection function picks out a single analysis for the entire passage. The phenomenology will be of *retrospective analysis* of what has gone before. This is the situation when the meter or key of a piece is determined some distance from the beginning.

2. Multiple possible analyses are present, and the selection function has chosen one as most salient; this one will be heard as the structure of the music up to this point, and it will generate prospective anticipations of what is to come. Then suppose an event arrives that causes reweighting of the analyses, so that the selection function changes its choice. The phenomenology will be of *retrospective reanalysis*: suddenly the whole previous passage changes structure like a Necker cube, producing the sensation of surprise remarked upon by Meyer and Narmour.

3. Multiple possible analyses are present, and one is designated as most salient. Then suppose an event arrives that is inconsistent with *all* the analyses being considered, so the selection function has no alternative to

fall back upon. The phenomenology will be of sudden bewilderment, "losing one's bearings." (The kind of passage I have in mind is the moment from which Mozart's "Dissonant" Quartet gets its name: the entry of the first violin in measure 2 on A-natural clashes violently and incomprehensibly with the (unstable) impression of A-flat major up to that point, and from there on all evidence for A-flat is decisively gone.)

Thus, various cases of prospective and retrospective hearing fall out from the assumption that STMM contains multiple analyses under scrutiny by a selection function. In particular, the fundamental notions of the implication-realization theory find a comfortable place within this account.

How might this approach meet the apparently fatal flaw in the implication-realization theory—that knowing a piece of music can increase rather than decrease its affect? There are two parts to the answer.

First, musical affect is not just a function of being satisfied or surprised by the realization or violation of one's expectations. That is only a small part of the musical experience, which involves the total effect of deriving in real time all details of the musical structures and of selecting among them, and which includes all the tensions engendered by the unconscious presence of conflicting structures. In any reasonably complex piece of music there are just too many details and too many large-scale considerations for a comprehensive structure to be developed on a single hearing. Repeated hearing is necessary before everything can be taken in and integrated in real time, and it is this full integration that makes the musical experience rich.

But why doesn't musical memory enable one to infer the correct structure immediately? It has to do with the nature of the processor. First of all, notice that one must verify that one is indeed hearing the same piece that one has stored in long-term memory. In order to be able to perform this comparison, the processor must derive the complete musical structure of the input—for the music could prove at any moment to deviate from what one remembers. Thus, the processor must be chugging away computing structure even for a known piece, in order to make sure that it is *still* the known piece.

To embellish this point, recall the discussion of "garden path" sentences such as (6.2) (*The horse raced past the barn fell*). The oddity of these sentences arises from the fact that the selection function cannot wait forever before committing itself to a decision, so it does the best it can on the basis of what it has so far. In (6.2) it settles on a structure with *raced* as main verb, which then turns out to be inconsistent with later evidence. Now notice that, even knowing the pitfalls of garden path sentences, (6.2) still sounds worse than *The horse that raced past the barn fell*. That is, memory does not entirely prevent the processor from constructing the erroneous structure, though it may provide a speedier resolution to the inconsistency once the processor detects it.

Suppose the musical processor works the same way. Then, for example, even if one knows consciously that a deceptive cadence is coming, the processor is innocent of this knowledge—it is "informationally encapsulated" in the sense of Fodor (1983). It is therefore likely to select as most salient a more stable structure with a full cadence, then be forced to reevaluate its choice when this structure is not realized. The conscious knowledge that a deceptive cadence is coming thus *does* diminish one's surprise, but it does not diminish the affect that comes from the activity of the processor deriving the structure autonomously. Hence the affect remains despite the absence of conscious surprise.

In short, the idea that musical affect arises from the formation of expectations, and from suspense, satisfaction, or surprise about the realization of these expectations, does not make sense if we think in terms of conscious expectations or a musical processor that has full access to one's musical memory. However, it does make sense if the processor is conceived as parallel to those for language and vision, made up of a number of autonomous units, each working in its own limited domain, with limited access to memory. For under this conception, expectation, suspense, satisfaction, and surprise *can* occur within the processor: in effect, the processor is *always* hearing the piece for the first time.

To sum up this section: We have not developed a theory of the algorithms used in the processing of music—in particular, the precise way the musical grammar is used, the number of hypotheses kept under consideration at once, the relative influences of top-down and bottom-up information over time, or a multitude of other questions. What we have seen is (1) how the levels of representation determine the logical course of processing, (2) how the problems faced by musical processing require a multiple-analysis parallel processor with a selection function, and (3) how such a processor could be responsible for certain previously unexplained aspects of the musical experience. Moreover, this sort of processor is altogether consistent in its overall form with those for language and for vision, suggesting that musical processing is of a piece with other psychological systems.

Chapter 12

The Modularity of the Computational Mind

We have now completed our survey of known levels of representation. Before returning to the issue of consciousness, I would like to draw together the results of this survey and extract some general conclusions about the overall organization of the computational mind. I will deal with both theory of structure and theory of processing, in that order. In particular, the view of processing developed here bears a strong resemblance to Jerry Fodor's in *The Modularity of Mind* (Fodor 1983). The details of the present analysis make possible a number of refinements and elaborations to Fodor's modularity thesis; these will be explored in the second half of the chapter.

12.1 Summary of the Levels

Figure 12.1 sums up all the levels of representation we have discussed. Each is characterized by a set of formation rules that enumerates its primitives and principles of combination. The levels are linked by correspondence rules that permit translation from one form of information into another. The correspondence rules we have discussed are symbolized by arrows in the figure; the direction of each arrow signifies the direction in which information may be translated in the course of processing.

Let me gloss figure 12.1 more completely, reviewing faculties one by one. In doing so, it is useful to distinguish a "broad" construal of a faculty from a "narrow" one. Under a *broad* construal a faculty includes all the levels of representation and all the correspondence rules that may be invoked while processing information within that faculty. The same faculty *narrowly* construed includes only those levels and correspondence rules that belong to it exclusively.

The *language faculty*, broadly construed, includes auditory input, motor output to the vocal tract, all the components of phonological structure, syntactic structure, conceptual structure, and, as shown in chapter 10, the 3D model level. It includes as well the correspondence rules that map between these levels.

Both ends of this chain of the levels are shared. At the peripheral end, auditory input also goes to the musical faculty, to voice recognition, and to

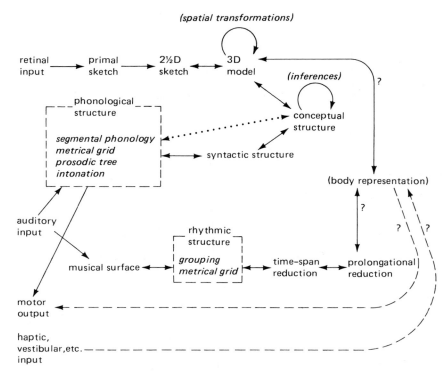

Figure 12.1
Organization of all levels of mental representation presented in parts II and III

general-purpose audition; motor output to the vocal tract is presumably also supplied by more general-purpose action representations that control breathing, swallowing, chewing, kissing, playing the clarinet, and so forth. At the central end, conceptual structure and the 3D model are representations accessed by many modalities, so they do not belong exclusively to language either. Thus the narrow construal of the language faculty includes only phonological and syntactic structure, plus the sets of correspondence rules that map between them, and from them to shared representations.

The *visual faculty* broadly construed includes retinal input, the primal sketch, the 2½D sketch, the 3D model, and, as shown in chapter 10, conceptual structure; it also includes the correspondence rules that map between these levels. Since the 3D model and conceptual structure are shared with language and probably the haptic and action faculties as well, the visual faculty narrowly construed includes everything from the retinal input up to and including the correspondence rules between the 2½D sketch and the 3D model, but not the 3D model itself.

The *musical faculty* broadly construed includes auditory input, the musical surface, grouping structure, the metrical grid, the two reductions, and the relevant correspondence rules. It may also invoke body representation, though this is at the moment a matter of speculation. The auditory input is of course shared with other faculties, and it appears likely that grouping structure is not peculiar to music but is a general characteristic of audition. Thus, the narrow construal of the musical faculty excludes these two levels, though it retains the correspondence rules that relate these levels to specifically musical information.

Figure 12.1 also includes, tentatively, the level of body representation, which participates in perception of one's body position in space and in the formation of action patterns. It also includes a tentative correspondence rule link between conceptual structure and phonological structure, bypassing syntax. This connection is present to account for the possibility of reading and of sign language, where categorization of visual rather than auditory inputs feeds the computation of phonological structure (section 10.7).

Finally, the central levels of 3D model and conceptual structure are subject to various sets of *intralevel* mapping principles. In conceptual structure these are the rules of inference, which permit the creation of new conceptual structures on the basis of old. In the 3D model, principles with parallel function include rules of spatial transformation such as the rotations, zooms, and changes of perspective described in the imagery literature (Shepard and Cooper 1982; Kosslyn 1980). As argued by Shepard and others, they are also involved in creating anticipations of changes in the spatial configurations of external objects or the viewing organism itself.

Other levels of representation and other sets of correspondence rules no doubt exist. Current understanding of the haptic and motor faculties, for instance, does not permit us to say anything about levels of representation that may serve as way stations in these faculties between the periphery and the central levels. I have also not included any of the correspondence rules necessary to the reading and performance of music, that is, the mappings from a visual categorization of symbols on a page of printed music to a specifically musical representation, and from there to the motor output necessary for playing the oboe or the viola da gamba or whatever. So figure 12.1 should be taken as a sketch only of the known structures of the computational mind, augmented by certain especially important avenues of speculation.

12.2 Hierarchies and Headed Hierarchies

Having worked out the organization of some dozen levels of representation in three faculties, we can begin to assess the extent to which there are general principles of organization in the computational mind beyond the division into autonomous levels linked by correspondence rules.

Let us look first at the general kinds of structures that appear in the levels of representation. At the lowest input levels—the acoustic signal and the retinal array—the organization of information is entirely local, consisting of unrelated elements linearly ordered in time and (in the retinal array) isotropically arranged in space. At the lowest output level, motor instructions, the information involves individual activations of muscles arrayed over time.

As we move up the levels, *hierarchies* appear: individual elements are grouped into larger constituents (for instance, syllables, visual boundaries, musical groups). Moreover, such grouping is recursive: groupings may themselves serve as elements of larger groups without thereby losing their own structural integrity. This sort of hierarchical grouping appears in all levels we have studied except the very lowest (those of the input and output transducers plus the musical surface).

As we move to the right in figure 12.1 the hierarchies tend to take on an additional property that I will call *headedness*. We may speak of a level of representation as a *headed hierarchy* if, in each constituent, the principles of combination assign to one of the elements a privileged role of *head*. By contrast, in a nonheaded hierarchy the elements of a constituent are all of equivalent status. The best-known example of a headed hierarchy is syntactic structure, where, for instance, a constituent labeled *noun phrase* must contain one specially designated element, the noun, as head.

Let us make a rapid survey of the faculties. In language *segmental phonology* is a nonheaded hierarchy: syllables are strung together to form words, and words are strung together to form phrases. The only possible headedness occurs within the syllable, where the vowel is often considered privileged. In the *metrical grid* the strong beats of any layer have a headlike privileged status; in the *prosodic tree* each constituent contains a privileged S (strong) element, and the rest of the elements are W (weak). There is no discernible notion of head in the *intonation contour* (and little evidence, in fact, even for a hierarchy). *Syntax*, as just observed, is the quintessential headed hierarchy. In *conceptual structure* functions (or predicates) play the role of heads, and the arguments of functions are nonheads.

In vision the (*full*) *primal sketch* contains recursive groupings, but the groups are nonheaded. It is not clear whether the *2½D sketch* is a headed hierarchy or not. (As pointed out in appendix B, Marr's formal description does not even accord it hierarchical structure, though his informal description does.) If the figure-ground distinction is represented at this level (as seems possible), the more "figural" member of a configuration might play a headlike role. In the *3D model* there is a clear notion of headedness in the decomposition of objects into their parts: the head of a configuration is that element whose coordinates most closely match those of the next coarser layer of description. For example, the torso is the head of the body configuration as a whole; the palm is the head of the hand configuration. (Recall the discussion of figure 9.6.)

In music, *grouping structure* is a nonheaded hierarchy: groups contained within a larger group are just strung together. On the other hand, in the *metrical grid* of music as well as in that of language the strong beats play a headlike role. The basic principle behind both *reduction structures* is that of one element in any grouping being the "most important" along certain dimensions, whereas the rest of the elements function as elaborations or ornamentations. Hence, the reductions are also headed hierarchies.

Thus, we find in each faculty a progression in the formal character of levels of representation: from ungrouped at the most peripheral levels, to hierarchically grouped at low to intermediate levels, to headed hierarchies at the intermediate to most central levels. I am inclined to suppose that this is no accident but instead reflects some rather important general property of the organization of the computational mind.

12.3 Fundamental Computational Principles

So far we have examined rather large-scale units: the levels of representation and their correspondences within faculties. Let us next look at one aspect of fine-scale organization.

A certain class of major disagreements in psychology can be characterized as disputes about the existence and nature of *fundamental computational principles* that pervade every aspect of mental activity. Associationist theory supposed that all relationships among ideas (or percepts or concepts) were built out of a single type of link, association, established through repeated exposure. Gestalt theory stressed the ubiquity of the differentiation between figure and ground. As mentioned in chapter 3, contemporary "information-processing" psychology often assumes the binary digit as the fundamental unit of information and a corresponding set of computational principles equivalent in power to a Turing machine.

Such hypotheses are just the sort of "horizontal" principles that Fodor (1983) decries as misguided attempts to overgeneralize mental function, to reduce all individual faculties to one generalized cognitive capacity. Our survey of faculties makes clear that Fodor is right in railing against the assumption that the mind is basically simple and undifferentiated. But, on the other hand, he has given no argument against the possibility that faculties share some fundamental computational principles yet differ in others. At the very least, of course, they *must* differ in the principles of the transducers, such as retinal versus cochlear cells.

More importantly, faculties might differ radically in how the fundamental units are organized, so that they compute and store differently structured information—just as a computer can compute radically different kinds of information by using various programs built out of the same primitive operations. To invoke Chomsky's (1975) "mental organ" analogy, the discovery that the entire body is built out of cells with virtually identical basic biological properties does not undermine the claim that the body contains highly differentiated organs, each with its own specific properties. Similarly, the existence of fundamental computational principles does not undermine the claim that the mind is highly differentiated. We are talking about different scales of organization.

What Fodor is more deeply concerned with, and rightly so, is showing that the differences among faculties are not learned. Again the biological analogy is helpful. To put it in Chomsky's (1975) terms, one no more *learns* to have a language faculty or a visual faculty than one *learns* to have arms rather than wings. (In turn, it is only by virtue of having a language faculty that one learns a language—recall the discussion of section 5.9.) Each faculty may be the product of a different organization built up out of fundamental computational principles; this organization, like the organization of cells into arms and hearts, may be partly or even largely innate. In short, differentiated innate faculties do not preclude common fundamental principles.

In the course of this investigation we have come upon the need for a principle of computation that seems pervasive in psychological systems: the *preference rule system*. As mentioned in section 8.3, its essential properties were discovered by Wertheimer (1923). A preference rule system is a means of producing a judgment or analysis on the basis of a number of discrete conditions. In any given field to which the system applies, each individual condition contributes a preferred analysis, with an intrinsic strength or weight of application. The overall analysis arrived at by the system is the one that receives the greatest weight from individual conditions. If an analysis results from the reinforcement of a number of conditions, and no competing analyses present themselves seriously, the analysis is a relatively stereotypical instance of its category. If two or more competing analyses receive approximately equal weight, an ambiguous or vague judgment results.

We have seen here preference rule systems as part of the organization of categories in conceptual structure (section 8.3), in Gestalt principles of visual organization (sections 8.3 and 9.3; see also Marr 1982, esp. section 3.5), and in the correspondence rule components for music (sections 11.4 and 11.5). The *content* of the preference rules varies widely from one domain to the next, but the characteristic *computational interaction* appears in every case. Lerdahl and Jackendoff (1983, section 12.2) and Jackendoff (1983, section 8.7) cite many further cases from the linguistic and visual literature that had not been previously recognized as instances of the same phenomenon. Thus, preference rule systems appear to be an important building block of mental computation that cuts broadly across domains of all sorts, irrespective of the actual content of the domains.

Among the systems we have cited here are the Gestalt principles of proximity and similarity, which, as observed by Wertheimer (1923), apply equally to spatial groupings and to temporal (including musical) groupings. Jackendoff (1983) concludes that these principles are stated over the modality-independent level of conceptual structure. However, this seems incorrect, inasmuch as Marr (1982) finds principles along very similar lines deep in the visual faculty, in the derivation of the full (recursively grouped) primal sketch from the raw (ungrouped) primal sketch; we would furthermore prefer musical grouping to be autonomous of conceptual structure. An alternative, more plausible conclusion in light of the present analysis of faculties is that proximity and similarity are "metaprinciples" that can be realized in any domain where grouping is accomplished. The content of the domains may differ widely, but as long as there are appropriate notions of distance and similarity among elements, these principles can be adapted and specialized to each of them.

Again, this need not mean that the domains, or the application of the metaprinciples to them, need be *learned*. Rather, the duplication of principles may be seen as evolution's way of using means already at its disposal for new purposes.

We next explore a more elaborate example of the same sort.

12.4 Larger-Scale Commonalities across Language and Music

Perhaps the most unexpected finding of Lerdahl and Jackendoff (1983) with respect to psychology as a whole was that the metrical grid and time-span reduction in music utilize structures virtually identical to the metrical grid and prosodic tree in language. We have already remarked on the parallelism of the metrical grids. Let us now expand on it somewhat and sketch the parallelism between the two tree structures; Lerdahl and Jackendoff (1983, section 12.3) work the parallels out in detail.

It has sometimes been claimed that musical meter is a natural outgrowth of biological periodicities such as the heartbeat, alpha brainwaves, or circadian rhythms. But such an explanation is overly facile, for two reasons. First, it does not explain how one can choose an arbitrary tempo, unrelated to biological rhythms, and maintain it over time. The regularity of musical meter is more likely to be attributed to an ability to replicate intervals of time (perhaps up to a couple of seconds), independent of preexisting physiological rhythms.

Second, the essence of musical meter is not just periodicity but *hierarchi-*

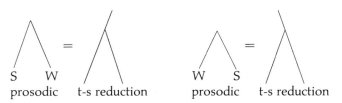

S   W   /\   W   S   /\
prosodic   t-s reduction   prosodic   t-s reduction

Figure 12.2
Translation between prosodic trees and time-span reduction trees

cal periodicity. In 4/4 time, for example, there are periodicities at every quarter note, every two quarters, and every four quarters; and the larger periodicities result in stronger beats. Such gradations of strength due to multiple periodicities do not occur in the biological rhythms usually attested as the basis of meter, so for this reason too they fail to provide an extrinsic basis for meter in music. It is the notion of hierarchical periodicity that is expressed by the use of a metrical grid in both music and language.

The linguistic grid differs from musical meter in that it is not usually isochronous; that is, there are not identical intervals of time between adjacent pairs of beats (see Prince 1983 for discussion). Though there may be some tendency toward a rough isochrony in ordinary language, the strict isochrony of music applies to language only in the recitation of certain kinds of poetry, such as nursery rhymes, limericks, and (it is thought) *Beowulf*.

Thus, the principles of metrical structure in music are probably assembled out of general metaprinciples of the metrical grid, shared with language, plus isochrony, plus a number of specializations to musical needs. It is difficult to imagine what other cognitive needs might be served by metrical grids, but the differences between meter in language and meter in music are substantial enough that they cannot be simply sharing a common structure.

Next let us briefly compare prosodic trees (section 5.6) and time-span reduction (section 11.5). Both are headed hierarchies. Both are based on a segmentation of the linear sequence of elementary units (phonological segments in language, notes or chords in music) into a nonheaded hierarchy (syllables, feet, and words in language, time-span domains in music). In each constituent of this segmentation one element is designated as head (*S* in language, Head in music) and the rest of the elements are designated nonhead (*W* in language, Elaboration in music). This parallelism in the structures can be made more explicit by an actual translation of the tree notations, according to the equivalency in figure 12.2. For instance, the prosodic tree for the word *reconciliation* (figure 12.3a) can be translated node by node into time-span reduction notation (figure 12.3b). Similarly,

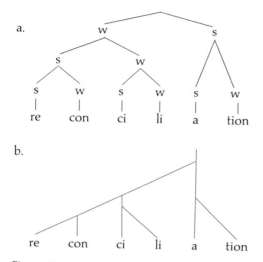

Figure 12.3
Translation of prosodic tree for the word *reconciliation* into time-span reduction notation

musical examples can be transcribed into prosodic tree notation. Thus, there is a strong substantive parallelism between these two tree structures.

The strength of the parallelism can be seen more vividly by comparing these trees to standard syntactic phrase structure trees, which have quite different properties—for example, domains that are labeled by name (Noun Phrase, Verb Phrase, and so on) rather than by relative importance. They differ as well from the prolongational reduction tree, also a headed hierarchy, in that they have only one way of combining elements of a domain (S–W or Head–Elaboration), whereas prolongational reduction has three (Head–Strong Prolongation, Head–Weak Prolongation, Head–Progression).

Further elements of parallelism emerge in the details of the grammars for these two structures. For example, the treatment of upbeats in music (notes in a group that precede the strongest beat or downbeat) is remarkably similar to that of unstressed syllables at the beginning of words in language. Moreover, the relation of time-span reduction to the musical metrical grid bears a distinct resemblance to the relationship between prosodic trees and the linguistic metrical grid. Thus, the grid-tree system as a whole appears in both faculties.

On the other hand, it is not possible to say that the two grid-tree systems constitute a single component of the computational mind, shared by the linguistic and musical faculties. That is, they are not like the 3D model–conceptual structure system, which is shared by language and vision and which is used to communicate between them. The reason is that the principles of this system in language involve such purely linguistic factors as vowel quality, number of consonants, morphological structure, and lexical marking; those in music involve musical factors such as harmonic consonance and dissonance, voice-leading, and relationship to prolongational reduction. Like the musical grid, the musical tree structure has some special structural adaptations (not described here) that play an important role in the regulation of phrase endings; such complexities are absent in language. Moreover, the role of stress in the two systems is somewhat different. For example, in language higher stress must fall on a strong beat and on the S member of an $S-W$ pair. A parallel correspondence is often present in music, but under various conditions higher stress instead falls on a weak beat or Elaboration.

Detailed examination of these structures, then, yields a complex picture. On the one hand, we have found two entire hierarchical structures whose application cuts across two distinct faculties, with relatively minor—but genuine—modifications. On the other hand, the way the structures are used and the principles by which they are computed from the input show considerable specialization in each domain. My judgment of the situation is that the two systems are distinct components of the computational mind, functioning in different processing systems, but that they each represent a particular realization (or adaptation) of a more general set of "metaprinciples" available for assiging structure to temporal patterns.

This conclusion does not seem implausible if we again appeal to the biological analogy. Compared to the kidney and the ear, for example, the fingers and toes have nearly identical morphology. Yet we would not hasten to conclude that the fingers and the toes are therefore the same organ. Rather, they are individual adaptations of a more general digital genotype. Why shouldn't the mind be like that too?

12.5 What Part of Music Is Specifically Musical?

At the beginning of chapter 11 the question was raised of why there should be a distinct musical faculty, given that there is no evident environmental pressure that would favor organisms possessing it. Though we are still not in a position to answer this question, a closer look has revealed that many aspects of musical cognition can be plausibly said to have been "borrowed" from other capacities or constructed from more general metaprinciples.

Musical grouping is largely not specific to music; as observed in section 11.4, many of its principles apply to any temporal sequence of events, presented in any modality. We dealt with metrical structure and time-span reduction in the previous section: they are music-specific adaptations of more general rhythmic functions. Because of the differences between the musical and linguistic adaptations of this machinery, we concluded that these structures are genuinely parts of the musical faculty, autonomous from, if similar to, the parallel parts of language.

The fourth musical hierarchy is prolongational reduction, the musical hierarchy that establishes domains of tensing and relaxing in the musical flow. This structure displays no formal affinities to other levels of representation developed so far. Section 11.8 speculated that it is most closely related to the level of body representation, but in the absence of any independent evidence about the nature of such representation, not much can be made of the point for now.

If there is a domain-specific germ around which a musical faculty could have evolved, it is probably the basic properties of tonal systems and their role in prolongational reduction. Central to most music is the notion of a maximally stable pitch that can serve as a point of departure and arrival and whose return can be recognized as a point of relaxation. Also central seems to be the notion of relative stability (consonance) or instability (dissonance) of the intervals between pitches. These aspects of music have no formal parallel in other cognitive capacities (imagine organizing colors or smells that way!), and they are essential to getting any musical system off the ground. (This stipulation probably even includes drum musics and gamelan, where the different pitches are perhaps inexact or indistinct but replicable and recognizable nonetheless.)

One of the livelier debates in the psychology of music has concerned the extent to which the choice of pitch collection is determined by factors extrinsic to music—in particular, by the natural pitches of the harmonic series and their effects on and within the ear. Looking at the musical idioms of the world as a whole and not just at Western music, it would appear that the salience of the octave, probably the fifth, and possibly the major triad are due to such extrinsic factors. In addition, the combinatorial possibilities of certain pitch collections (including the major scale and the most common form of pentatonic scale) enhance the recognizability of pitches of the scale, on the basis of their unique intervallic relationships to other pitches (see Balzano 1982). However, there is no cognitive *necessity* to adopt pitch collections with favorable properties, and among the musical idioms of the world there are many pitch collections—including the familiar minor scale—that deviate from acoustic or combinatorial optimality in various degrees. Thus, the choice of scale is at bottom a musical rather than acoustic or physiological matter, though it is shaped to a certain degree by such extrinsic factors.

Thus, just as one can think of phonology and syntax as having evolved in order to provide way stations in a translation between conceptual structure and its vocal expression, so it might be possible to think of metrical structure and time-span reduction as having evolved to provide a way to use a tonal system to express patterns of tension and relaxation over time. Again, the adaptive advantage of such an evolutionary course is completely mysterious. But at least we have begun to sort out the bits and pieces of the music faculty that are more specifically musical (and hence more mysterious) from those that may be adaptations of already existing machinery.

12.6 General Characteristics of the Processors

So far we have been talking about the information structures employed by the computational mind. What of the processes that produce and manipulate them?

Chapters 6, 9, and 11 argued (to the extent possible from the evidence) that the processors in each faculty we have examined are highly constrained in character and furthermore that processing in all faculties proceeds along similar lines. In turn, the proposed organization of the processors emerged in large part from the nature of the levels of representation and the logical connections among them.

Briefly, there are two kinds of processing components. For each set of correspondence rules that provides a translation from one level of representation L_i into another level L_j, there is a *translation processor* that automatically and compulsively translates whatever information is available at level L_i into information of level L_j, whenever such translation is possible. When a pair of levels is used bidirectionally in processing (such as the use of linguistic levels in both perception and production), I have supposed that there is a separate processor for translating in each direction; a better understanding of the translation process might well render the duplication unnecessary. In any event, we have seen that processing is bidirectional: in perception top-down evidence refines and fills in lower-level representations; in production bottom-up evidence guides choices in subsequent realization of the intended product (speech or imagery).

We have also seen that in order for such bidirectional processing to be possible, each level of representation must be regulated by an *integrative processor*. Each of these processors automatically and compulsively attempts to integrate into a coherent structure all the information it receives from whatever translation processors impinge on it.

By breaking up processing into these components, we can achieve the observed interpenetration of top-down, bottom-up, and intralevel holistic effects, without resorting to a chaotic unstructured free-for-all in processing; what we have instead is a very tightly structured free-for-all!

We have seen that the goal of processing in each faculty is the same: a single most coherent set of representations in short-term memory, one from each level of the faculty, maintained in registration with each other.

Recapitulating the argument: (1) All levels except the most peripheral in each faculty are available to be stored in long-term memory, so they must be produced in short-term memory in any event. (2) The levels must be maintained in registration with each other in order to allow feedback effects in the course of processing; such feedback effects have been shown to be necessary in a wide range of cases. (3) I have argued that each faculty contains a *selection function* that continually attempts to restrict the number of structures under consideration and that at each moment marks a particular candidate as most stable or salient. It is the selection function, rather than some superordinate general cognitive device, that is responsible for the fact that only one interpretation of an ambiguous field presents itself to consciousness at a time.

When motivating these characteristics of the processors, we spoke only of each faculty in isolation. Reconsidering in light of the entire layout of levels in figure 12.1, our view makes an interesting prediction. We have already seen that when levels are chained up by correspondence rules into a sequence, information put in at one end will propagate along the chain— from acoustic information to phonology to syntax to conceptual structure, for example. But suppose a chain splits in two directions. The prediction is that information will propagate automatically and compulsively along *both* directions of the chain and that all levels thus engaged will be kept in registration.

Reading provides one example of such a situation. Recall that the flow of information in reading starts at the retinal input and passes up through the visual system to conceptual structure, where the categorization of the visual inputs into letters and words is formulated. From there the information passes to the level of segmental phonology, where the forms of words are encoded, then back up through the linguistic system to conceptual structure, where the information is understood as language. (This is the primary direction of flow; like all the other processes we have discussed, it is presumably subject to feedback effects.)

Now what does it take to read out loud? This requires adding stress and intonation contour to the segmental phonology and mapping the whole into motor format. In other words, in reading aloud, the information fed into segmental phonology propagates in more than one direction, producing understanding and speech simultaneously. Moreover, *all* the linguistic levels are kept in registration, insofar as understanding what one reads produces a more enlightened performance: compare reading aloud in English to reading aloud phonetically in a language one does not understand.

The transfer can go in other directions too, over pathways of translation not included in figure 12.1. For instance, typing involves a learned translation from visual/linguistic patterns into motor patterns. It has been my experience (I have never compared notes to see if it is shared) that after a prolonged bout of typing I persist in realizing any language that I read, hear, or speak as (suppressed) typing motions. The translation goes on automatically.

Similarly, in humming a tune to myself, I often produce, simultaneously and unconsciously, the appropriate finger motions for playing the tune on the clarinet, for me a highly overlearned motor skill. I know I am not alone in this one: I used to know a trombonist who, when singing madrigals, would pump along grotesquely on an imaginary trombone. Still another linkage of outputs is well attested: certain famous pianists are notorious for their habit of humming along audibly during performance. In each of these cases musical production has split into the vocal pathway and the instrumental pathway, each yielding an independent mapping into motor output.

The point of such examples (and enterprising readers can doubtless come up with more) is that the automatic translation from level to level is not necessarily confined to the chain of levels that make up a particular faculty. Rather, to the extent that there are correspondence rules linking levels, any available connection can be invoked and can share in the overall set of levels produced, selected, and kept in registration.

Some of these connections are perhaps more subject than others to being turned on and off at will. One can choose to read aloud or silently. When not under duress, my friend could choose not to play along on his phantom trombone. But if a connection is exploited, its characteristics seem to be the same in every case.

12.7 Fodor's Modularity Thesis

Jerry Fodor's monograph *The Modularity of Mind* (1983) is one of the more prominent recent formulations of "faculty psychology"—the position that the apparent heterogeneity of mental life is supported by a genuinely heterogeneous collection of psychological mechanisms. According to faculty psychology, seeing, speaking a language, thinking, and remembering, for example, are not simply diverse uses of a single general psychological mechanism (be it association, stimulus-response connections, generalized problem solving, or whatever). Rather, there are specialized mechanisms, or *modules*, that subserve each function, each with its own characteristic task-relevant adaptations.

The position developed here is clearly a version of faculty psychology too, developed from much the same range of evidence as Fodor appeals to. It is therefore worth considering what revisions to Fodor's treatment might be suggested by our closer attention to the character of mental representations.

The mental faculties that Fodor wishes to characterize as modular are primarily what he calls *input systems*, in particular, visual perception and language perception. (He does not have much to say about output systems such as walking and language production except to hope that they are similar.) He contrasts input systems with what might be called "central cognition" or "thinking," which has quite different properties and which, he argues, is therefore not modular in his sense.

For present purposes, the relevant characteristics of modules are the following.

1. *Modules are mandatory.* One cannot choose not to organize visual input along the lines specified by the visual system, except by closing one's eyes. Likewise, one cannot hear a speech stream as mere sound, especially in a language one understands. By contrast, one can choose whether to follow up the logical consequences of a mathematical theorem or whether to inquire into the motivation behind someone's philosophical remarks—typical examples of "thinking."

2. *Modules are fast.* The time courses of visual and linguistic perception are measured in milliseconds, whereas thinking through a problem may take minutes or years.

3. *Modules have fixed neural architecture.* Associated with both language and vision there are known to be specific brain centers. By contrast, "thinking" appears to be diffused throughout the cortex. As a result, one finds that

4. *Modules suffer characteristic and specific breakdowns* due to brain injury, whereas "thought" seems (at least at present) more characteristically subject to degrees of generalized degradation.

These four are circumstantial symptoms of modularity. The characteristics with which Fodor is more centrally concerned, however, are these:

5. *Modules are domain specific.* Vision serves the function of delivering information about shape, color, three-dimensional spatial layout, and trajectory on the basis of retinal arrays. Language perception serves the function of delivering linguistic information on the basis of acoustic arrays (ignoring written language, to which we will return). Moreover, many characteristics of the acoustic array sound entirely different when heard as part of a speech stream than when heard in isolation; hence, there must be mechanisms specialized to speech per se that account for these differences in perception. By contrast, "thinking" can put to use information from any modality in order to interpret information from any other modality.

6. *Modules are informationally encapsulated.* The visual processes cannot make use of, say, linguistic information to arrive at an analysis of the visual scene; nor can one's phonological processing make use of information about color. Linguistic and visual facts may bear on each other in arriving at an *interpretation* of a perception—but this, Fodor argues, is a high-level inferential process, part of "thinking" and not a function of the input system itself.

Before we relate Fodor's position to the present work, it is worth noting that the perception of music also conforms to Fodor's criteria for modularity. It is mandatory: one cannot choose to hear music as mere sound, except by ceasing to attend to it altogether. Musical perception must be fast enough to deal with a rate of incoming musical events comparable to that of phonetic segments in a speech stream—eight to twelve notes or chords per second. Though little is known about the neural architecture underlying music processing, there are various sorts of specifically musical breakdowns due to brain damage (for a sampling, see Marin 1982).

Musical information is domain specific and does not on the whole mix even with other auditory perception, including speech perception. (There are various fuzzy cases involving the use of sirens and cannons in music, but 'these tend to be heard as intrusions into the music, not as integrated effects.) Finally, music is informationally encapsulated: there does not seem to be any nonmusical information, perceptual or cognitive, that pertains to the perception of music. Such information may influence the affect or interpretation of the music (for example, one may experience the *Eroica* Symphony differently upon learning that it was originally to have been dedicated to Napoleon), but this is altogether akin to the interpretive effects Fodor admits into the vision and language modules. And in general, we can make a distinction between the relatively fast and automatic processes of music perception and the relatively slow and willful processes involved in musical analysis, another example of "thought." Thus, we have a third example to bring to bear on issues of modularity.

12.8 A Finer-Grained View of Modularity

Given our discussion of processing in section 12.6, it appears that Fodor is right about the existence of modules and about their general properties, but he is wrong about the size of the modules. Rather than identifying entire input systems as modules, we are led toward smaller units of processing as the locus of modularity.

> *Representation-based Modularity Thesis*
> Each translation processor and each integrative processor is a module.

On the whole these processors satisfy Fodor's criteria for modules. The integrative processors are mandatory: they take whatever input they receive that has been translated into the proper format and attempt to create from it a unified representation. Many of the translation processors are also mandatory, including the ones that contribute to the main routes of information flow through the major faculties; others are capable of being turned on and off at will, as observed in section 12.6. Both kinds of processors are fast. In fact, the mandatoriness and rapidity of perception in each of Fodor's faculty-sized modules is, on our view, a product of the mandatoriness and rapidity of the component processors that collectively make up the faculty.

At the moment it is impossible to identify particular modules in my sense with particular areas in the brain. But it has always been clear, for instance, that Broca's and Wernicke's aphasias involve breakdowns in different aspects of language function, and parallel differentiations appear in visual impairments. Thus, Fodor has, if anything, carved things up too coarsely, in that he has not said anything about what sorts of breakdowns to expect. I might as well lay a great deal on the line and predict that, at least for a first approximation, different breakdowns will be found to be associated with different integrative or translation processors.

It is in terms of the issues of domain specificity and informational encapsulation that Fodor couches the claim that modules are "stupid"—that they can neither derive nor appeal to general knowledge. In the present framework these issues essentially concern the input and output formats of the modules. Each module in our sense is highly domain specific: the integrative processors deliver information only in the format to which they are devoted to integrating, and the translation processors deliver information only in the format that is the end product of their own translation process. Each module is also highly encapsulated: the integrative processors have access only to information in the format to which they are devoted, and the translation processors have access only to information in their specific input format. There are *no* processors that match up more than two levels. For instance, there could not be a single processor that directly used long-term conceptual information to help match phonological and syntactic structures (that is, a conceptually driven syntactic parser). Rather, such effects can arise only through the interaction of a number of different modules, each acting autonomously, as detailed in chapter 6.

What reason is there to believe in the modules proposed here rather than Fodor's "faculty-based" modules? I will offer three arguments beyond the representation-based theory's finer decomposition of mind into "stupid" components.

First, the representation-based modules proposed here make possible the bidirectionality of processing systems. The integrative processors for phonological and syntactic structure are used in both language perception and language production; the integrative processors for the 2½D sketch and 3D model are used in both visual perception and visual imagery. Many of the translation processors are used for the primary flow of information in perception and for feedback in production, or vice versa. Thus, representation-based modules exploit the fact that the same representations are used in both tasks. By contrast, Fodor's modular input systems bear no explicit relation to the modules that accomplish production. Fodor does not seriously consider what processes may be shared between hearing language and speaking it or between seeing the world and having visual images.

Second, there exist glaring exceptions to the domain specificity and informational encapsulation of faculty-based modules. *Reading* uses shape and configural information, supposedly domain specific to vision, to signal phonological and/or lexical distinctions that are supposedly informationally encapsulated within language processing. It does not matter whether reading is itself a module in Fodor's sense: the point is that it violates the domain specificity and informational encapsulation of the vision and language modules. If Fodor were right, there couldn't be such a thing as reading.

A similar argument arises with *American Sign Language*, in which visual-gestural information plays the role normally played by acoustic and phonological information in the lexicon and grammar. In this case the visual system breaks even more radically into the domain specificity and informational encapsulation of language. Moreover, even with the entirely different input-output modality, characteristics of a variety of standard linguistic aphasias appear in brain-damaged ASL speakers (Bellugi, Poizner, and Klima 1983). According to Fodor's view of modules, ASL shouldn't exist either. It appears, then, that faculty-based modularity is strictly speaking too constrained to account for the ways in which humans can derive and process linguistic information.

By contrast, in a representation-based theory of modules it is possible to account for reading and ASL by introducing a translation processor from visual or conceptual structure into phonological structure (the dotted line in figure 12.1). This processor is itself domain specific and informationally encapsulated, and it does not alter the specificity and encapsulation of the other processors. All goes on as before, except that there is one new path of information flow. (It is of course an empirical problem to determine exactly what translation processors are necessary. We have no reason, for instance, to suspect the existence of a primal sketch-to-phonological structure translation module.)

A third problem with faculty-based modules concerns the form of their outputs. Fodor, concerned with insulating information processing in input modules from the effects of thought, claims that the fast, mandatory input systems derive only shallow (that is, relatively peripheral) levels of representation, perhaps syntactic structure in language and the primal sketch in vision. But this view cannot be maintained. If Fodor is right, there still must be processes that translate the outputs of Fodor's modules into central levels of representation, and Fodor does not specify what these are. If we look at these processes, we find that they are fast, mandatory (and so on) as well; that is, they too have the properties of modules.

This difficulty arises because of the faculty-based treatment of modularity. On the one hand, the only parts of a faculty that are completely domain specific and informationally encapsulated are those that constitute the faculty *narrowly construed*, in the sense of section 12.1—those that do not interact with other faculties. On the other hand, what acts as a unified, fast, mandatory (and so on) process is the faculty *broadly construed*— all the levels and interconnections that are invoked during the exercise of that faculty. As discussed at length in chapter 6, language perception invokes all levels from acoustic information to at least conceptual structure; similarly, visual perception invokes all levels from retinal information to the 3D model and conceptual structure. Thus, strict domain specificity and informational encapsulation are violated at the central end of both processes.

Musical perception brings in a different such case. As noted, the principles of grouping structure are not domain specific to music but are in part more general to auditory perception. If this is the case, musical perception fails to be domain specific at the peripheral end of its processing, again a violation of Fodor's sense of modularity.

With a representation-based theory of modules these difficulties do not arise. Each integrative processor and each translation processor is totally domain specific and totally informationally encapsulated. It doesn't matter whether it deals with a central level of representation or a peripheral one, and it doesn't matter whether its inputs come from one or many sources: it just compulsively does its job, oblivious to the existence of the rest of the mind out there. What communication exists between faculties is a function of the existence of other, equally oblivious processors. Thus, it is possible to admit overlap among faculties and between them and "thought," without undermining the "stupid" nature of the individual processors.

To sum up, then, the representation-based modularity thesis presents an even more constrained view of domain specificity and informational encapsulation than Fodor can maintain. At the same time it permits a flexibility in the interaction among modules that enables the theory to deal with a wider range of phenomena, including output systems and systems that cut across modalities.

12.9 Central Processes

What of the processes that Fodor contrasts with the modular ones, those characterized as "thought"?

First consider the representations over which such processes operate. The level of conceptual structure was motivated specifically by the need for a form of information in which conceptual categories can be couched, without appeal to a further level of "meaning." Representations at this level are a primary goal of linguistic and visual processing as well as other perceptual processes; it is here that so many forms of input and output come to interact.

In addition to serving as input and output to various translation processors, conceptual structures are regulated in short-term memory by an integrative processor. This processor constructs the most coherent conceptual structure that can be maintained in registration with information arriving from other modules and makes this structure available for translation by other modules into action and into feedback to perception.

This integrative processor, however, does not perform operations on conceptual structure that we might construe as thought, such as problem solving or hypothesis confirmation. These, as Fodor observes, are processes that are much more diffuse in their effects than the construction of a single structure. Solving a problem may involve appeal to anything in one's far-flung network of knowledge and/or beliefs, and the solution in turn may have consequences that induce one to change one's beliefs, perhaps even radically.

Not only are these processes wide-ranging in the domains they can draw on and affect, they are also unpredictable in the time they may take. The solution to a problem may occur to one within a minute, or never, or only after years of intermittent attention. Integrating a novel solution into one's overall approach to the world may take years more. For convenience, then, I will call these processes "slow processes," by contrast with the "fast processes" of the modules of the previous section—although they may in fact range in speed from extremely slow to lightning-quick.

In his concentration on "rational thought," Fodor does not observe that, just as there are many distinguishable fast processes, there are many slow processes as well. Composing music, for example, hardly falls into the category of "belief fixation" with which Fodor characterizes central processes. But it does have the property of potentially drawing on all of one's musical knowledge and affecting the way one hears music subsequently— that is, it is as wide-ranging in its effects as, say, doing science. And it can be slow, even painfully so: the classic case is of course Beethoven, in whose sketchbooks one can follow the refinement of musical ideas over periods of years.

Thus, just as belief fixation is accomplished by slow processes that are domain specific to conceptual structure, so musical thought involves slow processes that are domain specific to musical representations. Similarly, creativity in the visual arts invokes slow processes over spatial and visual representations, and creativity in literature invokes slow processes over all the linguistic levels, not just conceptual structure.

What seems to emerge from even such a cursory look at slow processes is something like Gardner's (1983) view of "multiple intelligences": there is not one great slush of central processes, totally interactive in the sense Fodor envisions. Rather, there is some small number of relatively broad and independent domains over which distinct slow processes are defined.

Gardner speaks of two such domains in addition to those already mentioned. One is "bodily-kinesthetic intelligence," which is involved in dance and athletics and which in our terms invokes the presumed level of body representation. The other is "personal intelligence," which operates in the domain of interpersonal relations, and a talent for which is manifested by good teachers, therapists, and probably politicians. What representations this intelligence engages is an open question, but it is clear that intuition about how people work is quite distinct from intuition about how machines or deductive systems work; and it is equally clear that talent in one domain often does not carry over into another. Section 10.7.1 suggested that face recognition and voice recognition are specialized modules, parasitic on the spatial and auditory systems, whose purpose is to supply information that is specific to social cognition. Gardner's "personal intelligence" might then be seen as comprising the corresponding slow processes, the particular sort of thought that invokes and creates social concepts.

The upshot of this very brisk survey of varieties of "thought" is that there is likely some degree of modularity here as well. Fodor, by considering only the kind of thought appropriate to doing science and philosophy, has observed only one of a range of central domains. Just as there are distinct "fast modules" that subserve the creation and integration of short-term memory information and have various properties in common, so there may well be a system of distinct "slow modules," each adapted to the creation and integration of information in long-term memory.

A point of curiosity: Fodor, in arguing that central processes are non-modular, appears to agree entirely with the avowed "antimodularist" Anderson (1983). Anderson is intuitively convinced (1983, 1) that there is basically only one uniform kind of thought; but he is willing to concede the existence of specialized peripheral systems for input and output, coinciding more or less with Fodor's faculty-sized modules. Their major disagreement seems to be that Anderson thinks central processes can be studied precisely because they are uniform, whereas Fodor thinks central processes *cannot* be studied precisely because they are uniform! I am suggesting here that they are perhaps both off the mark. Central processes may be no more uniform in their characteristic domains than input-output processes, and the similarities among "slow" modules are like those among "fast" modules—general properties of a class of specialized devices. As in the "fast" modules, it may be that these processes can be properly differentiated only by paying attention to the representations on which they operate.

12.10 Acquisition of Modules: Innateness versus Learning

Finally, let us turn to the question of where modules come from. At bottom, I believe, Fodor's main concern is to counter associationist theory, in which language is said to be acquired either by its being taught, like facts of history, or else by mere association, like a conditioned reflex. The strong undertone to Fodor's position is that modules are innate: the fixed neural architecture is biologically determined.

This requires obvious qualification. Consider language. On the one hand, inasmuch as the overall organization of linguistic structure is innate, so is the overall organization of the processor. That is, since all the general principles and many particular principles of linguistic structure are either universally fixed or vary among a small number of options, the processor can be innately specialized to deal only with a restricted range of possibilities. We have already capitalized on this in delimiting the gross components of the processor, and one can obviously go much further.

On the other hand, there still remains the further specialization of the processor to a particular language: both the integrative and the translation processors must be sensitive to language-particular constraints. (Or, on Fodor's faculty-sized view, the language input module must be sensitive to the rules of the language it is processing.) Thus, to the extent that languages differ, so must the modules that process them. Hence, parts of the language modules must be learned—even if, as emphasized in chapter 5, such learning is not like either of the types from which Fodor rightly wishes to disassociate himself. Language learning—the specialization of the language modules to a specific language—is clearly to be thought of as a computational process too.

Language learning is sometimes called a species of "hypothesis testing," so let us compare it to the conscious process of testing scientific or logical hypotheses. What they have in common is that (1) they are computations over representations, (2) they have as input a number of alternatives and as output a preferred choice, and (3) they are "slow processes" in the sense of the last section. The first two of these are shared by virtually every process in the computational mind, so they don't count for any great similarity. Moreover, in view of the fact that the inputs and outputs of language acquisition—rules of grammar—are totally unavailable to consciousness, the alleged parallelism to rational hypothesis testing is rather slim.

There remains the third point of similarity—that they are both slow processes, altogether different in character from the "fast" modules whose time scale of operation is measured in milliseconds. Given the variety of slow processes, there seems no reason to subsume language learning under rational hypothesis testing in particular. Rather, language learning ought to be seen as a distinct and highly domain-specific variety of slow process, one concerned with the very restricted task of fixing language-particular parameters in the language modules.

This leads to a further question: Is language learning just another slow process of the sort discussed in the previous section, or is it a qualitatively different kind of slow process, with its own characteristics? The slow processes of the previous section can all be characterized as varieties of "thought"—the manipulation and creation of representations in long-term memory. Language acquisition, by contrast, involves the construction and/or fine-tuning of parts of a processing module. Are there other such processes?

Consider music. The processing modules for music perception bear the same relation to the grammar of a musical idiom as the language processors bear to the grammar of a language. Hence, the music processors can be thought of as innate just to the extent that musical grammar is universal. As discussed in chapter 11, becoming experienced in a musical idiom amounts to acquiring the idiom-particular rules of musical grammar. Like language acquisition, this is not a conscious process but appears superficially to be just a result of sufficient exposure. Within our framework, then, the acquisition of musical rules is a computational process that specializes the music modules to a particular idiom. The parallels to language acquisition are stronger than to any of the other processes, fast or slow, mentioned before. This begins to suggest the existence of a third distinct category of processes in the computational mind.

More controversially, consider fast processes that are clearly learned but behave in other respects much like modules, such as playing the bassoon. Here there is an "overlearned" mapping from the musical surface to a set of motor instructions. Compared to the mappings between linguistic levels, this mapping is relatively simple. On the other hand, it comes from a relatively unconstrained set of mappings: there is nothing innate about the fact that the bassoon is played with the vocal tract and the fingers, much less about what use is made of them in the mapping. About all that remains constant over musical instruments is (1) a temporal correlation between motor movements and changes of pitch and (2) if the instrument allows differences in volume, a correlation of greater volume with greater (apparent) motor effort. In order to learn to play the bassoon, then, one must acquire the bassoon-specific mapping, using a computational process that refines the relatively unconstrained potential correlations of motor activity to sound into a discrete and precise fast process. This may be a different sort of slow process than that responsible for language learning; or it may be the same sort, its relative difficulty compared to language learning being a consequence of the innately unconstrained nature of the music-to-motor mapping. I leave the issue open. Similar remarks pertain, of course, to the processes necessary for the acquisition of reading and ASL, not to mention "overlearned" motor tasks such as writing.

12.11 Summary

We have arrived at the view that the computational mind is differentiated along a number of dimensions. First and foremost is the differentiation among levels of representation, each of which defines an organized space of distinctions in terms of which information can be organized. The first half of this chapter explored some of the general characteristics of levels of representation, such as the prevalence of hierarchies, then of headed hierarchies, as one moves from peripheral to central levels. It was found that there are various degrees of similarity among levels, from very fine-scale similarities in the use of preference rule systems, to parallel principles like proximity and similarity in different levels, to very large-scale similarities like those between the two metrical grids. It was argued, however, that such similarities do not impugn the individuality of the levels, any more than similarities among organs of the body threaten the distinctions among them.

The second half of the chapter concerned the processes that create and maintain these representations. One important dimension in which they differ is the level(s) of representation they process: we have argued for a system of autonomous processors, each devoted either to maintaining and unifying a single level of representation or to translating from one particular level to another. Cutting across this dimension is the difference between "fast" processors—the present theory's counterpart of Fodor's modules—and "slow" processors. The latter category itself divides into at least two types: those that subserve "thought" in various domains, and those that are devoted to the construction and/or fine-tuning of "fast" processes. Further distinctions can be envisioned, but theories of the "slow" processes that are as substantive as those currently available for the "fast" ones await a great deal of future research.

We have seen that Fodor's view of modularity is incorrect in some major details. In particular, the proper size of "fast" modules is more likely to be the individual integrative and translation processor than an entire faculty; and central processing is likely to be as modular as input/output processing. However, if anything, our investigation substantiates and strengthens Fodor's overall position, namely, that the structures and processes of the computational mind are highly differentiated, as well as Chomsky's (1975) position that this differentiation must in large part be biologically determined.

12.12 Perception and Cognition

I suspect that some readers will have felt throughout this study that I have played too fast and loose for their taste with the terms "perception" and "cognition." I am finally at a point where I can defend my deliberate imprecision.

Probably everyone has his own definition of the perception-cognition distinction, either explicit or implicit, and I cannot pretend to speak to every version of it. The basic intuition behind the distinction, I think, is that parts of our experience of the world out there are entirely due to the character of the incoming signal, whereas other parts are a consequence of our "interpreting" the information in light of previous knowledge, belief, or experience. The process of perception is supposed to be responsible for the former aspects of experience, cognition for the latter. Those who take the distinction seriously generally presuppose that the two are autonomous processes and that perception precedes cognition. That is, one first perceives something in the world, then applies one's knowledge to categorize it and otherwise understand it.

Fodor's form of the modularity thesis embodies a version of this strong perception-cognition distinction. The input modules perform "stupid" knowledge-independent processing of inputs, that is, perception; it is only when information is passed on to central cognitive capacity that it is interpreted in light of beliefs. In fact, one can view Fodor's use of domain specificity and informational encapsulation as essentially a justification for isolating perception from cognition. (I am grateful to Gerald Balzano for pointing out this reading of Fodor.)

Under the view of processing developed here, the perception-cognition distinction is much less clear. In the course of getting information translated from the peripheral formats to central levels, one's "knowledge" intrudes in at least two ways, corresponding to what were called "top-down" and "holistic" processes in chapters 6, 9, and 11.

"Top-down" processes bring information from more central levels to bear on the analysis of more peripheral levels; they are carried out by top-down translation processors. "Holistic" processes make use of intrinsic constraints on particular levels to reduce indeterminacies in the information sent up from lower levels; they are one of the functions of integrative processors. In the case of vision these functions are presumably innate; in the case of language they involve the learned parts of one's language as well as innate constraints.

If there are any processes that can be considered "relatively pure" perception, then, they are just those carried out by the peripheral transducers and the bottom-up translation processors. (And even here, language perception beyond phonetics involves language-particular knowledge.) What there is not is a discrete *level* of perceptual representation, the output of perceptual processing and the input to cognition. Rather, as has been shown, each level of representation in short-term memory is derived by an interaction of bottom-up, holistic, and top-down processes. Thus, there is no perception-cognition distinction along traditional lines.

Yet this does not drive us into the arms of the "New Look" theorists (and much of the artificial intelligence community), who believe that perception is totally driven by top-down expectations. We have resolutely avoided cognitive "wild cards" that can indiscriminately regulate and monitor perception. Rather, conceptual structure can affect lower levels only through the mediation of the domain-specific and informationally encapsulated translation processors, a procedure much more highly constrained than usually imagined in discussion of top-down influences. That is, "cognition" can infect "perception" only in limited ways. As has happened elsewhere in the course of this study, a productive approach has emerged from acknowledging the intuitions behind two extreme views and seeking a coherent synthesis.

PART IV

The Phenomenological Mind and the
Computational Mind, continued

Chapter 13
Processing Precursors to Consciousness

We began this study by talking about consciousness. Then we reached a point where we had to detour into the details of the computational mind, an excursion so intricate and fascinating in its own right that one might justifiably have lost track of its original motivation. In order to step back into the larger context, let us briefly review chapters 1–4, now bearing the results of parts II and III in mind.

Before we plunge in, a word of caution. The discussion from here on relies heavily on the reader's assent to my description of the phenomenology. Aware as I am of the dangers of confabulation, I see no way to circumvent this situation, given the essential privacy of consciousness. All I can do is to be as careful as I can, and hope that disagreements about phenomenology can be settled in an atmosphere of mutual trust.

13.1 Review of *Theories I–III*

Our original problem was this: What is the relationship between the computational mind and experience? Our first try was Theory I (section 2.2).

> *Theory I*
> The elements of conscious awareness consist of information and processes of the computational mind that (1) are active and (2) have other (as yet unspecified) privileged properties.

The stipulation "active" was meant to exclude the contents of long-term memory from awareness, except when they are being actively remembered. The stipulation "other privileged properties" was to permit us to distinguish active elements that emerge into consciousness from those that do not. These two stipulations enabled us to define the "unconscious mind" as those elements of the computational mind that do not emerge into awareness.

We next observed that the term "consists of" in Theory I is too strong, inasmuch as it is unclear how a conscious experience could *consist of* a collection of computations. We considered three essential reasons why a computational theory alone cannot account for the phenomenological character of awareness: the problems of externalization (the experienced object is out there, it is not a computation in my head), of form (a square is not represented by a square set of computations), and of qualia (the sensations of blueness and saltiness are not represented by blue and salty computations). At best, it was argued, a computational theory can provide a set of computational distinctions adequate to support the distinctions present in awareness. What remains unexplained is how computations can result in experiences; we termed this the "mind-mind problem."

We therefore weakened Theory I to the form in Theory II (section 2.4).

Theory II
The elements of conscious awareness are caused by/supported by/ projected from information and processes of the computational mind that (1) are active and (2) have other (as yet unspecified) privileged properties.

The deliberately vague collection of predicates "caused by/supported by/ projected from" is intended to stand for the mysterious part of the mind-mind problem, the part I feel helpless to address. What we are treating as an empirical and potentially soluble problem is the refinement of stipulations (1) and (2): we are trying to discover precisely which components of the computational mind are responsible for the distinctions that cause/ support/project into awareness.

In setting the ground rules for investigation, we adopted the Hypothesis of Computational Sufficiency and the Hypothesis of the Nonefficacy of Consciousness (section 2.5).

Hypothesis of Computational Sufficiency
Every phenomenological distinction is caused by/supported by/ projected from a corresponding computational distinction.

Hypothesis of the Nonefficacy of Consciousness
The awareness of an entity E cannot *in itself* have any effect on the computational mind. Only the computational states that cause/ support/project E can have any such effect.

These hypotheses clarify Theory II. They say that the phenomenological mind subsists entirely on the support of the computational mind and that causality runs only from the computational mind to the phenomenological mind, not the other way about. Together they constitute rejection of an interactionist approach to the mind-mind problem, in which phenomenological states may have their own independent causal properties that can in turn influence behavior.

Chapter 4 distinguished the study of information structures in the computational mind from that of the computational processes that create and maintain such structures. Parts II and III further justified this bifurcation of theory, in the context of describing the computational mind itself. However, the distinction was also shown to be relevant to the theory of consciousness, as made clear by Lashley's Observation: *"No activity of mind is ever conscious."* We interpreted this as saying that the distinctions present to awareness are supported most directly by information structures—the consequences of processing—rather than by processing itself. Lashley's Observation leads to a narrowing of Theory II, so as to exclude processes from the elements of the computational mind privileged to support distinctions in awareness (section 4.4).

Theory III
The distinctions present in conscious awareness are caused by/ supported by/projected from information structures in the computational mind that (1) are active and (2) have other (as yet unspecified) privileged properties.

To go beyond Theory III, we must try to constrain further the set of representations that are privileged to support awareness. One way to accomplish this goal is to restrict the *form* of structures whose distinctions project into awareness. Another is to set more stringent criteria on the *processes* the privileged representations must be undergoing. We now turn to two refinements, one of each sort, the first in review and the second partly new.

13.2 The Role of Modality-Specific Levels: Review of *Theory IV*

Section 4.6 observed that experience is on the whole sharply differentiated by modality. The qualia of visual experience are totally unlike those of auditory or tactile experience, for example. A potential explanation was offered in terms of the Hypothesis of Levels (section 4.5).

Hypothesis of Levels
1. Each faculty of mind has its own characteristic chain of levels of representation from lowest to highest.
2. These chains intersect at various points.
3. The levels of structure at the intersections of chains are responsible for the interactions among faculties.
4. The central levels at which "thought" takes place, largely independent of sense modality, are at the intersection of many distinct chains.

One of the central tasks of parts II and III was to elaborate and justify this hypothesis. Inasmuch as we have been able to flesh out the details of a sizable number of levels in three faculties and to specify the points of intersection with a number of others, the hypothesis has been amply confirmed.

Here again is how the Hypothesis of Levels provides a potential computational account of the disunity of awareness. A faculty-specific modality of awareness can be achieved by including a faculty-specific level of representation among the representations that support that modality. For instance, visual awareness is to be projected from the level(s) of representation that make distinctions characteristic of visual qualia—color and shape, say, but not loudness or smell; qualia of loudness and timbre (sound quality) are to be projected from some level(s) of auditory representation in which these distinctions play a computational role; and so forth.

On the other hand, we have found two counterexamples to the disunity of awareness. One, noted in section 4.6, is taste, with which the sense of smell is inextricably linked in the phenomenology. The other is the sense of one's own body position and motion; section 10.2 pointed out that one cannot phenomenologically distinguish which aspects of this sense are contributed by visual cues, which by touch and pressure cues on the skin, which by muscle sensors, and which by the organs of balance in the ears. The Hypothesis of Levels provides for these cases too: such a modality of awareness is to be projected from a level of representation that lies at an intersection of chains of levels that have the requisite sense organs at their lower ends. At such an intersection the alphabet of distinctions available is (at least partly) neutral among the sense modalities that feed it, and therefore, by hypothesis, so is awareness.

This relationship between levels of representation and the form of awareness makes possible a refinement of Theory III on the basis of the *form* of privileged representations. It appeared in section 4.6 as Theory IV.

> *Theory IV*
> The distinctions present in conscious awareness are caused by/ supported by/projected from information structures in the computational mind that (1) are active, (2) are of privileged levels of representation, and (3) have other (as yet unspecified) privileged properties. In particular, each distinct modality of awareness is due to a distinct (set of) level(s) of representation.

13.3 Short-Term Memory and the Selection Function; *Theory V*

Section 6.9 proposed in preliminary form a different sort of refinement of the theory of consciousness. This one constrained the *processes* that make linguistic representations available to awareness. With the subsequent discussion of visual and musical processing, we can now state the constraint more generally.

The initial observation in chapter 6 was that linguistic awareness is supported by the structures created and maintained in registration in short-term linguistic memory. It was shown there that short-term linguistic memory often contains multiple sets of representations, each consisting of a phonological structure, a syntactic structure, and a conceptual structure in registration. These multiple sets arise during the course of perception when there are indeterminacies in the analysis of the input; in the processing of ambiguous sentences they remain in short-term memory even when processing is complete. Short-term memory is, however, regulated by a *selection function* that at each moment designates one of the sets as most coherent or salient. Section 6.8 argued at some length that the selection function is an intrinsic part of short-term linguistic memory, for it is involved constantly throughout processing in resolving low-level nitty-gritty details of linguistic structure.

Chapters 9 and 11 found that visual and musical short-term memories have parallel properties. In particular, they too are regulated by selection functions that designate at each moment a most coherent or salient set of representations.

The selection function has a phenomenological effect too. As mentioned in section 6.8, it has frequently been noted that one is aware of only a single interpretation at a time for an ambiguous visual figure or sentence. One notices an ambiguity only through the appearance of successive interpretations over time. This fact is often claimed to be a consequence of limitations on attention, or of processes in "higher-level" cognition, or of the function of consciousness itself. In fact, this phenomenology is one thing that gives rise to the widespread conception of consciousness as an executive function: "an instrument for the analysis of necessity and trouble" (Bruner 1983), the "supreme organizer" (Minsky 1968), "a plan for a total 'reconciliation' of the stubborn contradictions of the brain" (Lem 1981), "the comparison of [simultaneous possibilities] with each other, the selection of some, and the suppression of the rest" (James 1890). We have discussed this view and some of its inadequacies in sections 1.1, 2.2, and 4.4.

Here we have found another problem with this view. Our more detailed investigation has shown that perception does not send a multitude of half-baked analyses on to a higher capacity for adjudication. Rather, the selection of a single most salient analysis is localized right in the machinery that accomplishes perception itself, intimately intertwined with the other functions of the perceptual processors. Thus, we can incorporate the moment-by-moment singularity of interpretation in awareness into our theory simply by claiming that awareness is projected specifically from the set of representations designated by the selection function.

Theory V
The distinctions present in each modality of awareness are caused by/supported by/projected from the set of information structures that (1) are of the levels of representation appropriate to that modality, (2) are maintained in registration in the short-term memory STM_i for that modality, (3) are designated by the selection function of STM_i as most salient or coherent at the moment, and (4) have other (as yet unspecified) privileged properties.

Theory V refines the previous theories by replacing the notion "active" with "maintained in short-term memory." It further constrains the available representations to those chosen by the selection function; the rest of the representations in STM, though active, are still unconscious and can be detected only by experimental techniques.

The taxonomy of processes in chapter 12 yields an unexpected bonus for Theory V. Recall that short-term memory is the locus of "fast" processes of perception and production, the highly specialized integrative and translation processors that act as modules in Fodor's sense. Chapter 12 contrasted these with "slow" processes, which operate on information that is not in short-term memory. One type, which we call "thought," involves the integration and alteration of potentially large swatches of long-term memory; another type, which we call "skill learning" (for instance, language acquisition, learning to read or to play the bassoon) involves the construction and/or fine-tuning of the modules themselves. Theory V claims that awareness is supported by the contents of short-term memory. It therefore predicts that *slow processes have no direct phenomenological effects.*

This prediction appears to me to be correct. The stream of consciousness is projected from the structures being created and manipulated by fast processes; the contents of awareness change as these structures change. By contrast, the changes wrought by slow processes go on in secret. One discovers them only on the occasion of bringing the relevant structures into short-term memory, when they appear in awareness as a surprising and unexpected creative insight or as a sudden new facility at a skill. In other words, Theory V offers a possible explanation of the curious and frequently noted phenomenology of creativity and skill learning.

13.4 The Role of Attention in Awareness; *Theory VI*

Theory V also begins to make clear the role of attention in the system. Attention obviously has a phenomenological effect: it heightens or focuses awareness of the elements being attended. As observed in section 1.1, attention cannot be the cause of consciousness, for one can be *vaguely* aware of something, that is, aware of it without attending to it. On the other hand, it does not seem possible to pay attention to an element of the perceptual field without being aware of that element. Hence, availability to awareness seems a necessary condition for attention, rather than the other way about.

"Availability to awareness" now has a more direct definition: the faculty of attention can be applied to the set of representations in short-term memory that has been chosen as most salient by the selection function. That is, perceptual attention is restricted to the processor's current guess as to which set of representations encodes what is "actually out there."

All of this suggests a hypothesis about the computational effect of attention—roughly that material being attended to is undergoing especially intense and detailed processing. Under such processing the representations receive finer-grained parsing—they come to contain more highly articulated constituent structure. In turn, suppose that the selected set of representations becomes available to awareness only after being refined by attention. Then the richer structure of the attended portions of the field can project into a richer organization of distinctions in awareness; meanwhile, the unattended portions still project into awareness but are less differentiated or less vivid. Phenomenologically this account has he right flavor, though clearly a great deal remains to be fleshed out.

The view of attention as a high-intensity fine-grained processor might account for one of its widely remarked properties, its limited capacity. Mandler (1984, 99) tries to justify limited attentional capacity (erroneously conflating it with the limited capacity of *consciousness*), on the grounds that it "serves to reduce further the information overload that the physical world potentially presents to the organism." Actually, though, it would be ecologically advantageous to have a *greater* attentional capacity—the organism should want to take in and integrate as much information as possible. That is why the nervous system has become more complex throughout evolution. The real reason attention has a limited capacity is that attention is *expensive*. To perform the fine-grained fast processing characteristic of attention requires a lot of computational space and metabolic energy. This is the cost against which evolution weighs the advantages of parsing more of the perceptual field in such detail.

Another way that attention has often been noticed to interact with consciousness is in the learning of motor skills such as playing tennis or the piano, driving a car, and so on. The phenomenology is that as one improves at these skills, one pays less attention to the individual constituents of the action and in fact becomes virtually unconscious of them most of the time. This intuition again contributes to the view of consciousness as an executive system that takes care of "trouble spots" in perception and action— the idea is that as one gets better at a skill, there is less trouble, so consciousness is invoked less frequently to deal with problems.

Within the present framework we can separate the role of attention from that of consciousness. Clearly, what changes in the course of motor learning is that less *attention* is necessary. At the early stages of learning, where the constituents of the skill are still separate conceptual entities, a finely detailed high-level representation of the action must be produced and monitored in real time in order to perform correctly. This is only possible through the use of attention, whose function is to produce just such highly articulated representations. As learning proceeds, however, there are various ways this situation could change. One is that the high-level representations that direct action come to be better encoded in long-term memory, so they are easier to retrieve; another is that they become better integrated into larger constituents, so that a finely detailed high-level parse no longer has to be constructed in real time. (Notice, though, that the actual performance of the action requires the same motor movements, whether skilled or unskilled.) The upshot in any event is that less high-intensity processing—that is, less *attention*—is required after learning.

Now consider how this change affects the character of consciousness under the present account. If less attention is directed to the representations that support awareness, they will be less finely articulated. Hence, awareness of performing the action in question will be less vivid. One's awareness of the action does not go away altogether, and one *can* focus attention on it, but it need not be focal. This seems a fair description of the phenomenology, and it fits naturally within the present framework.

One final remark on attention. Beyond the selectivity exerted by the selection function, there is a further selectivity exerted by attention. This arises from its limited capacity: attention can only produce a fine-grained parsing for a small part of the perceptual field at a time. Thus there must be some mechanism that *directs* attention. Again, this is often described as a "high-level executive function," and it is usually not clearly distinguished from the selection function.

In the present framework, of course, this mechanism too must be a computational process. Like the mechanism directing eye movements, it is goal-directed, fast, and not open to introspection. I have little to say about is here except that it plays a different role from the selection function. The latter is responsible for the unitary character of awareness at any moment: it selects from the multiple sets of representations in STM one most salient or coherent set of structures. The direction of attention, however, is responsible for choosing which *portions* of the designated set of representations are to be subjected to high-intensity processing. Thus, one may conceive of the selection function and the direction of attention as successively narrowing the domain to which attention can apply.

It becomes clear, then, that the direction of attention should not be confused with consciousness either. It is true that the portion of the field picked out by this function will become more vivid in awareness, but we have already seen how this effect comes about: attention produces more highly articulated representations, which in turn project into richer awareness. In other words, the direction of attention is just another process that indirectly affects the form of the representations that support awareness. It may be mysterious, but that does not make it identical with consciousness.

We can sum up this section by appending an additional clause to Theory V (here, clause 4).

Theory VI

The distinctions present in each modality of awareness are caused by/supported by/projected from the set of information structures that (1) are of the levels of representation appropriate to that modality, (2) are maintained in registration in the short-term memory STM_i for that modality, (3) are designated by the selection function of STM_i as most salient or coherent at the moment, (4) have been selectively enriched by the high-intensity processing of attention, and (5) have other (as yet unspecified) privileged properties.

Chapter 14
The Intermediate-Level Theory of Consciousness

So far we have made rather simple observations about the character of awareness and found accounts for them in independently motivated properties of the computational mind. Lashley's Observation correlates with the exclusion of processes from awareness; the modality specific character of awareness correlates with the division of the computational mind into faculties; the singularity of interpretation in awareness at any moment correlates with the operation of the selection function in short-term memory; the vividness of attended portions of the phenomenal field correlates with the high-intensity processing of attention. Interesting though these correlations may be, they are only preliminaries to the business of this chapter: stating more precisely what forms of information project into awareness.

14.1 Some Theories of the Form of Awareness

Many treatments of consciousness in the literature recognize, at least incipiently, that consciousness is projected from mental information structures. Among the treatments I have encountered there can be discerned essentially three different theories of this sort. The first is a version of the theory of consciousness as executive, as stated by Johnson-Laird (1983, 465): "The contents of consciousness are the current values of parameters governing the high-level computations of the operating system." As observed in section 4.4, this differs from various other "executive" theories in that Johnson-Laird realizes that consciousness cannot just be a process but must be supported by representational content. Another (rather murky) statement of the same idea is offered by MacKay (1984, 309): "Conscious experience is the specific correlate of supervisory activity, ... the whole group of information-processing elements that are linked together by the flow of information in such a way as to exercise control of planning, representation, and evaluation, including evaluation of the system's *own* criteria of evaluation." However, neither of these proposals gives any serious consideration to what such parameters in the executive system should be like, nor how they might support the actual distinctions of the phenomenology.

A second theory is proposed by Marcel (1983) and endorsed by Mandler (1984). Marcel is arguing against a "threshold" theory of consciousness, in which a representation achieves consciousness by exceeding a certain threshold of activation, while competing representations are inhibited. He agrees with the present approach in believing that multiple representations are being processed simultaneously. He claims, though, that the representations responsible for consciousness are not simply selected from among those in STM but are rather translated into a qualitatively different form. He suggests (p. 256) that "the structural languages of conscious representations are not directly mappable onto those of nonconscious representations, i.e., they are neither commensurate nor coextensive." However, Marcel is totally unspecific about the formal character of any of the representations he discusses, beyond claiming that "perceptual" representations are relatively amorphous and unstructured compared to "conscious" representations. And with no theory of the form of representations it is obviously impossible to develop a theory of the translation between "perceptual" and "conscious" representations.

Johnson-Laird's and Marcel's theories, then, might be read as claiming that none of the levels of representation discussed here directly supports awareness—that we should be looking for yet another level. However, we will see shortly that the levels we already have are not only sufficient but in fact too rich to support the form of awareness.

By far the most frequently encountered position might be termed a "central-level" theory of consciousness: the idea that conceptual structure or something much like it is the form of representation that most directly supports awareness. Jerison (1973), for example, stresses that multimodal integration, a function of the central representations, is necessary for intelligence, then adds that he believes it essential to consciousness as well. Wilks (1982) hypothesizes that the contents of consciousness are provided by the uppermost level of mental representation. He uses "uppermost" here in the artificial intelligence sense of the programming language most distant (or abstract) with respect to machine language (recall the discussion of section 4.5), so his view might be taken as similar to Johnson-Laird's. On the other hand, it is clear from the context that Wilks has in mind something like conceptual structure as the locus of consciousness. Again, neither Jerison nor Wilks has anything to offer on the crucial issue of the actual form these central representations take.

Perhaps the most articulate exponent of a central-level theory is Dennett (1978a). In the functional architecture that he sketches for the mental processor, there is a buffer memory M that receives input from various modalities and whose contents are the input to speech acts. The contents of this buffer, he claims, are projected into consciousness. Though Dennett makes no reference to the notion of levels of representation and does not even address explicitly the form of representations, the characteristics he ascribes to the information in M appear to correspond most closely in the present framework to the conceptual structure(s) maintained in short-term memory.

An alternative reading of Dennett might be that the buffer M is the *whole* of short-term memory—that is, that all levels of representation in short-term memory are projected into consciousness. I find this "all-level" theory a less likely interpretation of Dennett, but it is a view worth considering on its own merits.

I now want to show, through a closer comparison of the phenomenology with the known levels of representation, that none of these views is correct. I begin again with language.

14.2 The Form of Linguistic Awareness; *Theory VII*

It is fairly clear to introspection that the constraints of Theory VI still make too much available to awareness. So far, the representations that support awareness have been restricted to the most salient set of representations in short-term memory, selectively enriched by attention. But in speaking or hearing language, I am not aware of three distinct coexisting organizations, one each from phonological, syntactic, and conceptual structures. In looking at the world, I am not aware of seeing it encoded simultaneously into primal sketch, $2\frac{1}{2}$D, 3D, and conceptual structures. In listening to music, I do not hear the musical surface plus four contrapuntal hierarchies.

This observation, of course, does not undermine the claim of psychological reality for these information structures, for, as emphasized throughout, they are justified on the grounds of their power to explain the character of perceptual judgments, behavior, and understanding—not the character of introspection or awareness. However, it does undermine the "all-level" theory of consciousness; and it shows that Theory VI is not restrictive enough, for it lets too much into awareness that does not belong there. So Theory VI must be narrowed further.

Let us first examine a variety of experience that we have not considered up to now and that has been almost entirely overlooked in recent discussion of imagery: linguistic (or verbal) imagery—hearing phrases and sentences in the head. The sheer quantity of linguistic imagery experienced by me and by others I query is astonishing. For many of us, the inner voice hardly ever ceases to comment, speculate, plan, or admonish. I'm hearing it now, trying out phrases to type.

What is interesting about linguistic images is that they must be generated from a full set of linguistic representations: they not only have a meaning, but they come complete with syntactic and phonological structures, down to details of stress and intonation. In other words, the information processing associated with the production of linguistic images is very likely the same as that in speech production, at least down to the phonetic level. Only the motor activity is missing. And in fact, as noticed as long ago as Watson (1913), linguistic images may even be accompanied by minor movements of the vocal tract.

Watson, in his behaviorist zeal, wanted to show by virtue of this fact that thought could be regarded as nothing but subvocal speech. There should be no need here to belabor the absurdity of his claim. Reasoning, inference, categorization, and the ability to talk about what we see are completely inexplicable in such terms. But there is a phenomenological insight lurking in Watson's claim: *thought is frequently experienced as a sequence of linguistic images.* That is, although linguistic images cannot be *identical* to thought, they often constitute our experiential evidence that thought is taking place.

Now let us ask, What linguistic structures most closely correspond to the phenomenological form of linguistic images? Examining each of the levels, we find that the most appropriate units of form seem to come from *phonological structure.* In particular, we experience the inner speech stream as segmented into words and possibly further into syllables or individual segments. In addition, the rhythm, stress pattern, and intonation of inner speech must come from phonological units as well. It is true that not *all* units of phonological structure are evident in awareness: we certainly do not experience phonological segments as composites of distinctive features. But those aspects of linguistic form that do present themselves to awareness seem indisputably phonological in nature.

By contrast, the units of syntax—nouns, verbs, prepositional phrases, and so on—do not present themselves to awareness at all. We do not *hear* syntactic categories in verbal images as we hear phonological categories. Still less are the units of conceptual structure available to awareness. They determine our *understanding* of verbal images, so we can judge that two sentences differ in meaning, or that one implies the other, or that one is a correct description of the visual scene and the other is not. But we cannot introspect the formal units that govern this understanding; their organization is entirely hidden from awareness. Thus, the form in which linguistic images present themselves to awareness is evidently most like phonological structure.

I have focused first on linguistic imagery rather than speech perception or production because the linguistic structure in this case seems so purely gratuitous. Why should thought be accompanied by syntactic and phonological structure? The answer comes from the nature of short-term memory: as soon as a conceptual structure is deposited into short-term memory, the fast processes of the language modules automatically translate it, insofar as possible, into linguistic form. It may seem even more strange, perhaps, that *awareness* comes clothed in phonological form. Yet this seems to be the case—we hear this inner voice speaking to us *in words*.

But in fact a parallel observation can be made of speech perception: the form in which we experience a heard utterance is as a sequence of discrete sounds that somehow bear meaning. Moreover, even the experience of speech production is auditory rather than motor: I experience the segmented sound of my voice speaking, not the (willed) motion of my vocal tract. (It takes training in articulatory phonetics to notice what the vocal tract is doing.) Hence, it appears that *all* uses of language present themselves to awareness in phonological form.

Let me be as blatant as I can about this claim, and see how far I can get.

Theory VII (preliminary form)
The distinctions of form present in linguistic awareness are caused by/supported by/projected from the phonological structure in short-term memory that has been designated as most salient by the selection function.

Theory VII claims that the *only* form of linguistic representation available to awareness is, of all things, phonological structure—far from what anyone would conceive of as "the parameters governing the operating system," as Johnson-Laird claims, and, despite Marcel, certainly commensurate with nonconscious "perceptual" representations. Moreover, Theory VII is not compatible with any version of the central-level theory or with the all-level theory. In fact, it may initially seem totally outlandish. I will argue for it by showing first that phonological structure alone can support linguistic awareness, then that conceptual structure alone cannot.

The first part of the argument is simple: nonsense syllables like *zup* and *riz* present themselves to awareness as some kind of linguistic form, even though they are patently meaningless. So do utterances in a language we do not understand, where we cannot map from phonology to meaning. In the latter case phonological structure will probably be fragmentary, because there is no holistic and top-down feedback in its derivation (recall the discussion of section 6.2). But there is still a form we are *aware of*, and it is doubtless language, even if totally incomprehensible.

One might object that English "sounds meaningful" and Armenian, say, does not. But what is meant by "sounds meaningful," other than that I understand it? As has been remarked for centuries, the meaningfulness of an utterance cannot be found anywhere in its palpable (that is, introspectively available) form. The difference lies only in the presence or absence of conceptual structure hidden behind the scenes (plus possibly in a different "feel" or "affect" associated with the utterance—an issue to which we return in the next chapter).

Suppose that, contrary to my claim, conceptual structure were the level most directly responsible for awareness, as in the central-level theory. This would leave no way of accounting for the fact that linguistic awareness is so sharply distinguished from visual awareness, since conceptual structure is common to the two faculties. We would not be able to tell whether we were seeing something or being told it. Language and vision would be phenomenologically as intertwined as taste and smell. What a weird idea. (Notice, in contrast, that we may not *remember* whether we were told something or actually saw it. But if long-term memories are stored predominantly in the form of conceptual structures, this is exactly what we would predict.)

On just these grounds, Theory IV claimed already that the modality-specific character of awareness is a consequence of its being projected from modality-specific levels of representation. We can therefore rule out a theory that claims that conceptual structure is the locus of linguistic awareness. At least one language-specific level must be included, as is the case in Theory VII.

One might try to save the central-level theory by proposing that conceptual structures are tagged by the modality in which they have been received. But this would miss the point, since the *non*modality of this level is one of its principal defining conditions. In any event, such a tactic is insufficient. Consider that we sometimes ask bilingual speakers which language they think in or dream in. That is, we seem to believe that one can *think in a particular language*. If conceptual structure, which is by definition language-neutral, were the sole support of linguistic awareness, this question would not make sense—linguistic images could not be distinguished by language. The fact that they can be argues again that *some* language-specific representations are involved in supporting the form of awareness.

Still, this argument shows only that phonological structure affects the form of awareness when it is present, not that the form of conceptual structure is *excluded* from awareness. To demonstrate this latter point, let us consider the frequently discussed "tip-of-the-tongue" experience, in which one is trying to say something but just can't think of the word, or one can precisely picture someone being talked about but can't remember her name. What could be going on in processing during this experience? Short-term memory must contain a conceptual structure, since one "knows what one intends to say"; there is likely a syntactic structure as well, since the desired word fits into a sentence. If there is an accompanying visual image, the representations to support that must be present too (see section 14.5). What is missing is the phonological structure, which for some reason the processes of lexical access have failed to supply. Sometimes part of the phonological structure is present—a rhythm, a stress, a few sounds per-haps—but not enough for one to be able to come out and say it.

Phenomenologically, I think it fair to say that in the tip-of-the-tongue situation one feels as though one is desperately trying to fill a void. (This is James's (1890) description too.) One is aware of *having* requisite conceptual structure ("I *know* what I want to say..."), and one can reject incorrect guesses at the desired word, but the content remains inarticulate. This is in fact exactly as Theory VII would predict: awareness is projected from the phonological representation—which in this case consists only of an empty set of brackets!

What of the awareness of having an unexpressed meaning, and the frustration at being unable to say it? These aspects of awareness have no form of their own, as words do, but are more like a "feel" to the experience. I don't want to push this part of the phenomenology yet; we will be more ready in the next chapter. For the moment, I will just distinguish the *form* of phenomenological entities from their feel or *affect*. The peculiarity of the tip-of-the-tongue experience is that it is all affect and no form. Theory VII, which addresses only the form of awareness, is therefore too narrow to characterize the experience fully. But what it says about form appears correct: linguistic awareness derives its form from phonological structure, and in the absence of phonological structure awareness is correspondingly formless.

The tip-of-the-tongue phenomenon, then, drives home the inadequacy of the central-level theory. The presence of conceptual structure is neither necessary for linguistic awareness (as in nonsense syllables) nor sufficient (as in tip-of-the-tongue). By contrast, phonological structure is both nec-essary (as shown by tip-of-the-tongue) and sufficient (in nonsense sylla-bles). Thus, Theory VII is supported not only by the phenomenology of ordinary speaking and listening and that of verbal imagery but by these slightly more unusual experiences as well.

One point from an unexpected quarter that reinforces Theory VII: What is linguistic awareness like in a language that lacks phonology, namely, American Sign Language? If awareness were projected from conceptual structure, we would expect no difference from ordinary language. But if Theory VII is right, we expect awareness to be like the representations that take the place of phonology in ASL. There are two possibilities. Awareness could be projected from visual representations, in which case ASL imagery should be something like seeing hands gesturing. Alternatively, awareness could be projected from body representations, in which case it should be something like feeling one's own hands moving. Interestingly, both pos-sibilities seem to occur, at least according to anecdotal evidence (Elissa Newport, personal communication). Evidently, deaf native speakers of ASL experience verbal imagery primarily as body sensations; hearing speakers, for whom ASL is a second language, have linguistic images primarily in the visual modality. I do not know what to make of this contrast, but it provides a surprising illustration of the fact that linguistic awareness derives its form not from conceptual structure but from levels of representation rather distant from thought.

14.3 The Form of Musical Awareness

Having justified Theory VII in the linguistic modality, we now seek a counterpart in the other two faculties whose levels of representation we have examined. The thrust of the generalization will be that awareness in general is supported by neither the most peripheral nor the most central representations in the computational mind, but by a collection of modality-specific intermediate levels.

Musical awareness is easily taken care of. Here direct awareness appears to parallel the *musical surface*, the linearly ordered sequence of pitch events (notes and chords): the notes are what we *hear*. The musical surface is not the lowest level of information structure involved in music perception, for, as detailed in section 11.2, a great deal of auditory processing has already taken place to discriminate pitches, pitch simultaneities, attack points, and temporal sequencing. On the other hand, the musical surface is far from the most central level of musical structure, since there are four higher levels of hierarchical musical structure that are responsible for the understanding of music.

If anything, the conclusion that awareness and understanding come from different levels is clearer in music than in language. This is because the central levels of music perception do not connect very directly to conceptual structure; they therefore do not evoke the verbal responses that we call "conscious thought." Without all the extra verbiage generated around it, musical understanding seems to us entirely mysterious and magical. Somehow a succession of notes may have an effect that seems to come unbidden from the depths of our being. This effect has no phenomenological form, only an ineffable "feel" associated with the musical surface. As in the case of language, I will describe this "feel" as the *affect* associated with awareness and will put it off to section 15.1. It is altogether distinct from the elements that give awareness its *form*, which in the case of music are quite clearly the elements of the musical surface.

As a parallel to the nonsense syllable case in language, consider the common reaction to much contemporary "classical" music. As Lerdahl and I show (1983, section 11.6), this type of music often has a musical surface so devised as to thwart all the principles of musical grammar; the result is that the listener cannot construct more than fragmentary and unstable representations of the music at the four hierarchical levels. Listeners hence frequently report the music as incomprehensible. But they certainly report *hearing* it—which would not be the case if central representations were essential for awareness.

It is not so easy to construct a musical analogue to the tip-of-the-tongue experience. We do sometimes have difficulty remembering a tune and experience only images of disconnected snatches of it. Unlike the linguistic case, though, it is not so obvious that the central representations are present in such circumstances. So I cannot display a case that shows that central musical representations alone do not support musical awareness.

Nevertheless, the evidence available is consistent with a musical counterpart of Theory VII and inconsistent with a central-level theory. What has not been definitively ruled out is an "all-level" theory—though the fact that one does not experience four simultaneous hierarchies while listening to music ought to be rather convincing.

14.4 The Form of Awareness in Visual Perception

The case of visual awareness is perhaps the most controversial, if only because it is so frequently taken as *the* form of awareness, to the exclusion of other varieties. Extending Theory VII, I will contend that *the level of visual structure most directly responsible for the form of visual awareness is the 2½D sketch*, the viewer-centered representation of visible surfaces.

To lend this position some initial plausibility, let us compare the elements in the 2½D sketch to those in the other levels of visual representation. The primal sketch does not contain enough organization to correspond to visual awareness; it does not even contain a complete partitioning of the visual field into surfaces. Moreover, visual awareness is unitary—we do not experience discrepant inputs from the two eyes; hence awareness must be projected from a level of structure where the information from the two retinas has been merged. This again rules out the primal sketch, since binocular fusion is a step on the way from the primal sketch to the 2½D sketch (recall section 9.3).

More intuitively plausible, perhaps, would be the claim that the 3D model is responsible for visual awareness. Yet there are a number of arguments against it, which depend on the formal character of the 2½D sketch and 3D model and their roles in the computational mind.

First, visual awareness is viewer-centered—one sees foremost from one's own point of view. In particular, one directly experiences only the presented side of objects in the visual field; the presence of the rear of objects is commonly said to be only an inference. The 3D model, however, encodes the *outcome* of the visual inference: it includes the whole of a viewed object, and it does not distinguish between "seen" and "unseen" portions. By contrast, the $2\frac{1}{2}$D sketch encodes just the right sort of visual information for this aspect of "raw awareness."

One might object that visual appearance is decidedly three-dimensional and that this therefore calls for a 3D model to support awareness. But recall that the $2\frac{1}{2}$D sketch does contain a great deal of information that is normally regarded as three-dimensional—that's why Marr didn't call it the "2D sketch." Far from being a flat "picture in the head," it encodes information about distance and orientation of surfaces with respect to the viewer and thus includes appropriate distinctions for visual awareness.

In addition, the formal nature of the 3D model has turned out to be less like visual awareness than might have been expected. 3D model representations are headed hierarchical structures that describe objects at many layers of detail, from coarse to fine. They are articulated in terms of axes and coordinate systems whose organization is definitely not present in direct experience: one sees the surfaces of objects, not the axes down their middles. Moreover, the 3D model is full of explicit elements for encoding spatial relations, such as regions and trajectories. None of these emerges in the form of awareness either. Thus, the 3D model, which subserves visual *understanding*, is if anything too rich to support the form of visual *awareness*, whereas the $2\frac{1}{2}$D sketch seems just rich enough.

There is a sense in which the 3D model is also too impoverished. Section 14.2 presented an argument against a central-level theory of linguistic awareness, based on modality specificity. We can construct a parallel argument for visual awareness. Recall that the 3D model is the level where all the spatial modalities intersect and exchange information, so that we can, for example, identify objects by either sight or touch. Thus, if the 3D model were the basis for visual awareness, the visual modality could not be sufficiently differentiated from other modalities. I could not tell whether I was seeing or feeling an object, for instance.

By contrast, my *memory* of an object's shape may be undifferentiated by modality—I may not be able to remember whether I actually touched it or just saw it. Such a difference between experience and memory is just what is to be expected if visual experience is based on the $2\frac{1}{2}$D sketch—a vision-specific level—but shape memory is encoded in terms of the modality-neutral 3D level.

The claim, then, is that the form of visual awareness—the way things *look*—is determined by the $2\frac{1}{2}$D sketch, whereas visual understanding—the "content" or "meaning" of visual awareness, what one is aware *of*—is determined by the 3D and conceptual structures in registration with the $2\frac{1}{2}$D sketch. Let me run through a few cases to illustrate this disparity between awareness and understanding.

First, I have already alluded to the perception of objects as solid. Their back sides and interiors are not present in the $2\frac{1}{2}$D sketch or in visual awareness; but they *are* represented in the 3D model, so that they can play a role in the inferences we make about the objects, the expectations we have about them, and the actions we perform on them. Now consider the case of totally occluded objects: what is the difference between seeing a bookcase and seeing a bookcase with a cat hidden behind it? There is *no* difference in the 2½D sketch, or in the form of visual awareness—the two situations *look* the same. But the 3D model includes the cat in the latter case and not in the former: one's understanding of the overall spatial layout is different. Hence, one responds differently to the two situations.

Note how our account of processing is crucial here. In order to use the 3D model to understand the 2½D sketch, the two structures must be maintained in registration with each other. One must encode, for instance, which parts of the 3D model correspond to the visible surfaces of the bookcase, as well as the fact that certain parts of the 3D model have no correlate in the current 2½D sketch. In other words, the notion of multiple levels of representation held in short-term memory and maintained in registration is central to the present view of the relation between awareness and understanding.

For another case, consider the classic example of the appearance of a stick halfway into a tub of water. The optical properties of the situation guarantee that (at most viewing angles) the viewer's 2½D sketch will contain a bend in the stick at the water's surface. If this bend is carried directly over into the 3D model, the viewer will simply report "The stick is bent in the middle." Suppose, on the other hand, that the viewer maintains a spatial and conceptual analysis based on previously derived attributes of the stick, or on his concept of rigid objects, or on his knowledge of optics. Then his understanding of the situation will involve a disparity between the current perceptually based analysis and preexisting conceptualization. In such a conflicted situation the viewer will report that "The stick *looks* bent, even though I know it's not." That is, in this case the disparity between visual experience and understanding becomes itself explicit in the viewer's understanding.

Next, consider a situation where one cannot make out a scene in the fog or cannot interpret a blurry picture. There is certainly visual awareness, but understanding is absent. (Perhaps this is an analogue to nonsense syllables in linguistic awareness.) At the sudden moment of recognition, when a 3D model is achieved, visual awareness too changes—there are boundaries and contours that one did not perceive before. This is because of the feedback the 3D model provides to visual perception, filling in 2½D structure that could not be derived from the retinal input alone. In such a case, then, understanding can inform awareness, through the two structures being maintained in registration.

A final remarkable example of the contrast between visual awareness and understanding comes from a pathological case quoted by Marcel (1983, 292–293). The patient reports such perceptions as these:

> ... there was what seemed to me to be one object which was partly motor car, partly tree and partly a man in a cricket shirt. They seemed somehow to belong together. More frequently, however, a lot of things which to any ordinary viewer would be parts of the same thing were parts of different things.... When one only saw a small object one could hardly say anything more than one saw a colored patch.... If there were a number of people in the picture at the same time it was very difficult to say how many there were or what they were doing....

From the perspective of the present theory this pathology seems functionally to consist of a failure to map properly from the 2½D sketch to the 3D model, or a failure to use 3D models in memory to properly regiment those derived from perception. All the regions and contours are present in the 2½D sketch, but the regions cannot be unified properly into identifiable objects. Again there is visual awareness; but understanding—and hence the ability to make linguistic reports—is defective.

14.5 The Form of Awareness in Visual Imagery; *Theory VII* Generalized

Next consider visual *imagery*, where the visual system is driven not by retinal input but by conceptual and/or 3D structures. The phenomenology of visual images has characteristics that again point to the 2½D sketch as the locus of visual awareness. Like visual perception, visual images present themselves as viewer-centered; that is, they are "seen" from a particular point of view. The "zooming" operations on visual images described by Kosslyn (1980) present themselves to awareness as the imaged object getting closer to or farther from the viewer—and this is experienced as distinct from the imaged object growing or shrinking. More crucially, in the mental rotations studied by Shepard et al., parts of the imaged objects are "seen" as occluding other parts, then themselves being occluded as the object continues to rotate. As in visual perception, the only level of representation that combines all these characteristics is the 2½D sketch.

Again, the 2½D sketch does not itself provide the information necessary for the understanding associated with the image. To use Fodor's (1975) example, based on an argument of Wittgenstein (1953), how is one to distinguish the images that go with the thoughts "John is fat" and "John is tall"? There is nothing intrinsic to the images that can draw attention to the property of fatness rather than height. However, in the present theory the requisite information appears in conceptual structure, in registration with the 2½D sketch from which the image is projected.

Like language, visual images have often been claimed to be a medium of thought. However, a well-known objection goes back to Berkeley: images are not general enough for the purposes in reasoning they must serve. The standard example is the concept "triangle," which, if it is realized as an image, must be some specific triangle of specific proportions. Fodor (1975) quotes Hume's reply to this objection: "The image in the mind is only that of a particular object, tho' the application of it in our reasoning be the same as if it were universal." In the present framework Hume's answer can be fleshed out more explicitly. The 2½D sketch by its nature must be explicit in matters of size and shape; hence, a particular token triangle must be chosen in order for an image to be formed at all. However, the understanding of this triangle as a representative of the category of triangles (or of scalene triangles, or of triangles with an angle of 75°, or of geometric figures in general) is due to the form of the 3D and conceptual structures with which the 2½D sketch is currently in registration; it is these more abstract and general structures that are used in reasoning. In short, the experienced image is evidence that visual thinking is taking place, but it is not itself the medium of thought.

The same approach applies to the common notion, mentioned in sections 9.4 and 10.4, that the meaning of a word like *chair* contains an image of a stereotypical instance. It was argued there that a fixed stereotype image cannot properly serve the purposes of spatial cognition, and what is really needed is the more flexibly specified 3D model representation. Now we can see that the image often evoked by the word *chair* is accounted for in the same way as Hume's triangle: it is projected from the 2½D sketch that is automatically created in short-term memory when the 3D model is recovered from the lexicon. Because the 2½D sketch must be formally specific in its details, the form of the image is fixed more closely than necessary or appropriate for understanding.

A sort of converse case, where the image is *less* specific than might be expected, is posed by Dennett (1969). He claims that if indeed a mental image of a tiger is something picture-like, we ought to be able to count the tiger's stripes; and of course we usually cannot. Fodor (1975) replies that one likely can't count the stripes in a blurry picture of a distant tiger either, so images are no worse than real pictures. But there is a better answer possible in present terms. One's ability to individuate stripes in the tiger's image depends on the 3D and conceptual structures in registration with the 2½D sketch, for it is over these structures that individuation and counting are defined. The stripes can be counted only if the higher-level representations contain a discrete constituent for each one of them. If, on the other hand, the stripes are conceptually represented as a texture, the stripedness cannot be discriminated into individual elements, and counting will be impossible.

Our conclusion, as with visual perception, is that the phenomenological form of visual images is most directly a product of the 2½D sketch level of representation. On the other hand, what one is aware *of* in an image is a product of the spatial and conceptual structures maintained in registration with the 2½D sketch that supports the image.

In each of three faculties, then, we have seen that awareness is supported not by the central levels of representation but by a level intermediate between the most central and the most peripheral. Theory VII can thus be generalized across the faculties.

> *Theory VII (Intermediate-Level Theory)*
> The distinctions of form present in each modality of awareness are caused by/supported by/projected from a structure of intermediate level for that modality that is part of the matched set of short-term memory representations designated by the selection function and enriched by attentional processing. Specifically, linguistic awareness is caused by/supported by/projected from phonological structure; musical awareness from the musical surface; visual awareness from the 2½D sketch.

14.6 Remarks on "Sensation," Touch, Pain, Hunger, and the Self

If the Intermediate-Level Theory is correct, it explains why it has never been possible to introspect "pure sensation." "Sensation" might be taken to mean the lowest-level, least processed form of input to sensory modalities. Under this interpretation the relevant levels are such things as retinal arrays and auditory information, which from the outset of our investigation we have seen to be totally unavailable to awareness. Alternatively, like "perception" (see section 12.12), sensation might be taken to mean a form of information derived exclusively by bottom-up processing, perhaps of a level lower than perception. However, the levels of representation available to awareness are already unavoidably affected by top-down processes as well as bottom-up. One cannot turn off the mandatory fast modules that contribute this top-down information, so as to be left solely with information that comes in from the environment. Hence, "sensation" in the intended sense cannot be separated from "interpretation" in awareness.

So far the only modalities for which we can verify the Intermediate-Level Theory are language, vision, and music, since these are the only ones for which we have a theory of levels. However, other modalities are suggestive. For instance, in the haptic modality, where we use the sense of touch to find our way around in the world, awareness takes neither the form of unintegrated arrays of pressure cues on the skin nor that of fully integrated spatial configurations. At least impressionistically, it seems to have the form of local judgments like "flat-surface here," "sharp-corner here," and so forth. This sounds a bit like a haptic analogue of the 2½D sketch's description of visible surfaces, which likewise must undergo further integration to yield full spatial form—in other words, like an intermediate level in the chain from touch to spatial understanding.

In a similar vein, section 11.8 speculated about the existence of a level of body representation, part of the chain leading from spatial understanding to motor activity. Something of the sort would be a possible locus for the representations supporting body sensations such as muscular effort, pain, and hunger. In the case of pain, at least, there are enough "cognitive" components involved in awareness and localization that one would be hard put to argue that pain simply is projected from the low-level pattern of pain receptor stimulations from the body. (See Dennett 1978c for discussion and references.) On the other hand, pain hardly seems to derive its effects from conceptual structure. Thus, some intermediate level of representation, perhaps body representation, again appears appropriate.

The distinctions made in the level of body representation are of course limited to the state of one's own body. This provides an almost trivial account of the fact that one can feel only one's own pain and hunger: the distinction "self's versus other's pain" is just not available in the way that "self's versus other's spatial position" is, simply because others' bodies are not represented at the relevant level.

Circumstantially, we might further suspect that the as yet unknown representations that are projected into awareness as emotion are still a different level. Unlike body sensations, emotions have no spatial localization at all but simply belong to the "self," whatever *that* is. This suggests that the relevant level of representation lacks spatial distinctions altogether; thereby the experience of emotion would be not only restricted to one's own person but also devoid of position in the body. If there are no *distinctions* of position, there is no *position*.

Finally, what of the "self"? William James (1890, 299–302) comes to this depressed conclusion:

> When I forsake ... general descriptions and grapple with particulars, coming to the closest possible quarters with the facts, it is difficult for me to detect in the activity [of the self] any purely spiritual element at all. Whenever my introspective glance succeeds in turning round quickly enough to catch one of these manifestations of spontaneity in the act, all it can ever feel distinctly is some bodily process, for the most part taking place within the head.... The 'Self of selves,' when carefully examined, is found to consist mainly of the collection of

these peculiar motions in the head or between the head and throat . . .
It would follow that our entire feeling of spiritual activity, or what
commonly passes by that name, is really a feeling of bodily activities
whose exact nature is by most men overlooked.

The Intermediate-Level Theory might explain these intuitions along the
following lines: The self must be represented explicitly in conceptual structure, as the privileged individual that is connected to body representations
and the instigation of action. However, the manifestations of self that
present themselves to awareness cannot come directly from this central
representation but must be projected from representations at a more peripheral level. But there is no such level where the notion of self appears as
a possible constituent; the closest is body representation, which projects
nothing but the tensions and twitches that James reports. Thus, a fundamental aspect of understanding is grossly underrepresented in awareness.

On a more metatheoretical plane, the Intermediate-Level Theory in a
sense provides a partial account of why the workings of the mind (in both
phenomenological and computational guises) have been so recalcitrant to
investigation. On the one hand, intuition suggests that awareness reveals
what is going on in the mind, including thought. On the other hand,
intuition suggests that awareness reveals what is going on out in the
world, that is, the result of sensation or perception. According to the
Intermediate-Level Theory, it reveals neither. Rather, awareness reflects a
curious amalgam of the effects on the mind of both thought and the real
world, while leaving totally opaque the means by which these effects come
about. It is only by developing a formal theory of levels of representation
that we could have come to suspect the existence of a part of the computational mind that has these characteristics.

14.7   The Unity of Entities in Awareness

In the Intermediate-Level Theory, each distinct modality of awareness
comes from a different faculty-specific level. Thus, as already noted, it
accounts more precisely for the "disunity of awareness" that was discussed
in section 4.6 and that motivated our earlier Theory IV. However, there
may be a lingering question: How is it that entities detected in multiple
modalities can be experienced as unified? For instance, when I look at
something and handle it at the same time, how can I experience it as the
same object, if my awareness is disunified into visual and haptic modalities?

The answer comes from the character of processing. The visual and
haptic representations that support awareness of the object are each in
registration with 3D model and conceptual structures that encode the
shape, identity, and category of the object. If it so happens that they are in

registration with the *same* 3D model and conceptual structure, then the two modalities will be understood and experienced as simultaneous manifestations of the same object. In other words, understanding again parses out experience, this time across modalities.

Though this solution falls readily out of the present approach, it is not necessarily intuitively obvious. As a spur to intuition, let me return to Marcel's (1983) pathological case. Here is another part of the transcript Marcel quotes (pp. 292–293):

> . . . (if somebody I knew was speaking to me) . . . it sounds quite absurd but there were two distinct things. One was that so and so was speaking to me and I could hear and understand what he said; two, that he was standing in front of me and I could see his mouth moving, but I noticed that the mouth moving did not belong to what I heard any more than a—than if one of the old talkie pictures would make sense if the voice tape had been the wrong tape for the conversation. That was absolutely quite fantastically exciting . . . . (Interviewer: Was this a failure to localize the source of the voice?) No. No. It was as though they were two different things. (Interviewer: They didn't belong together.) Didn't belong together at all.

Here, evidently, we have just the sort of disunity that Theory VII would predict *if* there were no registration among faculties, that is, if the central representations were not doing their job properly. At the same time awareness per se is (seemingly) intact—the person sees and hears. Thus, this pathology, where one (or more) of the links between faculties is apparently defective, provides an interesting source of evidence for the Intermediate-Level Theory and, more generally, for the role of unconscious understanding in unifying the separate modalities of awareness.

Chapter 15

Amplifications of the Intermediate-Level Theory

The Intermediate-Level Theory is, I believe, the key to describing the form of awareness and the disparity between awareness and understanding. There remain, however, certain problems in its account of the phenomenology. The task of this chapter is to face up to two of them and propose at least tentative approaches.

15.1 The Affects; *Theory VIII*

The first problem is this: Theory VII claims that both seeing and having visual images project into awareness from the 2½D sketch. Although this appears to account correctly for the forms of awareness in these two phenomena, it still provides no way to distinguish the two. If this were the whole story, we would not be able to tell whether there was really something out there or whether we had made it up! Evidently Theory VII has become too narrow.

The Hypothesis of Computational Sufficiency says that the difference between perception and imagery cannot be purely phenomenological but must be supported by a corresponding computational distinction. Moreover, since this difference also plays a role in reasoning and behavior—one is more likely to decide to run from a perceived tiger than an imagined one—the Hypothesis of the Nonefficacy of Consciousness likewise forces us to find a computational distinction between percepts and images. What is it?

One's first impulse might be that images are just vaguer or less substantial than perception. Yet one can have very clear images and one can perceive objects dimly through a fog, so this option is not open in general. Moreover, the essential similarity of visual images and visual percepts is emphasized by situations such as hallucination and dreams, where self-produced visual awareness is experienced as perception. Conversely, externally stimulated visual experience can also on occasion be experienced as imagery. This was demonstrated by Perky's (1910) experiments (described in Kosslyn 1980), whose subjects were instructed to imagine certain figures on a blank screen. Unbeknownst to them, faint figures were projected on the screen from behind; the subjects experienced these figures as their own imagery. Given these possibilities for confusion, then, it would appear incorrect to distinguish percepts from images on the basis of form.

Chapter 9 argued that the computational distinction between perception and imagery is not in the forms of information the two encode but rather in the processing that gives rise to them: perception is initiated from the periphery, whereas imagery is initiated from central representations. As a result, during visual perception there is information reaching the $2\frac{1}{2}$D sketch level from below, whereas during visual imagery there is not (under our assumption that the $2\frac{1}{2}$D sketch is the lower bound of bidirectional processing). Similarly, during visual perception the $2\frac{1}{2}$D sketch is activated earlier in time than the corresponding parts of the 3D model, whereas during visual imagery the reverse is the case.

How can these differences be put to use in supporting the phenomenology? The most immediate way is to take them as a limited kind of counterexample to Lashley's Observation—that is, to say that *this* distinction in awareness *is* supported by processing rather than by structure. Alternatively, suppose that the computational mind were to contain monitors or sensors that detect these processing differences and that the output of these monitors formed a new kind of structure. For concreteness, suppose that this structure were to take the form of a single binary feature *percept* versus *image*, whose value determined the character of awareness. Such a theoretical move would preserve Lashley's Observation intact, in that the most immediate support for awareness would again be a structure rather than a process.

Let us pursue this second alternative, if only speculatively. I will call the feature *percept* versus *image* a feature of *affect*. This feature has to do neither with the *form* of phenomenal entities nor with their *category*, but rather with how they "feel." It cuts across all distinctions of form, category, and even modality—for, as noted in section 4.6, one can have linguistic, musical, tactile, and olfactory images as well as visual ones.

An affect is not associated with the phenomenal field as a whole. Rather, it goes with an individual constituent of the phenomenal field. Recall the example in section 1.1 of the imaginary Martians coming in through the (real) window. Presumably, the Martians alone are represented with the affect *image*, whereas everything else in the scene is *percept*. Similarly, one can image the unseen source of a perceived (real) sound; and perceived smells often conjure up unbidden rich visual images of some past experience. Hence, the feature of affect must be integrated rather closely with the representations that support each entity in awareness, in order that perceived and imaged entities may be clearly distinguished.

Further, although a feature of affect may be derived by self-monitoring of processing, its phenomenological manifestation is not as a kind of self-awareness. Rather, the status of a phenomenological entity as percept or image is experienced as an objective fact about the entity itself—just like its size, form, and location.

The difference between percepts and images is, I think, only one of a family of distinctions of "feel" that appear in awareness. Here are some candidates for this family. Each is a binary distinction that is associated with individual entities in the phenomenal field but that belongs neither to phenomenal form nor to conceptual category. I have made an effort to make them as general as possible, though I am far from certain about their taxonomy.

1. *Outer versus inner.* This is a generalization of *percept* versus *image* to include output modalities. Percepts and actions carry the affect *outer*, and imaged percepts and imaged actions are *inner*. The processing factors that distinguish real actions from imaged actions are in part the same as those that distinguish perception from imagery; in particular, *inner* entities do not involve the most peripheral processors in either perception or action. In addition, of course, real actions give sensory feedback, since they produce changes in the sensory field, whereas imaged actions do not.

2. *Ego-initiated versus non-ego-initiated.* This has to do with the sense of will. The basic intuition is that actions are willed (*ego-initiated*), whereas perceptions are not—I see what is "out there," not what I want to see. But the distinction applies to other cases as well. Images can be *ego-initiated,* in which case one has the sense "I imagine this"; or they can be *non-ego-initiated,* in which case one has the sense "This image came to me." Furthermore, body motions can carry the affect *non-ego-initiated,* as in the case of involuntary twitches. Here one has the sense "My eyelid is twitching" or "My knees are knocking" rather than "I am twitching my eyelid" or "I am knocking my knees."

Table 15.1 charts the combinations of affects so far, to help keep them in

Table 15.1
Combinations of affects

	Outer		Inner	
	Ego-initiated	Non-ego-initiated	Ego-initiated	Non-ego-initiated
Input modalities	——	Perception	Willed perceptual images	Unwilled perceptual images
Output modalities	I'm moving	My body is moving	Willed action images	Unwilled action images

mind as things get more complicated. The only combination that is missing is willed perception, for (what appear to be) obvious reasons. (Even this case *might* show up—for instance, when one "deliberately sees" the vase-faces illusion in figure 6.7 as the faces rather than the vase.)

As we have not at all investigated the computational concomitants of the sense of will, I cannot suggest a source for this important distinction in affect. I should hope that this gap is not enough to warrant a reversion to know-nothing interactionism. Let us just say it is a crucial topic for future research and leave it at that.

One further point: *Hallucinations* can be classified as unwilled images that are for some pathological reason experienced as percepts. Within the scheme of table 15.1 their affect ought to be *inner, non-ego-initiated*, but what makes them seem real is that they are instead experienced with the affect *outer, non-ego-initiated*. In other words, hallucinations are an error of affect.

3. *Meaningful versus meaningless.* This feature was hinted at in the discussion of linguistic awareness. Basically, an utterance in linguistic awareness has the affect *meaningful* if the phonological structure that supports it is in registration with a conceptual structure, *meaningless* if there is no such connection. The factors in processing that support this affect are the existence and stability of structures in all the processors in short-term linguistic memory. Given a sensor that can detect these factors, we can explain why it is that one can sense an utterance to be meaningful without being able to explain the meaning: the affect *meaningful* and the phonological structure are present to awareness, but the conceptual structure is not.

This feature of affect occurs in other input modalities as well. We considered in section 14.4 the occasional experience of looking at a blurry picture or a dimly lit scene and being unable to "read" it. All the regions in the visual field are fairly clear, but the forms are still incoherent. Then, usually, one has the sense of the field clicking into place, and it suddenly is comprehended. The affect has changed from *meaningless* to *meaningful*, as a result of central representations being constructed.

Finally, the affect *meaningless* occurs in music as well—for instance, in many listeners' experience of contemporary "classical" music, as discussed in section 14.3, where the listener is unable to construct stable levels of representation more central than the musical surface. Hence this affect cuts across all three faculties. Whether it generalizes further—say, to a notion of *meaningful* versus *meaningless* action in the proper sense—is unclear to me.

4. *Familiar versus novel.* This pertains to access to long-term memory. I want to separate this feature of affect from the *conceptual* achievement of identification, because the two sometimes diverge. For instance, a déja vu experience, like a hallucination, is an error of affect: an experience carries the affect *familiar* even though there is nothing with which it can be

conceptually identified. For another example, consider the experience I'm sure everyone has now and then, reported as "I've seen that guy before, but damned if I know who he is!" Here the affect *familiar* appears, presumably properly, but actual identification in conceptual structure cannot be achieved for some reason. The opposite also occurs, namely, the experience of seeing something afresh, "as though altogether new." Here the affect is *novel*, even though conceptual identification has previously taken place.

This affect appears also in imagery, where one can experience a thought (in the guise of a verbal, visual, musical, or other image) as a memory (*familiar*) or a new idea (*novel*). I imagine it is also evident in action, especially to people who put store in the familiarity or novelty of actions, such as gymnasts or dancers.

5. *Easy versus effortful.* This pertains to rapidity and stability of short-term memory processing. A percept has the affect *effortful* if one must concentrate hard to get it, as when hearing through a noisy phone connection or seeing in dim surroundings. Section 6.2 spoke of what is going on in processing in such cases: the peripheral levels are providing limited and/or indeterminate information to short-term memory, so a great deal at intermediate levels must be filled in by holistic and top-down processes—best guesses as to what the message is. As mentioned there, though, the phenomenology is not of making guesses or inferences but rather of the object out there being hard to perceive. (The phenomenology of making inferences is different: it comes from new conceptual structures being produced in response to the conceptual structure derived from the incoming signal. These new structures in turn throw off their own linguistic images, which are responsible for the experience of inferences taking place.)

The affect *easy* versus *effortful* seems to pertain to actions as well as percepts, though without a theory of the relevant levels any account is pure speculation. But consider cases of complex motor coordination, such as reciting a tongue twister, or playing a difficult passage on the piano, or (for some of us klutzes) learning to waltz. The constituent actions are simple enough, but the whole cannot be brought off as a unit without intense concentration, if at all. The affect seems similar enough to perception of a degraded signal that one might try to account for it in terms of problematic mapping between levels. This time, information must be translated from higher to lower levels, but the central level, which initiates the action, does not provide enough information to fully specify the more peripheral levels, which direct and time muscle activations. The problem for short-term memory would be the same in both cases, the only difference being the desired primary direction of information flow.

6. *Neutral versus affective (+ or −).* This concerns the possible presence of emotional response: *affective (+)* is "It's nice" and *affective (−)* is "It's yucky." (*Affective* in general might be "It matters.") Notice that the affect is

again experienced as inhering in the phenomenal entity itself. Going to "I like it" or "I hate it" is (at least often) an intellectual rather than affective step. For example, prejudice is a result of *failing* to take this further step: the objects of hatred are seen as *objectively* offensive.

This affect is not limited to percepts. For instance, we may distinguish a reminiscence from an ordinary memory of past experience by the aura of *affective* (+) that it carries. As with other affects, the warmth seems somehow to inhere in the memory itself rather than being recognized as my subjective reaction to it.

For obvious reasons I am not ready to say anything about the factors in processing or memory that give rise to this affect.

7. *Congruous versus incongruous.* I have in mind here the curious and unsettling affect that comes with illusions and paradoxes. I would like to designate this as *incongruous*, by contrast with the affect *congruous* that comes with ordinary percepts. Notice how *incongruous* differs from *meaningless* in the sense intended here. In a *meaningless* utterance—say nonsense syllables or (for me) Armenian—no interpretation at all can be derived; by contrast, an *incongruous* utterance such as (15.1) has a meaning that fails to "make sense." Phenomenologically the affects are quite different.

(15.1)   This sentence is false.

The same distinction appears in the visual modality, where the affect of an uninterpretable or indistinct pattern is quite different from that of a "paradoxical figure" such as figure 15.1.

Sentence (15.1) and figure 15.1 involve incongruity of the central representations (conceptual and 3D, respectively) that go with the percept. The affect *incongruous* (or a close relative) also may arise from incompatibility

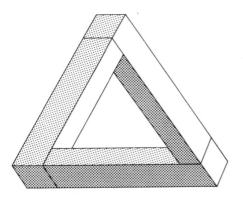

Figure 15.1
A paradoxical visual figure

between the central representation of the percept and the contents of long-term memory. As in the case of *familiar* versus *novel*, I am thinking of the nonconceptual detection of incongruity—the preintellectual feeling that something is amiss, as in "Something sounds funny in that motor—I'd better find out what it is," or "You don't look the way you should—I'd better call a doctor," or "Something sounds fishy in that argument—I'd better call a logician." These are all intuitive judgments of incongruity. They precede analysis and in fact are often what motivate one to undertake an analysis.

The affect *congruous* can produce a parallel preintellectual sense of conviction—for instance, in cases where one feels a statement to be correct in advance of supporting evidence (or even, unfortunately, in spite of counterevidence). For example, it is said that mathematicians often claim to sense the truth of a theorem long before being able to prove it. Less felicitous situations in which the affect *congruous* has accompanied patently false propositions—"irrational belief"—are probably too numerous to need mention.

This list of affects is intended only as a preliminary exercise in phenomenological description, hardly a full-fledged theory. I have essayed it, despite trepidation, with three goals in mind. First, by looking at a broad range of examples, I hope to stimulate a broader sensitivity to phenomenological description, both in myself and in readers. There are a lot of interesting phenomena right before our eyes if we think to look for them, and the affects provide a framework for a certain class of them. Second, something like affect is necessary to tie up various loose ends in the theory of awareness. In particular, whereas the Intermediate-Level Theory accounts for the distinctions among "modalities" of experience in the sense of section 4.6, the affects account for the distinctions among "varieties" of experience in the sense of section 1.1.

Third, I have tried to show that these loose ends together form a coherent system, much of which can be derived from already known properties of the computational mind. We then have three interacting systems of structure that contribute to the nature of experience and behavior: the intermediate levels provide its form, the central levels provide its content, and the affects provide its "feel." If my description above is anywhere near the mark, this third factor exerts a far greater influence on us than we intellectuals might like to admit, playing a crucial role in our senses of Reality, Truth, and Beauty—an issue to which we return briefly in section 16.1.

The suggested role of affect in awareness is incorporated into Theory VIII, our final emendation.

Theory VIII (Intermediate-Level Theory with Affect)
The distinctions present in each modality of awareness are caused by/supported by/projected from a structure of intermediate level for that modality that is part of the matched set of short-term memory representations designated by the selection function and enriched by attentional processing, plus the features of affect associated with the set. Specifically, phonological structure is responsible for the form of linguistic awareness; the musical surface for the form of musical awareness; the $2\frac{1}{2}$D sketch for the form of visual awareness; and the affects for the "feel" of phenomenal entities.

This is perhaps an appropriate place to bring up the controversial work of Jaynes (1976).[1] On the basis of the historical record and archaeological evidence, Jaynes claims that people of early civilizations, such as the Homeric Greeks and the Hebrews of the early Old Testament period, had radically different consciousness than we do. According to Jaynes, they did not experience themselves as thinking beings; rather, the verbal images that we experience as our own thought were experienced by them as the voices of external gods, much like the verbal hallucinations experienced by some schizophrenics today.

The reader is advised to consult Jaynes's work for the reasons behind this startling claim, and I leave the task of evaluating the historical evidence to others more capable than I. Suppose, though, that there is something to Jaynes's observations: what sense can we make then of the phenomenology he attributes to early civilizations? Jaynes himself claims that these people were literally unconscious and that their verbal images emanated from the right hemisphere of the brain, in the area corresponding to the normal speech areas in the left hemisphere—a physiologically unlikely possibility.

Within the present framework there is a less elaborate story available for the phenomenology: the differences appear in the affect system. In particular, suppose the verbal images these people experienced came with the affects *outer, non-ego-initiated, and congruous.* They would then experience their own thought as being produced by something in the external environment, like a perception; since the percept was *congruous,* its externality would seem okay to them, the way things should be. This is a relatively minor difference in the systems that monitor processing, even if it does produce a striking difference in the character of the experienced world. Such a minor difference is perhaps easier to contemplate as actually possible than Jaynes's radical reorganization of the brain.

Whichever account one adopts, Jaynes's or mine, the question arises, How could it come about that the computational minds of a whole society

---

1. I am grateful to Dan Dennett for encouraging me to discuss Jaynes. He doesn't know he did it.

gradually changed over some hundreds of years? There are two possibilities: biological change accompanying the cultural change (that is, natural selection imposed by the culture actually effecting changes in the brain) or cultural change alone. Jaynes (personal communication) believes the difference to be due to cultural change alone; no biological change has taken place. In this case the implication is that something as basic as the way one experiences one's own imagery—in our framework, the affects—is not totally innate but must be partly learned, like language, on the basis of one's cultural environment; moreover, the affect system, like the grammar of language, can change over time.

Now we are getting into deep water indeed. Yet, surprisingly, we are also approaching empirical testability. For now we can ask questions such as when children learn the difference between reality and imagination, on what evidence such learning is based (if any), and whether it might differ from one culture to another. Such questions are being asked in work such as that of Wimmer and Perner (1983), Olson (1986), and Astington, Harris, and Olson (in preparation). So perhaps by providing a framework in which Jaynes's claims can be stated in more modest terms, we will prove to be able to make some sense of them after all.

15.2 How is Introspection Possible?

The second problem for the Intermediate-Level Theory is something that I have taken for granted but have no right to, given my strong convictions: How is it at all possible to report on the form of awareness? I have taken care to account for why so many things can*not* be reported (we will review them in section 16.1), but there is as yet no mechanism to account for that fortunate residue that we *can* speak of.

What is the problem? One tends to think, Well, this stuff is in awareness, so *of course* we can talk about it. But let's unpack "so of course."

The fundamental difficulty with this answer is that talking about something requires *computational* distinctions, whereas being present in awareness is a *phenomenological* distinction. Hence, in order for awareness per se to make it possible to talk about something, a phenomenological distinction would have to cause a computational one, violating the Hypothesis of Nonefficacy of Consciousness. Put more traditionally, in order for something to be detected as present in awareness, there would have to be the magic "little man" or "mind's eye" observing the contents of awareness—the hopeless resort we have been continually trying to avoid.

The alternative offered by the Hypothesis of Nonefficacy of Consciousness is that introspection is possible not because of the presence of material in awareness but rather because of the presence of the particular information structures that support awareness. That is, the capacity for introspection does not feed on the phenomenology; it is to be accounted for entirely within the domain of the computational mind.

The information structures in question are of course just those that we have spent the last few chapters carefully picking out: the intermediate-level representations of each faculty that come from the most salient matched set in short-term memory, as enriched by attention and the affects—let's call these the *Privileged Representations*. But how do we manage to report their presence?

Section 2.1 mentioned Putnam's (1960) observation that being in a particular computational state is not equivalent to being *aware* of being in that computational state. A version of this argument is apposite here. Simply having the Privileged Representations in short-term memory (or some other place), so that they project into primary awareness, does not automatically make them available as the input for a linguistic report. Rather, as Putnam argues, a further computational mechanism must be invoked that detects the presence of the Privileged Representations and puts them to use.

To characterize this mechanism, let us first consider the forms of information it uses. The *inputs* to the device, the Privileged Representations, are of a variety of intermediate levels and also include the features of affect. Since the *output* of the device must be usable by the language faculty to construct reports of awareness, the logical choice of output form is conceptual structure. Thus, the device is to be conceived of as a kind of translation processor, or a collection of them—one per Privileged intermediate level.

A simple argument shows that this mechanism is distinct from any of the translation processors (or combinations thereof) that we have previously attributed to short-term memory. Consider language. The normal route of translation from the Privileged level of phonology to conceptual structure carries out language comprehension, that is, the association of a meaning with a phonological sequence. By contrast, we have stressed that introspective awareness of language is possible even for uncomprehended utterances such as nonsense syllables and Armenian; moreover, affect plays no role in comprehension but does turn up in awareness. Hence, the mechanism for introspection has to be able to bypass or shortcut the route from sound to meaning that accomplishes comprehension.[2]

2. It may be, though, that we have detected the need for this processor, in another connection. Section 10.7 observed that in order for reading and ASL to be possible, there must be a mapping from conceptual structure, which categorizes observed visual forms, into phonology, which is the entry into the language faculty. This mapping was shown as a dotted line in the diagram of levels at the beginning of chapter 12 (figure 12.1). The translation processor that performs this mapping at least invokes the proper levels of representation to be the processor for linguistic introspection; however, it remains to be seen whether there are stronger arguments that the two are more closely related.

Similarly, in vision the normal route of comprehension involves relating the Privileged level of 2½D sketch to a 3D model and thence to a conceptual structure. One of our reasons for concluding that the 2½D sketch is the Privileged level is that it can be reported even when visual meaning cannot be derived, as in viewing a blurry photo or a dimly lit scene. So the mechanism for introspection again must be distinct from that for comprehension. In musical awareness the situation is if anything even clearer. The processors responsible for musical understanding do not at any point invoke the level of conceptual structure, yet introspective report of music requires just such a mapping. So evidently a new processor is necessary here too.

Let me sketch the situation in grossly simplified fashion for the language faculty alone. Figure 15.2a shows the primary routes of information flow in language perception, ignoring all the complications of feedback, multiple sets of representations, the selection function, and attention. Figure 15.2b shows language production. The new parts here are the "affect monitors," with as yet unspecified sources of input, and the "introspection processor," the device we are now trying to characterize.

Other routes of processing have similar organization. Linguistic imagery is identical to figure 15.2b, except that the leftmost translation, from phonology into motor form, is absent. Visual perception is like figure 15.2a, with substitution of the relevant visual levels for linguistic levels ("2½D sketch" for "phonology," "3D model" for "syntax"). With the same substitutions, visual imagery parallels linguistic imagery. Music perception and imagery substitute the appropriate musical levels into figure 15.2, in particular, "musical surface" for "phonology." Significantly, the upper chain of processors in this case culminates in a prolongational reduction, not a conceptual structure; the introspection processor, however, still produces a conceptual structure.

The claim, then, is that the introspection processors produce conceptual structures distinct from those produced by normal routes; that is, they operate under different principles of translation than the translation processors involved in comprehension. Thus, they can produce an output even for music and for meaningless utterances or visual displays.

The need for a distinct conceptual structure (conceptual structure$_2$ in figure 15.2) is particularly evident in imagery. Here the conceptual structure involved in the primary flow of information (conceptual structure$_1$) is the *input* to the normal translation processors. On the other hand, the report of an image must be driven by the *output* of a translation from the Privileged level (in whatever faculty) to conceptual structure.

Consider also the "tip-of-the-tongue" phenomenon. Section 14.2 argued that this situation arises when for some reason the normal translation processors fail to translate an intended meaning into a phonological form,

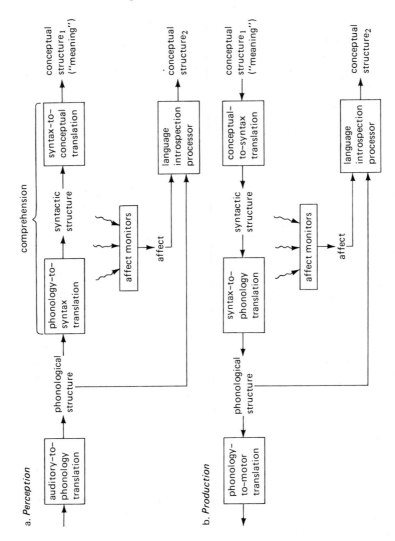

Figure 15.2
The flow of information in (a) language perception and (b) language production, with affect and introspection included

so that there is nothing in the Privileged level to support awareness. Under this analysis the intended meaning is conceptual structure$_1$, but conceptual structure$_2$ can report nothing in the way of form. However, the misfunction of the primary translation may produce the affect *effortful*; this will be available as input to the introspection processor, providing the grounds for a report of frustration at inability to find the word. Thus, the layout in figure 15.2b accounts in some detail for the phenomenology here.

What would happen if, in the course of perception, one's comprehension processors were to proceed more or less normally, but the introspection processors were to be disrupted? The result would be that one would understand the stimulus without being able to report its existence. This provides a possible mode of explanation for various phenomena of "subliminal perception." Consider, for instance, the experiments discussed by Marcel (1983), where a very brief presentation of a word on a screen was followed immediately by a masking stimulus. Subjects reported having seen nothing but the mask; however, lexical priming tasks (section 6.3) showed that the word had indeed been detected. We could account for this by making the minimal supposition that the introspection processor is somehow less sensitive (or has a higher threshold) than the comprehension processor; under the particular experimental conditions, then, only the latter would be triggered into action, and conceptual structure$_2$ would not be produced. Hence, no report.

One might speculate that a similar disruption is at work in the pathological condition of "blindsight," resulting from damage to geniculostriate visual pathways. Following the account of Marcel (1983, 275–277), such patients, though they deny seeing anything in the affected half of the visual field, nonetheless show signs of having detected things there. They can, under duress, point to objects they claim not to be able to see; they can reach for objects with appropriate preparatory grasping motions; they can even use words presented in the blind field to prime lexical decision tasks. Marcel therefore interprets the deficit not so much in terms of impaired visual comprehension as in terms of impaired recovery for awareness. Within the present framework this again suggests a malfunction of the visual introspection processor, with the comprehension processors comparatively intact. (I should acknowledge, with Marcel, that his interpretation is not universal; I leave the resolution to others better acquainted with the facts than myself.)

So far, then, we have established that there must be a system of introspection processors distinct from the normal processors for comprehension and production, and that the output of the introspection processors is a conceptual structure distinct from ordinary meaning. The next question is, What is encoded in conceptual structure$_2$—that is, what range of distinctions is available for introspective reports?

Without going into any detail, I want to suggest that the range of possibilities for conceptual structure$_2$ is quite limited—that is, that the introspection processors do not perform a very fine-grained translation. We see these limitations most clearly when the usual translation into conceptual structure does not take place, as in our standard cases of linguistic and visual perception under degraded circumstances and in the perception of music or body condition. In such situations it is often quite difficult to articulate what is being perceived, beyond designating it by the undifferentiated pronoun "that." Even people who by trade must be sensitive to form as well as content—poets, painters, photographers, musicians, dancers—tend to communicate all but the grosser distinctions of form by means of demonstration or metaphor rather than by literal description. This suggests that conceptual structure$_2$ is relatively rudimentary: it does not preserve anywhere near the full range of distinctions that exist in the Privileged Representations themselves.

Under more "normal" circumstances, of course, a Privileged Representation in language or vision is in registration with two distinct conceptual structures, as shown in figure 15.2: one that encodes its interpretation and one that encodes detection of the form itself by introspection. The two conceptual structures are thereby in registration with each other. When a report of introspection is produced, these two structures in fact tend to become conflated, so that the forms detected are categorized by their meanings. For example, "I see a dog" reports the detection of a Privileged visual form, but the description of this form is derived from conceptual structure$_1$, the category in terms of which the form is comprehended. That is, the introspective report in this case is relatively rich, but largely by virtue of the activity of comprehension rather than through introspection as such.

Still, even the limited translation performed by the introspection processors leads to *something* in conceptual structure, and we can thereby see the germ of truth in some of the more popular theories of consciousness discussed earlier. For example, various versions of the central-level theory are correct insofar as reportable awareness is indeed accompanied by central-level representations. However, the arguments of chapter 14 show that these central-level representations are not what most directly support the forms present to experience: the Privileged Intermediate-Level Representations are. The central-level representations supplied by introspection are only a pale translation of the true richness of form in consciousness.

This theory of introspection also contains counterparts of the "self-monitoring" and "looping back" that are fundamental characteristics of consciousness in many theories, among them Hofstadter's (1979). The introspection processors serve as the desired monitors on processing. They produce a conceptual structure which encodes "detection of a form in awareness" and which is quite distinct from conceptual structure$_1$, "what it is that I perceive." As observed above, these structures tend to be conflated in ordinary circumstances. However, they can be kept distinct, in which case the "detected form" functions conceptually as a different individual than its "interpretation." It can therefore be reported linguistically, producing another Privileged phonological structure that appears in awareness. Then, through the introspection processor, this new phonological form itself is encoded as a distinct individual, the "detection in awareness of a form reporting the detection of a form in awareness," in short, "awareness of being aware of something." Thus, the possibility of "higher-order" awareness is a straightforward consequence of the present account.

On the other hand, we have been able to maintain the Hypothesis of Nonefficacy of Consciousness: we do not have to ascribe higher-order awareness to some supervening magic of consciousness. In this system there is no such thing as literal awareness of awareness. Rather, introspection is a purely computational process, in general character little different from other translation processes. Higher-order *awareness* is simply projection, through the normal mysterious means, of the Privileged Representations derived from higher-order *concepts*. The mind-mind problem—what it means to "project a Privileged Representation into awareness"—still remains to be finessed, but at least it is no worse than before.

Chapter 16
Closing Thoughts

16.1 Inexpressible Thoughts and Knowledge

As remarked in chapter 1, common sense seems to tell us that awareness and thought are inseparable and that introspection can reveal the contents of the mind. Partly as a way to review the results of the present study, let me give a brief summary of the many varieties of unconscious and/or inexpressible thoughts and knowledge in the computational mind. By looking at what the Intermediate-Level Theory *excludes* from awareness and what the theory of introspection excludes from reportability, it will become obvious how powerful the unconscious is, should there be any remaining doubt.

First, it was emphasized throughout parts II and III that the formation rules and correspondence rules for all levels of representation are in principle inaccessible to consciousness and hence unreportable. Chomsky has always used the term "knowledge" to encompass such rules, whether learned or innate (see especially Chomsky 1975, 162ff.). Although I personally don't care too much about terminology here, there doesn't seem to be any especially better term.[1]

In addition, Lashley's Observation points to the necessary unawareness of the nature of information processing, no matter whether in perception, action, thought, or learning. Chapter 15 hedged his position slightly; it was suggested that those aspects of short-term processing that lead to distinctions of affect leave rudimentary marks on awareness. Still, on the whole one has no sense at all of the welter of complexity in processing.

Most of the information structures involved in processing do not appear in awareness either. We have spent a great deal of time showing that short-term memory in each of the faculties may develop multiple sets of structures for a given perceptual input, but that only the most salient of these is made available to awareness by the selection function. The others remain

---

1. On the other hand, we might do well to differentiate "knowledge" from what is often taken as its definition, "justified true belief." I would not want to say that a speaker of English "believes" the rules of English or of the primal sketch, or that the rules can be generally treated as the objects of propositional attitudes, as Fodor (1983, 5) claims.

totally unconscious. (In the case of fully ambiguous inputs, multiple sets of structures are retained in short-term memory and may take turns being chosen by the selection function—but the interpretations not in awareness at the moment still are present unconsciously in full detail.)

Moreover, of the matched set of structures chosen as most salient in each faculty, only one—the Privileged Intermediate-Level one—directly determines the form of awareness. In particular, one cannot introspect the form of thought. Our conclusion contrasts strongly with the two accounts of thought that appeal most to (nonphilosophical) common sense: either that thinking is like having visual images or that it is like talking to oneself. Even if both are hopelessly inadequate, for reasons in part detailed here, it is still very hard to shake free of them.

What lies behind their appeal is that visual and verbal imagery are the two most prominent ways in which the outcome of thought is revealed to awareness. The stream of consciousness, made up of such images, is usually copious enough for us to be intuitively satisfied that it in itself constitutes thought. But it does not: visual and verbal images are projected from intermediate-level representations, which are in turn generated from thought by the mandatory fast processing modules in short-term memory. Hence, as suggested in chapter 14, the stream of consciousness is essentially nothing but our evidence that thought is taking place; both the process of thought and its content are inaccessible to awareness.

In addition to all these aspects of the computational mind that are totally unconscious, there are various ways in which one can know one has information but cannot express it in linguistic terms. One such case arises when thoughts are articulated in terms of levels of representation that correlate only imperfectly with conceptual structure, the input level for speech. For example, the 3D model structure can accurately represent the details of an irregular shape (such as the exact contour of a swan's neck, the precise pattern of a tiger's stripes, or the shape of the Armenian letters in example (4.5)), and the 3D model can be mapped into a 2½D sketch that supports an image. But at the same time, because the shape is so irregular, there are no preexisting type concepts that match the constituents of the 3D model. Since the meanings of words are generally type concepts, there thus will be no appropriate words to describe the desired details except through paraphrase, circumlocution, or the pointing out of examples. In music the situation is if anything more extreme, since there is little (pretheoretic) communication between the more central musical structures and conceptual structures. Still, visual and musical images may be extremely detailed and explicit; the experience will hence be one of "I know exactly what I have in mind, but I can't tell you." Such experiences may also arise in attempts to report introspection and affect, which, as seen in chapter 15, are poorly translated into conceptual structure.

A second possibility is that the thought or knowledge does appear in conceptual structure, but it is constituted in such a way that it cannot be translated accurately into a syntactic structure and thence into speech. If this is for lack of an appropriate lexical item (say, in identifying a new species or devising a new theoretical concept), the lack can be remedied by inventing a new word. If it is for lack of an appropriate syntactic structure (say, because the most appropriate one violates the Coordinate Structure Constraint of section 4.3—"What do you like your pizza with pepperoni and?"), the problem can often be circumvented by a paraphrase that conveys at least a closely related thought ("What do you like on your pizza along with pepperoni?").

On the other hand, there is the possibility that the internal structure of the concept simply is not decomposable into linguistic units. The kind of case I have in mind is the interaction of conditions in a preference rule system (section 8.3). Such conditions can be incorporated into a word meaning; but they apparently cannot always be decomposed into independent words that in turn can be recombined by syntactic devices. This is the reason that although one knows a word's meaning operationally, one often cannot provide a definition—a syntactically expressed decomposition —that accounts for intuitions about the word's use. In cases like this the experience may vary from "I don't know what it means" (while using the word correctly) to "I know but I can't explain it" to "I know what it means" (and coming up with a spurious explanation).

Yet another sort of case arises in the seemingly infinite regress of logical justification pointed out by Wittgenstein (1953), Polanyi (1958), and Lewis Carroll (1895). The problem is that every time one states a putative principle of justification for an inference, it is possible to ask, But what is the principle of justification for *that*? (For instance, why do you believe the Law of Noncontradiction?) And the reply is, I just *know* it's true. (*Why* is it true?) Beyond a certain point logical justification never seems to get any closer to being explained. Here is a tentative account of why.

Macnamara (1986) suggests that theories of logical inference and justification are best understood as hypotheses about humans' logical competence—that is, they are claims about principles of computation over certain aspects of conceptual structure. Like rules of grammar, such principles can be revealed indirectly by examining intuitions, in this case intuitions of warrantability of logical arguments. (Macnamara argues further that these rules are largely innate: one could not *learn* the Law of Noncontradiction without first *invoking* it.)

Following Macnamara, principles of logic should have the same sort of psychological status as the formation rules and correspondence rules that determine and relate all levels of representations. In particular, the rules of logic are used by the processors that derive new conceptual structures from old and that check the mutual consistency of multiple conceptual structures. (This view has been hinted at without much comment in sections 7.1, 7.2, and 12.1.)

Under this view principles of logic, like rules of grammar, are in principle unavailable to awareness. On the other hand, *hypotheses about* principles of logic, because they are overtly stated, are by necessity internalized as conceptual structures—the inputs and outputs of principles of logic and not the principles themselves. They therefore cannot serve as their own justification. In other words, in the very act of stating possible principles of logic, one must necessarily couch them in a form in which they cannot fulfill their intended function, while the principles in the form in which they are actually used are inexpressible.

We can perhaps go a little further. What is there in awareness that signals the difference between a good logical argument and a bad one? Clearly, it does not lie in the overt form. The difference between good arguments and bad arguments lies in their conceptual structure—but that, unfortunately, is not open to awareness, which is why logicians are still in business devising theories about it. What *is* in awareness is this ineluctable "feeling" of a difference—what section 15.1 characterized as the affect *congruous* versus *incongruous*. However, the presence of an affect in awareness reveals even less about the nature of logical justification than the linguistic form does. The affect is just a binary feature; it makes the same distinction as does prefixing "It is true that . . ." or "It is false that . . ." to the putative logical argument.

Now recall from section 15.2 that affects can be reflected in conceptual structure through the operation of the introspection processors. This suggests the possibility that the meanings of the words "true" and "false" are basically conceptual reflexes of the affect *congruous* versus *incongruous*. Bizarre though this hypothesis may sound (Do I really think truth is a *feeling*?), it fits the symptoms disturbingly well. The grounds for finding a sentence true or false are ultimately not expressible; rather, they eventually reduce to nothing but an inner feeling of certainty or indubitability. Moreover, even if it is the case that truth is experienced as an objective property of the sentence, it is no different in this respect from the experienced objectivity of other properties such as color or shape. It is just another manifestation of the same old problem: the externalization of location, form, qualia, and now affect in every aspect of experience.

We thus arrive again, from a different angle, at the issue of the goals of semantic theory, discussed in section 7.5. The present perspective, even if highly tentative, reinforces my claim there that semantics cannot begin with a primitive unexplained notion of "objective truth in the Real World." We have begun in this study to lay the foundations for an alternative: Conceptual Semantics deals with the content of propositions, and the theory of affects deals with the experienced inevitability yet inexpressibility of the grounds for judging truth.

16.2 How Does Language Aid Thought?

Much of what has been said here tends to undermine the often presumed centrality of language to the nature of thought. The processes that we generally call "rational thought" are computations over conceptual structures, which exist independently of language and must in fact be present in nonlinguistic organisms. Other kinds of thought, such as spatial thinking and musical thinking, involve structures even more distant from the language faculty. Moreover, as just shown, having language does not make it possible to express the principles of thought.

Still, it seems undeniable that although language is not the source or the cause of thought, it might well facilitate it. But how could computations over conceptual structure be helped by the presence of two peripheral levels of representation, over which it is clearly impossible to state rules of inference? What could syntax and phonology possibly have to do with reasoning? Here are a couple of possibilities.

First, recall the discussion of section 4.2, where we observed that the imposition of any kind of structure at all seems to aid learning and memory. It follows that if a conceptual structure can be placed in registration with a syntactic structure and a phonological structure—that is, if it can be expressed linguistically—it is thereby stabilized in memory (probably both short-term and long-term). This would make individual concepts as well as their combinations more robust, making it easier to keep them in mind or recover them accurately when needed.

Second, the verbalization of a conceptual structure creates a phonological structure, which is a possible object of awareness. This alone cannot aid thought (because of the Nonefficacy of Consciousness); but, because it is a Privileged Representation, the phonological structure in turn is mapped into a second conceptual structure that identifies the object of awareness. Thus, the original thought has yet more structure in registration with it, which further helps stabilize the thought in processing and in memory.

One especially important effect of language in this respect is that it helps differentiate concepts more clearly. Two or more very similar concepts can be placed in registration with clearly distinct phonological structures and thereby be themselves kept distinct in memory and reasoning. Think, for instance, how much easier it is to stabilize thoughts about the physical interaction of objects if one has terminology such as *force, power,* and *momentum* to help keep the relevant concepts identified and differentiated. On the other hand, this advantage has its pitfalls too—for instance, leading one to believe in sharp distinctions where there is really continuity between the ranges of concepts (recall the discussion of preference rules in section 8.3). Moreover, since the language is not always systematic in assigning one word per concept, one is sometimes led to conflate two or more concepts that ought to be differentiated for the purposes at hand, because they happen to be associated with the same word (case in point: *consciousness*). Nevertheless, the free availability of linguistic forms to keep conceptual distinctions straight is on the whole of great value in the stabilization of thought.

In a sense, visual imagery provides similar advantages to spatial thinking: being able to visualize something helps one remember it too. But language can stabilize a much wider range of concepts. A visual image must be of an object in the spatial modality, and it must be relatively specific as to shape and proportion, even if it stands for something general. The translation of conceptual structures into language is much more flexible. Linguistic structures are the only peripheral levels with distinctions that correspond (albeit sometimes only roughly) to basic conceptual elements such as the type-token distinction, predication, negation, and hypotheticals; they are also the only ones that can pare away all features from a concept other than the bare identity expressed by the pronoun *that*, and the only ones that can explicitly encode affects (such as *true* and *false*). Thus, language is the only peripheral faculty that can stabilize the kinds of concepts we most strongly associate with logical reasoning.

These are reasons why language might make it easier to think the thoughts one would have anyway. But language also enriches the range of concepts one can have: since phonological structures are (partially) available to introspection, they can be treated in conceptual structure as new token concepts—as new "objects" in their own right. They can then be collected into types expressed by terms such as *syllable*, *word*, and *sentence*. Furthermore, phonological structures can be differentiated not only by form but also by the conceptual structures with which they are in registration—that is, by meaning. It thus becomes possible to have concepts about concepts and, through language, to stabilize the resulting abstractions. In turn, phonological expression of such higher-order concepts can again be introspected, reexpressed, stabilized, and combined with other concepts.

What makes this recursion especially powerful is that the fundamental concepts of predication, identity, and so forth can undergo the process, themselves being identified, categorized, and negated. Without a more substantial formal analysis than we have at this point it is hard to say precisely what the resulting system is like; but it seems likely that this recursion is what produces the essential elements for formulation and verification of explicit *theories*, the hallmarks of rational thought.

These remarks are perhaps not so different from things that are often said about how language aids thought. (One could add, of course, the cultural advantages of having language available to communicate to one's colleagues and descendants the *results* of thought.) What is important is that these hypotheses can be formulated within severer constraints than are usually imposed on the relations between language, thought, and awareness. Specifically, (1) language is not a medium of thought, only conceptual structure is; (2) awareness has direct access only to phonological form, not to conceptual form; (3) having something in awareness per se cannot in any event affect computation. Nevertheless, even within these constraints it proves possible to ascribe to language a significant role in facilitating thought.

It follows, then, that the thought of nonlinguistic organisms will be lacking all the metaconcepts that stem from the linguistic modality. In addition, many other concepts will be more difficult to process and recall, because of the absence of accompanying linguistic structures to stabilize them. On the other hand, spatial and motor concepts will still have rich peripheral structures to go with them, so we can imagine spatial and motor thought qualitatively not unlike our own (though no doubt subject to different limitations on short-term memory capacity and the like).

16.3 Last Overview

If there is any overall moral to be drawn from the present study, it is a justification of the goal of cognitive science to study the mind in computational terms. Even if some investigators have been overenthusiastic in identifying the phenomenological mind with the computational mind, studying the latter does help us understand the former. More specifically, the degree to which we have been able to match phenomenological distinctions with computational ones vindicates the strategy of dividing cognitive science into theory of structure and theory of processing, for it is in the information structures of the computational mind that the character of experience is most directly determined. And despite the many areas where we have been forced to speculate for lack of evidence, the whole hangs together in a way that I find exciting and promising.

Standing back from the mass of empirical detail that has been adduced in formulating and justifying the Intermediate-Level Theory, we arrive at what seems to me a startling conclusion. Consciousness has proven not to be an especially high-level process, as everyone has always wanted it to be. In particular, it is not what makes us human. Rather, if we assume that evolutionary continuity in the computational mind parallels (and is derived from) evolutionary continuity in the form of the body, it follows that the higher animals likely have levels of representation something like ours. In turn, it follows from the Intermediate-Level Theory that their computational minds are capable of supporting forms of awareness something like ours, projected from corresponding levels.

There are of course differences. In particular, people have a richer conceptual structure, which parses out the content of awareness more finely and supplies it with more highly articulated meaning: we are aware *of* more things than other animals. Moreover, people have the modality of awareness provided by language, with all the metaconceptual advantages that language confers. But dogs likely have a more differentiated olfactory awareness than we do, arising from a richer registration between conceptual structure and the more detailed sensory input. (Imagine perhaps having as vivid an awareness of Harry from the scent of his trail as from seeing his face!) And bats and dolphins likely have a whole chain of levels dealing with echolocation, a chain that terminates in the 3D model level. Following the Intermediate-Level Theory, some level in this chain ought to support a modality of awareness entirely alien to us.

Generally, though, as we go down the phylogenetic scale, we would expect less and less structure in the computational mind; accordingly, awareness will become progressively attenuated from our point of view. However, since nothing is yet known about levels of mental representation in, say, turtles or trout—even if their behavior and brain organization lead us to impute to them a computational mind—it is folly to speculate what their awareness, if any, is like. (Given the essential privacy of awareness, the furthest we can go *empirically*, of course, is to understand the computational minds of other organisms. Statements about their awareness will always remain purest speculation. Nevertheless, it's fun to indulge once in a while.)

Could a computer be conscious? The organization of present-day computers does not include anything like our hard-wired faculty-specific levels of representation. I have argued here that no degree of conceptual complexity alone can produce awareness as we know it; rather, the chains of levels leading to the periphery are necessary, and at best these provide the computational distinctions necessary for awareness. In addition, we still have left unsolved the essential mystery of the mind-mind problem (and the mind-body problem before it): how a computational or physical state could possibly be related to an experience. So the possibility of computer awareness, even if a computer were to simulate all details of human computation, remains problematic.

Many readers will no doubt still find the Intermediate-Level Theory unsatisfying, even if it has been shown empirically more adequate than the in some sense more intuitively plausible central-level and "executive" theories. Why in heaven's name should consciousness be driven by this haphazard collection of intermediate levels of representation that reflect nothing but way stations between sensation and understanding? And why should the introspection processors hook up at these levels instead of directly to conceptual structure, as has nearly always been assumed? I myself find this apparent pointlessness of consciousness somewhat disturbing.

One possible answer to these questions is that the Privileged Representations serve as a kind of "early warning system" for comprehension: it might be crucial to have introspection processors in order to compare what is detected with what is understood, so that attention can be directed to problematic portions of the field. Another possibility, not mutually exclusive with the first, is that the organization of awareness represents a throwback to a stage in evolution when the counterparts of our intermediate-level representations were the most highly differentiated structures in the computational mind, interacting only weakly through a rudimentary conceptual structure. Under this supposition the introspection processors are a relic of the form of thought in earlier organisms, and our more highly developed processes that lead to a rich conceptual structure are the evolutionary innovation. If so, this turns on its head the common notion that intelligence is a precursor of awareness; quite the opposite is the case.

All this is conjecture of the most blatant kind regarding how the Intermediate-Level Theory might make sense in some larger context. What does not seem to me legitimate by this point is to impugn the theory on the grounds that it does not explain what consciousness might be for. The theory has been worked out carefully step by step, on the basis of a wide range of evidence from many aspects of the computational and phenomenological minds. This evidence is directed toward what consciousness *is*, not what it is *for*. We are thus somewhat in the position of an anatomist who has discovered the structure of an organ but has not yet determined its function in the context of the whole organism. It is only a prejudice to regard this as an achievement in the case of, say, the parathyroid gland but not in the case of consciousness; it is just that we hold our consciousness so much dearer. My suspicion, anyway, is that the actual function of consciousness can be revealed only by understanding its structure first.

Appendix A

A Second Correspondence Rule between Intonation and Syntax

The problem to be accounted for here is the disparity between syntactic structure and intonational phrasing in the following examples (where (A.1a, b) = (5.15b, c), (A.2) = figure 5.9, and (A.3) = (5.16)).

(A.1)   a.   This is [$_{NP}$ the cat [$_S$ that chased [$_{NP}$ the rat [$_S$ that ate [$_{NP}$ the cheese]]]]]

        b.   [$_{IntPhr}$ This is the cat] [$_{IntPhr}$ that chased the rat] [$_{IntPhr}$ that ate the cheese]

(A.2)   a.   [$_{NP}$ Harry] [$_{VP}$ disliked [$_{NP}$ organization]]

        b.   [$_{IntPhr}$ Harry disliked] [$_{IntPhr}$ organization]

(A.3)   a.   [$_{IntPhr}$ Abernathy gesticulated]

        b.   [$_{IntPhr}$ Abernathy] [$_{IntPhr}$ gesticulated]

(A.4)   a.   [$_{IntPhr}$ *Sesame Street* is a production of] [$_{IntPhr}$ the Children's Television Workshop]

        b.   [$_{IntPhr}$ *Sesame Street* is a production] [$_{IntPhr}$ of the Children's Television Workshop]

(A.1a) has a deeply right-recursive syntactic structure associated with a flat phonological structure (A.1b) that cuts across syntactic boundaries. The first IntPhr in (A.2b) corresponds to a nonconstituent of the syntactic structure (A.2a). (A.3) and (A.4) show two possible phonological structures associated with the same syntactic structure. (Both the structures in (A.4) are attested: Big Bird says (A.4a) and Susan says (A.4b).)

     Here is a correspondence rule, a partial mapping between syntactic and phonological structure, that accounts for these possibilities.

> A phrasal constituent (NP, S, VP, PP) at the *end* of a sentence *may* be treated as an Intonational Phrase.

This rule optionally cuts off a constituent at the end of the sentence, leaving the material before it, whatever its syntactic structure, as another Intonational Phrase. The optional application of this rule is responsible for the variation between (A.3a) and (A.3b). In (A.3a) the rule has not applied, so there is only one IntPhr. In (A.3b), though, the rule has applied to the VP *gesticulated*, leaving only *Abernathy* remaining for the other IntPhr. In (A.2) the rule has applied to the final NP *organization*, leaving the syntactic nonconstituent *Harry disliked* for the remaining IntPhr. Since the rule does not specify *which* final constituent of the syntactic structure is eligible to be detached, either the final NP or the final PP may be detached in (A.4), yielding the phrasings in (A.4a) and (A.4b), respectively.

The phrasing of (A.1b) results from applying this rule twice. On the first application the S *that chased the rat that ate the cheese* is segregated, leaving the nonconstituent *this is the cat* as the first IntPhr. On the second application the S *that ate the cheese* is segregated from *that chased the rat that ate the cheese*, leaving the nonconstituent *that chased the rat* as an IntPhr. Other intonational variants can be produced by applying the rule in different ways. However, there seems to be a general preference for Intonational Phrases of roughly equal length in a sentence, which is why (A.1b) is the favored phrasing.

Although the rule says nothing about the syntactic structure of the left-hand residue, it does require the right-hand IntPhr to be a syntactic constituent. Hence, it cannot produce a phrasing like (A.5).

(A.5)   [The man] [in the yellow hat gesticulated]

This seems a correct prediction, and it is borne out in much of the discussion by Gee and Grosjean (1983) and Selkirk (1984, chapter 5)—although they propose rather different rules to account for the phenomenon.

Appendix B
Possible Enrichment of the 2½D Sketch

As a linguist, I hate to stick my neck out, but Marr's formal account of the 2½D sketch strikes me as excessively improverished, actually a regression from his stated intention of describing visible surfaces. All it describes is the depths and local orientations of visible *points* of surfaces; it lacks integration in much the same way as the original retinal array does. One possible reason for this is that Marr is more concerned with what can be derived directly from the primal sketch—that is, with the correspondence rules between the primal and 2½D sketches—than with the constraints that might be placed on the 2½D sketch by its own intrinsic formation rules. This is a way that his program of research superficially looks much different from linguistics: linguists tend to neglect correspondence rules and focus more heavily on formation rules.

In an effort to promote a more balanced view to both enterprises, let me offer a possible approach to enriching the 2½D sketch. In addition to the bit map posited by Marr, let us introduce a 2½D *structural description* imposed on the bit map, among whose primitive notions are *boundary* and *region*. An insight of the early Gestaltists such as Rubin was that a visual boundary is not simply a division between one region and another: in a sense it "belongs to" the figural region it bounds but not to the adjacent ground. We will follow a suggestion of Shiman (1975), who expresses this insight topologically by treating boundaries of his equivalent of the 2½D structural description as obligatorily *directed* toward the regions to which they belong.

To understand the notion of directed boundary, consider figure B.1. If we take the arrow attached to a boundary as pointing into the region the boundary belongs to, figure B.1a expresses the reading of the figure in which the circle is a disk superimposed on the square, which in turn is seen against the background of the page. That is, the circular boundary belongs to the circular region and plays no role in the understanding of the square. By contrast, figure B.1b expresses a reading in which the square has a circular hole in it, through which the background is visible; here the circular boundary is part of the square region's shape.

Figure B.1
The significance of directed boundaries: (a) a square with a disk in front of it; (b) a square with a circular hole in it

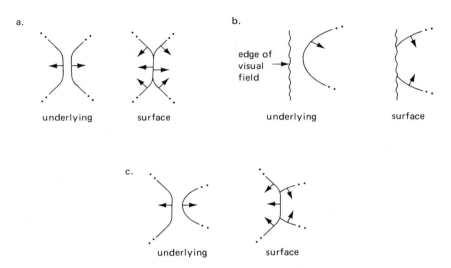

Figure B.2
Transformations from underlying to surface 2½D structure: (a) abutting; (b) overflow; (c) occlusion

The fundamental constraint on the 2½D structural description then may be stated as follows.

2½D Well-formedness Constraint
The visual field must be exhaustively partitioned into regions, each with its own closed directed boundary, plus a background that lacks boundaries.

There are many obvious counterexamples to this constraint. I propose to deal with them by introducing a distinction between *underlying* and surface 2½D structure, related by transformation-like operations. The surface structure is in closest correspondence with the bit map, whereas the underlying structure expresses one's sense of the decomposition of the field into regions. It is over underlying structure that the 2½D Well-formedness Constraint applies.

Three of the important transformations of 2½D structure are illustrated informally in figure B.2. These sketches are to be understood topologically—that is, in terms of the relative configurations of boundaries and regions but not in terms of shape.

The operation of *abutting* produces a segment of a surface boundary that is simultaneously directed in two directions. Such a boundary occurs where two surfaces of an object join or where two surface markings abut. For instance, the most likely interpretation of figure B.3a is as two squares sharing a side, as indicated by the structural description in figure B.3b. The underlying structure satisfies the 2½D Well-formedness Constraint, in that each square has its own boundary.

Overflow provides for closure of regions that extend outside the field of vision. In underlying structure the region is closed, but part of the boundary is absent in surface structure. Crucially, the boundary strikes the edge of the visual field at two points. *Occlusion* is similar, except that the region altered by the transformation is cut off by a directed boundary instead of by the edge of the visual field.

Applying these transformations recursively to an underlying decomposition of the visual field, one can produce the complex pattern of overlapping regions characteristic of the real visual field. But why adopt this treat-

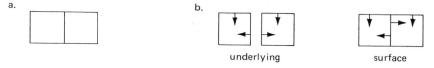

a.   b.

underlying   surface

Figure B.3
Part (a) is most likely seen as two abutted squares, as shown by 2½D structural description in part (b)

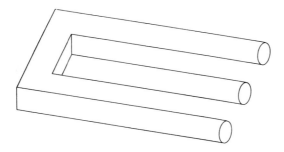

Figure B.4
The "trident": a figure with a globally inconsistent 2½D structure

ment? What is the virtue of imposing the 2½D Well-formedness Constraint if one must then subject the structure to so much machinery to derive the surface 2½D structure?

One reason is given by Shiman. He shows that there are important topological constraints on the global configuration of directed boundaries in the visual field. These can be used to explain mathematically the ill-formedness of such well-known figures as the "trident" (figure B.4), in which consistent directed boundaries cannot be assigned for the entire configuration. (Shiman does not develop his constraints in terms of deep and surface structures, but the effect is similar and, unlike the treatment offered here, mathematically rigorous.)

Another reason is implicit in Marr's work. He speaks here and there of the problem of putting into the 2½D sketch parts of boundaries for which there is no supporting evidence in the primal sketch. For instance, in seeing one tree in front of another, it often happens that there are bits and pieces of the seen boundary at which there are no intensity differences to support primal sketch boundary elements. Similarly, a part of an object in deep shadow may not be clearly distinguished from the background at every point of its boundary. In such cases the 2½D sketch must "fill in" a continuous boundary—and we see one—even where local external information is not present. The 2½D Well-formedness Constraint is what motivates this filling in, instead of letting us tolerate fragmentary boundaries.

The sorts of structural descriptions that can be built up by these means are reminiscent of the "blocks world" of Waltz (1975), which Marr explicitly eschews but every now and again glances at sidelong. A major difference between the present conception and the blocks world is that here the boundaries in the structural description are constructed in various ways rather than given in advance.

The most important source of boundaries, of course, is the information derived from the primal sketch, including depth and orientation inform-

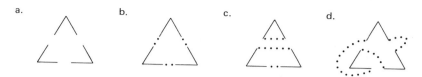

Figure B.5
Filling in of missing intervals in boundaries: (a) is most likely seen as a defective version of (b), not of (c) or (d).

ation. A discontinuity in depth, for example, maps into a boundary segment directed toward the nearer region. A discontinuity in orientation alone, as at the edge joining two faces of a cube, maps into an abutted boundary segment directed toward both adjoining regions. A discontinuity in intensity without depth or orientation information maps into a boundary segment of unspecified directedness.

A second source of boundaries comes from the filling in of missing intervals between boundary segments. The principles governing this filling in are essentially the Gestalt laws of good form and good continuation. For instance, gaps in a boundary are filled in with the "simplest" curve consistent with both the 2½D Well-formedness Constraint and the directedness of the segments to be joined. Figure B.5a is normally seen as a version of figure B.5b, not as a version of figure B.5c or figure B.5d.

The overflow and occlusion transformations provide a third source of boundaries—boundaries unseen in the surface form but present in underlying form. Again, these boundaries are filled in by principles obeying the Gestalt laws.

A fourth source is the process discussed by Hoffman (1983a, b), which uses texture gradients to find contours of maximum curvature in a surface —essentially, rounded edges. The effectiveness of this process is demonstrated by Hoffman's "cosine surface," in which one vividly sees a series of concentric circular ridges separated from each other by boundaries at the bottom of the valleys, even though no segmentation is explicitly present (figure B.6).

A fifth source is the related process discussed by Hoffman and Richards (1984), which decomposes regions into parts on the basis of projecting portions in the boundary contour. Such projections are in turn defined by maxima of concave curvature in the boundary. Notice that what counts as concavity depends on the directedness of the boundary—it is convex on one side, concave on the other. As a result, figures with boundaries of ambiguous directedness may have ambiguous part-decomposition as well. An example pointed out by Hoffman and Richards is the vase-faces illusion. If the faces are figure, "the concavities divide the boundary into chunks corresponding to a forehead, nose, upper lip, lower lip, and chin [figure

Figure B.6
Hoffman's "cosine surface" (Reprinted, by permission, from D. D. Hoffman (1983a). Representing shapes for visual recognition. Doctoral dissertation, MIT.)

Figure B.7
The part-boundaries of the faces (a) fall at different points than the part-boundaries of the vase (b)

B.7a]. If instead the [vase] is taken to be figure then the [concavities] reposition, dividing the curve into new chunks corresponding to a base, a couple parts of the stem, a bowl, and a lip on the bowl [figure B.7b]. It is probably no accident that the parts defined by [these criteria] are often easily assigned verbal labels" (Hoffman and Richards 1984, 82). Across these concavities appear "virtual" part-boundaries, indicated by dashed lines in figure B.7. In the present treatment these are abutted boundaries, and the parts are separated off in underlying 2½D structure. This decomposition into 2½D parts is an important source of information for the eventual three-dimensional decomposition into parts described in section 9.4.

All of these boundaries must be supplied with directedness. As noted, some come with directedness specified; but others do not. Here is where the constraints of Waltz (1975) on intersections of boundaries prove useful. (Marr alludes to these from time to time but does not show how to work them in.) For example, the "Y-junction" shown in figure B.8a is likely to be the intersection of three abutting surfaces, as shown in the structural

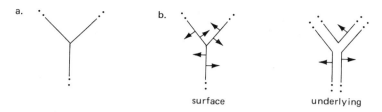

Figure B.8
A "Y-junction" (a), and its likely 2½D structural description (b)

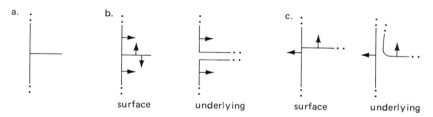

Figure B.9
A "T-junction" (a) and two possible 2½D structural descriptions (b) and (c)

description in figure B.8b. A "T-junction" (figure B.9a) is likely to be either two abutting regions (figure B.9b) or one boundary occluded by another (figure B.9c).

Importantly, if a boundary direction is adopted without supporting depth evidence from the primal sketch, depth is seen anyway. This is what accounts for the alternating sensations of depth in the vase-faces illusion, for example. When the faces are figural, the boundaries are directed toward them (figure B.7a) and so they are seen in front of the background. When the vase is figural, the directedness of the boundary is reversed (figure B.7b) and so is the sensation of relative depth of the regions.

These principles for deriving boundaries and their directedness are modulated, of course, by the 2½D Well-formedness Constraint, which requires that the total assignment of directed boundaries be globally consistent. Again, it is the unified notion of 2½D sketch that makes it possible for all these processes and constraints to operate in relative independence yet produce an integrated result. For instance, the primitive *directed boundary* can be the result of any number of different computations; but whatever its source, a boundary is a boundary is a boundary.

Connoisseurs will no doubt see further possibilities, such as hierarchical arrangement of parts, difference in treatment between surfaces per se and surface markings, and above all, doing the whole thing in multiple scales like those of the primal sketch—an aspect of Marr's theory I have wholly omitted from the present exposition. One would also want to supplement the theory of the 2½D sketch to include surfaces seen through other surfaces (such as a tree seen through the living room window or a fish seen through the surface of a pond), as well as "virtual surfaces" such as the surface defined by the bars of a cage. And of course the whole thing wants formalization.

This gives an idea of how the description of visible surfaces might be extended beyond Marr's bit map. Along the way we have seen how the theory might incorporate insights from other approaches to vision that did not have a comfortable home in Marr's approach.

References

Ackley, D., G. Hinton, and T. Sejnowski (1985). A learning algorithm for Boltzmann machines. *Cognitive Science* 9, 147–169.

Akmajian, A., R. Demers, and M. Harnish (1984). *Linguistics*, 2nd ed. Cambridge, MA: MIT Press.

Anderson, J. A. (1984). Neural models and very little about language. In D. Caplan, A. R. Lecours, and A. Smith, eds., *Biological perspectives on language*. Cambridge, MA: MIT Press.

Anderson, J. R. (1978). Arguments concerning representations for mental imagery. *Psychological Review* 85, 249–277.

Anderson, J. R. (1983). *The architecture of cognition*. Cambridge, MA: Harvard University Press.

Anderson, J. R., and G. H. Bower (1973). *Human associative memory*. New York: V. H. Winston and Sons.

Arbib, M. A. (1982a). From artificial intelligence to neurolinguistics. In Arbib, Caplan, and Marshall (1982), 77–94.

Arbib, M. A. (1982b). Perceptual-motor processes and the neural basis of language. In Arbib, Caplan, and Marshall (1982), 531–552.

Arbib, M., D. Caplan, and J. C. Marshall, eds. (1982). *Neural models of language processes*. New York: Academic Press.

Armstrong, S. L., L. R. Gleitman, and H. Gleitman (1983). On what some concepts might not be. *Cognition* 13, 263–308.

Arnheim, R. (1974). *Art and visual perception (The new version)*. Berkeley, CA: University of California Press.

Astington, J., P. Harris, and D. Olson, eds. (in preparation). *Developing theories of mind*.

Baker, C. L., and J. McCarthy, eds. (1981). *The logical problem of language acquisition*. Cambridge, MA: MIT Press.

Balzano, G. J. (1982). The pitch set as a level of description for studying musical pitch perception. In Clynes (1982), 321–351.

Bartlett, F. C. (1932). *Remembering*. Cambridge: Cambridge University Press.

Barwise, J., and J. Perry (1983). *Situations and attitudes*. Cambridge, MA: MIT Press. A Bradford book.

Barwise, J., and J. Perry (1985). Shifting situations and shaken attitudes. *Linguistics and Philosophy* 8, 105–161.

Bellugi, R., H. Poizner, and E. S. Klima (1983). Brain organization for language: Clues from sign aphasia. *Human Neurobiology* 2, 155–170.

Berwick, R., and A. Weinberg (1984). *The grammatical basis of linguistic performance*. Cambridge, MA: MIT Press.

Bever, T. G., J. M. Carroll, and L. A. Miller, eds. (1984). *Talking minds: The study of language in the cognitive sciences*. Cambridge, MA: MIT Press.

Black, J. W. (1951). The effects of delayed side-tone upon vocal rate and intensity. *Journal of Speech and Hearing Disorders* 16, 56–60.

Block, N. (1978). Troubles with functionism. In Savage (1978), 261–325.

Blum, D. (1977). *Casals and the art of interpretation*. Berkeley, CA: University of California Press.

Bolinger, D. (1965). *Forms of English: Accent, morpheme, order*. Edited by I. Abe and T. Kanekiyo. Cambridge, MA: Harvard University Press.

Bradley, D., M. Garrett, and E. Zurif (1980). Syntactic deficits in Broca's Aphasia. In Caplan (1980), 269–286.

Brady, M., and H. Asada (1984). Smoothed local symmetries and their implementation. A. I. Memo 757, Artificial Intelligence Laboratory, MIT.

Brandt, R. B. (1960). Doubts about the Identity Theory. In Hook (1960), 62–70.

Bransford, J. D., and J. J. Franks (1971). The abstraction of linguistic ideas. *Cognitive Psychology* 2, 331–350.

Bregman, A. A., and J. Campbell (1971). Primary auditory stream segregation and perception of order in rapid sequences of tones. *Journal of Experimental Psychology* 89, 244–249.

Bresnan, J. (1978). A realistic transformational grammar. In Halle, Bresnan, and Miller (1978), 1–59.

Bresnan, J., ed. (1982). *The mental representation of grammatical relations*. Cambridge, MA: MIT Press.

Bresnan, J., and R. M. Kaplan (1982). Introduction: Grammars as mental representations of language. In Bresnan (1982), xvii–lii.

Brugman, C. (1981). Story of *over*. M. A. dissertation, University of California, Berkeley; Bloomington: Indiana University Linguistics Club.

Bruner, J. S. (1957). On perceptual readiness. *Psychological Review* 64, 123–152.

Bruner, J. (1983). *In search of mind*. New York: Harper & Row.

Caplan, D., ed. (1980). *Biological studies of mental processes*. Cambridge, MA: MIT Press.

Carey, S. (1978). The child as word learner. In Halle, Bresnan, and Miller (1978), 264–293.

Carey, S. (1979). A case study: Face recognition. In E. Walker, ed., *Explorations in the biology of language*, 175–202. Cambridge, MA: MIT Press. A Bradford book.

Carey, S. (1982). Semantic development: The state of the art. In Wanner and Gleitman (1982), 347–389.

Carey, S., and R. Diamond (1980). Maturational determination of the developmental course of face encoding. In Caplan (1980), 60–93.

Carroll, L. (1895). What the tortoise said to Achilles. *Mind* 4, 278–280. Reprinted in Hofstadter (1979), 43–45.

Castellano, M., J. Bharucha, and C. L. Krumhansl (1984). Tonal hierarchies in the music of north India. *Journal of Experimental Psychology: General* 113, 394–412.

Cheney, D. L., and R. M. Seyfarth (1985). Social and non-social knowledge in vervet monkeys. *Phil. Trans. R. Soc. Lond.* B 308, 187–201.

Chomsky, N. (1957). *Syntactic structures*. The Hague: Mouton.

Chomsky, N. (1965). *Aspects of the theory of syntax*. Cambridge, MA: MIT Press.

Chomsky, N. (1970). Remarks on nominalization. In R. Jacobs and P. Rosenbaum, eds., *Readings in English transformational grammar*, 184–221. Waltham, MA: Ginn.

Chomsky, N. (1972). *Studies on semantics in generative grammar*. The Hague: Mouton.

Chomsky, N. (1975). *Reflections on language*. New York: Pantheon.

Chomsky, N. (1981). *Lectures on government and binding*. Dordrecht: Foris.

Chomsky, N. (1986). *Barriers*. Cambridge, MA: MIT Press.

Chomsky, N., and M. Halle (1965). Some controversial questions in phonological theory. *Journal of Linguistics* 1, 97–138.

Chomsky, N., and M. Halle (1968). *The sound pattern of English*. New York: Harper & Row.

Churchland, P. M. (1984). *Matter and consciousness*. Cambridge, MA: MIT Press. A Bradford book.

Churchland, P. S. (1983). Consciousness: The transmutation of a concept. *Pacific Philosophical Quarterly* 64, 80–95.

Clark, H. H. (1973). Space, time, semantics and the child. In T. E. Moore, ed., *Cognitive development and the acquisition of language*, 27–64. New York: Academic Press.

Clark, H. H., and W. G. Chase (1972). On the process of comparing sentences against pictures. *Cognitive Psychology* 3, 472–517.

Clynes, M., ed. (1982). *Music, mind, and brain: The neuropsychology of music*. New York: Plenum.

Clynes, M., and N. Nettheim (1982). The living quality of music: Neurobiologic basis of communicating feeling. In Clynes (1982), 47–82.

Clynes, M., and J. Walker (1982). Neurobiological functions of rhythm, time, and pulse in music. In Clynes (1982), 171–216.

Coleman, L., and P. Kay (1981). Prototype semantics: The English verb *lie*. *Language* 57, 26–44.

Collins, A., and M. Quillian (1969). Retrieval time from semantic memory. *Journal of Verbal Learning and Verbal Behavior* 9, 240–247.

Cooper, L. (1976). Demonstration of a mental analog of an external rotation. *Perception and Psychophysics* 19, 296–302. Reprinted in Shepard and Cooper (1982), 159–170.

Craik, F. I. M., and R. S. Lockhart (1972). Levels of processing: A framework for memory research. *Journal of Verbal Learning and Verbal Behavior* 11, 671–684.

Crook, J. H. (1980). *The evolution of human consciousness*. Oxford: Clarendon Press.

Cutting, J. (1981). Six tenets for event perception. *Cognition* 10, 71–78.

Dawkins, R. (1981). Selfish genes and selfish memes. In Hofstadter and Dennett (1981), 124–146.

Deliege, I. (1985). Les règles préferentielles de groupement dans la perception musicale. Dissertation, Université Libre de Bruxelles.

Dennett, D. C. (1969). *Content and consciousness*. London: Routledge & Kegan Paul.

Dennett, D. C. (1976). Are dreams experiences? *Philosophical Review* 73, 151–171. Reprinted in Dennett (1978d), 129–148.

Dennett, D. C. (1978a). Toward a cognitive theory of consciousness. In Savage (1978), 201–228. Reprinted in Dennett (1978d), 149–173.

Dennett, D. C. (1978b). Two approaches to mental images. In Dennett (1978d), 174–189.

Dennett, D. C. (1978c). Why you can't make a computer that feels pain. *Synthese* 38.3. Reprinted in Dennett (1978d), 190–229.

Dennett, D. C. (1978d). *Brainstorms: Philosophical essays on mind and psychology*. Cambridge, MA: MIT Press. A Bradford book.

Dennett, D. C. (1984). *Elbow room: The varieties of free will worth wanting*. Cambridge, MA: MIT Press. A Bradford book.

Deutsch, D. (1980). Music perception. *Musical Quarterly* 66, 165–179.

Deutsch, D., ed. (1982a). *Psychology of music*. New York: Academic Press.

Deutsch, D. (1982b). Grouping mechanisms in music. In Deutsch (1982a), 99–134.

Dowling, W. J. (1973). The perception of interleaved melodies. *Cognitive Psychology* 5, 322–337.

Epstein, W. (1961). The influence of syntactical structure on learning. *American Journal of Psychology* 74, 80–85.

Epstein, W. (1962). A further study of the influence of syntactical structure on learning. *American Journal of Psychology* 75, 121–126.

Farah, M. J. (1984). The neurological basis of mental imagery: A componential analysis. In

Pinker (1984a), 245–271.

Fauconnier, G. (1984). *Mental spaces: Aspects of meaning construction in natural language.* Cambridge, MA: MIT Press. A Bradford book.

Feldman, J. A., and D. H. Ballard (1982). Connectionist models and their properties. *Cognitive Science 6*, 205–254.

Finke, R. A. (1986). Mental imagery and the visual system. *Scientific American 254.3*, 88–95.

Fodor, J. A. (1975). *The language of thought.* Cambridge, MA: Harvard University Press.

Fodor, J. A. (1983). *The modularity of mind.* Cambridge, MA: MIT Press. A Bradford book.

Fodor, J. A. (1984). Why paramecia don't have mental representations. Ms., MIT; to appear in *Midwest Studies in Philosophy.* Minneapolis: University of Minnesota Press.

Fodor, J. A., T. Bever, and M. Garrett (1974). *The psychology of language.* New York: McGraw-Hill.

Fodor, J. A., M. Garrett, E. Walker, and C. Parkes (1980). Against definitions. *Cognition 8*, 263–367.

Fodor, J. A., and Z. Pylyshyn (1981). How direct is visual perception: Some reflections on Gibson's "ecological approach." *Cognition 9*, 139–196.

Forster, K. I. (1979). Levels of processing and the structure of the language processor. In W. Cooper and E. Walker, eds., *Sentence processing: Psycholinguistic studies presented to Merrill Garrett*, 28–85. Hillsdale, NJ: Erlbaum.

Frazier, L., and J. D. Fodor (1978). The sausage machine: A new two-stage parsing model. *Cognition 6*, 291–325.

Frith, C. D. (1981). Schizophrenia: An abnormality of consciousness. In G. Underwood and R. Stevens, eds., *Aspects of consciousness*, vol. 2, 149–168. New York: Academic Press.

Fromkin, V. (1971). The non-anomalous nature of anomalous utterances. *Language 47*, 27–52.

Fromkin, V., and R. Rodman (1974). *An introduction to language.* New York: Holt, Rinehart & Winston.

Gallistel, C. R. (1980). *The organization of action: A new synthesis.* Hillsdale, NJ: Erlbaum.

Gardner, H. (1983). *Frames of mind.* New York: Basic Books.

Garrett, M. (1975). The analysis of sentence production. In G. H. Bower, ed., *Psychology of learning and motivation*, vol. 9, 133–177. New York: Academic Press.

Garrett, M. (1982). Remarks on the relation between language production and language comprehension systems. In Arbib, Caplan, and Marshall (1982), 209–224.

Gee, J. P., and F. Grosjean (1983). Performance structures: A psycholinguistic and linguistic appraisal. *Cognitive Psychology 15*, 411–458.

Gee, J. P., and J. A. Kegl (1982). Semantic perspicuity and the locative hypothesis: Implications for acquisition. *Journal of Education 164*, 185–209.

Gelman, R., and C. R. Gallistel (1978). *The child's understanding of number.* Cambridge, MA: Harvard University Press.

Gibson, J. J. (1966). *The senses considered as perceptual systems.* Boston: Houghton Mifflin.

Gibson, J. J. (1979). *The ecological approach to visual perception.* Boston: Houghton Mifflin.

Gleitman, H. (1981). *Psychology.* New York: Norton.

Gleitman, L., and E. Wanner (1982). The state of the state of the art. In Wanner and Gleitman (1982), 3–48.

Globus, G. G. (1976). Mind, structure, and contradiction. In Globus, Maxwell, and Savodnik (1976), 271–294.

Globus, G. G., G. Maxwell, and I. Savodnik, eds. (1976). *Consciousness and the brain: A scientific and philosophical inquiry.* New York: Plenum.

Goldsmith, J. (1976). Autosegmental phonology. Doctoral dissertation, MIT. Reprinted by Indiana University Linguistics Club, Bloomington, IN.

Gregory, R. L. (1970). *The intelligent eye.* New York: McGraw-Hill.

Griffin, D. R. (1981). *The question of animal awareness*. Revised and expanded edition. Los Altos, CA: William Kaufman, Inc.

Grimshaw, J. (1979). Complement selection and the lexicon. *Linguistic Inquiry* 10, 279–325.

Gruber, J. S. (1965). Studies in lexical relations. Doctoral dissertation, MIT. Reprinted by Indiana University Linguistics Club, Bloomington, IN. Reprinted (1976) as part of *Lexical structures in syntax and semantics*. Amsterdam: North-Holland.

Halle, M. (1978). Knowledge unlearned and untaught. In Halle, Bresnan, and Miller (1978), 294–303.

Halle, M. (1983). On distinctive features and their articulatory implementation. *Natural Language and Linguistic Theory* 1, 91–106.

Halle, M., J. Bresnan, and G. Miller, eds. (1978). *Linguistic theory and psychological reality*. Cambridge, MA: MIT Press.

Halle, M., and S. J. Keyser (1971). *English stress*. New York: Harper & Row.

Halle, M., and J.-R. Vergnaud (1978). Metrical structures in phonology. Unpublished mimeo, MIT.

Hankamer, J., and I. Sag (1976). Deep and surface anaphora. *Linguistic Inquiry* 7, 391–428.

Hayes, B. (1982). Extrametricality and English stress. *Linguistic Inquiry* 13, 227–276.

Helmholtz, H. von (1867). *Treatise on physiological optics*. Vol. 3. English translation: New York: Dover, 1962.

Herskovits, A. (1985). Semantics and pragmatics of locative expressions. *Cognitive Science* 9, 341–378.

Hochberg, J. (1978). *Perception*. 2nd ed. Englewood Cliffs, NJ: Prentice-Hall.

Hoffman, D. D. (1983a). Representing shapes for visual recognition. Doctoral dissertation, MIT.

Hoffman, D. D. (1983b). The interpretation of visual illusions. *Scientific American* 249.6, 154–162.

Hoffman, D. D., and W. A. Richards (1984). Parts of recognition. In Pinker (1984a), 65–96.

Hofstadter, D. (1979). *Gödel, Escher, Bach: An eternal golden braid*. New York: Basic Books.

Hofstadter, D., and D. C. Dennett, eds. (1981). *The mind's I: Fantasies and reflections on mind and soul*. New York: Basic Books.

Hook, S., ed. (1960). *Dimensions of mind*. New York: Collier Books.

Howell, P., and A. Archer (1984). Susceptibility to the effects of delayed auditory feedback. *Perception and Psychophysics* 36, 296–302.

Hubel, D. H., and T. N. Wiesel (1962). Receptive fields, binocular interaction and functional architecture in the cat's visual cortex. *J. Physiol. (Lond.)* 166, 106–154.

Hubel, D. H., and T. N. Wiesel (1968). Receptive fields and functional architecture of monkey striate cortex. *J. Physiol (Lond.)* 195, 215–243.

Hudson, S., and M. Tanenhaus (1984). Ambiguity resolution in the absence of contextual bias. In *Proceedings of the Sixth Annual Conference of the Cognitive Science Society*.

Huyghe, P. (1983). Of two minds. *Psychology Today* 17.12, 26–35.

Jackendoff, R. (1976). Toward an explanatory semantic representation. *Linguistic Inquiry* 7, 89–150.

Jackendoff, R. (1977a). *X̄-Syntax: A study of phrase structure*. Cambridge, MA: MIT Press.

Jackendoff, R. (1977b). Toward a cognitively viable semantics. In C. Rameh, ed., *Georgetown University Round Table on Languages and Linguistics*, 59–80. Washington, D.C.: Georgetown University Press.

Jackendoff, R. (1978). Grammar as evidence for conceptual structure. In Halle, Bresnan, and Miller (1978), 201–228.

Jackendoff, R. (1983). *Semantics and cognition*. Cambridge, MA: MIT Press.

Jackendoff, R. (1985a). Information is in the mind of the beholder. *Linguistics and Philosophy* 8, 23–33.

Jackendoff, R. (1985b). Multiple subcategorization and the θ-criterion: The case of *climb*. *Natural Language and Linguistic Theory* 3, 271–295.

Jakobson, R. (1941). *Child language, aphasia, and phonological universals*. Trans. by Allan R. Keiler. The Hague: Mouton, 1968.

Jakobson, R., G. Fant, and M. Halle (1952). *Preliminaries to speech analysis*. Cambridge, MA: MIT Press.

James, W. (1890). *The principles of psychology*. New York: Dover [reprint], 1950.

Jaynes, J. (1976). *The origin of consciousness in the breakdown of the bicameral mind*. Boston: Houghton Mifflin.

Jenkins, J. J., J. Wald, and J. B. Pittenger (1978). Apprehending pictorial events: An instance of psychological cohesion. In Savage (1978), 129–164.

Jerison, H. J. (1973). *Evolution of the brain and intelligence*. New York: Academic Press.

Johansson, G. (1975). Visual motion perception. *Scientific American* 232, 76–88.

Johnson-Laird, P. (1983). *Mental models*. Cambridge: Cambridge University Press.

Joos, M., ed. (1957). *Readings in Linguistics I*. Chicago: University of Chicago Press.

Julesz, B. (1971). *Foundations of cyclopean perception*. Chicago: University of Chicago Press.

Julesz, B., and J. J. Chang (1976). Interaction between pools of binocular disparity detectors tuned to different disparities. *Biological Cybernetics* 22, 107–120.

Kahn, D. (1976). Syllable-based generalizations in English phonology. Doctoral dissertation, MIT.

Kandel, E. R., and J. H. Schwarz (1981). *Principles of neural science*. New York: Elsevier/North-Holland.

Katz, J. J. (1977). A proper theory of names. *Philosophical Studies* 31, 1–80.

Katz, J. J. (1981). *Language and other abstract objects*. Totowa, NJ: Rowman and Littlefield.

Katz, J. J., and P. M. Postal (1964). *An integrated theory of linguistic descriptions*. Cambridge, MA: MIT Press.

Keiler, A. (1978). The empiricist illusion. *Perspectives of New Music* 17, 161–195.

Kintsch, W. (1984). Approaches to the study of the psychology of language. In Bever, Carroll, and Miller (1984), 111–146.

Kiparsky, P. (1977). The rhythmic structure of English verse. *Linguistic Inquiry* 8, 189–248.

Klima, E. S., and U. Bellugi (1979). *The signs of language*. Cambridge, MA: Harvard University Press.

Koffka, K. (1935). *Principles of Gestalt psychology*. New York: Harcourt, Brace & World.

Köhler, W. (1927). *The mentality of apes*. London: Routledge & Kegan Paul.

Köhler, W. (1929). *Gestalt psychology*. New York: Liveright.

Köhler, W. (1940). *Dynamics in psychology*. New York: Liveright.

Köhler, W. (1960). The mind-body problem. In Hook (1960), 15–32.

Kosslyn, S. (1980). *Image and mind*. Cambridge, MA: Harvard University Press.

Krumhansl, C. (1983). Perceptual structures for tonal music. *Music Perception* 1, 28–62.

Krumhansl, C., and E. J. Kessler (1982). Tracing the dynamic changes in perceived tonal organization in a spatial representation of musical keys. *Psychological Review* 89, 334–368.

Labov, W. (1973). The boundaries of words and their meanings. In C.-J. N. Bailey and R. W. Shuy, eds., *New ways of analyzing variation in English*, vol. 1. Washington, D.C.: Georgetown University Press.

Lackner, J. R. (1981). Some contributions of touch, pressure, and kinesthesis to human spatial orientation and oculomotor control. *Acta Astronautica* 8, 825–830.

Lackner, J. R. (1984). Some influences of tonic vibration reflexes on the position sense of the contralateral limb. *Experimental Neurology* 85, 107–113.

Lackner, J. R. (1985). Human sensory-motor adaptation to the terrestrial force environment.

In D. Ingle, M. Jeannerod, and D. Lee, eds., *Brain mechanisms and spatial vision.* Dordrecht: Martin Nijhoff.

Lackner, J. R., and P. DiZio (1984). Some efferent and somatosensory influences on body orientation and oculomotor control. In L. Spillman and B. Wooten, eds., *Sensory experience,* 281–301. Hillsdale, NJ: Erlbaum.

Lackner, J. R., and A. Graybiel (1983). Perceived orientation in free-fall depends on visual, postural, and architectural factors. *Aviation, Space, and Environmental Medicine* 54, 47–51.

Lackner, J. R., and A. Graybiel (1984). Perception of body weight and body mass at twice earth-gravity acceleration levels. *Brain* 107, 133–144.

Lackner, J. R., and M. Levine (1978). Visual direction depends on the operation of spatial constancy mechanisms: The oculobrachial illusion. *Neuroscience Letters* 7, 207–212.

Lackner, J. R., and A. B. Taublieb (1984). Influence of vision on vibration-induced illusions of limb movement. *Experimental Neurology* 85, 97–106.

Lackner, J. R., and B. Tuller (1976). The influence of syntactic segmentation on perceived stress. *Cognition* 4, 303–307.

Landau, B., and L. Gleitman (1985). *Language and experience: Evidence from the blind child.* Cambridge, MA: Harvard University Press.

Landau, B., E. Spelke, and H. Gleitman (1984). Spatial knowledge in a young child. *Cognition* 16, 225–260.

Langacker, R. W. (1986). *Foundations of cognitive grammar.* Vol. 1. Stanford, CA: Stanford University Press.

Lasher, M. (1981). The cognitive representation of an event involving human motion. *Cognitive Psychology* 13, 391–406.

Lashley, K. (1951). The problem of serial order in behavior. In L. A. Jeffress, ed., *Cerebral mechanisms in behavior,* 112–136. New York: Wiley.

Lashley, K. (1956). Cerebral organization and behavior. In H. Solomon, S. Cobb, and W. Penfield, eds., *The brain and human behavior,* 1–18. Baltimore: Williams & Wilkins.

Lem, S. (1981). Non serviam. In Hofstadter and Dennett (1981), 296–317.

Lenneberg, E. (1967). *Biological foundations of language.* New York: Wiley.

Lerdahl, F., and R. Jackendoff (1983). *A generative theory of tonal music.* Cambridge, MA: MIT Press.

Lewis, D. (1972). General semantics. In D. Davidson and G. Harman, eds., *Semantics of natural language,* 169–218. Dordrecht: Reidel.

Liberman, A., and M. Studdert-Kennedy (1977). Phonetic perception. In R. Held, H. Leibowitz, and H.-L. Teuber, eds., *Handbook of sensory physiology. Vol. 8: Perception.* Heidelberg: Springer-Verlag.

Liberman, M. (1975). The intonational system of English. Doctoral dissertation, MIT.

Liberman, M., and A. Prince (1977). On stress and linguistic rhythm. *Linguistic Inquiry* 8, 249–336.

Lightfoot, D. (1982). *The language lottery.* Cambridge, MA: MIT Press.

Linden, E. (1976). *Apes, men, and language.* New York: Penguin Books.

Lorenz, K. (1965). *Evolution and modification of behavior.* Chicago: University of Chicago Press.

McCulloch, W. S., and W. H. Pitts (1943). A logical calculus of the ideas immanent in nervous activity. Reprinted in W. S. McCulloch (1965). *Embodiments of mind,* 19–39. Cambridge, MA: MIT Press.

MacKay, D. M. (1984). Mind talk and brain talk. In M. S. Gazzaniga, ed., *Handbook of cognitive neuroscience,* 293–317. New York: Plenum.

Macnamara, J. (1978). How do we talk about what we see? Mimeo, McGill University.

Macnamara, J. (1986). *A border dispute.* Cambridge, MA: MIT Press. A Bradford book.

MacNeilage, P., and P. Ladefoged (1976). The production of speech and language. In E. C. Carterette and M. Friedman, eds., *Handbook of Perception*, vol. 8, 75–120. New York: Academic Press.

Makeig, S. (1982). Affective versus analytic perception of musical intervals. In Clynes (1982), 227–250.

Mandler, G. (1984). *Mind and body*. New York: Norton.

Marcel, A. J. (1983). Conscious and unconscious perception: An approach to the relations between phenomenal experience and perceptual processes. *Cognitive Psychology* 15, 238–300.

Marcus, M. (1980). *A theory of syntactic recognition for natural language*. Cambridge, MA: MIT Press.

Marin, O. S. M. (1982). Neurological aspects of music perception and performance. In Deutsch (1982a), 453–478.

Marr, D. (1982). *Vision*. San Francisco, CA: Freeman.

Marr, D., and H. K. Nishihara (1978). Visual information processing: Artificial intelligence and the sensorium of sight. *Technology Review* 81 (October), 28–49.

Marr, D., and L. Vaina (1982). Representation and recognition of the movements of shapes. *Proc. R. Soc. Lond.* B 214, 501–524.

Martin, J. G. (1972). Rhythmic (hierarchical) versus serial structure in speech and other behavior. *Psychological Review* 79, 487–509.

Mervis, C., and J. Pani (1980). Acquisition of basic object categories. *Cognitive Psychology* 12, 496–522.

Meyer, L. B. (1956). *Emotion and meaning in music*. Chicago: University of Chicago Press.

Meyer, L. B. (1973). *Explaining music*. Berkeley: University of California Press.

Michotte, A. (1954). *La perception de la causalité*. 2nd ed. Louvain: Publications Universitaires de Louvain.

Miller, G. A. (1962). Some psychological studies of grammar. *American Psychologist* 17, 748–762.

Miller, G. A. (1980). Trends and debates in cognitive psychology. *Cognition* 10, 215–225.

Miller, G. A., and P. Johnson-Laird (1976). *Language and perception*. Cambridge, MA: Harvard University Press.

Miller, G. A., and K. A. McKean (1964). A chronometric study of some relations between sentences. *Quarterly Journal of Experimental Psychology* 16, 297–308.

Minsky, M. (1968). Matter, mind, and models. In M. Minsky, ed., *Semantic information processing*, 425–432. Cambridge, MA: MIT Press.

Minsky, M., and S. Papert (1969). *Perceptrons*. Cambridge, MA: MIT Press.

Montague, R. (1970). English as a formal language. In *Formal philosophy*, 188–221. New Haven, CT: Yale University Press.

Montague, R. (1973). The proper treatment of quantification in ordinary English. In K. Hintikka, J. Moravcsik, and P. Suppes, eds., *Approaches to natural language*, 221–242. Dordrecht: Reidel.

Moore, E. F., ed. (1964). *Sequential machines: Selected papers*. Reading, MA: Addison-Wesley.

Moulton, W. G. (1947). Juncture in modern standard German. *Language* 23, 212–226. Reprinted in Joos (1957), 208–214.

Nagel, T. (1974). What is it like to be a bat? *Philosophical Review* 83, 435–450.

Narmour, E. (1977). *Beyond Schenkerism*. Chicago: University of Chicago Press.

Neisser, U. (1967). *Cognitive psychology*. Englewood Cliffs, NJ: Prentice-Hall.

Neisser, U. (1976). *Cognition and reality*. San Francisco, CA: Freeman.

Olson, D. (1986). The cognitive consequences of literacy. *Canadian Psychology* 27, 109–121.

Olson, D., and E. Bialystok (1983). *Spatial cognition*. Hillsdale, NJ: Erlbaum.

Onifer, W., and D. A. Swinney (1981). Accessing lexical ambiguities during sentence comprehension: Effects of frequency of meaning and contextual bias. *Memory and Cognition* 9, 225–236.

Osherson, D. N., and E. E. Smith (1981). On the adequacy of prototype theory as a theory of concepts. *Cognition* 9, 35–58.

Osherson, D. N., and E. E. Smith (1982). Gradedness and conceptual combination. *Cognition* 12, 299–318.

Padden, C. (1983). Interaction of morphology and syntax in American Sign Language. Doctoral dissertation, University of California, San Diego.

Perky, C. W. (1910). An experimental study of imagination. *American Journal of Psychology* 21, 422–452.

Peterson, P. (1985). Causation, agency, and natural actions. In Chicago Linguistic Society, *Proceedings of 21st Regional Meeting and Parasession on Causatives and Agentivity.* Chicago: Department of Linguistics, University of Chicago.

Piaget, J. (1952). *The child's conception of number.* New York: Norton.

Pinker, S., ed. (1984a). *Visual cognition.* Cambridge, MA: MIT Press. A Bradford book.

Pinker, S. (1984b). Visual cognition: An introduction. In Pinker (1984a), 1–63.

Piszcalski, M., and B. A. Galler (1982). A computer model of music recognition. In Clynes (1982), 399–416.

Polanyi, M. (1958). *Personal knowledge.* Chicago: University of Chicago Press.

Popper, K. R., and J. C. Eccles (1977). *The self and its brain.* New York: Springer International.

Postal, P. (1972). The best theory. In P. S. Peters, ed., *The goals of linguistic theory.* Englewood Cliffs, NJ: Prentice-Hall.

Povel, D.-J., and P. Essens (1985). Perception of temporal patterns. *Music Perception* 2, 411–440.

Prince, A. S. (1983). Relating to the grid. *Linguistic Inquiry* 14, 19–100.

Putnam, H. (1960). Minds and machines. In Hook (1960), 138–164.

Putnam, H. (1975). The meaning of "meaning." In K. Gunderson, ed., *Language, Mind, and Knowledge,* 131–193. (Minnesota Studies in the Philosophy of Science 7.) Minneapolis: University of Minnesota Press.

Pylyshyn, Z. (1973). What the mind's eye tells the mind's brain: A critique of mental imagery. *Psychological Bulletin* 80, 1–24.

Pylyshyn, Z. (1981). The imagery debate: Analog media versus tacit knowledge. *Psychological Review* 88, 16–45.

Pylyshyn, Z. (1984). *Computation and cognition.* Cambridge, MA: MIT Press. A Bradford book.

Ristau, C. A., and D. Robbins (1982). Language in the great apes: A critical review. In J. S. Rosenblatt, ed., *Advances in the study of behavior,* vol. 12, 142–255. New York: Academic Press.

Rorty, R. (1979). *Philosophy and the mirror of nature.* Princeton, NJ: Princeton University Press.

Rosch, E., and C. Mervis (1975). Family resemblances: Studies in the internal structure of categories. *Cognitive Psychology* 7, 573–605.

Ross, J. R. (1967). Constraints on variables in syntax. Doctoral dissertation, MIT.

Rumelhart, D., and D. Zipser (1985). Feature discovery by competitive learning. *Cognitive Science* 9, 75–112.

Sachs, J. S. (1967). Recognition memory for syntactic and semantic aspects of connected discourse. *Perception and Psychophysics* 2, 437–442.

Sasanuma, S. (1974). Impairment of written language in Japanese aphasics. *Journal of Chinese Linguistics* 2, 141–157.

Savage, C. W., ed. (1978). *Perception and cognition: Issues in the foundations of psychology.*

(Minnesota Studies in the Philosophy of Science 9.) Minneapolis: University of Minnesota Press.

Schank, R., and L. Birnbaum (1984). Memory, meaning, and syntax. In Bever, Carroll, and Miller (1984), 209–252.

Searle, J. (1958). Proper names. *Mind* 67, 166–173.

Searle, J. (1980). Minds, brains and programs. *Behavioral and Brain Sciences* 3, 417–424.

Searle, J. (1983). *Intentionality.* Cambridge: Cambridge University Press.

Seidenberg, M., and L. Pettito (1978). Signing behavior in apes: A critical review. *Cognition* 7, 177–215.

Selkirk, E. O. (1982). *The syntax of words.* Cambridge, MA: MIT Press.

Selkirk, E. O. (1984). *Phonology and syntax: The relation between sound and structure.* Cambridge, MA: MIT Press.

Shannon, C. E., and W. Weaver (1949). *The mathematical theory of communication.* Urbana, IL: University of Illinois Press.

Shepard, R. N. (1984) Ecological constraints on internal representation: Resonant kinematics of perceiving, imagining, thinking, and dreaming. *Psychological Review* 91, 417–447.

Shepard, R. N., and L. A. Cooper, eds. (1982). *Mental images and their transformations.* Cambridge, MA: MIT Press. A Bradford book.

Shepard, R. N., and S. Hurwitz (1984). Upward direction, mental rotation, and discrimination of left and right turns in maps. *Cognition* 18, 161–193.

Shepard, R. N., and S. A. Judd (1976). Perceptual illusion of rotation of three-dimensional objects. *Science* 191, 952–954. Reprinted in Shepard and Cooper (1982), 267–272.

Shepard, R. N., and J. Metzler (1971). Mental rotation of three-dimensional objects. *Science* 171, 701–703.

Shiman, L. (1975). Grammar for vision. Doctoral dissertation, MIT.

Simmons, R. F. (1973). Semantic networks: Their computation and use for understanding English sentences. In R. Schank and K. Colby, eds., *Computer models of thought and language,* 63–113. San Francisco, CA: Freeman.

Singer, A. (1974). The metrical structure of Macedonian dance. *Ethnomusicology* 18, 379–404.

Sloboda, J. A. (1982). Music performance. In Deutsch (1982a), 479–496.

Sloboda, J. A. (1984). Experimental studies of music reading: A review. *Music Perception* 2, 222–237.

Sloboda, J. A. (1985). *The musical mind: The cognitive psychology of music.* Oxford: Clarendon Press.

Smith, E. (1978). Theories of semantic memory. In W. K. Estes, ed., *Handbook of learning and cognitive processes,* vol. 5. Hillsdale, NJ: Erlbaum.

Smith, E., E. Shoben, and L. J. Rips (1974). Structure and process in semantic memory: A featural model for semantic decision. *Psychological Review* 81, 214–241.

Spencer-Brown, G. (1969). *Laws of form.* London: George Allen & Unwin.

Sperry, R. W. (1976). Mental phenomena as causal determinants in brain function. In Globus, Maxwell, and Savodnik (1976), 163–178.

Sternberg, S., R. L. Knoll, and P. Zukofsky (1982). Timing by skilled musicians. In Deutsch (1982a), 182–240.

Sudnow, D. (1978). *Ways of the hand.* Cambridge, MA: Harvard University Press.

Supalla, T. (1982). Structure and acquisition of verbs of motion and location in American Sign Language. Doctoral dissertation, University of California, San Diego.

Swinney, D. A. (1979). Lexical access during sentence comprehension: (Re)consideration of context effects. *Journal of Verbal Learning and Verbal Behavior* 18, 645–659.

Swinney, D. A. (1982). The structure and time-course of information interaction during speech comprehension: Lexical segmentation, access, and interpretation. In J. Mehler,

E. Walker, and M. Garrett, eds., *Perspectives on mental representation*, 151–167. Hillsdale, NJ: Erlbaum.

Szigeti, J. (1969). *Szigeti on the violin*. New York: Dover [reprint], 1979.

Talmy, L. (1980). Lexicalization patterns: Semantic structure in lexical forms. In T. Shopen et al., eds., *Language typology and syntactic description*, vol. 3. New York: Cambridge University Press.

Talmy, L. (1983). How language structures space. In H. Pick and L. Acredolo, eds., *Spatial orientation: Theory, research, and application*. New York: Plenum.

Talmy, L. (1985). Force dynamics in language and thought. In Chicago Linguistic Society, *Proceedings of 21st Regional Meeting and Parasession on Causatives and Agentivity*. Chicago: Department of Linguistics, University of Chicago.

Tanenhaus, M. K., J. M. Leiman, and M. S. Seidenberg (1979). Evidence for multiple stages in the processing of ambiguous words in syntactic contexts. *Journal of Verbal Learning and Verbal Behavior* 18, 427–440.

Tarski, A. (1956). The concept of truth in formalized languages. In *Logic, semantics, and metamathematics*, 152–197. London: Oxford University Press.

Todd, N. (1985). A model of expressive timing in music. *Music Perception* 3, 33–58.

Trubetzkoy, N. S. (1939). *Grundzüge der phonologie*. Trans. as *Principles of phonology*. Berkeley, CA: University of California Press, 1969.

Tulving, E. (1972). Episodic and semantic memory. In E. Tulving and W. Donaldson, eds., *Organization of memory*. New York: Academic Press.

Turkle, S. (1984). *The second self: Computers and the human spirit*. New York: Simon and Schuster.

Tyler, L. K., and W. D. Marslen-Wilson (1977). The on-line effects of context on syntactic processing. *Journal of Verbal Learning and Verbal Behavior* 16, 683–692.

Tzeng, O., and W. S.-Y. Wang (1983). The first two R's. *American Scientist* 71 (May), 238–244.

Ullmann, S. (1979). *The interpretation of visual motion*. Cambridge, MA: MIT Press.

Vaina, L. (1983). From shapes and movements to objects and actions. *Synthese* 54, 3–36.

Von Neumann, J. (1958). *The computer and the brain*. New Haven, CT: Yale University Press.

Vos, J., and R. Rasch (1982). The perceptual onset of musical tones. In Clynes (1982), 299–320.

Waltz, D. (1975). Understanding line drawings of scenes with shadows. In P. H. Winston, ed., *The psychology of computer vision*, 19–91. New York: McGraw-Hill.

Waltz, D. (1979). On the function of mental imagery. *Behavioral and Brain Sciences* 2, 569–570.

Wanner, E., and L. Gleitman, eds. (1982). *Language acquisition: The state of the art*. Cambridge: Cambridge University Press.

Wanner, E., and M. Maratsos (1978). An ATN approach to comprehension. In Halle, Bresnan, and Miller (1978), 119–161.

Warren, R. M. (1970). Perceptual restoration of missing speech sounds. *Science* 167, 392–393.

Wason, P. C., and P. N. Johnson-Laird (1972). *Psychology of reasoning*. Cambridge, MA: Harvard University Press.

Watson, J. B. (1913). Psychology as the behaviorist views it. *Psychological Review* 20, 158–177.

Wertheimer, M. (1923). Laws of organization in perceptual forms. In W. D. Ellis, ed., *A source book of Gestalt psychology*, 71–88. London: Routledge & Kegan Paul, 1938.

Wilks, Y. (1982). Machines and consciousness. Paper CSCM–8, Cognitive Studies Centre, University of Essex.

Wimmer, H., and J. Perner (1983). Beliefs about beliefs: Representation and constraining function of wrong beliefs in young children's understanding of deception. *Cognition* 13, 103–128.

Wittgenstein, L. (1953). *Philosophical investigations*. Oxford: Blackwell.

Wolf, T. (1976). A cognitive model of musical sight-reading. *Journal of Psychological Research* 5, 143–171.

Woods, W. A. (1982). HWIM: A speech understanding system on a computer. In Arbib, Caplan, and Marshall (1982), 95–114.

Zadeh, L. (1965). Fuzzy sets. *Information and Control* 8, 338–353.

Index

Ackley, D., 34
Acoustic signal in music, 218–219, 247–248
Acoustic signal in speech, 57–59, 66, 98, 100
Action, 7, 34, 67, 124, 195, 199–200, 212, 234–236, 239, 248, 259–260, 269–270, 281–282, 305, 307, 325
Affect ("feel" of experience), 290–292, 303–311, 313–315, 319, 322–323
Affect (musical expressiveness), 235, 236–239, 240, 244–245, 292
Akmajian, A., 57
Ambiguity, 279, 320
  in language, 116–118
  in music, 243–244
  in vision, 115, 189–190
American Sign Language (ASL), 210–212, 264, 270, 291
Anderson, J. A., 33
Anderson, J. R., 47, 90, 112, 183–184, 267
Animal cognition and awareness, 30–32, 89–90, 135, 209, 325–327
Aphasia, 110, 211, 263
Arbib, M., 98, 115
Armstrong, S., 143, 147
Arnheim, R., 234
Attention, 6, 116, 280–283, 310, 312
Auditory feedback, 108

Balzano, G., 257, 271
Bartlett, F., 111
Barwise, J., 126, 132
Bat sonar, 3, 196, 326
Beethoven, L. v., 216, 224–225, 232
Behaviorism, 10, 14, 288
Bellugi, U., 211, 212, 264
Berkeley, G., 12

Berwick, R., 39, 110
Bharucha, J., 217
"Blindsight," 315
Block, N., 18
Body awareness, body representation, 3–5, 195–196, 238–239, 248, 257, 267, 278, 299
Bolinger, D., 76
Bradley, D., 110
Brady, M., 178
Brain localization, 34–35, 208, 211, 261–263, 310–311
Brandt, R., 14
Bregman, A., 239
Bresnan, J., 39, 73
Brugman, C., 142
Bruner, J., 6, 27, 46, 99, 279

Carey, S., 127, 208
Carroll, L., 40, 321
Casals, P., 236
Castellano, M., 217
Categorization, 135–147, 156, 194, 198–200, 297, 316
Causality, 8–10, 25–26, 157–158, 276
"Central-level" theory, 286–287, 289–290, 293, 326
Cheney, D., 209
Chomsky, N., 38, 39, 41, 42, 44, 60, 65, 71–74, 77, 88, 96, 168, 183, 252, 270, 319
Churchland, P. M., 11
Churchland, P. S., 52
Clark, H., 202, 204
Clynes, M., 239
Coleman, L., 142
Collins, A., 138
Competence, theory of, 38, 168, 214
Complex NP Constraint, 106–107

Computers, 15–17, 19, 29–31, 33–36, 50, 326
Conceptual structure, 73–74, 102, 121–159, 186–189, 193–194, 198–208, 248, 250, 255, 286–287, 289–291, 300–301, 306, 312–317, 320–326
Connectionist computers, 34, 148
Cooper, L., 19, 179–183, 249
Coordinate Structure Constraint, 42–44, 88, 99, 100, 106, 321
Craik, F., 50, 98
Creative use of categorization, 137–138, 146
Creative use of language, 41, 84, 86
Crook, J., 6
Cutting, J., 151, 177

Dawkins, R., 6
Déja vu experience, 306–307
Deliege, I., 221, 239
Dennett, D., 5, 6, 7, 9, 17, 183, 286–287, 297, 299, 310
Descartes, R., 8, 12, 20
Deutsch, D., 221, 239
Distinctive features (phonology), 58–60, 64–65
Dowling, W., 239
Dreams, 4, 127, 130–131, 290
Dualism. See Epiphenomenalism; Interactionist dualism; Parallelism

Eccles, J., 8, 26, 46
Echoic memory, 111–112
Emotion, 5, 35, 209, 236–239, 299
Epiphenomenalism, 8–10, 22, 24
Episodic memory, 50
Evolution of mind, 31–32, 87, 90, 130, 209, 256–258, 325–327
"Executive" theory, 17, 46, 279, 281, 285–286, 289, 326

Face recognition, 208–209, 267
Farah, M., 188
Feldman, J., 34, 148
Figure-ground opposition, 48, 250, 251
Finke, R., 184
Fodor, J. A., 21, 29, 30, 58, 73, 90, 99–102, 119, 137, 140, 142, 146, 167, 245, 246, 251, 252, 260–271, 280, 296, 297, 319
Forster, K., 102

Frazier, L., 97, 243
Freud, S., 14
Frith, C., 17, 46
Fromkin, V., 41, 57, 105
Functionalism, 15, 20

Gallistel, C., 31, 151
"Garden path" sentences, 97, 117, 244–245
Gardner, H., 267
Garrett, M., 41, 58, 73, 105–106, 140, 146
Gee, J., 76, 212, 330
Gelman, R., 151
Gestalt psychology, 13, 48, 144, 167, 189, 220, 251, 252–253, 331
Gibson, J., 13, 167
Gleitman, H., 14, 143, 147, 197
Gleitman, L., 86, 127, 143, 147
Globus, G., 32
Goldsmith, J., 76
Gregory, R., 164, 167
Griffin, D., 5, 6, 26
Grimshaw, J., 151
Grouping structure (music), 219–221, 224, 229, 236, 239, 248, 251, 253, 256
Gruber, J., 152, 154, 202

Halle, M., 41, 47, 60, 65–67, 72, 74, 77
Hallucinations, 4, 12, 127, 131, 306, 310–311
Hankamer, J., 148
Haptic (tactile) perception, 51–52, 194–195, 197, 248, 294, 298, 300
Hayes, B., 77
Headed hierarchies, 70, 176, 227, 230, 249–251, 254, 270
Helmholtz, H., 167, 218
Herskovits, A., 203
Hierarchical information structures, 65, 69, 172, 174–176, 208, 219–232, 249–251, 253, 270
Hochberg, J., 167
Hoffman, D., 178, 335–336
Hofstadter, D., 6, 18, 316
Hubel, D., 168
Hudson, S., 116
Hume, D., 13, 297
Hypothesis of Computational Sufficiency, 24–26, 276, 303
Hypothesis of Levels, 49, 51, 277–278

Hypothesis of the Nonefficacy of Consciousness, 25–26, 46, 276, 303, 311, 317, 323

Iconic memory, 111–112
Identification of objects, 163–164, 176–177, 194, 198–199
Identity theory, 10–11, 22–24
Illusions, 4, 13, 52. *See also* Muller-Lyer illusion; Necker cube; Vase-faces illusion
Imagery. *See* Mental imagery
Inference, 123–124, 139, 249, 261, 321–323
"visual inference," 293–295
Information-processing psychology, 37–38, 110–112, 125, 251
Information theory, 96
Innateness Hypothesis, 87–90, 138, 214, 215, 268–270, 321–323
Integrative processors, 102, 108–110, 186–188, 241, 258, 260, 262–265, 268, 280
Intentionality, 19–20, 128
Interactionist dualism, 8, 22, 25, 46, 276, 306
Intermediate-Level Theory, 285–301, 303, 309–310, 319, 325–327
Interrogative sentences, 42–44, 71–72
Intonation contour, 75–76, 81–83, 118, 250, 288, 329–330
Introspection processors, 312–317, 327

Jackendoff, R., 71, 126, 142, 144, 151, 152, 157, 202, 203, 252, 253
Jakobson, R., 47, 60, 66
James, W., 14, 17, 27, 279, 291, 299–300
Jaynes, J., 6, 310–311
Jenkins, J., 151
Jerison, H., 6, 286
Johansson, G., 178
Johnson-Laird, P., 17, 46, 123, 202, 285, 286
Julesz, B., 166, 188, 190

Kahn, D., 75
Katz, J., 73, 126, 143, 146
Keiler, A., 240
Kintsch, W., 39
Kiparsky, P., 66
Klima, E., 211, 212, 264
Koffka, K., 167
Köhler, W., 5, 13, 90, 151, 167

Kosslyn, S., 47, 181–184, 189, 249, 296, 303
Krumhansl, C., 217, 239, 240
Kuhn, T., 133, 200

Labov, W., 140
Lackner, J., 117–118, 195–196
Landau, B., 127, 197
Langacker, R., 202
Language acquisition, 66, 84, 86–90, 126–127, 214, 268–269
Lasher, M., 205
Lashley, K., 45–46, 67, 97, 105, 277, 304, 319
Lashley's Observation, 46, 277, 304, 319
Learning, 214–215, 252–253, 268–270, 281–282, 311. *See also* Language acquisition
Lem, S., 279
Lenneberg, E., 67, 88
Lerdahl, F., 144, 214, 252, 253, 292
Levels of representation/structure, 47–52, 63–64, 85, 182–185, 209–211, 247–258, 270, 326. *See also* Conceptual structure; Grouping structure (music); Metrical structure in language; Musical surface; Phonological structure; Primal sketch; Prolongational reduction; Syntactic structure; 3D model; Time-span reduction; 2½D sketch
Lévi-Strauss, C., 60
Lewis, D., 126, 129–132
Lexicon, 83–85, 103–104, 124, 200–202, 321
Liberman, A., 58, 66
Liberman, M., 76, 77, 79
Lightfoot, D., 57
Linden, E., 90
Logical Structure of Language Processing (LSLP), 91–95, 100–104, 106
Logical Structure of Musical Processing (LSMP), 240–242
Logical Structure of Visual Processing (LSVP), 186
Long-term memory, 112–113, 198–202, 244, 265–267
Lorenz, K., 88

McCulloch, W., 33
MacKay, D., 285
Macnamara, J., 124, 193, 321

Makeig, S., 236
Mandler, G., 17, 281, 286
Marcel, A., 116, 286, 296, 301, 315
Marcus, M., 97, 168, 243
Marin, O., 262
Marr, D., 38, 39, 44, 47, 101, 167–178,
    185, 188, 190, 193–195, 197–199, 206,
    207, 234, 250, 252, 253, 294, 331, 334,
    336–338
Martin, J., 223
Mental imagery, 4, 6, 12, 19, 26, 52, 127,
    130–131, 305, 320
  in ASL, 291
  in language, 287–290, 310
  in music, 235
  in vision, 19, 177, 179–185, 187–189,
    249, 263–264, 290, 296–298, 303–304,
    324
Mentalist Postulate, 121–122, 126–128,
    138
Mervis, C., 143
Metrical structure in language, 77–79, 250,
    253–256, 270
Metrical structure in music, 221–224, 229,
    236, 239, 248, 251, 253–256, 270
Metzler, J., 179–181, 189
Meyer, L., 240, 242, 243
Michotte, A., 151
Miller, G., 25, 73, 202
Mind-body problem, 7–14, 20–21
Mind-mind problem, 20–27, 52, 276
Minsky, M., 17, 33, 35, 46, 148, 279
Modality-specificity of consciousness, 51–
    52, 277, 290, 294, 300–301
Modularity of mind, 100–102, 108–110,
    173, 191, 245, 247–272
Montague, R., 126, 137
Moore, E., 31
Morphology, 74–75, 83–85, 212
Motor control, motor skills. See Action
Moulton, W., 65
Mozart, W. A., 216, 219–221, 224, 225,
    228, 230–232, 244
Muller-Lyer illusion, 99
Musical performance, 214, 222–223, 227,
    234–236, 260
Musical surface, 217–219, 221–222, 234,
    248, 292–293, 298, 310

Nagel, T., 11, 27
Narmour, E., 240, 243

Necessary and sufficient conditions, 139–
    143, 146
Necker cube, 115–117, 145, 164, 243
Neisser, U., 98, 99, 111–113, 167, 198
Neuroscience, 32–33, 35–36
"New Look" psychology, 99, 272
Newport, E., 212, 291
Nishihara, H., 168, 174–175
Nonsense syllables, 39–40, 42, 289, 292,
    295, 317

Olson, D., 204, 205, 311
Onifer, W., 104
Ontological categories, 148–152
Osherson, D., 147

Pain, 3, 5, 12, 18, 19, 299
Papert, S., 33, 148
Parallelism, 9–11, 22
Perceptrons, 148
Perky, C., 303
Perry, J., 126, 132
Peterson, P., 199
Phoneme restoration effect, 99, 114
Phonological structure, 57–67, 72, 73–85,
    248, 250, 288–291, 298, 306, 310–317,
    323–325
Piaget, J., 151
Pinker, S., 168, 184
Piszcalski, M., 219
Poetry, 66, 119, 234, 236, 254, 316
Polanyi, M., 7, 321
Popper, K., 8, 46
Postal, P., 73, 183
Povel, D.-J., 239
Pragmatic anaphora, 148–149
Pragmatics, 121
Prague Circle, 47
Preference rule system, 143–148, 220, 223,
    229, 252–253, 270, 321, 324
Primal sketch, 170–172, 186–189, 190,
    248, 250, 293, 334
Primary awareness, 4–7, 16
Prince, A., 77, 79, 254
Privileged Representations in short-term
    memory, 312–316, 320, 323
Projection of experience, 23–27, 276
Prolongational reduction, 224, 229–232,
    248, 251, 257
Propositional attitudes, 7, 128, 319n
Prosodic trees, 79–81, 250, 254–256

Prototypes, 142, 146, 147, 177, 297
Psychological reality, 42, 64–66, 129, 219,
    225
Putnam, H., 16, 20, 126, 140, 142, 312
Pylyshyn, Z., 119, 167, 182–184

Qualia, 13–14, 18, 276, 277–278

Reading of language, 209–211, 259–260,
    264, 270
Reading of music, 214, 234–236
Reduction Hypothesis, 225
Reflective awareness, 4–7, 16, 18, 315–
    317
Registration of levels in short-term mem-
    ory, 258–260, 280, 298, 306, 310
  in language processing, 113–115, 118
  in musical processing, 242–243
  in visual processing, 188–189
Retinal array, 48, 163–165, 248
Richards, W., 335–336
Ristau, C., 90
Rorty, R., 14
Rosch, E., 143
Ross, J., 43
Rubin, E., 331
Rumelhart, D., 34, 148

Sasanuma, S., 211
Schank, R., 39, 94
Schenker, H., 225, 230
Searle, J., 19–20, 29, 128, 143, 147
Seidenberg, M., 90
Selection function, 259–260, 278–280,
    282, 298, 310, 312, 320
  in language processing, 115–120
  in musical processing, 243–245
  in visual processing, 189–190
Self, 299–300
Self-awareness, self-consciousness. See
    Reflective awareness
Selkirk, E., 60, 75–77, 330
Semantic networks, 138
Semantic structure. See Conceptual structure
Seyfarth, R., 209
Shannon, C., 38, 96
Shepard, R., 19, 167, 179–184, 188, 189,
    205, 249
Shiman, L., 331–334
Short-term memory, 278–280, 282, 286–
    288, 290, 298, 307, 310, 312, 320

for language, 110–120
for music, 242–245
for vision, 188–190
Simmons, R., 138
Singer, A., 222
Situation semantics, 126, 132
Sloboda, J., 214, 223, 236
"Slow processes," 266–270, 280
Smell, 3, 51–52, 278, 326
Smith, E., 138, 143, 146, 147
Social cognition, 131, 157, 209, 267
Spatial cognition, cross-modal, 194–197,
    202–208, 239
  in language, 152–158
  in vision, 163–164
Speech errors, 41–42, 104–106
Speech perception, 57–59, 66, 92–104,
    108–110, 288–289
Speech production, 67–68, 92–95, 105–
    110, 288–289. See also Speech errors
Spencer-Brown, G., 48
Sperry, R., 8
Spoonerisms. See Speech errors
Stereopsis, 165–167, 168, 173
Stereotypes. See Prototypes
Sternberg, S., 236
Stravinsky, I., 233
Stress, musical, 223–224
Stress, phonological, 77–81, 212, 288
Sudnow, D., 234
Supalla, T., 212
Swinney, D., 104, 117, 243
Syllable structure, 40, 59–61, 65, 74–75
Syntactic structure, 42–44, 68–74, 212,
    248, 255, 288, 290, 323, 329–330
  production of, 106–107
Szigeti, J., 236

Talmy, L., 157, 202–206
Tanenhaus, M., 104, 116
Tarski, A., 128, 132, 140
Taste, 7, 51, 278
3D model, 174–178, 184–190, 193–212,
    248, 250, 255, 293–297, 300–301, 304,
    313, 320
Time-span reduction, 224–229, 248, 251,
    254–256
"Tip-of-the-tongue" experience, 290–291,
    313–315
Todd, N., 236
Tonality (music), 216–217, 229, 257

"Top-down" influences on processing, 271–272
  in language, 96, 98–103, 109–110, 114–115, 258–260
  in music, 241–242
  in vision, 187–188, 191
Touch. *See* Haptic (tactile) perception
Translation processors (bottom-up and top-down), 102, 108–110, 186–188, 241, 258–260, 262–265, 268, 272, 280, 312–317
Trubetzkoy, N., 47, 60
Truth, truth-conditions, 128–133, 322–323
Tulving, E., 50
Turkle, S., 15
2½D sketch, 172–174, 177, 184–190, 248, 250, 293–298, 304, 310, 313, 320, 331–338
Tyler, L., 94, 102
Tzeng, O., 211

Ullman, S., 173, 177
Unconscious, 14, 16, 17, 26, 275, 319–323
Underlying vs. surface phonological structure, 61–63
  syntactic structure, 71–74
  2½D sketch, 333–338

Vaina, L., 176, 199, 201
Vase-faces illusion, 115–116, 164, 335–336
Von Neumann, J., 33
Vos, J., 219

Waltz, D., 169, 184, 334, 336–337
Wang, W., 211
Wanner, E., 86, 97, 127, 243
Warren, R., 99
Wason, P., 123–124
Watson, J., 288
Wertheimer, M., 144, 167, 220, 252, 253
Wilks, Y., 286
Will (volition), xiv, 5, 8–9, 17, 305–306
Wimmer, H., 311
Wittgenstein, L., 7, 142, 146, 296, 321
Wolf, T., 214
Woods, W., 98, 115, 243
Word, possible, 40–41
Wundt, W., 14

Zadeh, L., 147